METHODISTS AND THEIR MISSIONARY SOCIETIES 1900–1996

This book examines the contribution of the Methodist Missionary Society (and its predecessors before 1932) to world-changing movements, from the remarkable mass conversions in south-west China and west Africa early in the century to the controversy over grants to liberation movements in the 1970s and 1980s. This is a ground-breaking study of the Methodist Missionary Societies in the twentieth century, how it adjusted to changing circumstances - including the forced withdrawals from China and Burma - and developed new initiatives and partnerships.

Ashgate Methodist Studies Series

Methodism remains one of the largest denominations in the USA and is growing in South America, Africa and Asia (especially in Korea and China). This series spans Methodist history and theology, exploring its success as a movement historically and in its global expansion. Books in the series will look particularly at features within Methodism which attract wide interest, including: the unique position of the Wesleys; the prominent role of women and minorities in Methodism; the interaction between Methodism and politics; the 'Methodist conscience' and its motivation for temperance and pacifist movements; the wide range of Pentecostal, holiness and evangelical movements, and the interaction of Methodism with different cultures.

Methodists and their Missionary Societies 1900–1996

JOHN PRITCHARD

ASHGATE

Published by
Ashgate Publishing Limited
Wey Court East
Union Road
Farnham
Surrey, GU9 7PT
England

Ashgate Publishing Company
110 Cherry Street
Suite 3-1
Burlington, VT 05401-3818
USA

www.ashgate.com

British Library Cataloguing in Publication Data
Pritchard, John.
    Methodists and their Missionary Societies 1760–1900. –
    (Ashgate Methodist Studies Series)
    1. Methodist Church – Missions – History – 19th century. 2. Methodist Church –
    Missions – History – 20th century. I. Title II. Series
    266.7'1–dc23

The Library of Congress has cataloged the printed edition as follows:
Pritchard, John, 1941–
    Methodists and their Missionary Societies 1760–1900 / by John Pritchard.
        pages   cm
    Includes bibliographical references and index.
    1. Missions – Societies, etc. 2. Wesleyan Methodist Church – Missions – History –
    19th century. 3. Wesleyan Methodist Church – Missions – History – 20th century.
    4. Methodist Church in Ireland – Missions – History – 18th century.
    5. Methodist Church in Ireland – Missions – History – 19th century. I. Title.
    BV2550.P75 2013
    266'.75–dc23   2012051545

ISBN   9781472409140 (hbk)
ISBN   9781472409157 (ebk-PDF)
ISBN   9781472409164 (ebk-ePUB)

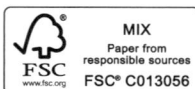

In gratitude to
Ralph and Dorothy
my parents
Harry Morton and Philip Potter
my elders and betters
summa cum laude

Contents

List of Illustrations

Endnotes

[1]   Photo: William Baillie – SOAS Collection, MMS/West Indies/Photographs/Box 1200, file 6, item 3*

[2]   Photo: Frank D. Walker, from an album, Storm and Sunshine in Mid China: Our Work in the Hupeh District – SOAS collection, MMS/China/Photographs/Box 1197a, file 2, item 15*

[3]   Photo: Mark Howard

[4]   Photo: S.S. Kemp – The Kingdom Overseas, February 1940, p. 27

[5]   NOW, November 1972, p. 11

[6]   NOW, March 1985, p. 8

[7]   One of a set of lantern slides entitled Stone Gateway, c. 1949 – SOAS collection, MMS/Home/Glass Lantern Slides/Box 83, slide 21

[8]   Unknown photographer

[9]   Photo: Keith Horton – NOW, May 1991, p. 8

[10] The Foreign Field, 1919, p. 130

[11] Photo: Elliot Kendall – SOAS collection, MMS/China/Photographs/Box 1197b, file 40, item 1*

[12] Photo: Frank D. Walker, from Storm and Sunshine in Mid China – SOAS collection, MMS/China/Photographs/Box 1197a, file 2, item 9*

[13] Photo: Albert Mosley – NOW, December 1987, p. 12

[14] Photo: James Walton – SOAS collection, MMS/ West Africa/Photographs/Box 1195a, file 3, item 10*

[15] Photo: Frank D. Walker – SOAS collection, MMS/West Africa/Photographs/Box 1195a, file 10, item 17*

Note: All images © Trustees for Methodist Church Purposes, used by permission.

* These and many other images from the SOAS collection may be viewed on-line at the International Mission Photography Archive.

List of Maps

All maps © Trustees for Methodist Church Purposes, used by permission

Abbreviations

AACC	All Africa Conference of Churches
AIM	Africa Inland Mission
AMPLA	Anglican-Methodist Project in Latin America
ANC	African National Congress (South Africa; also Zambia)
BBC	British Broadcasting Corporation
BC	Bible Christian
BCC	British Council of Churches
BFBS	British and Foreign Bible Society
BMC	Black Methodist Consultation (MCSAfrica)
BMS	Baptist Missionary Society
CBMS	Conference of Missionary Societies in Great Britain and Ireland
CCAR	Church of Central Africa in Rhodesia (Zambia)
CCC	China Christian Council
CCD	Christian Citizenship Department (of British Methodism)
CCN	Christian Council of Nigeria
CCSA	Christian Concern for Southern Africa
CEVAA	Communauté Evangélique d'Action Apostolique (Evangelical Community of Apostolic Action)

CIEMAL	Consejo de Iglesias Evangélicas Metodistas de América Latina y el Caribe (Council of Evangelical Methodist Churches of Latin America and the Caribbean)
CLS	Christian Literature Society
CMS	Church Missionary Society
CNI	Church of North India
CPD	The Constitutional Practice and Discipline of the Methodist Church
CSI	Church of South India
CWM	Council for World Mission
CWME	Commission on World Mission and Evangelism (of WCC)
DMBI	Dictionary of Methodism in Britain and Ireland
DSR	Division of Social Responsibility
ELTSA	End Loans to South Africa
FRCS	Fellow of the Royal College of Surgeons
FTM	Feed The Minds
FRELIMO	Frente de Libertação de Moçambique (Liberation Font of Mozambique)
HMD	Home Mission Division (of British Methodism)
HOD	Home Organisation Department (WMMS/MMS)
IMC	International Missionary Council
IRA	Irish Republican Army
JMA	Juvenile/Junior Missionary Association (later, Junior Mission for All)
LMS	London Missionary Society

MAYC	Methodist Association of Youth Clubs
MCCA	Methodist Church of the Caribbean and the Americas
MCN	Methodist Church Nigeria
MCOD	Methodist Church Overseas Division
MCSA	Methodist Church of South Asia / Methodist Church of South(ern) Africa
MCUB	Methodist Church in Upper Burma
MCZ	Methodist Church Zimbabwe
MEC	Methodist Episcopal Church (US)
MIH	Methodist International House
MLMM	Methodist Laymen's Missionary Movement
MMS	Methodist Missionary Society
MMU	Ministers' Missionary Union
MNC	Methodist New Connexion
MR(D)F	Methodist Relief (and Development) Fund
NCH	National Children's Home (Action for Children)
NGO	Non-governmental Organisation
NMAs	Nationals in Mission Appointments
OAU	Organization of African Unity
OTF	Overseas Training Fund
PCC	Presbyterian Church of Cameroun
PCR	(WCC) Programme to Combat Racism
PM(AMS)	Primitive Methodist (African Missionary Society)

PMS	Paris Missionary Society (Société des missions évangéliques de Paris)
PNG	Papua New Guinea
PROCMURA	Programme for Christian-Muslim Relations in Africa
RC	Roman Catholic
SIUC	South India United Church
SOAS	School of Oriental and African Studies, University of London
SPCK	Society for Promoting Christian Knowledge
SPG	Society for the Propagation of the Gospel
SWAPO	South-West Africa People's Organization
TAEC	Tikonko Agricultural Extension Centre (Sierra Leone)
TSPM	Three-Self Patriotic Movement (China)
UCA	United College of the Ascension
UCNI	United Church of North India
UCZ	United Church of Zambia
UDI	Unilateral Declaration of Independence (Rhodesia)
UM, UMC	United Methodist Church (in Britain, 1907–1932; in USA and associated Conferences, from 1968)
UMCA	Universities' Mission to Central Africa
UMCB	United Missions in the Copperbelt (Zambia)
UMFC	United Methodist Free Churches
UMN	United Mission to Nepal
UN	United Nations

UNIP	United National Independence Party (Zambia)
US	United States
USCL	United Society for Christian Literature
USPG	United Society for the Propagation of the Gospel
UTC	United Theological College (Bangalore)
VSO	Voluntary Service Overseas
WA	Women's Auxiliary (WM)
WAY	World Affairs Youth
WCC	World Council of Churches
WD	Women's Department (WM)
WDM	World Development Movement
WDO	Wesley Deaconess Order
WHS	Wesley Historical Society
WLMM	Wesleyan Laymen's Missionary Movement
WMC	World Methodist Council
WMF	Women's Missionary Federation (PM)
WM(MS)	Wesleyan Methodist (Missionary Society)
WW	Women's Work
YMA	Youth Missionary Association
ZANU	Zimbabwe African National Union
ZAPU	Zimbabwe African People's Union

Brief Glossary of Methodist Terms

Chairman of the District: The minister appointed by the Conference to oversee a District and chair the Synod. Overseas, the title 'Chairman of the District and General Superintendent' was often used to make clear that the Chairman did not merely chair Synod meetings. This book normally abbreviates to 'Chairman'.

Circuit: A group of Methodist societies in a given area.

Class: The basic unit in Wesleyan Methodism: all members were expected to meet regularly in a group with a designated Class Leader for prayer, testimony and mutual exhortation.

Class ticket: Issued quarterly to all members as proof of their good standing, of use especially when away from home. It served as a ticket of entry to meetings; in many places to Holy Communion; and was often placed in a member's coffin as a ticket of entry to heaven...

Committee: Here used, unless otherwise defined by the context, to denote the General or managing Committee of the Society in question.

Conference: The central governing body of the denomination, meeting annually.

Connexion: The network of local churches, circuits and districts governed by the Conference.

District: A sub-unit of the Conference, normally comprising a number of circuits, governed by a Synod.

President of the Conference: In Britain, an annual appointment.

Quarterly Meeting: The ministers and lay representatives of all the societies in a Circuit, meeting four times per annum to conduct the affairs of the Circuit, with the superintendent minister in the chair (in British Methodism post-1976, the Circuit Meeting, held at least twice per annum.)

Secretary: With a capital S, a Secretary of the Missionary Society in question (the Wesleyan Secretaries were styled 'General Secretary' from 1843).

Society (1): Used in this book with a lower case s, the original and enduring term for a local Methodist congregation – Methodists at first avoided using the term 'church' in order to make it clear they were not competing with the local parish (Anglican) church.

Society (2): With a capital S, the particular Missionary Society in question (most often the WMMS).

Stations: A list, published annually, of the Circuits and other appointments to which ministers had been assigned by the Conference.

Steward: A lay leader: the term was used for a variety of roles, the chief being Society Steward (in current usage Church Steward) and Circuit Steward.

Place Names

Since, in accordance with common usage, Deutschland is in these pages invariably referred to as Germany, and Xianggang as Hong Kong, the same principle has been applied to most other names, however they are rendered locally. Thus, for example, Mumbai, Chennai and Kolkata are referred to as Bombay, Madras and Calcutta. The principle has not been applied consistently however. Sri Lanka, Ghana, Zambia and Zimbabwe are Ceylon, the Gold Coast and the Rhodesias at first, but the contemporary names, once adopted, are preferred, while the people of the Gold Coast are Ghanaians from the outset.

The Ivory Coast is an interesting case: tired of shunting from I to C at international meetings, depending on the language according to which seating was arranged, the government decreed that even in English the country is Côte d'Ivoire. This occurred right at the end of the period and so Ivory Coast is here used throughout. Kenya on the other hand did not alter the spelling at independence, but the colonial pronunciation Keen-ya was changed to Ken-ya (in Kiswahili the Lord's Prayer ends *kenya mwa kenya*, 'for ever and ever').

Chinese names present their own problem. In 1958 a new system of romanizing Chinese characters, known as *pinyin*, was officially endorsed, replacing the Wade–Giles spelling previously used. To enable readers to locate places on modern maps, *pinyin* is used, even though the old spelling is used in the Societies' records. Peking, for example, is thus Beijing, and Canton is either Guangzhou, for the city, or Guangdong, for the province. To use Hong Kong's familiar name may be considered an anomaly; the alternative would be bizarre. Personal names, on the other hand, retain the spelling found in the records.

Foreword

The most important development in modern church history is one that has only lately begun to receive scholarly attention commensurate with its importance, and is still often overlooked. In the twentieth century the demographic and cultural base of the Christian faith was transformed. In 1900 the vast majority of the world's professing Christians lived in Europe and the Americas; Christians constituted a small fraction of the population of Africa. For some centuries past, Christianity had been both a Western religion and the religion of the West. The traditions that gave the different communities of Christians their identity, and regulated their forms of expression and government, had emerged from the Christian history of Europe; the languages and intellectual and cultural history of Europe supplied the vocabulary and the categories in which their theology was articulated and their worship carried out; and Western life and literature, arts and music carried the impress of centuries of Christian teaching and imagery. Before the end of the twentieth century, however, the majority of professing Christians were Africans, Asians, Latin Americans, or people from the Pacific. Exponential growth had occurred in the numbers of Christians in sub-Saharan Africa and elsewhere, while Christian profession in the West, and especially in Europe, was in decline, and with it the Christian impress on European culture. Christianity is becoming increasingly a non-Western religion, with issues and influences from Africa and Asia increasingly likely to shape its theology, worship and agenda.

What brought about this shift in the composition of the Christian Church – more considerable, perhaps, than in any earlier hundred year period of Christian history other than the first? Certainly many forces and processes, varying in nature in different locations, were at work, as the pages that follow make clear; and those forces were often indigenous to Africa or Asia or the Pacific; key initiatives and developments often arose among people indigenous to those continents. But it is impossible to overlook the catalytic presence of Christian missions from the West. They were not the creator of contemporary World Christianity, but the detonator of many of the explosions that brought it about.

The missionary movement from the West, often applauded and sometimes reviled, was rarely a high priority in the life of the churches of the West. It first took recognizable form in Catholic southern Europe in the first half of the sixteenth century. Not until the early years of the eighteenth century did Protestants produce anything comparable. The nineteenth century saw both Catholic and Protestant activities greatly expanded, and the movement firmly established in the consciousness of the Western churches; the early twentieth century saw its climax. By the end of the twentieth century, however, Western missions in every continent were peripheral to indigenous Christian churches and indigenous

Christian movements; African, Asian and Latin American missionaries abounded, and some of them were working for the renewal of Christian faith in the West. Within a hundred years, Christian missions had been transformed, and so, to a significant degree through their agency, had Christianity itself.

The present volume grapples with this important theme, illustrating it from one substantial sector of the missionary movement, and providing the first comprehensive survey of that sector. Methodist missions offer a lens through which to view the whole missionary movement and the outcome of its work. Methodism began as a missionary movement within British Christianity concerned to make the all-but-universal profession of Christianity in Britain vital in ordinary life. John Wesley called the mission 'spreading scriptural holiness throughout the land'. The Methodist churches that grew out of the movement developed institutions and forms of organization designed to maintain that vital religion – in fact, radical Christianity. Methodist missions beyond Britain came into being as a result of Methodists – typically lay people – maintaining the lives of devotion and witness to others that they believed constituted scriptural holiness. The need for organizational frameworks for missions came later; and in his earlier work on the eighteenth and nineteenth centuries John Pritchard showed how British and Irish Methodist missionary activity significantly antedated the foundation of the first Methodist missionary society.

That volume described how Methodist missions came to every continent, the growth of the different branches of missionary work and service, the effect on missionary work of events and issues in the British churches, and the converse. These matters feature also in the present volume, as the story continues into the twentieth century; the century that saw the emergence, with all its crucial potentialities, of contemporary World Christianity. The Methodist branch of the missionary movement is revealed as a microcosm of the processes that produced this turning point in Christian history.

The story evolves against the background of other world events; for the history of the missionary movement and of the rebirth of Christianity as a world faith runs parallel with other stories: that of mass migration from Europe, for instance, and the resultant building of new nations; and the rise and fall of the Western maritime empires and the building of other new nations as those empires dissolved. This is a story of interaction, for missionaries were both representative Westerners and representative Christians; and, since Christian faith is embodied faith, theirs was necessarily shaped by the history and conditions of Europe. But they were involved in a process of engagement, interaction and exchange, and the outcome has been the embodiment of Christian faith within widely different cultures across the world, where it is taking new shapes under the influence of other histories and other conditions.

John Pritchard writes as an insider of insight and sympathy, but with critical detachment. He has known missionary life at first hand, and personally witnessed many of the processes recorded here. He knows the workings of Methodism, and steered its missionary society at a crucial phase of its history. We could wish for no better interpreter of the place of British and Irish missionary activity within the complex of events that has issued in the World Christianity of the twenty-first century.

ANDREW F WALLS

University of Edinburgh, Liverpool Hope University and
Akrofi-Christaller Institute, Akropong, Ghana

Preface

On 9 July 2013 the British Methodist Conference determined 'that the Methodist Missionary Society (MMS) be wound up with immediate effect'. This was one of a raft of resolutions which committed the Methodist people in Britain and in Ireland to engage actively in mission both locally and globally, in a spirit of partnership, collaboration and mutuality with sister Churches across the world. The international dimension of Methodism's calling to share in God's mission, which was embedded long before the formal creation of the Wesleyan Methodist Missionary Society (WMMS) in 1818, was a given that the demise of the MMS would not undermine in the globalized twenty-first century. Since 1973 (as chapter 17 of this book relates) the Missionary Society had been coterminous with, and better known as, the Methodist Church Overseas Division (MCOD)[1] and in 1996 the Overseas Division was merged with the six other Divisions that had been created in 1973 into a unified headquarters team for the British connexion. In 2009 the last remaining Overseas District of the British Conference, The Gambia, became autonomous. That event constitutes a postscript to my narrative, which otherwise ends with the 1996 restructuring. Some of the essays in this volume will be found to end somewhat abruptly, like Mark's Gospel, at the point when the new connexional team was appointed and the last General Secretary was replaced by a different style of leadership and administration.

The period covered by my account of *Methodists and their Missionary Societies, 1760—1900*,[2] which saw the birth and rapid expansion of the Protestant missionary movement, was an age of discovery in many fields: geographical exploration, technological innovation, the biological and geological sciences. The explorers, inventors and scientists in question were men — and a handful of women — of European stock, as were the missionaries (a growing number of missionary women as the nineteenth century advanced). The indigenous peoples of other continents found their own ways and wisdom scorned by Europeans, who occupied their lands, hired their labour for a pittance, and sold them mass-produced articles at inflated prices. Africa, China, South Asia and the Caribbean were the regions where British Methodists were investing their missionary funds and personnel; by the year 1900 all bar China had largely fallen under European rule. Manufactured imports, coins and paper currency, schools and taxes transformed all but the most remote and inaccessible communities, and some lives were changed yet more fundamentally by the preaching of the gospel.

---

[1]   In referring to the post-1973 period MMS and MCOD are one and the same.

[2]   J.R. Pritchard, *Methodists and their Missionary Societies 1760–1900* (Aldershot, Ashgate Publishing, 2013).

While the speed and extent of change in the nineteenth century were unprecedented, they were outpaced in the twentieth. A graph with a line rising almost imperceptibly for millennia and then soaring exponentially in the twentieth century might depict many things: the distance a person could travel in an hour, the size of the audience a speaker could address, the number of people that a single warrior could kill, as well as the size of the global population, which grew four-fold in a hundred years, from 1.5 billion to 6 billion. It was also the century which saw such rapid worldwide growth of Christianity that Christians in Europe and North America were eventually outnumbered by those living to the south; in 1900 one African in ten was Christian, by the year 2000 one in two. The decades after 1945 saw the erstwhile Protestant mission fields become self-supporting Churches, even as the former colonies became independent nations (though in both cases some remained firmly in the category of client states).

Tracing the evolution of Methodist missionary activity in this context has been an enthralling task, imperfectly accomplished. Earlier histories covered hardly more than the first third of the century. Allen Birtwhistle wrote a substantial chapter for volume three of *A History of the Methodist Church in Great Britain* (1983).[3] He began with the Wesleys and got no further than 1932, when the overseas work of the three Methodist Churches which united that year was merged as the Methodist Missionary Society; for reasons of space the editors had to condense what was already hardly more than a general overview and the twentieth century got short shrift. Cyril Davey's *The March of Methodism* (1951)[4] was commissioned by the Literature Committee of the MMS, which asked for 'a popular and easily readable account of our work'. He divided it into three parts: 'How it began: 1786–1820' describing the origins of Methodist work in the British colonies, 'On to Victory: 1820–1900', including a brief mention of the non-Wesleyan Missionary Societies, and 'Twentieth Century: 1900–50'. The third part comprised studies of women's work, medical and educational missions, 'mass movements' and contemporary problems and opportunities. Davey's *Changing Places* (1988)[5] was as much a work of propaganda as of history.

In this volume I have approached the task through a series of thematic essays rather than a chronological account or a geographical survey, though within most essays there is a geographic structure and the passage of time generally moves towards the present rather than backwards. They are no more than introductory essays. Too many people, institutions and issues are — again due to constraints on length — given scant attention or totally ignored. Some of the topics span the entire period, while others relate to particular segments. Certain events, such as the upheavals in China, are treated in several chapters, not necessarily in

---

[3]   R.E. Davies, A.R. George, G. Rupp (eds), *A History of the Methodist Church in Great Britain* (4 vols, London, Epworth Press, 1965, 1978, 1983, 1988).

[4]   C.J. Davey, *The March of Methodism* (London, Epworth Press, 1951).

[5]   C.J. Davey, *Changing Places* (London, Marshall Pickering, 1988).

chronological sequence. To set them in order is the role of church historians; the object here is to set them in the context of MMS policy and activity.

Like so many other students of mission history, I am deeply indebted to Professor Andrew Walls. Alongside numerous other responsibilities, he organized a dozen annual conferences and associated seminars on the contribution of British and Irish Methodism to world mission beginning in 2002. Many of the papers delivered there have informed my understanding. Annual reports[6] and the magazines *The Foreign Field, The Missionary Echo, Advance, The Kingdom Overseas, Women's Work* and *NOW*, which can all be consulted at the University of London School of Oriental and African Studies (SOAS), highlight the key events of the century. Many of the books listed in the bibliography, although long out of print, can be accessed at SOAS. The British Library's Oral History section holds a collection of taped interviews with serving and former missionaries and mission partners recorded since 1970, listed as the Methodist Church Oral Archive project. I have been privileged to consult a massive amount of archival material at Methodist Church House which has not yet been weeded, transferred to SOAS, catalogued and made generally accessible, and is therefore not as fully referenced in the footnotes as I would have wished.[7] A questionnaire to former missionaries about their selection and preparation informed chapter 9, and personal communications from people who worked abroad – in the main from the 1950s onwards but from 1916 in the case of Bill Platt, with whom I last spoke on his hundredth birthday – have filled in important details.

I have refrained from inserting 'sic' after every mention of 'man', 'brotherhood', and terms such as 'kaffirs' and 'coolies' where they appear in quotations; it must be taken as read.

I am greatly indebted to Lance Martin, the archivist at SOAS with a prodigious knowledge of the MMS archive, for his encouragement and advice; to Albert Mosley, former General Secretary of the MCOD, for many details and explanations and for the monumental database of almost every Methodist missionary that ever was, which he has compiled in retirement; and to Norman Taggart, another former officer of MCOD and past President of the Methodist Church in Ireland, for his advice on the Irish contribution. Others whose help I gratefully acknowledge include Lesley Anderson, Ruth Angove, Ruth Anstey, Meg Bailey, Brian Beck, Brian Brown, John Clapham, Kenneth Cracknell, David Cruise, Howard Dalziel, Trevor Durston, Maureen Edwards, Audrey Facey, Joy Fox, Deborah Gaitskell, Alison Geary, Bill Gibson, Jenny Gibson, Dorothy Graham, Elizabeth Harris, Jo Hibbard, Peter Howson, Graeme Jackson, Martin James, Mike Leigh, John Lenton, Alison Lewis, Shelagh Livingstone, Sandra Lopez, Eric Lott, Timothy Mark, Colin Morris, George Mulrain, Kirsty Murray, John Neal, Peter Nockles,

---

[6] Annual reports were not published until several months into the ensuing year. Footnotes refer to the year reported on; in some instances, for the avoidance of doubt, the date of publication is also mentioned.

[7] Footnotes prefixed MCH refer to this material.

Mabel Nyazika, Don Pickard, Jennifer Potter, Henry Rack, Edward Royle, Israel Selvanayagam, Geoffrey Senior, Rosemary Seton, John Simmonds, Keith Slatter, John Stedman, Jan Sutch Pickard, David Temple, Juliet Ushewokunze, Betty Venner, John Vickers, Martin Wellings, John Young and the great number of hosts who enlightened me and enlivened my visits to sister Churches in the 1980s and 1990s. To Pat, my partner for half a century, without whose constant attentions this book would not have been started, let alone finished, I owe more than words can express.

JOHN PRITCHARD
12 July 2013

Chapter 1
A New Century: High Hopes and Ill Omens

In the year 1900 Britain was at war in South Africa; at the end of 1914, in Europe. In 1900 China was torn by the Boxer uprising with Christians the chief target of the insurgents; by 1915, the last Emperor had been dethroned, the first Republic destabilized, and the disintegration of China at the hands of rival warlords and Japanese invaders had begun. In 1900 Sir Frederick Hodgson, the governor of the Gold Coast, was besieged in the fort in Kumasi; by 1914 British rule was firmly established and a swift campaign was mounted to wrest neighbouring Togo from Germany. Half-way through this brief period Mahatma Gandhi had his first taste of prison, in Johannesburg; in 1914 he was back in India to lead the struggle for Home Rule.

The early years of the century, before Europe was engulfed in conflict, saw remarkable instances of conversions of village people *en masse* in India, China and Africa. The formation of the South India United Church in 1901 was the first step towards a unified Church of South India (CSI), while the World Missionary Conference at Edinburgh in 1910 was a milestone in the history of the ecumenical movement. The first decade saw too the start of missionary training in Selly Oak, Birmingham, heralding a new and more thorough style of preparation for overseas service.[1]

There was still much pioneering evangelism to be done. The slogan 'the evangelization of the world in this generation', coined at a missionary conference in Shanghai in 1877 and popularized by the Student Volunteer Movement from 1883, was enthusiastically adopted.[2] Methodist mission fields gradually – sometimes rapidly – enlarged their terrain. Meanwhile the churches already planted had to be nurtured. Roland Allen's thesis, that the missionary becomes dispensable at an early stage in the life of a young church and should then move on just as the apostle Paul did, was first published in 1912;[3] it did not commend itself to mission society executives, who were busily fashioning churches modelled on their own – or, less harshly put, their missionaries were engaged

> in teaching those whose emotions had been so profoundly stirred what is involved in discipleship … in gathering believers together for corporate prayer

---

[1]   See chapters 6, 9 and 11.

[2]   T. Yates, *Christian Mission in the Twentieth Century* (Cambridge, Cambridge University Press, 1994), pp. 17–20.

[3]   R. Allen, *Missionary Methods: St Paul's or Ours?* (London, World Dominion Press, 1912).

and worship … in training workers to preach, to teach in Sunday Schools, to hold office in the Church and care for its spiritual activities and its buildings; and … to offer willingly of their substance…[4]

It would be a much longer road to the selfhood of indigenous churches than Allen envisaged and advocated.

Primitive Methodists in Africa

In 1903 *The Record* – the organ of the Primitive Methodist (PM) Home, Colonial and Foreign Missionary Society – published a table listing the income of the several Methodist denominations earmarked for Home and Foreign Missions. Wesleyans, numbering 501,963 members, gave on average 7s 6d each the previous year; Bible Christians, the smallest body with 33,098 members, gave 3s 8d; the 96,436 United Methodist Free Church (UMFC) members also contributed 3s 8d a head, and 42,744 New Connexion (MNC) members 3s 1d. The 198,395 Primitive Methodists, however, averaged only 1s 9½d.[5] *The Record's* purpose in publishing the figures was of course to urge its readers to give more. Four slide sets were available to borrow promoting the work of PM missionaries: in the Spanish colony of Fernando Po, Archibongville (named the 'Southern Nigeria Missions' in 1903), Aliwal North in South Africa and Zambesi (southern Zambia).

The island of Fernando Po (renamed Bioko after independence) is small but the interior was inaccessible. There were four stations, not always fully staffed, all on the coast, and reached by sea. The mission contended with four problems in particular. The climate took its toll and fever took lives. Hostile Spanish priests put endless difficulties in the way, especially when Methodists wanted to acquire land. The liquor trade thrived – imported rum and gin did much more harm than local palm wine – and the white traders were sworn enemies; one attempted to get the Fernandian minister, William Barleycorn, banished from the island. Even more disruptive was the failure of the cocoa harvest.

Cocoa superseded palm oil as the island's main crop towards the end of the nineteenth century but at the start of the twentieth there was a succession of bad seasons and an economic crisis. The plantations were worked largely by contracted labourers from the mainland, who were left unpaid; their situation was later found by a League of Nations investigation to be akin to slavery. The PM mission had invested in cocoa, both as a means of employment for converts and as a source of income; not only did the commercial return suffer, the giving of hard-hit members fell too. But cocoa recovered. In 1910 Jabez Bell obtained land for an 'industrial Christian and

---

4   A.E. Southon, *Gold Coast Methodism* (London, Cargate Press, 1934), p. 97.

5   7 shillings and 6 pence in 1902 was the equivalent of £31.80 at 2010 prices, and of £127 if calculated by average earnings; 1 shilling and 9 pence was the equivalent of £7.41 using the Retail Price Index, £29.70 using average earnings.

non-liquor colony', with a large farm and facilities for drying and storing the crop. Notwithstanding the low price of cocoa it proved a worthwhile venture.[6]

As the century advanced, the missionaries rejoiced to see some of the indigenous Bubi people, hitherto resistant to the gospel, beginning to respond. However, Methodist membership, and the encouraging attendance at class meetings and prayer meetings, was still drawn mainly from the settlers and migrant workers from the mainland. Several young men were sent for training to the Oron Institute in Nigeria, and one, Ben Twajo, was by 1911 the Vice-Principal of the Institute, with C.P. Groves[7] as Principal.

Southern Nigeria was rapidly becoming the more important of the two West African PM operations. The Oron Institute was established in order to turn the brightest schoolboys into teachers, and in the hope that some of them might eventually become ministers. £1,000 was needed to get it started; the PM Christian Endeavour branches in England raised the money. It opened in 1905.

At this period PM attentions were directed to the Efik and Ibibio peoples of the coast and creeks. In 1902 a new station was built, with difficulty, at Idua.

> When the house materials were landed, we had to sort and stack them high above the ground, so as to put them beyond the reach of millions of white ants. Even then we have had to watch most vigilantly, or they would have climbed the wood posts and set about their destructive work. To guard against these pests our united energies have been taxed to the full. I am happy to inform you we have beaten the ravenous creatures, numberless though they are.[8]

It is unsurprising that ants were frequently mentioned in letters and reports from many parts of the world.

At Jamestown a Girls' Institute was begun by George Hanney, who arrived in 1902 and worked in Nigeria until 1949, retiring at the age of 70. *The Herald* – successor to *The Record* – announced in 1908 that there were now seven girls in residence and a teacher and a matron were needed. Amy Richardson, who promptly offered her services, was the first single woman missionary appointed by the PM mission and had reached her post by the time the Women's Missionary Federation (WMF) was officially founded at the 1909 Conference. The last leg of her long journey, from Oron to Jamestown, was by a dilapidated launch which had long been 'eligible for superannuation', as she put it. It was wrecked in a tornado not long after, but one of the WMF's earliest achievements was to raise the money for a replacement, which Amy launched at Worthing while on furlough in 1910.

Meanwhile the Southern Nigeria Mission was making contact with villages further from the coast. William Christie reckoned there were 50,000 people in

---

[6]   Boocock, N., *Our Fernandian Missions* (London, W.A. Hammond, 1912), p. 94.

[7]   Groves was later to hold the chair of mission at Selly Oak (see p. 130) and write *The Planting of Christianity in Africa* (4 vols, London, Lutterworth Press, 1948–1958).

[8]   PM Annual Report 1902, p. xxxix.

the area and calculated that to create 'three white stations' would cost £1,000 for the buildings and £1,000 for salaries and expenses. In 1907 he made his way to Ikot-Ekpene, a two-day cycle ride from Oron. The village had a reputation for wickedness – in 1909 fifty people were tried for murder at the Ikot-Ekpene assizes. None the less Christie was well received, and the chief gave him a well-placed hill on which to build. By 1909 he reported four churches, three schools and a mission house, and 800 present every Sunday. Then, leaving William Groves to take his place, he moved on to the Igbo town of Bende, and learned that somewhere called 'Ozakoli' was a promising place to settle. Uzuakoli was to become a major Methodist centre.[9] In 1910 *The Herald* carried a photograph of six missionaries enjoying a Christmas party 'in a Swamp at Ikot-Ekpene' – among them Fred Dodds, soon to be the District Chairman, and a recently arrived teacher, Grace Fisher, who was destined to become his wife. The brief report of the party told that

> Government officials even went so far as to offer the use of a motor-car, which shows how rapidly civilisation is making inroads upon the barbarism of the West Coast.[10]

In South Africa there were above 1,000 PM Christians when the Boer War broke out. In the course of the hostilities several chapels were destroyed and over 600 people were scattered, while many others died. But it was reported that

> Not even the panic of war could make them forget their 'Church Notes'. They might have to leave some of their household effects behind, as many of them did, but their Church note was altogether too precious to be left and when they reach their destination, one of the first things they do is to find a minister and deposit their Church note. It is touching to see how much care they lavish on their 'note'. It is usually ... carried in the belt or bosom, or some other place of equal safety, and it is handled with great care. There is no superstition about this, it simply shows their high value of Church membership. That little piece of paper, written in a language which many of them cannot read, is the instrument which is to admit them to ... Christian fellowship, as found in the class meeting and the Lord's Supper.[11]

By 1903, the membership return was back up to 1,332. The end of the conflict, however, saw a renewed tide of migration to the illusory 'streets paved with gold' of the Witwatersrand. George Butt made an exploratory visit to Johannesburg but concluded that it was not the time to start a PM Congregation there, since there

---

[9]   A.J. Fox, *Uzuakoli, A Short History* (London, Oxford University Press, 1964), pp. 93–102.

[10]   *The Herald* vol. VI no. 3 (1910): p. 41.

[11]   PM Annual Report 1900, p. xliv.

was an abundance of churches and because of 'the almost certainty of the near-coming of Methodist Union in the whole of South Africa'.[12]

North of the Zambezi, on the other hand, there were unlimited opportunities to extend the mission. In 1904 William Chapman made a journey, the equivalent, he said, of going from Berwick-on-Tweed to Land's End, to the newly-discovered copper mines, said to be the largest in the world. Chapman was a man of considerable stamina: during the war when he could obtain no transport he had walked from Aliwal North all the 500 miles to Bulawayo. The copper fields were already attracting migrant workers but it was to be many years before Methodism began work there. For the moment there was enough to do among the Ila, where Chapman was based, and the Tonga in the Zambezi valley; the staff of the mission had not grown since the pioneers left England in 1889. Edwin Smith, one of the team in Central Africa between 1902 and 1915, lamented the lost opportunity. But before long the gospel was taken to the Copperbelt, not by European missionaries but by African mineworkers who brought their faith from their villages.[13]

Smith was a scholar who lost no time in getting to grips with the Ila language. After a year he could preach without an interpreter and he was soon producing Ila literature. With a colleague, John Price, and many Ila assistants, he translated the New Testament; he also produced an *Ila Phrase Book for the use of Sportsmen and Settlers* (1911) – the sport in question being game hunting rather than football.[14] He found himself at odds with the General Missionary Committee in London, however; in 1915 he left Africa and went on to a distinguished academic career. He clashed fiercely with Arthur Guttery, the Secretary of the Committee, over the complaint that the mission in South Central Africa was far more costly than in Southern Nigeria. So it was, in monetary terms; the cost of getting goods to these outposts in shipping and rail charges, customs dues, agency fees and then porters for the last two hundred miles from the Zambezi was exorbitant. But it was costly not only in financial terms. Smith's predecessor Arthur Baldwin pointed out that the missionary

> must get his wood from the forest, his thatching grass from the plain and make all his own bricks, in fact he must build his own house and church out of the materials that nature supplies.[15]

Ila people, added Smith, had no concept of voluntary work and even wage labour was alien to them. Baldwin also described the cost in terms of loneliness: 'For some years our nearest neighbours lived about 200 miles away and never

---

[12]   In the event union was achieved some thirty years later, in 1932.

[13]   W.J. Young, *The Quiet Wise Spirit,* (London, Epworth Press, 2002), p. 51.

[14]   E.W. Smith, *An Ila Phrase Book for the use of Sportsmen and Settlers* (Livingstone, Administration Press, 1911).

[15]   A. Baldwin, *A Missionary Outpost in Central Africa* (London, PM Young People's Missionary Department, 1914), p. 95.

came to see us'.[16] There was also the cost in human life: his wife was one of those whose lives were cut short.

In 1914 the Committee approved the start of medical work at Kasenga on the Kafue river, the station Smith had opened in 1909. Smith, who had done a short medical course at Livingstone College in London, valued the training and put it to good use; in the annual report for 1904 he wrote:

> One day a woman presented herself at the station with a fearful gash in her arm and several cuts in her neck. She had been ruthlessly assaulted by a man as she was working in her fields, and speared without any provocation. As I was away, my wife bound up the arm temporally, and on my return I sewed it up. After several weeks the wound healed soundly.[17]

But he recognized both the inadequacy of his training and the limited time he could devote to medical matters. For fifteen years he had been urging the Committee to appoint qualified medical workers; Elizabeth Barlow, a nurse, arrived just before the Smiths departed and Dr Herbert Gerrard shortly after.

United Methodists

The UMFC, MNC and Bible Christians (BC) united in 1907 but did not finish bringing their missionary committees and accounts together until 1909. The exercise was likened to three small boats tying up at a landing-stage and transferring their passengers to another, larger and more powerful – yet there is still bound to be a loss of speed until the bigger boat gets properly under way.

All three uniting churches had work in China, where the anti-foreign and anti-Christian Boxer uprising was quelled by a foreign relief army in 1900 but new calamities followed. The 1901 Peace Protocol exacted crippling reparations. Popular disillusion with the Qing dynasty, in power since 1644, grew with the realization of China's backwardness and weakness, particularly by comparison with Japan which seized control of the north-east in 1905; ironically, such modernization as went on – the railways, postal and telegraph services and education – all served to spread dissatisfaction rather than contain it. Through these troubled years, leading to the dethronement of the last Emperor in 1913, the MNC worked steadily and faithfully in Shandong and Tianjin, with its ambitious watchword, 'Every Christian a missionary and every home a church'. None was more faithful than John Robinson, who had come to China in 1877; his death in 1905 was attributed to 'the harrowing experiences of the Boxer days, and the stupendous task of reorganization that followed after 1900.'[18] Another who died

---

16   Ibid.
17   PM Annual Report 1904, p. xliv.
18   J. Hedley, *Our Mission in North China* (London, Geo. Burrows, 1907), p. 48.

in 1905 was Mrs Hu, the widow of the first Chinese MNC minister and herself a tireless worker who was listed on the stations as a 'female agent' to the day she died, aged 97. At union, there were 322 MNC chapels or meeting places, 3,120 members and eleven ministers, 53 elementary schools and the hospital at Laoling which in 1907 saw 2,387 outpatients and 241 admissions. The Training Institution in Tianjin thrived until 1912, when the Chinese New Year saw riots in both Beijing and Tianjin. The students did not return after the New Year break. Later in the year, however, the Institution reopened in Beijing.

For the Bible Christians in Yunnan province in the south-west, 1904 and 1905 were the dramatic years when thousands of Miao people became Christians.[19] After the Boxer Rising there was no return to Kunming, the capital of Yunnan, for many years, but in Zhaotong a girls' school was opened in 1903, a training school for teachers and evangelists in 1904 and a hospital in 1905. By 1907 the District had 2,867 members and another 2,552 under instruction, the vast majority of them newly-baptized Miao.

On China's eastern seaboard the UMFC (known in China as the English Methodist Free Church Mission) opened numerous country chapels. In most places, however, the Christians met for worship in private houses; in some villages it was possible to make use of an ancestral hall and praise God in surroundings which traditional culture venerated. A fold-out map of Wenzhou County included in the annual report for 1903 showed 112 Free Methodist outstations, and a note that there were at least 3,000 more villages without preaching places. In Ningbo, the older of the two UMFC Districts, a hospital was started in 1899 and the Ningbo College in 1906; in Wenzhou, the second District, the 1897 hospital was expanded in 1900 thanks to a gift from Henry Blyth of Great Yarmouth, after whom it was named, and a College was opened in 1903. In the two Districts there were 209 chapels or meeting places, 4,118 members, six ministers and 107 Chinese preachers.

The UMFC's work in Jamaica, never strong, was weakened by a hurricane in 1903 which destroyed or severely damaged sixteen churches and schools, and destroyed banana plantations with long-term consequences for the economy and for the livelihoods of church families. In 1907 an earthquake devastated Kingston: over 1,200 died and 3,000 were made homeless, and the family of William Griffith (a supernumerary minister, who had been fifty-five years in Jamaica by the time he died in 1915) was 'marvellously preserved, having vacated the house a few seconds before it was utterly demolished'.[20] Not a church of any denomination was left standing. The previous year the UMFC's Annual Assembly had discontinued grants to Jamaica and, although a disaster relief appeal was made, that decision of principle was not reversed. A Jamaican minister, R.H. McLaughlin, had been appointed as General Superintendent in 1906 and in 1907 the principle of autonomy was carried further in that the choice of Superintendent was left to the local people. At the time there were 3,890 members in all, fewer than when

---

[19]   pp. 67–70.
[20]   *Missionary Echo* April 1907: p. 75.

disaffected Wesleyans had separated nearly seventy years before. The Jamaican societies, and the daughter mission in Panama, transferred their allegiance to the Methodist Episcopal Church (MEC) in 1912.

In Sierra Leone there were 2,426 members in the Freetown churches, which were largely self-directed, and just 84 in the Mende mission inland. Charles Goodman[21] survived the ravages of the Mende War but his Krio colleagues, like his home and church in Tikonko, did not; when he departed in 1901 his successor, Albert Greensmith, re-energized and extended the work. For years Greensmith was the only European missionary in the District. In East Africa, after forty-five years of endeavour, there were just 404 members; the first two African ministers were ordained in 1899 and 1904, but they were the last until 1930. Around 1905, the attempt to plant the faith among the Galla, the original *raison d'être* of the mission, was effectively abandoned. But in 1905 the capital of the Protectorate was moved from Mombasa to the rail-head in Nairobi and other missions were beginning work inland; in due course Methodism would follow.

The birth of the United Methodist Church (UMC) coincided with a tragedy in China, where the hill village of Shimenkan had become the centre of a far-flung circuit.[22] There were still villages hostile to the gospel, however, and, although nurturing the new Christians was a full-time task, Samuel Pollard believed fervently that to be a disciple is to be an evangelist and the most important thing was to set them the example. He sent Miao evangelists out two by two and himself visited dozens of unbelieving villages. By then he could speak Miao as fluently as any of them, with all the cadences and the proverbs. In April 1907, as preparations for the uniting Conference were being finalized back in England, Pollard and three companions led a service in a little hut, in a hamlet where just a handful had been converted and had been ill-treated as a result. At midnight the house was surrounded by a mob – most of them Chinese and a few local Miao – who dragged them out to beat them up. Pollard made a dash for it, which allowed the others to escape, but he was caught and savagely battered, leaving him with broken ribs, a punctured lung and severe lacerations. A runner took the news to the BC hospital in Zhaotong, normally two days away – but within two days Dr Savin with a government escort was on the scene. In great pain and near to death Pollard was taken to the hospital. Miraculously, he survived; and amazingly, before July was over he was back in Shimenkan, touring the villages again. In 1908 he left for England, a long journey by the new Trans-Siberian Railway; it was his second furlough in twenty years. He had delayed his departure because he knew his story had prompted a wave of sympathy and he had no wish to be fussed over or lionized.[23]

After twelve months with his family in England, Pollard returned alone to Yunnan. He resumed his rounds and revisited the scene of his beating; he recorded in his diary that he 'had a basin of *hsi-fan* with them, to show there was no ill-

21   Pritchard, *Methodists and their Missionary Societies 1760–1900*, p. 196.
22   pp. 68–9.
23   R.E. Kendall, *Beyond the Clouds* (London, Cargate Press, 1948), pp. 108–118.

feeling'.[24] At the end of 1913, eight years after the first Miao baptism, there were 4,800 adult communicant members and more than 5,000 preparing for baptism. By 1915 there were over seventy chapels, built at an average cost of five pounds. But he was always dissatisfied with the progress. In June 1915, the day after he had 'baptized seventy-five Miao, fourteen Nosu, one Chinese', he wrote 'There is not much advance among the unbelievers here; as in so many places, the work is standing still'.[25] A month later typhoid came to Shimenkan and in September Pollard succumbed.

Before he was contacted by the Miao, Pollard's interest was in the Nosu people and in 1908 there was sufficient Nosu interest in the Christian faith to warrant a full-time missionary appointment among them. Clement Mylne took up the challenge. With the revolution of 1912 came persecution for Nosu Christians, yet in that year 313 were baptized. Mylne's policy was to let them 'manage everything, or nearly everything, for themselves', looking forward to a time when they would be both self-governing and self-supporting. So at the annual meeting they adopted stringent regulations on Betrothal and Marriage Customs, and on Sunday Observance: 'So marked was the feeling,' wrote Mylne, 'that any member or enquirer failing to comply with the new rules is to be summarily ejected'.[26] Even so the Christian community grew, as it did among another minority people, the Kopu, where Miao evangelists led the way and there were 2,000 enquirers by 1914.

In Africa the year 1912 saw work begun in Meru on the foothills of Mount Kenya which would transform the character of Kenyan Methodism. John Griffiths had been pressing the UMFC Committee to establish new work inland since 1900. It was the UMC Committee which eventually took the decision, after he had obtained the Governor's permission to make a start in Meru and reported on an initial visit to the area. So he returned in 1912 with an agriculturalist, Frank Mimmack, and spent a month clearing a site and building a thatched log-cabin in Kaaga township. Meanwhile the Committee selected an enthusiastic young minister, Reginald Worthington, to pioneer the new mission with Mimmack. After some medical training at Livingstone College, he arrived in Kaaga in 1913. With the help of a Kimeru-speaking catechist, he wasted no time in opening a school but there was a tragic setback in 1914 when a dormitory fire killed five of the first twelve boys. It was a misfortune which for a while affected the attitude of the Meru. Worthington's own confidence was shaken but his convictions were not; his perseverance was rewarded by the first eleven baptisms in 1916.

---

[24]   Diary entry for 24 January 1911, quoted in R.E. Kendall, *Eyes of the Earth* (London, Cargate Press, 1954), p. 135.

[25]   Ibid., p. 170.

[26]   UM Mission Report for year ended April 1913: p. 46.

Wesleyans reach a Centenary

There were two areas of special concern at the start of the century. The Methodist Church of South Africa was autonomous, but the Transvaal and Swaziland District was still the responsibility of the Wesleyan Methodist Missionary Society (WMMS) and the Boer War disrupted its life as it did the PM work. Many chapels were requisitioned as temporary hospitals; most missionaries were compelled to vacate their stations. However some of the African ministers were able to remain at their posts and hold their congregations together, and between 1898 and 1902, although the number of chapels was reduced, the number of members actually rose. After the hostilities came to an end, activity was resumed to such good effect that at each of the next two Synods, in 1903 and 1904, a membership increase of over 3,000 was reported.

In the West Indies, the autonomous Conference proved to be administratively and financially unmanageable; in 1903 it was dissolved and the Districts again became Districts of the British Conference, under WMMS direction. Despite the management problems, which had plagued the autonomous Conference throughout its twenty-year life-time, there was said to be 'no sign of decline or decay, but life and growth'.[27]

The twentieth century was to see the centre of gravity of the Christian world shift decisively from the North Atlantic southwards; in Wesleyan circles, that movement was evident from the earliest years. Throughout the decade reports of conversions came from near and far, and the annual report for 1910 noted with joy some striking statistics: in ten years, 28 per cent growth in Ceylon; 68 per cent in Hyderabad; in Bengal, 82 per cent; in Burma, over 100 per cent; in the Gold Coast 74 per cent (including a rise from eight members to 914 in Ashanti); in the Lagos District 69 per cent; in the Transvaal, 131 per cent; in Rhodesia 140 per cent; and in China 72 per cent – the 432 adult baptisms recorded in the three Chinese Wesleyan Districts in the year 1910 were few by African and Indian standards but extraordinary by comparison with the 281 members which the first quarter-century's efforts in China brought into the fold. One remarkable conversion took place in the Seychelles, where Nana Prempeh, the Asantahene, was exiled from the Gold Coast in 1893; he was converted and baptized in 1904. Subsequently he was confirmed in 1921, and permitted to return to Kumasi in 1924 where the first thing he did was command all his family to put themselves under instruction for baptism; a few months later he chaired a Wesleyan missionary meeting.

The thousands of baptisms in Hyderabad[28] were exceptional; elsewhere the conversion of a handful of individuals could be significant enough to feature in the Society's annual reports. In some instances these were hailed, if not in so many words, as trophies: as when four Buddhist priests in Ceylon became Christians, or when some Brahman students at the college in Negapatam were converted.

----

27   WMMS Annual Report 1904, p. 3.
28   pp. 64–6.

That event so aroused the ire of other Brahmans that a group of them proceeded to destroy the church at Mannargudi. While the vast majority of baptisms in India were of Dalit converts, it was also in the Negapatam District that 'a community of caste people invited the missionary to their village that they might hear and discuss Christian principles, and … over 200 of them attended an evangelistic service in the street which was conducted by means of a magic lantern.'[29] From Italy, where British and American Methodists and the Evangelical Free Church came together in 1904, came reports of Roman Catholic converts: 179 of them in 1909, plus an 'anarchical Socialist long under police surveillance' whose family were now 'good citizens and zealous church members'.[30] In Italy too, a diminutive minister in the slums of Naples, Riccardo Santi, began his work with street-children when, on his birthday in 1905, two children living under the arches at the station tried to sell him matches. Instead, he took them home to tea, and they became the first of hundreds who lived with the Santis, initially in their little manse and, as numbers rapidly grew, in 'Casa Materna'. The name became widely known, and later it was rehoused in a villa bought by American Methodists.

During this period schools and hospitals in many parts of the world were being opened, refurbished, extended. The bills were affordable partly because the Society's income rose steadily and in 1906 shot up to a new high of £174,000, but primarily thanks to the contributions of so many more members on the spot.

The joy was tempered by a series of disasters and disappointments, especially in the Caribbean. On St Vincent, where a third of the island's 30,000 inhabitants were Methodists, the eruption of the Soufrière volcano in 1902 left 2,000 people dead and thousands more – including two of the four ministers – homeless. In Jamaica, not only did frequent hurricanes wreak damage to life and property, the 1907 earthquake destroyed Kingston and the daughter of George Lockett, 'the oldest English missionary in the active service of our Society', was among the dead.

The earthquake did, however, lead many Jamaicans to reconsider their priorities, and membership rose by 1,269 that year. The hurricane of 1912 rendered 100,000 Jamaicans homeless; five Wesleyan chapels were destroyed and another five severely damaged. Honduras experienced an outbreak of yellow fever in 1905, and two revolutions in 1910. Haiti suffered a series of calamities. There were repeated uprisings and revolts; Haiti had eight Presidents between 1902 and 1915, when it was occupied by American marines. The rebels often resorted to arson. Fires ravaged Petit Goâve in 1902, Port-au-Prince in 1908 and Aux Cayes in 1911; Methodist members and property were not spared. The Port-au-Prince premises – chapel, schools, manse and other buildings – together with books, schedules and records were lost. The church was utterly dispirited. The saga of destruction continued with a disastrous hurricane in 1915 which 'reduced much of the population to despairing poverty and caused some Haitians to look

---

[29]   WMMS Annual Report 1912, p. 83.
[30]   WMMS Annual Report 1910, p. 38.

Figure 1.1   George Lockett at the grave of his daughter Emily: Kingston, Jamaica 1911

upon the arrival of the American marines as a deliverance of God'.[31] These were far from the last of Haiti's trials; but in Haiti and throughout the Caribbean the Methodist people were, like St Paul, 'afflicted but not crushed ... struck down but not destroyed'.[32] In British Guiana, Harold Yates was appointed in 1912 to work among the East Indian labourers after a thirty-year interval; over the next thirteen years he trained catechists and saw membership increase from half-a-dozen to 250. In 1913 work began among Guaymi Indian groups in Panama.

     In China, with the Boxer uprising overpowered by foreign intervention, the life of the church resumed – but in conditions which included cholera in Hunan, floods in Guangdong, lawlessness in the cities, brigands in the countryside and riots over the price of rice. Yet when the 1909 Prayer Manual reported on the riots, Gilbert Warren, Chairman of the Hunan District, whose house had been ransacked, wrote:

---

     [31]   L.J. Griffiths, *History of Methodism in Haiti,* (Port-au-Prince, Imprimerie Méthodiste, 1991), p. 197.
     [32]   2 Corinthians 4:8, 9.

I am sorry the new *What to Pray For* has put the interruption to our work so strongly ... The missionary oversight was in great part withdrawn – happily our work does not consist of merely the work that missionaries do.[33]

Under the terms of the 'Unequal Treaties' the WMMS had the right to claim compensation for riot damage, and had indeed done so after earlier incidents. On this occasion however, Warren felt, and the Committee agreed, that no claim should be made; a sign of embarrassment at the extent to which they were compromised by the protection of the western powers.

The days of the Qing dynasty were numbered. In 1911 unrest became widespread and a military revolt in Wuhan toppled the regime. Sun Yat-sen, himself a Christian, was elected provisional President of Republic of China and circulated an appeal for the prayerful support of the churches and missions. It seemed that a great opportunity was at hand; Wesleyans baptized another 500 believers in the year. At this juncture one of the Society's Secretaries, Henry Haigh, visited the three Districts and saw for himself that after sixty years the work still rested on very shaky foundations: inadequate premises, insufficient staff, too little educational work to produce Chinese ministers and catechists in any numbers. He made the bold recommendation to add to the staff of each District one evangelistic worker, one medical worker and one educational worker. The Society did even better, and did it quickly; in the autumn of 1913, a party who were known as 'the Methodist eleven' set sail. (For the WMMS eleven was a lot, though there were by then over 5,000 Protestant missionaries across China.) Another result of Haigh's visit was the College[34] in South China, where Haigh had found just one elementary school with twenty-six pupils. It was built in Foshan, near the hospital, and opened in 1914. Although post-Imperial China was riven with factionalism from day one, it was for Christian missions a time of optimism.

In Burma there were by 1913 over 500 members, but it was apparent that Burmese Buddhists were unlikely to forsake their ancient faith in numbers. In the hills north-west of Mandalay, however, were Shan and Chin people, long-time foes of the Burmese who had never adopted Buddhism; it was there that efforts should be concentrated, if only there were the people – European or Burmese – to do it; but there were not. Two attempts were doomed to failure. First, Edgar Bradford conceived the idea of a motor vessel to reach the villages along the Chindwin river and its tributaries, and in 1912 wrote a letter to the *Methodist Recorder* which so impressed a Mr Booth of Dublin that he arranged for a boat to be built to Bradford's specifications. Bradford then took advice locally, realized the specifications needed modifying, and discovered that it could be built in Burma for £120. Booth generously agreed to sell the half-built boat and send the

---

[33]   M. Sheaff, *From Tortoise Hill* (Leominster, Orphans Press, 2007), p.91.
[34]   Originally named after Haigh, it later became Wa Ying College.

engine and £185 to Burma. The vessel was completed in 1913.[35] Mervyn Young, a minister who had his master's certificate, was put in charge and took it upriver. Before long, however, spare parts were needed and they proved difficult to obtain. In 1915 Young joined the Indian Army Reserve, the boat fell into disuse, and it was sold in 1918.

Map 1.1   Burma

For years the missionaries had wanted to start medical work; plague, cholera and smallpox were rife. Out of the blue, a gift from a 'generous friend' in 1914 made it possible and Dr Percy Stocks and his wife volunteered their services. The couple prepared for their new adventure excitedly, indicating in letters that they were intrepid travellers and even planned to bring with them a touring kit and a folding piano. Dr Stocks made it clear that his wife, a trained nurse, was as determined as he was to abandon home comforts and to travel in hostile territory.[36] There was a dispute in the District over whether to start in the Shan Hills or the

    [35]   SOAS, WMMS/Correspondence/Burma/FBN1, Phillips to Hartley, 8 December 1913; Hartley to Booth, 2 March 1914.

    [36]   SOAS, WMMS/Correspondence/Burma/FBN1, Stocks to Hartley, 28 February 1915.

Chin Hills; Stocks said he was prepared to look at both. But this amenability disappeared the moment they set foot in Burma, in September 1915. Within two days of arriving in Mandalay, Stocks tendered his resignation; and though he was persuaded to withdraw it and go to the Shan Hills where a beautiful house was rented for him, he was soon complaining, on the one hand that the house was inadequately furnished and on the other that it was too costly to rent and it was 'against his Christian and moral principles' to divert funds from evangelistic work. In any case, he said, it was his duty to join the army – and they departed. Their life in Burma lasted from 26 September to 21 October.[37]

Happily this was an uncommon experience, even before candidates were put through a more rigorous selection process. A year earlier Dr John Stephens had arrived in Nigeria with the backing of the Wesley Guild and Dr Sydney Osborn was sent to Rhodesia.[38] They were the first medical missionaries appointed to Africa. Medical and educational work were now seen as integral to Christian mission and not merely as strings to the evangelistic bow; healthy bodies, lively minds and practical skills were a universal birthright. African schools were better resourced than formerly; one of the notable early twentieth century innovations was the arrangement to station small teams of deaconesses at the girls' schools in Freetown, Cape Coast, Accra and Lagos, taking furlough in turns so that, in principle, there were always two *in situ*, sharing both the teaching and the pastoral care of boarders. Sunday Schools too flourished in West Africa. William Balmer wrote of them in 1911:

> … it has been my lot to visit Sunday Schools in which method, discipline, energy, and smoothness of working, and that undefinable essential of a good school called 'tone', were all present … And that is true all the way down from the Gambia to the Niger.

In a Sunday School in Freetown, he was impressed by the 'swift, quiet registration of present scholars, and prompt visitation of absentees'. He found 'neatly printed plans of lessons, devotional meetings, and prayer-leaders'. In the Gold Coast, he reported, 'The Ga community (around Accra) seems to have a special genius for this kind of work, which they cultivate assiduously'.[39]

Access to the West African interior was becoming easier with developing road, rail and telegraph networks. Missionaries were eager to establish bases inland, not least because the influence of Islam was spreading southwards on the same routes; every Muslim trader was an evangelist for his faith. Robert Gush, in Sierra Leone early in the century, was visited by a deputation from a remote Mende village asking him to go and live there as their teacher. He was obliged to disappoint them. A few

---

[37] M.D. Leigh, 'Cowboys and Indians: Methodist Missionaries in the imperial high noon of Upper Burma', paper delivered at MMS History Conference 2005.

[38] pp. 91–2.

[39] *The Foreign Field* May 1911: pp. 252–3.

months later they returned asking for an African teacher, but there was none to spare. A third approach was equally fruitless. Two years later Gush learned that the chief had become a Muslim, the church they had erected was a mosque, and a Muslim teacher was living in the house they had built hoping for a Methodist evangelist.

It was clear that Christian evangelism would be best undertaken by Africans, and that in any case there would never be an adequate supply of Europeans. To build a corps of well-equipped evangelists and teachers was paramount. The Lagos District responded by opening a training institution 120 miles inland at Ibadan, with four students when it was built in 1905 and twenty by 1913. Somewhat later the Gold Coast District would follow suit in Kumasi, once the scene of frequent human sacrifices. In 1911 the Gold Coast Chairman, William Griffin, and his colleague Frederick Ekuban made an exploratory journey through the northern territories of the Protectorate; they were met by delegations asking for Christian teachers, and were offered land. The Synod received their report enthusiastically and promptly appointed two missionaries to the area, but the venture was short-lived and another forty years elapsed before the Northern Ghana Mission became a reality. In the French territories, the church in Porto Novo, the administrative capital of Dahomey (later the Republic of Bénin) and a renowned centre of Vodun (voodoo[40]) practice, celebrated its Jubilee in 1912 with a congregation of 1,500. The mass conversions in the Ivory Coast, prompted by the preaching of the Liberian revered as Prophet Harris in 1913–1915, were unknown to the Society for another decade.[41]

The Rhodesia District was also looking northward. Chikala, a mineworker from the north, now Zambia, was converted in the south, Zimbabwe, and wanted his people to hear the gospel. The Chairman, John White, undertook an exploratory mission in 1909, and in 1912 three catechists were appointed to begin work. In the same year a joint committee of the Rhodesia and Transvaal Districts proposed to open a station in the Belgian-controlled mining area of Katanga. Douglas Gray, who had come to Africa two years earlier, was earmarked for the job, but the Society vetoed the venture. Gray went instead to Zambia and in July 1913 settled in Chipembi, north of Lusaka; his outstanding ministry of almost fifty years made it a notable Methodist centre. In Mashonaland too new stations were established. The farm at Epworth was extended with the purchase, in 1905 and 1908, of two adjoining farms comprising over 6,000 acres; some of the land was used for specifically church purposes, much of it rented to tenant farmers. Other new stations were given English names, such as Sandringham (1913) and Marshall Hartley (1914) – a tribute to the long-serving WMMS Secretary. At Gatooma, a mining centre which drew many Europeans, services were at first held in billiard rooms and boarding houses but soon a church was built for the Europeans with a resident minister, and four school-churches for the Africans with an evangelist

---

[40]   Vodun, the Fon word from which 'voodoo' is derived, can be translated as 'spirit' or 'god'.

[41]   pp. 72–7.

in charge. As in the cities, segregated worship was the norm for many years. Language made that inevitable – interpreters were few and in any case Europeans were not prepared to endure interpreted sermons. John White, who had first gone to the Transvaal in 1892 and served in Rhodesia from 1894 until 1932, began translating the New Testament into Shona as soon as his grasp of the language allowed, assisted by Jonas, the son of Chief Chiremba of Epworth. Later he wrote:

> I was without any settled abode, and spent most of my time travelling from place to place, superintending the work of our evangelists. Whilst the oxen rested ... we sought shelter from the burning sun, and under some friendly tree or under our wagon, rendered St Mark's Gospel into the Shona Language.[42]

The whole New Testament was published in 1907 and a Shona hymn-book of sixty hymns, composed or translated by White and his colleague Avon Walton, in 1908.

The Wesleyans of Britain and Ireland never lost their interest in 'the foreign field' but as the centenary year approached a surge of enthusiasm was evident. In 1902 the Conference appointed 'the first Monday in October to be observed throughout the Connexion as an Annual Day of Intercession for Foreign Missions'. In the same year the Ministers' Missionary Union (MMU), independent of the Society, was founded, with a statement of intent which read:

> The Members of the Union will make it their aim:-
> To pray for Foreign Missions
> > in private devotions
> > in family worship at least once a week
> > in the Public Services of the Church
> To preach on Foreign Missions at least once in every six months – not omitting on these occasions to appeal for the consecration of young men and women to work on the Foreign Field
> To encourage, and wherever possible, personally to conduct, the Missionary Prayer Meeting of the Church.

The MMU produced a four-page monthly bulletin *For the Missionary Prayer Meeting*. A flavour of the style is found in the subjects for thanksgiving included in July 1902:

> For the King's happy progress towards recovery, for all the blessings of our favoured land and empire, and for the splendid opportunities our power and place afford of spreading the light of the Gospel throughout the world.

---

[42] C.J.M. Zvogbo, 'An overview of the Methodist Church' in C.S. Banana (ed.), *A Century of Methodism in Zimbabwe* (Harare, Methodist Church in Zimbabwe, 1991), p. 12.

Over the lifetime of the MMU, which disbanded in 1978, the frequency of the bulletin was gradually reduced, its style evolved and its theology of mission moved on.

A decade later Wesleyan laymen in their turn organized themselves to support the Society.[43] Primitive Methodists had set an example a year earlier when they founded the Laymen's Missionary League. At the 1912 WM Conference a hundred members were invited to a dinner at which the Wesleyan Laymen's Missionary Movement (WLMM) was founded. It arranged an annual conference at Swanwick in Derbyshire, where it continued to meet well into the twenty-first century (having changed its name to Methodists for World Mission after women were belatedly admitted in 1972).

The Society's centenary celebrations lasted for three years. At the 1911 Conference an appeal was made for 'not less than 250,000 guineas' and its target was surpassed, thanks to collecting boxes in homes and to collections at centenary meetings held in every District and in almost every circuit. Three books came out for the use of local study groups in 1910, 1911 and 1912, on China, Africa and India respectively. The week beginning 28 September 1913 was marked throughout the connexion as a week when thanks were offered, in the words of William Goudie – home from Madras and secretary of the Centenary Committee – 'for the wisdom given to the Conference in 1813, when, casting providence to the wind, it resolved to fund Missions in Ceylon and India'. The grand climax was a gathering in the Royal Albert Hall on Monday 6 October. All that remained was to publish the Centenary History which had been in preparation since 1907; its five volumes appeared at last between 1921 and 1924.[44]

Edinburgh 1910

In many ways the outstanding event of this period was not a specifically Methodist one. The World Missionary Conference[45] brought together over 1,000 delegates, all but a handful from Europe and North America. It met just fifty years after the first – but much smaller and very largely British – such event, held in Liverpool. There had been other gatherings in the interval, including an Ecumenical Missionary Conference in New York in 1900, with 2,500 official members, and practically 200,000 people attending its meetings over ten days. But most of these were popular conventions aimed at stimulating public interest and support. Liverpool 1860 and Edinburgh 1910 were *confer*ences designed to enable missionaries and mission board executives to confer about strategies. Missionaries in India and

---

[43]   J.R. Pritchard, '1913 and All That' in P. Forsaith and M. Wellings (eds), *Methodism and History* (Oxford, Applied Theology Press, 2010), p. 148.

[44]   Ibid., pp. 141–146.

[45]   B. Stanley, *The World Missionary Conference, Edinburgh 1910,* (Grand Rapids, Eerdmans, 2009).

China had held such meetings from time to time. At Shanghai in 1907, on the centenary of Robert Morrison's arrival in China, 1,200 delegates assembled. It was a forward-looking conference, characterized by the opening address of John Campbell Gibson, the chairman:

> While planting the church we have also reproduced in China the unhappy divisions of our western Christianity … Let us recognize that Chinese Christianity is bound to seek two things and to regard them as intimately related, namely independence of the control of foreign Churches and union among their own.

He referred to 'the time-honoured formula in which we all agree that the Church in China should be self-supporting, self-governing and self-propagating'.[46] Ironically there were very few Chinese participants, which limited the value of the discussions on training the Chinese ministry and the whole day spent debating 'Ancestral Worship'. Edinburgh 1910, it has often been remarked, suffered in the same way from a dearth of Asian, African, Pacific and Caribbean participants.

The World Missionary Conference was masterminded by the American Methodist layman John Mott, who convened a planning meeting in 1907. This followed the example of the Shanghai Centenary Conference organizers and established eight commissions to prepare the ground; each conducted two years of meticulous research and produced a substantial report, which was distributed to all delegates before they headed to Scotland. The eight themes were: Carrying the gospel to all the non-Christian world; The Church in the Mission field; Education in relation to the Christianization of National Life; The Missionary Message in relation to non-Christian Religions; The Preparation of Missionaries; The Home Base of Missions; Missions and Governments; Co-operation and the Promotion of Unity. Each report formed the basis of a day's deliberations in Edinburgh.

There were over fifty British Methodist participants: two PMs, six from the UMC, thirty-nine from the WMMS – nine of them currently stationed overseas – and five from the WM Women's Auxiliary.[47] Among them were John Ritson, James Hope Moulton and William Findlay. Neither Ritson nor Moulton was a missionary himself. Ritson was one of the two General Secretaries of the British and Foreign Bible Society (BFBS); he was also the honorary secretary of the MMU. Another of his commitments was to convene the London Secretaries' Association which brought representatives of several missionary societies together regularly to address matters of common concern. In that capacity he was asked to join the organizing committee of the Conference and later to lead its finance committee. In Edinburgh, he was one of the two recording clerks; one of his tasks was to press a concealed button to warn speakers their time was up. He was a member of the 'continuation committee' which eventually led to the creation of the International

---

[46]   *China Centenary Missionary Conference Records* (New York, American Tract Society, 1907), p. 8.

[47]   There were 144 Methodists from North America.

Missionary Council (IMC). At that committee's second meeting the London Secretaries' Association was asked to take forward the idea of a 'collective and representative body' of the British Societies and he convened a gathering in York, in June 1911, as a result of which the Conference of British Missionary Societies (CBMS) began life at Swanwick in 1912. Ritson chaired its Standing Committee for six years. Moulton came from a family of Methodist ministers. His uncle and son both worked overseas and he once had a long conversation with David Hill about being a missionary, but he took a different path: he was an eminent scholar and the first nonconformist to be elected a Fellow of a Cambridge college. He became an expert on Zoroastrianism; returning from a seventeen month-long lecture tour in India in 1917 his ship was torpedoed in the Mediterranean and he died from exposure after three days in an open boat. He and Findlay were passionate enthusiasts for the message of Edinburgh. Findlay, who had worked in south India from 1881 to 1900 and was a Secretary of the Society from 1900 to 1910, was deputed to spend the next year touring British Methodism to spread the message. He was to have given the Fernley lecture in the Centenary year, but fell ill and Moulton was hastily called upon. Moulton chose as his subject *Religions and Religion*, influenced heavily by the work of the Commission on the Missionary Message in relation to other Religions.[48]

Some of the insights and affirmations which emerged from the Conference shaped missionary thinking and practice in the years that lay ahead; others failed to make much impact – the deficiencies of the report on Education, for example, became evident as time passed.[49] The issue of the place of other religions in God's purposes was controversial and the sympathy, generosity and humility evident at Edinburgh were not widely shared for many years to come. There was a welcome stress on the imperative to educate women as well as men. There was anger at the opium and liquor trades and at forced labour; caste was not condemned so forthrightly, and incipient apartheid in South Africa was passed over. The need to eliminate duplication of effort, to avoid competition between agencies in any given area and to co-operate in activities such as publishing and higher education was emphasized but the prospect of church union (among Protestants – there was no Roman Catholic participation) was aired without agreement. Indeed, only after considerable debate was a continuation committee established to maintain the ecumenical momentum.

The Conference's closing message was quoted, by Findlay's brother and niece, in the final paragraph of their *Wesley's World Parish* (1912), published in time for the WMMS centenary:

---

[48]   J.H. Moulton, *Religions and Religion; a Study of the Science of Religion, Pure and Applied* (London, Charles H. Kelly, 1913). Moulton's theology of mission and faith-to-faith encounter is discussed in K.R. Cracknell, *Justice, Courtesy and Love* (London, Epworth Press, 1995), pp. 270–282.

[49]   Stanley, pp. 200–201.

We are called to make new discoveries of the grace and power of God, for ourselves, for the Church, and for the world; and in the strength of that firmer and bolder faith in Him, to face the new age and the new task with a new consecration.[50]

But even as Wesleyans celebrated, dark clouds were gathering over Europe and the continent was soon plunged into an ugly conflict which raised a massive question mark over the moral right of Europeans to preach to others and shook their confidence in the progress of the missionary enterprise to the core. Western missionaries, having come together at Edinburgh, found themselves on opposite sides of a bloody war. If western cultures were supposed to be examples of Christian ideals, then it was hardly surprising that for many people the gospel appeared to be 'bad news'. From the vantage point of 1996, the message of the latest conference on world mission and evangelism reviewed the intervening years:

> ... the first comprehensive ecumenical mission conference ... stated 'The work [of mission] has to be done now. It is urgent and must be pressed forward at once.' The work of mission, however, did not turn out to be straightforward. Within four years of that conference the world was engulfed in war. Since then it has known massacres and mass deportations, another world war, the development of new forms of colonialism, life under nuclear threat, the destruction of ecosystems by human greed, the growth and collapse of the Soviet bloc, violent and separatist ethnic struggles, rampant capitalism leading to an ever-greater gap between rich and poor.[51]

Yet the theme of that 1996 conference in Brazil was *Called to One Hope.* A hope justified, in spite of the multiple traumas of the twentieth century, by Christianity's dramatic demographic shift to the 'global south'. This was a movement in mission in which Methodists played a full part.

---

[50]   G.G. and M.G. Findlay, *Wesley's World Parish* (London, Hodder & Stoughton, 1912), p. 224.

[51]   C. Duraisingh (ed.), *Called to One Hope* (Geneva, World Council of Churches, 1998), p. 20.

Chapter 2
Changing Patterns of Missionary Life

The life of a missionary in the new century was very different from the experience of those who sailed with Thomas Coke a hundred years before. Most now knew something, before departure, of the land, if not the specific destination, for which they were bound. They had heard and been stirred by missionaries on furlough. They were better equipped to face the rigours of climate, and the mosquito had been identified as an enemy to avoid. Many would be living and working alongside missionary colleagues rather than in isolation. Their number increased steadily for fifty years before beginning to dwindle. The number of women missionaries, boosted by the development of the Wesley Deaconess Order (WDO), grew noticeably, due in part to the lack of husbands after the carnage of the Great War.

The life of a mission partner at the end of the twentieth century was vastly different again from what their Edwardian predecessors knew. Now many could telephone the family whenever they chose. It was usual to make visits home much more frequently than of yore. The majority enjoyed water and electricity, if not always on an uninterrupted basis. But the biggest changes, by far, were in the nature of their relationships with their indigenous colleagues and national church leaders: changes that were effected slowly, and at times painfully, over the course of many years.

The Deaconesses

The WDO was founded by Thomas Stephenson in 1890. Three years earlier a similar order had already been formed in the German Methodist District. The *Martha-Maria Verein* was founded by G.J. Ekert in 1887. By the time that District was transferred to the MEC, under American oversight, in 1896, there were some three dozen sisters working in Nuremberg, Munich, Magdeburg and Vienna. They ministered to the sick, to the dying and – as in London – to destitute children. Stephenson's sisters were initially attached to the Children's Home which he also founded. Before long, however, the Order had a clear identity of its own, and the sisters were appointed to serve in circuits both at home and abroad. Those who went overseas did not necessarily go under the auspices of the Women's Auxiliary (WA), or even to places where the WMMS was working. One in Christchurch, New Zealand, later another in Lima, Peru, and some brief appointments in Canada are recorded; while in 1910 a request to supply a deaconess for the Falkland Islands was received, but could not be met for want of a suitable volunteer.[1]

The first deaconess to serve abroad was Evelyn Oates, who volunteered to work in South Africa and sailed in 1894. In Johannesburg she named her home 'Stephenson Cottage', and wrote:

> The Committee voted me the magnificent sum of £20 to furnish – my bedstead and bedding cost about £10, leaving a very small amount to be spent on the sitting room, and kitchen necessaries. However, there is such a thing as sanctified ingenuity, and a cosier little place than I am now writing in would be hard to find.[2]

In 1896 Sister Evelyn was sent to Australia 'on a mission of extraordinary delicacy and difficulty' the details of which neither she nor Stephenson revealed. Back in South Africa the tasks to which she was called included vital ministrations to Boer War victims and culminated in her appointment to head the new Kilnerton institution 'for the training of native girls' in Pretoria – though ill health cut short her service there.[3]

In 1897 the Order undertook to send two deaconesses to Puttur, in North Ceylon. Gertrude Nettleship, the first, was there until 1931; she had a string of colleagues and successors, doing medical and evangelistic work and training Tamil deaconesses. The Order established a Ceylon Fund which supported their work for fifty-five years.

Early in the twentieth century teams of three were sent to run the Girls' High Schools in Freetown, Cape Coast, Accra and Lagos, on the basis that at any one time two would be on duty and the third on furlough. In view of the rigours of the climate, the WMMS agreed to provide £10 per annum to the superannuation fund for each deaconess. Stephenson insisted that all should be volunteers; his statement that 'the call to duty will be cheerfully answered' was amply vindicated. The rotation system worked well; the posts were staffed by the Order, rather than the individual. Tragically just as Sister Agnes Reed, who had been working for some years to obtain a science degree and teaching qualifications in readiness for this work, arrived in Accra in 1913, yellow fever broke out. She and Sister Nellie Hopewell nursed the pupils until they both were taken to hospital. She died within a month of her arrival; the funeral was attended by the entire European population of Accra and over 1,000 Africans.

Deaconess appointments were at first administered jointly by Stephenson and the Secretaries, and not by the WA. In 1927 however, when the Auxiliary became the WMMS Women's Department (WD) and moved its offices back to

---

[1]   E.D. Graham, *Saved to Serve* (Peterborough, Methodist Publishing House. 2002), p. 239.

[2]   *Highways and Hedges*, October 1895, quoted by Graham, p. 100.

[3]   R. Aitchison, 'The Wesley Deaconess Order in the Transvaal', in *WHS Proceedings* 58 (May 2011): pp. 62–7.

Bishopsgate, they came under the care of the WD Secretaries. There were then thirty-four deaconesses overseas, compared with just four thirty years earlier. Among these were two who had qualified as nurse-midwives and gave particularly long service: Ethel Tomkinson in Mysore from 1914 to 1964, Gladys Stephenson in Wuhan from 1915 to 1951.

Sister Ethel went to India as a sister-tutor and worked at the Holdsworth Memorial Hospital in Mysore for eighteen years. In the next phase of her service she led a team of Indian Biblewomen, engaged in evangelistic and pastoral work among women in the Mysore circuit. There was plenty to be done in the city but as much and more in the surrounding villages, and she moved to Kastur where she established an ashram with the name Premalaya, or House of Love, sharing the simple life of the villagers in a ministry of prayer and service. At an age when she could have retired she began a new chapter, restoring a derelict jungle mission station which she turned into another ashram, a retreat centre with a little dispensary. Later still, at a time of drought and famine, she returned to Premalaya and rescued it from threatened closure, building it up until it comprised a nursery school, a hospital, a food distribution point, a retreat house and a home for retired workers. But she herself would not retire. She was still a practising midwife on occasion, especially when no-one else would attend a mother with leprosy. And when Premalaya was well established and the jungle ashram at Mandagadde was left short-staffed through illness, back she went again and stayed until she was 75.

Sister Ethel completed her training at the Deaconess House in Ilkley before she trained as a nurse, whereas Sister Gladys, likewise persuaded of her missionary calling from her teenage years, became a nurse first. From Ilkley she went initially to Anlu, in Hubei Province. When she arrived she found the hospital sparsely furnished, with a quartet of untrained boys as her nursing team. Over the years she and her doctor colleague transformed it. The hospital became a recognized Nurses' Training School, with such a reputation that she herself became President of the Nurses' Association of China. In 1926 she was sent by the Association to the United States to study the latest approaches to nurse education. She could not return to Anlu, now occupied by the Communist Red Army, and was posted instead to the new Union Hospital in Hankou, which soon became the largest teaching hospital in China.

Her experiences there included the floods of 1931–1932 when the Yangtze burst its banks, 20 million people were made homeless, and the waters reached the middle floor of the hospital. 40,000 square miles of central China were inundated for months. Cholera inevitably followed, and Sister Gladys was put in charge of the nursing staff at seven temporary hospitals on higher ground. After a few years of relative normality came the Japanese invasion. The hospital remained open throughout the war years, but in 1941 she was interned for the duration of the war. She later described her life during those years:

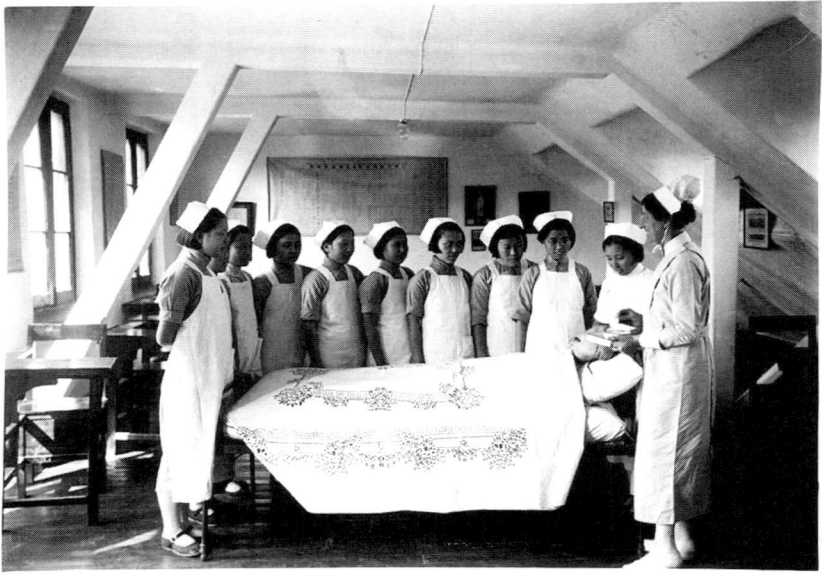

Figure 2.1   Sister Gladys Stephenson teaching Chinese nurses: Hankou. c. 1937

> We ran a school for four hundred children and a small hospital of twenty beds
> where I worked … We ran a Sunday School as well as services, and an evening
> intercession period which became very precious to a small group of us.[4]

On her release Gladys Stephenson returned to Hankou and resumed her duties until,
after Mao Zedong came to power, she and all missionaries had to leave the country.

Jessie Kerridge was another long-serving missionary deaconess. She was a
trained teacher and active in the Guide movement; from Ilkley she went in 1928
to Jamaica where she ran leadership courses for women. In time she was asked to
develop deaconess work throughout the Caribbean and travelled tirelessly across
the region. The Deaconess House in Kingston, her home for thirty years, became
the headquarters and training centre of the West Indian Order. The WDO's link with
Puttur was concluded in 1953, since the work there was now well established, and
the Ceylon Fund became the Overseas Deaconess Fund, expressly to resource West
Indian developments. Eventually the House, and Sister Jessie with it, moved to the
campus of the United Theological College where deaconesses trained alongside
ministerial students. By the time she retired to England in 1965 there were West
Indian deaconesses in eight countries. One of these was Julia Davis, who spent
years in the squalid slums of west Kingston where she set up Operation Friendship.[5]

---

4   Quoted more fully in Graham, pp. 208–9.
5   p. 249.

Many others served for shorter periods and had less remarkable ministries; each made her own contribution to the life, growth and social witness of the world church. After 1973, when after much vacillation Methodist women were at last admitted to the ministry of word and sacrament, diaconal vocations dwindled and recruitment to the Order ceased in 1978.[6]

Women's Work

Organizationally, Methodist Union in 1932 brought the three women's auxiliaries together as Women's Work (WW), and later the oversight of WW missionaries was integrated more closely with the administration of the MMS as a whole. As the twentieth century advanced, WW activities tended to become more institutionalized and more regulated. When they moved around, it was often on foot; in towns, perhaps by rickshaw; for longer journeys, by public transport – train, boat or overcrowded buses of disparate shapes and sizes. Men missionaries were provided with their own cars long before most women, though from the 1960s a militant WW team at the Mission House remedied that wherever travel was a requirement of the post.

An unprecedented number of women offered themselves for service overseas in the 1930s and 1940s, and the combined resources of the women's networks in the uniting churches made it possible to support them. When the Society celebrated the centenary of the Wesleyan 'Ladies' Committee' in 1958, there were 218 women workers on its books. The majority, still, were either teachers or medical workers, but increasingly they were appointed to teacher-training, sister-tutor and kindred posts, preparing the way for national independence and church autonomy. Others were village or urban evangelists, on the front line of mission, and key support-workers, such as District administrators. The greatest concentration of women workers, as of ministers, was for many years in India – though within India they were widely dispersed, in the many Methodist hospitals, schools and circuits, and some, from 1947, in institutions of the CSI begun by other denominations.

Gwen Ash, who was the Secretary of the Girls' League[7] between 1937 and 1944, sailed at the end of that year for the Gold Coast. It was a nervous voyage: the Elder Dempster line had lost several boats to enemy action. The convoy took three weeks to reach Takoradi. She described her first impressions of Africa, jammed in a mammy wagon on her way to Cape Coast, in her diary.

---

[6]   Ten years later the surviving deaconesses were incorporated in a new Methodist Diaconal Order. Graham, pp. 98–240, is a much fuller account of deaconess service overseas. There are chapters on Kerridge, Stephenson and Tomkinson in P.M. Webb, *Women of our Time* (London, Cargate Press, 1963).

[7]   pp. 56–7.

When the lorry driver drove off I saw for the first time the palms and strange tropical plants and flowers, the women sitting at the roadside with oranges and nuts to sell, and naked brown children running to and fro – and I realised that this was Africa. I could have wept for sheer thankfulness. God had brought me here. Although the long ride was a strange experience, I felt at peace and full of wonder that it had come to pass.

Her temporary destination was Wesley Girls' High School, where she attended worship the same day.

The service with the dark skinned blue-clad schoolgirls seemed oddly familiar, and yet strange. The view from the windows, yellow sand, palms and the heavy surf are all too much like a missionary poster to be real.[8]

Margaret James, who arrived in Secunderabad a matter of weeks after Indian independence and the inauguration of the CSI, described her first impressions in a letter home:[9]

I have been shown all round the hostel, domestic quarters and compound row; it is all very interesting and so utterly different from an English school. The girls sleep on mats on a big verandah and eat on another one; of course no tables or chairs are needed there. The washing arrangements, etc. seem very primitive to me, but are a lot different from those in their village homes, where they are often, as such, non-existent. Mother would be interested in the store-room, where all the food stuff is in the raw – great bags of rice, grain, wheat, etc. … in the kitchen all the cooking is done over fire; I don't know how they bear it in the hottest weather.

Our servants' houses in the compound are typical of ordinary Indian homes, and take some getting used to; they are made of mud and stone and each is just one small window-less room in which the entire family sleeps – on the floor, of course. They cook over a small fire and there is no outlet for the smoke; only very primitive lighting, if any. They bolt the door at night, and I just can't think what it must be like.

There is a Dhobi family living on the compound who do all the washing: they have done my first lot beautifully – the art is 'in the family' so to speak, as they and their ancestors will have been at the same job for ages. If we just want something pressed we send it over to them. I watched them ironing with huge irons which have burning coal in them and are so heavy that I could not lift them.[9]

---

[8]   G. Ash, *Ninety-Nine Not Out!* (private publication, 2008), pp. 43–4.

[9]   E.M. James, letter to her parents, 2 November 1947 (James family papers).

Although Women's Work at home had its distinctive organization, its own recruitment and training arrangements, and funds dedicated to supporting its missionaries, overseas the missionaries were under the direction of the church leaders, invariably male, and the discipline of the District Synod or autonomous Conference. They were immediately accountable to the heads of their institutions or to circuit superintendents; as the years went by these were increasingly men or women of their host nation. In time new missionaries came to see themselves no longer as 'WWs' but – in all but name – mission partners.

Becoming Mission Partners

Even before Overseas Districts became autonomous churches, many had indigenous Chairmen[10] and the leadership of the church passed out of missionary hands. Senior missionaries who stayed on made their experience available to their successors; they would not wish to be thought of as the power behind the throne, though that was sometimes the case. New arrivals found themselves under local direction and stationed by committees and Synods which were, at least in majority, composed of national members. Although the term 'mission partner' was not formally adopted until 1995, it was how many described themselves. They went, and were received, as ministers or lay professionals seconded for a period to serve the partner church. Tours of duty varied with the climate: two years in West Africa, three in the Caribbean, four in East Africa, five in India (where local leave in the hills brought relief from the oppressive heat of the plains) and Central Africa. The receiving Church determined, whenever a missionary went on furlough, whether or not to extend an invitation to return for a further period.

The forty years from the mid-1950s were a time of accelerating change. Most post-1960 missionaries, and all post-1970 missionaries, would fly to and from their appointments. There was no longer time for language study or Bible study on deck, or in cabin. Landing just hours after departure, they emerged from the cool of an aircraft into what was, for most, a steamy heat. First-timers would have a few days, at best a few weeks, of orientation before being thrust into their work. If a foreign language was a requirement of the job, some would have done a crash course before departure; structured language study *in situ* gradually gave way to intensive pre-departure courses at SOAS in London or the Alliance Française in Paris. With a better-educated population than in the past, much of their work could be done in the colonial language, and reasonably competent interpreters in other tongues were available where necessary.

Housing varied from palatial to simple, but more often than not – and in places later rather than sooner – water was available on tap and electricity on switch. MMS policy was to provide essential domestic equipment and furniture if it were lacking. 'Essential' could well include a cooker, fuelled by a butane gas bottle, and

---

[10]   Appendix 2.

a fridge, but not a washing machine; washing could be done by hand, probably the hand of a domestic servant. Grants were still made to support a compound-worker and a night-watchman, if local conditions made that advisable, but other domestic help would be paid for out of the missionary's pocket.

Depending on the nature of the appointment, the missionary might well be provided with a car. Most circuit ministers still had many churches to serve and many miles to travel, and in this respect expatriates were often better off than their national colleagues who had to use public transport, frequently un-timetabled and unpredictable. On the other hand, they were unlikely to have air-conditioned vehicles although that became the norm for church leaders. (It should be borne in mind that while references to heat and air-conditioning apply to most of Africa, Asia and the Caribbean, it was otherwise in the highlands of East and Central Africa or Bolivia.)

Contact with home was becoming much easier, cheaper and frequent. In the 1970s it was unusual to phone home other than at a time of family crisis. By the 1980s many places had reliable telecommunications and missionaries in Tonga could ring their parents – though it was still a complicated procedure – with the news that a baby had been born 'at 4 o'clock tomorrow morning'. In rare cases of serious illness or injury evacuation could be arranged rapidly, though a very few fatalities – child deaths, road accidents – brought missionary service to a tragic end. The 1990s saw the advent of email. The first mission partners to use it were in places where airmail was slow to arrive and the telephone system unreliable, namely Nepal and Bolivia; they were emailing home before the Mission House in London was equipped to receive and respond.

In the second half of the twentieth century it became possible in some situations for married women to take paid employment. Using their qualifications professionally was fulfilling, and their income was a welcome supplement to the missionary allowances. It was, however, still the most common thing, to the end of the century, for a spouse to give unpaid service. Winnie Tovey described her life in Mysore in the 1950s and 60s as 'wife, mother, hospital driver, physiotherapist, stenographer, librarian, sick visitor, church organist and food aid distributor'.[11] It was possible because 'Each servant had his or her own allotted duties and on no account was I allowed to cook or clean'.

An awkward divergence between European and local ministers on matters of theology and pastoral practice became more noticeable, and a difficult and sometimes stressful balancing act could be needed between sensitivity and respect for colleagues, and personal integrity. Many of the attitudes and practices which missionaries found unpalatable had been fostered by their predecessors; others owed more to local custom. Examples of the former included the use of the office of Morning Prayer with its archaic language – in places poorly translated – each Sunday, and the practice of seeing and signing a membership card before allowing

---

[11]   W.E.Tovey, *Cor Blimey! Where 'ave you come from?* (Northampton, Little Knoll Press, 2011), p. 99.

anyone into the church for Holy Communion. An example of the latter would be harsh treatment of subordinates by ministers (though similar behaviour by missionaries had not been unknown) which even ran, in at least one instance, to punitive beatings of theological students by their teachers. Other unfamiliar aspects of church life, such as a steward with a long pole ready to prod anyone who started nodding off during the sermon, or worshippers wandering over to an open window to spit outside, or baptizing infants as they suckled at the breast, could be taken in the missionary's stride. There were churches which had not yet abandoned the expectation that every man would come on Sunday clad in jacket, collar and tie, and others which insisted on ordering expensive choir robes from England made of material totally inappropriate for the climate. There was nothing to be done other than point out the incongruity without attempting to impose a veto. A more likely source of tension, debated in ministers' and preachers' meetings, lay in how the Bible was understood – a feature of home circuits as well, except that even the most conservative of missionaries could be pained at the way some of their colleagues treated the text. Yet these differences were not generally allowed to affect the relationship between national and expatriate colleagues; mutual respect, and sometimes close friendships, made possible creative dialogue on issues that would otherwise have been irredeemably divisive.

The back-up support of MMS staff was an important factor in the life of the missionary. There were sometimes complaints, as there had been ever since Coke's party reached Ceylon. It was not always possible for a Secretary visiting a country to meet every missionary there and some felt neglected. But the care provided by those responsible for personnel and finance became progressively more extensive. It was mandatory to make a will before departure, and that could be done in-house. National insurance and pension provision were safeguarded. Furlough accommodation for families was available. Help towards the costs of children's education was given, whether through home tuition, schools overseas or boarding in Britain or Ireland. There was a full medical check-up at the start of furlough, and any treatment was promptly arranged. Those such as diabetics, with particular medical requirements, if these could not be reliably met abroad, could have their medication sent from London regularly. The export department shipped supplies for missionaries as readily as for institutions, at cost. For some years an *Annotated Booklist* of recent publications was sent to each missionary; books were classified as 'worth buying', 'for your furlough reading list' and 'for specialists, colleges and school libraries'. There were furlough conferences, and eventually intensive courses for those on final furlough to assist their re-entry into British society and church life. Yet post-service care was variable: one who came home with an alcohol problem was found work for a time at Mission House where an eye was kept on him as he 'dried out'; much later another, who came back after thirty years' service suffering from serious depression, received – as he saw it – virtually no help from the Mission House once he was no longer on the books.

Those who returned full of enthusiasm for the new work they would be doing in Britain or Ireland could find reintegration difficult. Reverse culture shock was a traumatic experience for many. Ruth Anstey recorded that:

> The cost of the dinner I enjoyed in a London hotel on the evening of my arrival back in London in 1962 was greater than in our Hostel in Dharapuram we had spent on one day's food for a month. I developed a massive sense of guilt. It was not alleviated by the waste, and the apathy and intolerance towards the Third World, which I was to see around me. This sense of guilt has never left me...[12]

She was not alone. Many returned missionaries became energetic workers for Christian Aid, the World Development Movement, Traidcraft and kindred causes, besides their continued interest in the churches or institutions they had served and in the wide spectrum of the Society's activity.

The number of ministerial missionaries fell rapidly in the last half-century, from 327 in 1946 to 185 in 1971 to nineteen in 1996. There were 230 single women and sixty laymen in 1946 but in 1996 just thirteen single laywomen (eight of the ministers were women as well) and sixteen laymen. The autonomous Churches had come of age. They could staff their own circuits and institutions, train their own ministers. In the 1960s the Indian government began to refuse visas to missionaries, and in 1967 the Society reported:

> With other Societies we have had great difficulty in returning missionaries [to India] from furlough, and for new missionaries, especially those appointed to evangelistic work, the difficulties have been even greater.[13]

In the 1970s there were vociferous demands in various quarters overseas for a 'moratorium' on missionaries.[14] But they were not widely shared and went largely unheeded. In time, however, the most common practice was for autonomous Conferences to seek a mission partner for a specific appointment such as a hospital, theological college, social welfare or agricultural post, or serving an English-speaking congregation.

Identification

In the mid-1980s the matter of the relationship between missionaries and those amongst whom they work was revisited. A Voluntary Service Overseas (VSO) worker in Sierra Leone had caught lassa fever and been repatriated at a cost approaching £250,000. The Secretaries had to consider whether, had it been a

---

[12]   *Indo-British Review*, vol. XIV (1986): p. 10.
[13]   Agenda of the Methodist Conference 1967: p. 220.
[14]   pp. 263–5.

missionary, MCOD would have done the same; whether insurance should be taken out for missionaries in areas of risk, for very high premiums; or whether missionaries should be withdrawn from such areas. These questions highlighted wider issues of principle, which were addressed in a discussion paper:

> In the Incarnation Jesus came to earth and shared totally the life of human beings. He calls us to share in his mission – he is our example. What does it mean in the 1980s to partake in the Incarnation? ... As we struggle over questions concerning a car for this missionary, an annual leave because of family circumstances for that missionary, or because of the children's education for another missionary ... what is involved in being identified with the local church and the local culture? ... Personnel with government agencies and businesses abroad have a different approach to life and work in another country. The expectations of people in Britain in many areas of life have become much higher ... Are we being challenged to a different view of life and death? Do we need to relearn that life is transitory and death is part of life?[15]

The use of the Incarnation as a model for cross-cultural mission raised difficult questions for the then General Secretary, Albert Mosley. It would mean that 'a missionary going to Haiti, to Zimbabwe, to Sri Lanka must seek to become a Haitian, a Zimbabwean, a Sri Lankan in the way that Christ became man in the incarnation. It will not be possible for her/him to do it completely, but it is an ideal at which the missionary must aim' if the incarnational model is followed. But there are weaknesses in the model:

> Some of the reasons why missionaries cannot become Haitians, Zimbabweans, Sri Lankans are ...
>
> They will never have the right colour of skin and other physical characteristics.
>
> They can never go through the formative experiences which Haitians, Zimbabweans, Sri Lankans go through in their early years ...
>
> They can never become members of the blood-related communities in which Haitians etc live their lives.
>
> Perhaps because they have been shaped by the living standards, education etc of their early lives there are limits to how far they can adapt to different living standards, to being themselves without some of the books, music etc on which they have come to rely.

---

[15]   MCH: Elizabeth Hale, paper circulated within MCOD, 1985.

These are insuperable barriers which prevent missionaries getting anywhere near the ideal this model sets before them.

Furthermore, observed Mosley:

> Suggesting to missionaries that they must strive towards this ideal – which they can never get near to because of these insuperable barriers – creates a great deal of unhealthy guilt. It makes missionaries wish they could become Haitians etc. It makes them try to pretend to be what they are not.

> This guilt prevents missionaries from seeing that they have a very positive, creative contribution to make because they are 'strangers'. It is possible both in the Bible and in Church history to trace a very special role which 'strangers' play in God's mission.[16]

The issue, sharply focused in the relationship between missionary and indigenous colleague, had much wider implications. In a world where extremes of wealth and poverty co-exist, how were rich-world Churches to relate to poor-world Churches? Were they to redouble their charity or, as the proponents of a moratorium argued, to wind down? How were rich-world Christians, from the security and comfort of their rich-world homes, to express their solidarity with poor-world Christians? What were the Christians of the poor world and their Churches to make of their rich-world fellow-believers?

The Kenyan Methodist, Zablon Nthamburi, writing more in sorrow than in anger, brought an African perspective to the debate:

> I grew up near a mission station where for many years I interacted and rubbed shoulders with missionaries. At that time, missionaries were the only people who had good and decent houses, clean piped water, telephones, electricity, and serviceable automobiles. They were able to employ quite a number of people in the neighborhood as cooks, ayahs, gardeners, messengers and menials of various kinds who did many of the more tedious household chores for them ... The missionary was, by local standards, a very wealthy person. People could not understand why, with so much wealth, the missionary seemed unwilling to share with those who were poverty stricken...

> ... it is only discerning missionaries who are able to realize the degree to which their lifestyle contradicts the biblical message. The effectiveness of the gospel is hindered by insensitive affluence that makes social relationships not only difficult but embarrassing; for as long as there is an economic gap between missionaries and their converts, fraternal fellowship is difficult to maintain. In

---

[16]   MCH: Albert Mosley, paper circulated within MCOD , 1985.

the end, the gospel that the missionary tries to proclaim is watered down, not intentionally but watered down nonetheless.[17]

Though Methodists were not insensitive to the contrast, they could only plead guilty as charged. The Society did its utmost to prepare 'discerning missionaries', but the dilemma was not resolved. In the particular dilemma raised by the risk of life-threatening illness, it had to be recognized, in the words of one of the thought-provoking posters that MCOD produced at the time, that 'Mission is Risk' – and the physical risks run by missionaries in the late twentieth century were fewer by far than those run by their nineteenth century predecessors.

International partnership in mission still had its own significance; as another Kenyan, Lawi Imathiu, put it in 1988:

> We shall continue asking for missionaries ... indefinitely, even when we have enough ministers, doctors and nurses. Why? Not because they have anything

Figure 2.2   Lawi Imathiu, Presiding Bishop, Methodist Church Kenya and Chair of the World Methodist Council

---

[17]   Foreword to J.J. Bonk, *Missions and Money* (New York, Orbis Books, 1991), p. xiv.

new to give us, but they will be a kind of window to bring fresh air into our Church. A Church that does not receive people from outside becomes stuffy.[18]

---

[18]   L. Imathiu, in conversation; reproduced in one of a series of posters entitled *Power to Change*, MCOD 1989.

Chapter 3
Twentieth Century Martyrs

The Methodist missionaries who met a violent death on active service in the twentieth century were all, directly or indirectly, victims of war, rather than martyrs in the classic sense that they were executed for refusing to renounce their faith. But it was their obedient response to what they believed to be a divine call that placed them in situations of danger.[1]

The death of Heber Goldsworthy in 1938 was indirectly caused by the Sino-Japanese war. The Japanese invasion began in 1937 and all Chinese soldiers were called to the front, leaving the west of China vulnerable to the roving bands of brigands who infested the region. Since 1921 Goldsworthy had been working in south-west China, where Methodist mission was begun by the Bible Christians. Born into a Methodist family, he had been inspired in his youth by Samuel Pollard's account of the mass movement among the Miao people.[2] He offered himself for the ministry of the UMC, in which the Bible Christians had joined in 1907, expressly for overseas work. For sixteen years he served in circuits in Yunnan, including the capital Kunming (then still known as Yunnanfu) and Zhaotong where a Miao deputation had appeared in 1904 entreating Pollard to share the gospel with them. The Miao have numerous sub-groups and Methodist work was primarily among the A-Hmao, or 'Flowery Miao', in the hills around Shimenkan in the adjoining province of Guizhou. Goldsworthy's hope was to develop work among the Chuan (River) Miao, and saw his appointment to Shimenkan in 1937 as a step towards that goal. He was excited to be living in the very place of which he had heard Pollard speak in his youth. Miao evangelists were still spreading the word to their neighbours, and in his first year itinerating in Guizhou province he baptized 2,300 new Christians. In addition he had oversight of the boarding school in Shimenkan, which is where he met his death.

Bandits attacked the mission station in March 1938. The identity of the raiders was never determined. They may have been a marauding gang of Muslims: the Muslims of Yunnan had been subdued with great cruelty in 1873 and some had lived from hand to mouth ever since. Heber Goldsworthy, with a Miao colleague, was killed trying to protect the students in the boarding house. He was buried alongside the grave of Samuel Pollard. These graves were desecrated in the course of China's 'cultural revolution' some time after 1966, but over twenty years later they were restored by the government and in a moving ceremony in 1995, in the

---

[1]   The deaths in 1906 of George Maddison in South Africa and Roderick Macdonald in south China were recorded in Pritchard, *Methodists and their Missionary Societies 1760–1900.*

[2]   See pp. 67–71.

presence of Goldsworthy's children who knew him only via their mother's stories, the site was declared to be a permanent County Monument.

A year after Goldsworthy's death Albert Leigh was killed in an air-raid in Hunan, and in December 1941, as Japanese forces overran Hong Kong, Eric Moreton was hit by a shell. In the war years that followed, China and its missionaries had much to endure, and many were interned. None of the Methodists died in internment, though Grace Ridge, who had worked in Hankou since 1923, died in Shanghai as the Hubei missionaries, with permission to leave the country, waited for a passage to Mozambique, and Sadie Laird, an educationist interned after the fall of Hong Kong, was mistakenly reported to be dead.[3] Nor were any missionary lives lost in the turbulent period preceding and following China's liberation by Mao Zedong's Red Army, which led to the departure of all missionaries.

Albert Leigh had worked in Hunan since 1930. Early in 1939, he returned from furlough to Pingjiang, leaving his wife and four-year-old son in England because of the hostilities. Pingjiang was thirty miles from the front, still in Chinese hands, but the target of Japanese air-raids. The Japanese authorities had prescribed that all foreign properties should be identified with a signal clearly visible from the air, and the Methodist mission was marked by a large Union Flag. Within weeks of his return, an air raid warning prompted Leigh to join a group of frightened schoolchildren in a colleague's house on the compound to comfort and reassure them. But reassurance was vain. For some reason the air signal was ignored and ten bombs hit the compound. Three fell on the house where Leigh was sheltering; he and a Chinese colleague were killed.

Eric Moreton was the grandson of Robert Moreton, the pioneer missionary in Portugal; his father was the BFBS agent in Portugal. His first missionary posting was to Haiti. His station at Aux Cayes was isolated; he became depressed and lost his sense of call. He returned to London, and became an active layman. In 1936 he re-entered the ministry, and in 1938 he offered to supply an urgent vacancy in the Hong Kong English circuit, with special responsibility for the Soldiers and Sailors Home in Wanchai. He married Norah in 1939 and in November 1941 their son was born. In December the Japanese attacked both Pearl Harbor and Hong Kong. Moreton was wounded driving an ambulance that was hit by a shell. He died of his injuries on Christmas Day.

Two who died in 1941 have no grave. Alec Fenby and Herbert Williams both died at sea when their convoy was attacked by enemy aircraft. They were returning from West Africa. Both had earlier served at Uzuakoli College in Eastern Nigeria, where Williams as Principal had built up the institution, designed new buildings, formed its traditions, and left it with a full range of departments from primary classes to teacher-training. He then became the Chairman of the Eastern Nigeria District, while Fenby moved to the Gold Coast as head of the prestigious Mfantsipim School

---

[3]   When she read her own obituary in the *Methodist Recorder* she pronounced it 'most interesting': W.G.B. Ream, *Too Hot for Comfort: War Years in China 1938-50* (London, Epworth Press, 1988), p. 21.

in Cape Coast. Another victim of the war was Ernest Taylor. He had put aside his doctoral studies to answer an urgent call from the Séminaire Protestant in Porto Novo where ministers for the French West African Districts were trained. He was arrested by the French authorities in October 1941 and charged with assisting persons to leave the Vichy-ruled territory. He was sent for trial to Dakar and imprisoned there in unhealthy conditions. He died of typhoid fever in the Military Hospital in Dakar in April 1942 at the age of 29. Thus two more distinguished ministries and one full of promise were brought to an untimely end.

In 1965 the Rhodesian government unilaterally declared its independence from Britain, determined to retain the white power and privilege which elsewhere had been forfeited to the African majority in the course of decolonization. Most African leaders took an unequivocal stand for 'NIBMAR' – No Independence Before Majority African Rule. Their liberation movements were gradually making the country ungovernable. One night in 1978 freedom fighters surrounded the Methodist School at Thekwane,[4] south-west of Bulawayo, and compelled 400 students to walk across the border into Botswana. Their plan was that some of the students would become teachers in the refugee camps they were running, and others would fight in the liberation army. The school's head teacher, Luke Kumalo, insisted on going with them. Kumalo was born into the Ndebele royal family; he was directly descended from Mzilikazi who founded the Ndebele nation. But he did not seek royal privileges. He trained as a teacher and taught geography at Thekwane. He took charge of the boys' hostel and exercised a quiet influence for good as one generation of boys after another passed through the school. In all he gave twenty-six years' service. Some of the boys he taught went on to be cabinet ministers, others to important professional responsibilities. He exercised discipline firmly and fairly. He was a man of sound judgement, as it proved on this occasion. By his courage and strength of character he compelled the abductors to release the children, and almost all of them went back to the school.

In 1969 a missionary teacher from England, Jean Gosling had come to Thekwane. Jean had previously worked in Eastern Nigeria. Trained at Southlands College and then at Kingsmead, she went to Nigeria in 1957 at the age of 25. She was on furlough when the Biafran War broke out ten years later and, unable to return to Nigeria, she was redeployed to Rhodesia. Jean and Luke fell in love. There was a great deal of racial tension in the country and many people advised them to break off their relationship. But they eventually married in 1972. Their life together witnessed, in an unpromising context, to the truth that racial differences were no barrier to human relationships, even of the most intimate kind.

Because of the danger that Thekwane, an isolated compound, might be attacked again, the school was moved into the city of Bulawayo. The buildings were left empty. Later they were used as an army camp; villagers took away the furniture and the library books were burned.

---

[4] Known to Europeans as Tegwani, and so called in all the literature prior to 1980.

The Kumalos were on sabbatical in England when the war ended and Zimbabwe became independent. Together with Andrew Ndhlela, the President of the Methodist Church in Zimbabwe (the church officially used the name before the nation could adopt it) they were given rousing applause at the 1980 British Conference. Then they returned to Thekwane. It had been badly vandalized – windows broken, doors pulled off their hinges, holes in many of the roofs, water pipes smashed. Luke himself was going blind. The situation seemed hopeless but he did not give up hope and was determined that, with Jean's encouragement and support, the school should be rebuilt. The students moved back and life began there again. Luke inspired them to work with their hands and repair the buildings whilst they were also doing their studies.

In the immediate post-independence years the different political parties were jostling for power. Each one tried to gain Kumalo's support, but he refused to take sides. This led to threats, but he stood his ground and was unafraid. In 1985 he got into trouble with the authorities for refusing to comply with military orders to close down the school food shop; one of the army's counter-insurgency tactics at the time was to inhibit the flow of food into affected areas.

At the close of that school year, Luke Kumalo led the end-of-term service and told the students that all he had accomplished had been through the power of Christ. He urged them to have courage and to be faithful. He reminded them that among that year's leavers were some who had come back from Botswana with him seven years before. He was full of hope. For the first time next term there would be a full complement of staff. But the following night, 25 November, a group of armed men went to the school, asked for the Kumalos, shot and killed them both and burned their house to the ground. Eyewitnesses described the attackers as numbering about twenty-five and being clean and in uniform. A nearby army unit failed to intervene. They were said, officially, to have been tracking a dissident unit which they suspected was responsible for the attack. But if the army was aware of a rebel presence in the area, its failure to intervene was all the more incomprehensible. No plausible explanation was ever uncovered for what happened. It was not an attack on missionaries or on white people: there were others on the staff who were not harmed, though an 18-year-old Irish volunteer was seriously injured. Speculation as to the identity of the killers and their motives ranged from dissident groups bent on destabilizing the country to government agents bent on eliminating potential rivals.

The Kumalos were buried at Thekwane. On their graves were placed two simple crosses with the words, 'Father forgive'.[5]

---

[5]   *Zimbabwe:The Killing of Luke and Jean Kumalo* (London, Amnesty International, February 1986); *NOW*, July-August 1986, p. 29.

Chapter 4
Life at the Mission House

Church, manse, school, clinic – and sometimes graveyard – were in many places clustered together on 'the mission compound'. This was a plot that had been allocated by, or bought from, the local government, whether traditional or colonial, or a landowner. Frequently it was situated a little away from the town or village it served, often on a hillside which was preferred on health grounds. Sometimes it was large enough for converts to build houses there, especially in situations where converts were ostracized by the local community. In common parlance, 'the mission' denoted not the task but the place. The missionary's home was known as the mission house.

The Mission House – initial capitals – was the place from which the Wesleyan enterprise was managed. The 'Centenary Hall' at Bishopsgate, refurbished and re-opened in 1903, together with the warehouse nearby at Carlisle Avenue, served the Society well. In 1908 *The Foreign Field* reported that the warehouse was using seventy-two miles of string and sixteen acres of brown paper per annum. The smaller branches of Methodism had virtually no centralized headquarters, apart from a Book Room/Publishing House in London; missionary Secretaries worked from manses dispersed around the country.[1]

For a while after Methodist Union in 1932, Bishopsgate remained the headquarters of the much enlarged MMS, with other work conducted no longer from Carlisle Avenue but from Holborn Hall, the old PM offices. But before long the time came when the Centenary Hall, like its predecessors, was no longer fit for purpose. Its value had soared and it was sold to the Bank of India in 1938 for £320,000; this sum paid for a site on Marylebone Road, the erection of a brand new building with eight floors and two levels below ground, and a large injection of capital into a Plant Fund for use on property development overseas.

The new Mission House was only half-finished when war broke out in 1939, but the lower floors were occupied, some by the BBC. The work was completed after the war and the staff from Holborn Hall joined their colleagues in 1951. In 1996 the offices of most of the connexional staff were centralized there, after a long debate as to whether they should move out of London altogether, and the building was renamed Methodist Church House.

---

[1]   The PM Office and Publishing House was at Sutton Street, 1848–1894, Aldersgate Street 1895–1909 and at Holborn Hall, Clerkenwell Road from 1910; the UM Publishing House was at 12 Farringdon Avenue.

Figure 4.1 The new Mission House on Marylebone Road, London, being built, 1939

The People

The earliest officers of the WMMS were appointed in 1814: two Secretaries and a Treasurer, all of them ministers in London. A lay Treasurer was appointed in 1815 – the first lay connexional officer. (Thomas Farmer, lay Treasurer for twenty-five years from 1836, had as a child accompanied Thomas Coke begging from door to door for the missionary cause.) In 1816 the Conference approved the employment of a permanent clerk to assist the officers. From these small beginnings the staff at headquarters grew to over a hundred in the 1970s. The number of Secretaries quickly became three, one being resident at the Mission House; by 1932 the WMMS had five and one from each of the other uniting Churches joined the team. After reorganization in 1973 there were as many as ten: a General Secretary, three Area Secretaries (earlier known as Field Secretaries, but the term 'the mission field' was no longer used), a Secretary dealing with candidates for overseas service and another concerned with missionary affairs such as furlough, return to Britain and retirement, a Home Education Secretary, an Editor, a Children's Secretary and a Secretary shared with the Division of Education and Youth to stimulate young people's interest in world affairs and mission. Some of these responsibilities had for years been carried by less senior staff and undervalued.

The Secretaries were often men – and belatedly women – of considerable distinction. Not a few, from Richard Watson and Jabez Bunting to Harry Morton and Colin Morris, served as President of the Conference and four, in the thirty years from 1965, as Vice-President. Two, Elijah Hoole and Marshall Hartley, served as WMMS Secretaries for no less than thirty-one years. In the other branches of the Methodist family, by far the most notable of the bureaucrats was Charles Stedeford. A staid and sedate figure, he became Foreign Missions Secretary of the Bible Christians in 1904 and then served in that role throughout the life of the UMC. He was known as a great encourager. He had not himself served abroad, but his Secretarial duties took him to Africa and to China, and he was President of the UM Conference in 1928.

The redoubtable Edgar Thompson spent his entire ministry in the service of the Society. For twenty-five years he worked in the Mysore District in South India. On furlough in 1911, speaking on behalf of his South India colleagues at Conference, he proposed some notable revisions to the WMMS constitution. The debate was still remembered many years later as 'Thompson's great battle in Conference against the dictatorship of Marshall Hartley'.[2] In 1919 he returned to England as one of the General Secretaries, and as chairman of the Officers' Meeting from 1930 to 1934 he oversaw the merger of the uniting Churches' overseas work. At the time he retired, the practice was for retired Secretaries to become Honorary Secretaries and retain a seat on the Committee; he continued to take an active and, some said, over-intrusive part in MMS affairs. He helped to draft the Conference Declaration on Racial Policy in 1950 and in 1955, at the age of 84, penned a succinct account of *The Methodist Missionary Society: Its Origin and Name,*

---

[2]   If there was any personal animus between the two it was not evident at the 1928 opening of the new Mission House chapel, when Thompson wrote of Hartley's 'last appearance in the House of which for thirty-one years he had been so efficient and so distinguished a servant': E.W. Thompson, *The Methodist Mission House: its history and its treasures* (London, WMMS, 1933?), p. 11.

arguing the case which persuaded a later generation to celebrate the Bicentenary of Overseas Missions in 1986.[3]

Another Thompson took charge in 1958. Douglas Thompson, who worked in China 1925–1940, was not the Committee's first choice[4] but proved an inspired appointment. Until his time all departmental Secretaries throughout British Methodism were ministers; he persuaded the Committee to appoint laymen and women to senior posts. Since 1927 the WW Secretaries had been members of the Officers' Meeting but their responsibility was clearly defined as being for 'work by and for women'. That changed in 1966: there would no longer be two Secretaries, one man and one woman, for each part of the world. Instead there would be one 'Field Secretary', either man or woman, per area, with responsibility for all missionaries and for all relationships with the Churches of the area. The Society's Editor, Pauline Webb, was the first female Secretary. She had hit the headlines at the 1957 Conference when, just back from making a film in India about the CSI, she made an impassioned speech about global poverty which prompted the press to dub her 'the angry young woman'.[5] She was angry too about prejudice against women, and re-opened the dormant issue of women's ordination. She was a tireless campaigner against apartheid and in favour of Church unity. She was Vice-President of the 1965 Conference: all this while editing *The Kingdom Overseas*. Her post in the Society gave her a platform which she used to great effect, and the Society wisely saw her wider activity as an extension of its own ministry. After an interval, during which she added to her commitments the role of Vice-Moderator of the World Council of Churches' Central Committee, she returned to Mission House as Area Secretary for the Caribbean in 1973. That year the Society was rebranded as the Methodist Church Overseas Division (MCOD), a name with which she said she was far more comfortable. After six years she moved on to be Organizer of Religious Broadcasting for the BBC World Service.

Another inspired appointment was made under Douglas Thompson's guidance in 1961. Philip Potter from Dominica was the first overseas minister to become a Secretary. He succeeded Tom Beetham who moved to the Africa Desk of CBMS. Beetham had always insisted that, however onerous the task, the Africa Secretary should relate to the whole continent. Potter's appointment made that impossible: the Rhodesia District said it would be utterly impractical, in the political context,[6] for a black person to take the job. Harry Morton took responsibility for East and Central Africa, Potter for West Africa. Both went on to key positions in the ecumenical

---

    [3]   J.R. Pritchard, 'The Untidy Beginnings of Methodist World Mission', *Epworth Review,* 26/4 (1999): p. 70.

    [4]   J.R. Pritchard, *Edward Rogers: Portrait of a Christian Citizen* (Evesham, Wesley Historical Society, 2008), pp. 12–13.

    [5]   P.M. Webb, *World-Wide Webb* (Norwich, Canterbury Press, 2006), p. 39.

    [6]   UDI – a Unilateral Declaration of Independence – was soon to enforce white rule 'in perpetuity'.

Figure 4.2   Philip Potter, Secretary for West Africa and the Caribbean, 1961–1966

movement, Morton as General Secretary of the British Council of Churches (BCC) and Potter as General Secretary of the World Council of Churches (WCC).

The first General Secretary of the 'Overseas Division' was Colin Morris, like Webb no longer quite so young but every bit as angry about injustice and discrimination. As a young minister on the Copperbelt, before Zambian independence, he had courted hostility by proclaiming 'this church is colour blind'. He described himself as a 'political parson' and was in one of the delegations to the Lancaster House Conference in 1961 that worked on Zambia's constitution. He became a supporter and friend of Kenneth Kaunda, Zambia's first President in 1964, and was himself the first President of the United Church of Zambia (UCZ), inaugurated a few weeks after independence. He was a prolific writer and powerful preacher. He clothed his passionate impatience with a light-hearted style. Like Webb, Morris joined the BBC on leaving the Mission House. He became Head of Religious Television and later Controller of BBC Northern Ireland, but was best known not as an administrator but for his regular and incisive 'Thought for the Day' on Radio 4.

The post-war world was thus very different from former days. There were still 'giants in the land' but they no longer expected to give a life-time's service to the MMS. It became the general, though not unbroken, rule that connexional Secretaries

– in the Overseas and all other Divisions – should serve for a maximum of nine years and then put their talents to work elsewhere, in local church or wider world.

That restriction did not apply to most of the Mission House staff. Some of the back-room men and women did their jobs for decades. Stanley Sowton, for instance, was on the staff from 1906 to 1942. Earlier, while a banker in Plymouth, he had been influential in transforming the Juvenile Missionary Association (JMA) into a dynamic children's movement. He invented the JMA medals, which from 1903 were awarded to those who collected £5 (then a considerable sum) for missionary funds. He was good with words as well as figures and had begun writing in the children's magazine *At Home and Abroad* under the by-line 'Uncle Ned', a name familiar to thousands for half-a-century. In the run-up to the 1913 centenary celebrations he wrote regular articles in *The Foreign Field,* promoting in lively fashion the successful appeal for 'not less than 250,000 guineas' to mark the occasion. He fostered the use of 'overseas' rather than 'foreign' in the Society's terminology. After the centenary he became assistant secretary for finance, which for him was no desk job. He travelled widely and spoke often, and produced a steady stream of books and booklets, especially for JMA collectors.

Cyril Bennett, who had joined the Society in 1930, was the Finance Secretary from 1954 to 1975. His was a very influential position but without a voice in the Officers' Meeting. Perhaps for that very reason, he was a father-figure and confidant to missionaries. He promoted the establishment of Methodist International Houses (MIH), Dabou Hospital in the Ivory Coast and the Laymen's Capital Fund.[7] He was Vice-President of the Conference in 1976, the year he retired; for the previous year he was seconded to set up the Ecumenical Development Co-operative Society[8] under the auspices of the WCC, a permanent and revolving capital resource designed to foster partnership between wealthy and poor nations, and bring about economic growth, social justice and self-reliance. It was a cause which united three of his motivating passions: money, development and mission.

Lending their support to the Mission House team were the Committees. The 1818 'Laws and Regulations' of the WMMS prescribed a General Committee appointed by Conference, consisting of the President and Secretary of Conference and forty-eight other members, 'at least one-third of whom ... shall be selected from the Country Circuits', the rest 'resident in or near London'. In addition, a remarkable provision (not removed until 1884) to the effect that 'Those of the Methodist Ministers who are Annual Subscribers to the Missions of One Guinea, and one Treasurer, Secretary, or other principal Member from every Auxiliary District Society, who may be in London occasionally, shall be entitled to meet and vote with the Committee'.

Subsidiary committees inevitably multiplied: as well as a Finance and General Purposes Committee, the MMS inherited from the Wesleyans an Eastern and a Western Committee, set up in 1912 and comprising people of experience and

---

[7]   See pp. 231-2 for MIH, pp. 99-100 for Dabou and p. 55 for the Capital Fund.

[8]   Subsequently renamed Oikocredit.

influence. The extent to which these committees exercised delegated powers was often discussed and occasionally changed. A Pastoral Committee made recommendations to the Conference about probation, retirement, disciplinary cases and permission to serve other organizations. There were Literature, Medical, Candidates, Home Organization and numerous other sub-committees as well. The committees for women's work met separately. In the post-Union era there was a large WW Committee on Tuesday, followed by a large General Committee on Wednesday, almost every month of the year, until these were merged in 1970. The size and frequency of its meetings were gradually reduced in the interests of economy, and the Eastern and Western Committees were replaced by Area Advisory Groups for the Caribbean & Latin America, Africa, and Asia & the Pacific. Between them the various committees were at any one time tapping the knowledge, wisdom and interest of hundreds, many of whom had personal experience of living overseas.

The Role and Relationships

Secretarial responsibilities evolved steadily. The spiritual and theological preparation of new missionaries became the task of the college tutors. Administrative duties were increasingly devolved as the clerical staff expanded. But the number of fields and of missionaries multiplied. The number of Secretaries was enlarged, but the range of their duties was undiminished. By the middle of the century the then Africa Secretary listed his role as:

1. Reading about Africa and the World Church

2. Bringing to the notice of the Church in Africa experience of the Church elsewhere, in pastoral work, education and community welfare

3. Keeping in touch with African visitors to London and with Societies where African problems are discussed

4. Keeping in touch with Methodists in Government and other service and with Associate teachers in Methodist schools

5. Interpreting the African Church to the Home Church, by speaking and writing

6. Field Administration: grants, appointment and personal affairs of missionaries.[9]

Tom Beetham's self-assessment was that he was able to attend very little to five of the six because the bulk of his time and energy went on the last. Field

---

[9]   MCH: T.A. Beetham, memo to the MMS Officers' Meeting, 26 April 1953.

Secretaries exchanged numbered 'paragraphs' with the Chairman of each District on a wide range of topics: property repairs, grant requests for new projects, vehicles for missionaries, equipment for their manses and, not least, reports on ministerial students and probationers. Until an overseas District became autonomous, it was the British Conference which approved, or retarded, their progress towards ordination, and it fell to the Field Secretary to vet and transmit the District Synod's recommendations. Then there were committees to sit on, sometimes in the chair, and the many weekends spent away from home, 'maintaining the indispensable invisible asset of the Society, the confidence of the Home Church'. Beetham described a typical weekend: Saturday night welcome, two Sunday services, afternoon Sunday School, evening Youth Group, Monday Women's Meeting in the afternoon and another meeting in the evening – all of which had to be prepared.

A generation later, many of the issues which loomed so large in 1953 were resolved. Autonomy removed the British Conference's responsibility for national probationers, and the Secretary's responsibility for many of the issues treated in the 'paragraphs'. A weekend generally consisted of no more than a Saturday meeting and one or two services. And there was now a Personnel Department working alongside the Area Secretaries in recruiting, training, deploying and caring for missionaries, and their first point of contact.

But other things had changed. The rapidity of air travel made possible more frequent Secretarial visits to sister Churches. For 200 years inter-continental journeys had been made by sea, and although steam-power cut the time, no Secretary had travelled as frequently as Thomas Coke until flying became the norm. Until then, overseas visits had necessarily been of many weeks' or months' duration, at intervals of several years. Now the time spent away from home and family was much reduced, but it was common to travel several times a year, maintaining and developing relationships with the leaders of the overseas Churches, and assessing jointly the challenges and opportunities for partnership in mission. Equally, there were many more 'flying' visitors to be met in London – lay Methodists on business as well as church leaders on church business. There were ministers of sister Churches serving in British circuits[10] or on shorter visits, and while other staff handled the detailed arrangements it was important to be in touch with them.

The other major change was in the scale of ecumenical activity. The Society had never been a go-it-alone organization. The CBMS, formed in the wake of the World Missionary Conference in Edinburgh in 1910, was an organization with its own staff, including some notable Methodists over the years, and with Methodist representation on its committees and working-groups. From the 1960s there were increasing numbers of ecumenical meetings abroad at which it was useful to be present, such as the periodical Assemblies of the different continent-wide Councils of Churches and round tables convened by the united Churches in

---

[10]   p. 265.

India and Zambia to co-ordinate partnership – and in between meetings, a volume of correspondence.

Lobbying MPs and government circles had always been part of the job: over the slave trade, the annexation of Fiji and the opium trade in the nineteenth century, for forty years of the twentieth over apartheid in Africa and for even longer over the racism in Britain to which immigrants from the 'mission fields' were subjected. Not only politicians but banks and businesses trading in, or investing in, southern Africa, were pressured and the ethics of investment was a matter over which the Overseas Division lobbied the Conference and its Central Finance Board.

The tools for the job evolved, the copperplate penmanship of nineteenth century ledgers and letters giving way to typewriters and eventually computers. It was a shock to the Finance Secretary who was used to waiting at least three weeks for a reply to his letters to the Caribbean, when he first sent a fax and got a reply within three hours. The advance in technology softened the effects of a steady – and occasionally steep – reduction in staff numbers, necessitated by a decline in real income in the last quarter of the century. From around a hundred staff in 1973, the establishment had fallen to forty-seven in 1996.

Some of the policy developments were reflected in the wording of the Society's constitution, which not only guided the Secretaries and the Committee but was drafted by them. The original WMMS *Laws and Regulations*, drafted by Bunting and Watson, said no more than that

> The object of this Society is to excite and combine ... the exertions of ... Methodists (and of others, who are friends to the conversion of the Heathen World, and to the preaching of the Gospel, generally, in Foreign Lands) in the support and enlargement of the Foreign Missions, which were first established by the Rev John Wesley, AM, the Rev Thomas Coke, LLD and others..[11]

Subsequent to Methodist Union the MMS constitution declared:

> The aim and endeavour of the Methodist Missionary Society is to bring to Christ people who know him not; and, as fruit is granted to its labours, to assist in the establishment of Churches overseas which shall maintain and spread the Faith in their own countries and among their own kindred ... assisting in the nurture and growth of Churches which have not yet attained the stature of full self-support and self-direction.

and in 1974 the 'aim and endeavour' were restated as:

---

[11]   Clause 2 of the *Laws and Regulations,* printed annually from 1818 to 1932, with only slight changes of wording, in the WMMS Annual Report.

To proclaim and offer Christ to the peoples of the world; and to assist in the resulting establishment of churches overseas which themselves become the instruments of this great work both within their national boundaries and beyond.[12]

A consultation in 1992 produced a declaration that:

God's love is for the whole created order. God calls the Church into being to share in the accomplishment of that loving purpose through

- Bearing witness by life-style and proclamation to the way of Jesus

- Calling people of all races into discipleship and nurturing their growth

- The caring and healing of needy and broken individuals and communities

- Acting for justice, peace and the harmony of creation

- Lifting up in prayer the world's pain and suffering; and celebrating its hopes and joys.

- Particular tasks for the Overseas Division, in partnership with others in these islands and elsewhere, are:

- To promote and facilitate the interchange of resources for mission – people, finance and other resources such as insights, experience, prayer…
      between churches around the world,
      all receiving and all contributing
      all listening and all learning
      in mutual questioning and encouragement

- To make people increasingly aware of the world-wide implications of the Gospel – encouraging and promoting personal encounter between people of different countries and cultures and faiths and challenging all to a deeper commitment to sharing in God's mission through prayer, study and action.[13]

This 'restatement of purpose' did not find its way into the constitutional documents, but informed the change made in 1996 when the *purposes of the Missionary Society* were more comprehensively defined, as:

---

[12]   The constitution was not printed in MMS annual reports but in *The Constitutional Practice and Discipline of the Methodist Church* (*CPD*) from its first appearance in 1951.

[13]   Central Committee minutes, 21 March 1992.

Figure 4.3   The Mission House, 25 Marylebone Road, in 1984

To initiate, maintain and encourage Christian mission in other countries

To encourage the establishment of Churches overseas which will themselves undertake that mission both within and beyond their own borders

To engage in a continuing relationship of mutual help and enrichment with churches (including united churches) in the life of which Methodist missions have played a part

To foster and take part in ecumenical relationships in the field of world mission, including the work of the World Council of Churches and the Churches' Commission on Mission [as the Conference of British Missionary Societies had become]

To bear witness to the global character of Christian mission by supporting work with and among ethnic minority communities in Britain and Ireland which have had their origin in other countries

In furtherance of these purposes to engage in education, advocacy and fund-raising.[14]

The task was as challenging as ever, but as the Mission House became Methodist Church House it was time to tackle it in new ways.

---

[14]   MMS Constitution, clause 3, found until the Society was wound up in 2013 in *CPD*, vol. 2: Book IV B, Part 3.

Chapter 5
Nurturing Support

Late on Easter Sunday 1924, William Platt wrote an excited letter to his parents. For a fortnight he had trekked through southern Ivory Coast, astounded by the welcome he received from vast numbers of African Christians of whom European Missionary Societies had no knowledge.[1] At the end of a full account he wrote:

> Talk about a big job !!! I prayed for it and you two dear ones consecrated yourselves and your offspring to it !!! … However it's [thanks] to you two – your lives and love, that these thousands whose constant saying to me was 'We had no one to open our eyes and give us light' will now be cared for. So even though <u>your</u> Headquarters are 15 Welbourne Grove [Horwich], your outposts are in West Africa. God is good.[2]

By then hundreds of Methodist families and congregations had 'outposts' abroad: men and women they knew personally, prayed for daily and supported generously. It was not so in the early eighteenth century, when there was as yet a much smaller number of missionaries, whose news reached home only after long intervals. But the support mechanisms put in place at the outset paved the way to more elaborate ways of stimulating interest, prayer and finance and forging enduring links between 'outposts' and 'headquarters' – not only the Mission House but Methodist homes throughout Britain and Ireland.

Money

Thomas Coke's haphazard fund-raising and carefree book-keeping had to be turned into a *methodical* system. The WMMS constitution of 1818 spelt out in detail:

> The Monies raised in any Circuit for the Methodist Missions, by Branch Societies … shall be regularly paid, once in every quarter or oftener, into the hands of the Treasurer of the Auxiliary Society for the district in which the said Circuit is situated, with the deduction only of such sum as may have been disbursed for the incidental and local expenses of the Branch Society…[3]

---

[1]   pp. 74–7.

[2]   J.R. Pritchard, paper delivered to MMS History Conference, November 2009, quoting a copy of the letter to Platt's parents received from the writer.

[3]   Laws and Regulations, clause V.

The annual reports of the WMMS, and the missionary reports of the other branches of Methodism, devoted half their pages to listing the amounts and sources of moneys received, so that benefactors and treasurers could satisfy themselves that none had gone astray.

Locally, subscribers were encouraged to make regular contributions. In the Society's infancy, Jabez Bunting, for whom 'domestic and foreign missions were not mutually exclusive but mutually reinforcing', described how

> In Leeds, we have a private regulation, that no Leader shall allow a member to subscribe to the Missions, unless such Member previously subscribe to the Class-Money; & some have actually begun to pay class-money, in order to purchase the privilege of giving an additional penny per week to the Missions.[4]

Before long 'missionary boxes' were designed, to be emptied towards the end of the financial year if not oftener. Missionary meetings, which in principle were held annually in every church, and whenever a good speaker could be booked at other times, always included a collection – taken up after the speaker had delivered a stirring address. Special appeals were made to the whole connexion from time to time. At the WMMS Jubilee in 1863, £180,000 was raised. £37,500 bought Richmond College in Surrey where ministers destined for overseas work would train, £30,000 was set aside for its maintenance, £63,000 was spent on buildings overseas, and £30,000 was invested for 'the support of disabled and superannuated Missionaries, and of Missionaries' widows and orphaned children', while over £15,000 was used to provide working capital to obviate the need for costly overdrafts when money had to be spent before it was received – pleas to circuits to forward income more promptly were a constant refrain in the Society's history. The WMMS Centenary in 1913 was not, Methodists were assured, primarily an excuse for fund-raising, but none the less 130,000 little red 'Thanksgiving boxes' were produced, in the hope that they would be used in every home over a hundred weeks. The Centenary appeal raised £283,000.

The other Societies had their boxes, bazaars, collecting cards and benefactors too. The Jubilee of PM African Missions was celebrated by setting up an African Jubilee Thanksgiving Fund after World War One. The aim was to raise £50,000; by 1923 £66,000 had been contributed. The principal benefactor over many years, as for all PM causes, was Sir William Hartley who, shortly after opening his first jam factory in 1874, had vowed to devote a tenth of his gross annual income to religious and charitable purposes. In 1884 he promised £1,000 to help liquidate a formidable £5,000 debt on condition the other £4,000 was raised, and in 1909 he contributed half of the start-up costs of the new Central African mission station at Kasenga. But the bulk of the mission funds, year in and year out, came from the efforts of not-very-well-off Primitive Methodists.

---

    [4]   Letter to S. Taylor, 10 March 1814, cited in D. Hempton, The Religion of the People (London, Routledge, 1996), pp. 104–5.

From 1951, if not earlier,[5] a Standing Order required that one Sunday's collection each year should be allocated in its entirety to the MMS, and Overseas Missions Sunday was duly celebrated in most churches; in 1979 this requirement was replaced when a new form of assessment for a connexional Mission and Service Fund was introduced. Between 1961 and 1975 the Laymen's Missionary Movement (MLMM), inspired by the Society's Finance Secretary, Cyril Bennett, raised £256,000 as a working capital fund, desirable because, as in 1863, while expenditure continued throughout the year, most of the income arrived only at the year's end when boxes were emptied and local accounts closed.

Another considerable source of income was legacies. The most helpful to the Society were those which carried no restrictive provisions, but many were endowments for very specific 'outposts', which could not always be sustained and in after-years were a problem to the finance officers. For example, in 1935 a cheque for £100 was received with a letter from the benefactor's friend saying:

> She wishes the money to be invested in Trustee Stock and the interest therefrom to be invested in perpetuity to the Methodist General Hospital at Hankow to be used as the doctors in charge see fit.[6]

In 1960 Cyril Bennett wrote to the friend explaining that it was now impossible to use the annual income in that way and asking if, in her opinion, the testator would have approved its use for work among Chinese people in other parts of the world. She replied saying that as long as only the interest was used, she was sure that her friend would wish to give the officers a free hand provided it went to help sick Chinese. The officers decided it should be used for refugee and relief work in Hong Kong; in 1995 the meagre sum of £16.99 was sent. By that year restricted invested funds, small and large, had a book value of over £4 million.

Among other benefactors who boosted the Society's funds over the years were two self-made millionaires, Joseph Rank and William Leech. Rank, a flour miller, supported numerous Methodist causes. His first Settlement on the Missionary Society was made in 1919, and was followed by many supplemental deeds over the next twenty years. In 1995 the market value of the Rank investments was over £7 million. Leech, who in 1921, with ten shillings to his name, built a ladder and started window-cleaning, became a successful house-builder and philanthropist. In 1955 he selected five charities which, thanks to astute and complex management

---

5   SO 111 in *CPD* (first published in 1951) required that '(a) the whole proceeds of one Sunday's collections, or their equivalent, shall be contributed each year from every Chapel and Preaching-place throughout the Connexion. On that Sunday special sermons shall be preached and appeals made in furtherance of the work of the Society; (b) an Overseas Missionary Meeting, at which a collection shall be taken and subscriptions received on behalf of the General Fund of the Society, shall be held on a weekday in every Chapel and Preaching-place throughout the Connexion…'

6   MCH: financial correspondence.

of his donation, soon began to benefit at undreamed-of levels. The five were the Salvation Army, BFBS, SPCK, CMS and MMS. Each received £573,000 in 1995/96.

Yet the Society depended principally on the giving, year after year, of the Methodist people. Monetary donations were sometimes accompanied by other tangible gifts, from the implements Samuel Leigh assembled for a Maori mission[7] to the roller skates for which the Uzuakoli leprosy colony appealed in 1954 'to relieve the dullness of life in a long-stay institution'. Important contributions came from women and from children. Enthusiasm for the Easter Offerings begun in 1883 never flagged, though other titles and structures changed often, and long after Women's Work finances were merged with the General Fund in 1970 the Easter Offerings continued to contribute significantly to the Society's funds.

In a few places there were, even before the WMMS came into being, children's auxiliaries as well. The *Missionary Notices* for June 1816 told of 'Juvenile Missionary Societies' in Leeds and at the City Road chapel in London. Other missionary societies also developed children's branches, with a variety of names and organized differently from place to place. As the twentieth century opened, the WM Juvenile Missionary Association was still not rigorously organized and while some churches forwarded all the money for overseas work, others shared it between home and foreign missions. There were some churches who divided it into three, with one third for local use.[8] In 1903 Stanley Sowton[9] introduced medals with the motto 'For Zeal for Christ', awarded to those who collected at least £5. JMA boxes for the smallest children, subscription books for older collectors, certificates, ribbons to hold bars for successive years, all enhanced the scheme and in the 1980s the annual total raised reached almost £1 million. By then £5 had become much easier to collect: the qualifying amount was doubled in 1981 and abolished in 1991. Collectors were to be found overseas as well as in the British Isles; on the Caribbean island of Dominica, a small boy with big ears who used to waggle them in return for his pennies was Philip Potter, the future General Secretary of the WCC!

JMA supported the parent Society – by the end of the nineteenth century some 20 per cent of WMMS income derived from JMA. At the time of its Jubilee in 1908, the WA started its own junior branch, the Girls' League; members played their part in raising the £28,000 which, *inter alia*, helped to establish a pension fund for women missionaries. For a few years this movement specifically supported a women's hospital at Akbarpur in North India, as the Girls' Medical League, but 'Medical' was dropped by 1914. The League was far more than a fund-raising organization. Many branches met regularly to hear speakers, study literature – including the League's own magazine, *The Lamp* – and pray together. The League

[7]   Pritchard, *Methodists and their Missionary Societies 1760–1900*, p. 70.

[8]   Following Methodist Union four-fifths were allocated to Overseas and one-fifth to Home Mission.

[9]   p. 46.

was the main reason why the number of women candidates for missionary work was so large in the 1930s and 1940s, although the death toll of men in war must have played a part. By 1945 there were sixty-one missionaries who had grown up in the Girls' League. Both the new Methodist Youth Department and the new Women's Fellowship envied its achievements and courted its involvement.[10] A Young Laymen's League initiated by the MLMM had an active programme but never attracted large numbers; renamed the Young Men's League in 1946, it had in 1949 just two hundred members. The two Leagues were merged in 1953 as the Youth Missionary Association (YMA), redesignated World Affairs Youth (WAY) in 1976. Although YMA and WAY had their special fund-raising projects, their primary *raison d'etre* was not money but to implement one of the guiding principles of the Methodist Association of Youth Clubs (MAYC): 'Members should be helped to develop a global view of the world in which they live – to live on a large map'.

The funds raised from all these sources were considerable, though giving ebbed and flowed. It was affected by the state of the economy, by church politics, by theological doubts and convictions. In the 1990s, as giving bounced back from one of the periodical financial crises, MCOD was listed among the top fifty fund-raising charities in Britain. Live giving from Britain and Ireland amounted to £306,000 in 1933 when the funds were consolidated after Union, and £3,360,000 in 1995/96. Total income, including legacies and investments, rose from £414,000 in 1933 to £5,709,000, with the William Leech charity contributing 10 per cent of that, in 1995/96. The balance sheet that year-end showed £32,000,000 in endowments, reserves, designated and restricted funds: the fruit of generations of sacrificial giving and prudent investing.

But giving in Britain was only part of the story. From the earliest days the overseas Churches provided for many of their needs themselves, and supported new ventures as well. In 1850, for example, a missionary meeting was held in Fiji, with Captain Buck, the captain of the *John Wesley*, in the chair. 'The White residents assisted with handsome subscriptions; the Natives contributed a wonderful assortment of gifts, including clubs and spears, combs and fans, a pillow and a pig!'[11] In 1878, Thomas Wakefield described the first UMFC missionary meeting in Africa. It was a commissioning service for a Kenyan family:

> Aba Shora was set apart for the work at Sigirso among his own countrymen, and
> the speeches and prayers in behalf of this good man and his mission aroused a
> deep interest in the hearts and minds of the people. The collection amounted to
> … about 12s, a small beginning, but proportionately a good collection.[12]

---

[10]   *The Lamp*, May 1945, pp. 14–15.

[11]   G.G. Findlay and W.W. Holdsworth, *The History of the Wesleyan Methodist Missionary Society* (5 vols, London, Epworth Press, 1921–1924), vol. 3, p. 450.

[12]   E.S. Wakefield, *Thomas Wakefield: missionary and geographical pioneer in east equatorial Africa* (London, Religious Tract Society, 1904), pp. 148–9.

In monetary terms alone, the giving of the Wesleyan Districts overseas equalled the income of the WMMS at home by 1902. By one estimate, MMS support for churches abroad (not including the cost of missionary personnel) in 1961 came to £370,000 and local income (excluding government grants for institutions but including school and hospital fees) to £1,477,000[13] – but monetary calculations are insignificant when set against the gifts in kind and in dedicated service.

Prayer

It was often remarked that 'those who pray, give, and those who give, pray'. The Societies encouraged prayer as much as they encouraged giving, and did their best to ensure it was informed praying. The early Wesleyan missionaries had been ordained with prayers that they would be faithful to their calling and that their ministry would be fruitful. But what else did their colleagues, families, friends and congregations pray for as they made ready to depart? In valedictory services, and those emotional moments on the quayside just before they embarked, what did they ask? In the prayers of those who sailed towards an unknown future, and as they reached the other side of the world, and in all the daily and nightly prayers of those who had been left behind, what was their petition? The essence of all their requests was twofold: that God would keep them safe, and that God would prosper their mission. The first, something very precise, was frequently disappointed, while the second was extremely imprecise.

All concerned knew that their prayer for safety might not be granted. Dietrich Bonhoeffer used to rally the German pastors who struggled against the Nazi regime in the 1930s by recalling Richmond College. 'I am not asking you to do or suffer anything new,' he told them. 'This has always been the way of witness. What, over there in Richmond College there are boards with the names of the Methodist missionaries who died on the field, and when one fell there was another to take his place.'[14] Well into the twentieth century those who went abroad had to reckon with the chance that they would never come home. In the days when the normal period of service in the Pacific was twenty years before furlough became due, it was not so much possible as likely. Yet for all that, there is no evidence that people questioned the efficacy or bemoaned the futility of their prayers. The prayer for safety was nothing less than committing the future into God's hands, whatever the outcome. There was no thought of turning on a magic tap that would ensure God's protection against every danger. They simply shared with God, as with a friend, their most heartfelt longings.

---

[13]   K. Slatter, unpublished seminar paper 2004.

[14]   N.A. Birtwhistle, 'Methodist Missions' in R.E. Davies, A.R. George, G. Rupp (eds), *A History of the Methodist Church in Great Britain*, *vol. 3* (London, Epworth Press 1983), p. 19.

The second prayer had to be vague and imprecise, at least as far as the pioneers were concerned. Since nothing was known of the situations to which they were going, or of the individuals they would encounter, they could ask nothing more than a general prayer for God's blessing. When the missionaries arrived at their appointed station, their prayers became much more specific. But those left at home might wait a long time for news: two years or more from the Pacific. Had children been born? Many couples left as newly-weds and many wives arrived in a strange climate after a rough voyage further weakened by pregnancy. Were they alive or dead? Ignorance of the answer made the prayers of folk at home that much more fervent, but that much more uncertain.

In time, however, news from abroad began to flesh out the praying at home. The initial Wesleyan instructions to missionaries required them to send home regular reports of their work, and many were published, particularly in the widely read *Missionary Notices*, which appeared regularly from 1816 through to 1904, when they were superseded by the magazine *The Foreign Field*. They contained ample material for prayer. David Hill, who served in China from 1865 to 1896, conceived of a Prayer Union with a regular bulletin for its members. In this he was greatly encouraged and assisted by the staff of The Leys School, Cambridge, which he visited during his furlough in 1881. For a yearly subscription of a shilling members received a newsletter several times a year.

> The object of this Prayer Union is to hasten by united intercession the coming of the Kingdom of Christ in Central China, and to this end the Members of the Union agree to devote a given portion of time each day to earnest prayer on this behalf; whilst the Missionaries on the spot will, from time to time, communicate with our friends at home with regard to any cases of answered prayer, or any department of their work specially calling for the intercession of God's people. A further object of the publication of this letter is to give information and awaken interest in the work of our Mission in Central China.[15]

In 1911 the scope of the Prayer Union was extended to cover 'the Wesleyan Mission of South and Central China'. The letter continued to be published until 1932.

David Hill's idea was bound to be imitated and in 1897 the WMMS Secretaries set up a Helpers' Union to encourage prayer for the entire range of its work. A *Prayer Manual* was produced annually from 1906. Entitled *What to Pray For*, it had thirty-one sections for use through the month. It listed each missionary by name; it began to mention the number of 'ministers in local connexion' only in 1934, although in 1908 it had pointed out that 'the work is done mainly (and most suitably) by native preachers, paid and unpaid'. The Manual long outlived the Helpers' Union, which was disbanded in 1949, and in 1988 it was merged with a similar Home Mission tool to become the *Prayer Handbook of the Methodist Church*. It was inevitable that such tools were out of date even before they were

---

[15]   The Central China Wesleyan Mission Prayer Union Letter no. 75, July 1897.

published. The provision of blank pages for handwritten additions and corrections was an encouragement to users to be alert: the Manual needed to be used alongside newspapers, reports and letters. On one occasion in the 1980s it was being used in prayers at the Mission House and the leader, reaching the name of a particular missionary, included a clause relating to the fact that she was expecting a baby. The prayer was promptly interrupted by a better-informed member of the group: 'Twins', he said.

Telling the Story

Through print and picture, public meeting and private conversation, Methodists learned how God was using their ambassadors and partners around the world. The conversations were especially informative and fruitful. Often the missionary on furlough or Secretary of the Society would be taken, after speaking or preaching, to a host family for a meal, a bed – and an interrogation. Bright youngsters with endless questions were fired with an enthusiasm which resulted in life-long Christian service at home or abroad. The public meetings nurtured the enthusiasm. As well as the local church's missionary meeting, there were annual District Rallies, and the May Meetings of the Society in London attracted large numbers to hear notable speakers. These were long meetings with several addresses. The tradition grew into a week-long series of events, including the Women's Work and Medical meetings, a Saturday afternoon Children's Rally at Central Hall Westminster with a Youth gathering to follow, missionary sermons across London on the Sunday, culminating in a Great Thanksgiving Meeting in the Royal Albert Hall on Monday night. The Meetings continued, latterly hosted by Districts beyond London with a shorter programme, until 1985. There were also packed public meetings in connection with the Methodist Conference every year.

At local and circuit events, speakers with first-hand experience were not always available, and a leaflet entitled *Hints for Missionary Speakers*[16] was produced by Frank Deaville Walker, the WMMS Editor from 1912 to 1945 and a prolific author. In his youth he was challenged to dedicate his camera to Christian service and his books and articles were frequently illustrated with the photographs he took on his travels. Early in the 1920s the Society launched a publishing arm, the Cargate Press (from its two offices, at Carlisle Avenue and Bishopsgate). Around 250 Cargate titles appeared in the next half-century, including accounts of mission and church growth overseas, biographies and socio-political studies, plays, poems and prayers, some written for an adult and some for a younger readership. The Primitive Methodists published some twenty books relating to their overseas enterprise under their Holborn Hall imprint, and the United Methodist Publishing House and its predecessors produced a number on China and East Africa; after 1932 the Cargate imprint took over.

---

[16]   No date; probably early 1920s.

The mainstays of the Societies' literature, however, were the magazines. The Wesleyan *Missionary Notices* were accompanied by *Work and Workers in the Mission Field* from 1892 to 1904 when both were succeeded by *The Foreign Field*. The Irish poet, John Hewitt, told in a poem *Going to Church* how the pages of the *Foreign Field* caught his attention as a youth, a diversion from 'those yawning mornings' spent at Sunday worship in Belfast. The magazine, according to Hewitt, afforded 'fancy freedom in a cruise along the Congo' while 'other voyages promised pagodas' and 'pig-tailed Chinamen'. 'I swore to be a missionary then', he confessed.[17] *At Home and Abroad* was offered gratis to all juvenile collectors raising ten shillings or more in the year. The PMs had *The Herald* 1905–1922 and *Advance* 1923–1932 and the UMFC's *Missionary Echo* (1894) became the UM organ from 1908. They were amalgamated at Methodist Union as *The Kingdom Overseas*. There was a separate quarterly *Women's Work* magazine. In 1970 the two were replaced by *NOW.*

From 1915 the Home Organisation Department (HOD) produced its own Newsletter (the name varied and became *Ways & Means* in 1970) which publicized resources available, offered tips as to how they might be used and announced the arrival of missionaries on furlough who could be booked for meetings. When the HOD became the Home Education Department it produced *Facets*, which was distributed along with *NOW*, and other leaflets, study packs, posters and resources were published regularly or occasionally. As names changed to reflect a changing world and new understandings of the mission imperative, each new name had a shorter life-span than its predecessor. *NOW* was merged in 1992 with the organs of other connexional departments in the quarterly *Connect*. This proved an error of judgement as *Connect* failed to capture Methodist imagination and left many feeling deprived of an invaluable resource.

The twentieth century magazines were lavishly illustrated with photographs. They were much more attractive than the *Missionary Notices* of old, and more effective at putting readers 'in the picture'. The camera made possible other styles of communication as well. From the turn of the century sets of lantern slides, generally hand-tinted, could be borrowed from the HOD. Pictures of indigenous Christian workers conveyed, as mere words could not, the reality that the task of mission was now firmly in their hands. Lantern slides were still being produced as late as 1945, but by then it was the turn of the film-strip, needing a less bulky and more readily available projector. In the 1950s the Society again caught up with technology and dispatched Pauline Webb, its Editor, to make a movie about the CSI.[18] *Bright Diadem* was shown on television as well as at local missionary meetings and other films followed, but they were expensive to produce. Missionaries

---

[17]   F. Ormsby (ed), *The Collected Poems of John Hewitt* (Belfast, Blackstaff, 1991), pp, 291–2, quoted by N.W. Taggart in 'Irish Methodism and World Mission in the Twentieth Century' (unpublished monograph, 2012). Hewitt became Keeper of Art at the Ulster Museum and an agnostic.

[18]   Webb, *World-Wide Webb,* pp. 17–25.

began using their own 35mm cameras and creating their own colour slide shows. The Home Education Department (later renamed yet again as the Department for Education in World Mission) continued to publish regular resource packs which occasionally included slide-sets or a video. The aim was mainly awareness raising – sharing with the Home Church a better understanding of the World Church. This included challenging racist and more subtle paternalistic attitudes, through published resources and through District Training weekends. The deputation visits by missionaries on furlough and people from Mission House continued right up to 1996 and beyond, but the number available declined and other ways had to be found of stimulating interest in the life and mission of the church worldwide.

The language of outposts and headquarters had long gone. It was no longer a question of harnessing support for a foreign enterprise. The story now told was of partners in mission at home and abroad, prayerfully sharing their resources and concerns.

Chapter 6
Mass Movements and Group Conversions

Evangelism was generally a slow process, and sometimes disheartening. To excite the curiosity of people with no knowledge of the gospel was not difficult, but to draw them from curiosity to serious interest was much harder. If interest was sufficiently aroused, then the evangelist could retell the Bible stories and apply them to the life of the listener – all the more effectively if it was an indigenous preacher rather than a missionary. One by one individuals came to ask for baptism; when the first had taken the plunge, others were encouraged to follow suit; little by little the church grew. The motives of converts were often mixed. Privileged contact with white people in the early days of colonization, rice in times of famine, educational opportunities and material advantage were the incentive for some. But cynicism is easily overdone; they were motivated as well, or wholly, by a desire to serve the God revealed in Jesus and to follow his example of holy living and his love for others expressed in practical action. However small the number of converts – and in some places it was many years before they reached double figures – missionaries could and did share the 'joy in heaven over one sinner who repents'; the longer the wait, the greater the rejoicing.

But sometimes a different dynamic was at work. In India, in China, in Africa there were periods when people turned to Christianity in large numbers. These were not revival movements like those within Christendom stimulated by Jonathan Edwards, George Whitefield and John Wesley in the eighteenth century, Dwight Moody and William Booth in the nineteenth. In Asia and Africa there were no dormant seeds to be revived; these were seeds newly broadcast.

India

The 'mass movement' label came from India, where it was used in both a political and religious context. The movement of tribal people to Christianity did not compare numerically with the massive support given to nationalist independence movements, but it gave a new shape and impetus to the Indian church. After years of patient activity yielding, in terms of conversions, meagre results, missionaries in places wide apart were faced with villagers coming as a body to request baptism. These were not the farmers and the artisans, some of whom had allowed their sons – and even their daughters – to attend a mission school. They were, rather, from the euphemistically-called 'Depressed Classes'. Their homes might be close to the villages of caste Indians, but they were outcastes. They lived squalid lives in squalid conditions. They were completely subjugated to the will and the whim of caste people: 'untouchable' in every way except as rape victims, restricted to the most menial, filthy and demeaning tasks in a society built on concepts of purity and pollution. Economically they were at the mercy of their caste neighbours. Born into untouchability, their miserable existence had been passed on from generation to generation, with no chance of escape. The name they chose for themselves in the twentieth century, in defiance of the labels given them by others, was Dalits – denoting downtrodden and oppressed.

The Dalit mass movements[1] began in different parts of India in the 1860s and 1870s. They impacted on Methodist work somewhat later, particularly in Hyderabad and to a less spectacular extent in Trichinopoly, Madras and Bengal. Dalits who had heard Christian preaching did not despise the gospel, as many Hindus did, but at first they believed it could not apply to them: they were beyond the pale. It was practical action, not preaching, which convinced them. Epidemics and famines invariably hit those on the bottom rung earliest and hardest. When missionaries demonstrated a care for their plight they had never known before, they began to view their situation in a different light. If they were valued by these foreigners, who came as God's servants, then perhaps they were valued by the God they served. From this epiphany sprang the movement in which the Dalits themselves, not the missionaries, took the initiative. The missionaries struggled to respond at several levels.

At one level a 'mass movement' meant far more requests for a teacher than they could handle. The village teacher was the crucial figure in the mass movements: any response had to be on a sustained, not a hit-and-run, basis. Time and again the reluctant reply was 'Wait'. Some villages had to wait a very long time. The wisdom of the policy was debated: while superficial conversions were to be deplored, so were lost opportunities.

Secondly they had to adjust their thinking to an unfamiliar process in which a 'decision for Christ' was taken by the community rather than the individual. In any matter concerning the whole village the elders would discuss, perhaps over a long period, what course to take. Once their decision was made, the whole village acted. Not all had the same degree of conviction and commitment. Not everyone was in the same spiritual or moral condition. And when a teacher came, everybody did not learn at the same rate, absorb the teaching with the same measure of understanding, or feel the same way about it. And after months of teaching, when the time was ripe for baptism, it was the business of the community, not the catechist or missionary, to determine who was ready.[2] It remained a personal decision in so far as baptism was administered one by one, and there were some who absented themselves on the appointed day, for baptism was never in secret, and when they gathered at the river bank, their landlords would be there too, not out of curiosity but out of spite. Dalits who became Christians knew they would find the antipathy of the caste

---

[1]   J. Webster, *Dalit Christians: A History* (Delhi, ISPCK, 1992).

[2]   A similar process among the Maasai is described in V. Donovan, *Christianity Rediscovered* (London, SCM, 1978), pp. 91–2.

community increased and their daily hardships redoubled. They could be denied any share in the harvest and any land to cultivate, so rather than see their children starve some drew back. A sample of the spitefulness with which they were treated was experienced by Lesslie Newbigin, one of the first bishops of the CSI:

> I am constantly asked to help untouchable groups to get permission for the use of wells. On one occasion I was so foolish as to approach the caste people on their behalf. With as much delicacy as possible I spoke of the terrible difficulties of the outcaste group who were compelled to collect their water in a muddy pool, into which filth from the refuse heaps was constantly draining, while there was a fine deep well close by which they were not allowed to use. The only result of the conversation was that, when I left, the caste people raided the outcaste quarters and beat up the people there.[3]

The third issue related to the reasons for Dalit conversions. Were there economic motives? Was it an attempt to climb socially, to win the favours of bishops, or 'find a way out of a religion which had kept them in servitude for centuries'?[4] Walter Noble, one of the MMS Secretaries, was unequivocal:

> It was not told them … that the acceptance of (Christ) would bring them release from their burden of serfdom to their overlords, or from the debts which hung so heavily round their necks, or that Christianity would make two meals appear where there had been only one before. They were not lured by false or unrealisable promises of economic release. They were offered the redeeming grace of Christ.[5]

It is true that some missionaries offered food, especially at times of famine, but at those times they were especially reluctant to baptize. They brought education too, with its capacity to uplift the most degraded lives – though a 1997 survey of 'The Plight of Christian Dalits' found that 'in only half of Christian Dalit households was anyone literate'.[6] Their greatest gift however was the affirmation of the dignity and worth of the most downtrodden. Dalit villages remained squalid, but their inhabitants' reputation as liars, thieves and drunkards was no longer deserved.

Fourthly, there was in some quarters a degree of ambivalence about the community movements. If the depressed classes really did become Christian *en masse*, it would undermine the decades of painstaking work among the higher castes, by confirming their suspicion that Christianity was after all only for the poor and ignorant. As the twentieth century progressed, however, missionaries

---

[3]   L. Newbigin, *A South India Diary* (London, SCM, 1951), p. 48.

[4]   F.J. Balasunderam, *Dalits and Christian Mission in the Tamil Country* (Bangalore, Asian Trading Corporation, 1997), p.134, quoted in D.A. Haslam, *Caste Out* (London, CTBI, 1999), p. 24.

[5]   W.J. Noble, *Flood Tide in India* (London, Cargate Press, 1937), p. 32.

[6]   Haslam, p. 39.

came to see more clearly what Dalits themselves had long realised: the gospel was 'relevant to the emancipation of the underdogs'.[7]

The mass movement in Hyderabad began in 1893 with the accession of the first Mala villages. It began slowly but spread steadily. When Charles Posnett arrived in 1895, the baptized community numbered 4,254; when he left in 1933 it was 121,098. Those recorded as church members were far fewer, since a distinction was made, as it was in British Methodism, between the baptism, even of adults, and their reception into full membership. Membership required much more preparation, in terms of both Bible knowledge and sustained evidence of a converted life-style. In the Trichinopoly District, where Wesleyans had been working for over seventy years – the first chapel was opened by James Lynch, one of Coke's 1813 missionary pioneers – there was a baptized community of just 1,430 in 1896. The growth which began at that time, especially in and around Dharapuram, was not as spectacular as in Hyderabad, but represented a steady stream of conversions. Around 2,000 in 1906 became over 3,000 in 1916, more than 13,000 in 1926, and in excess of 28,000 in 1936. In the Madras area the rate of baptisms had not risen above a hundred or so per annum for decades, but there too they reached a thousand and more annually by 1936 – few enough by comparison with Hyderabad, but the result of 'community' if scarcely 'mass' accessions.

That distinction was equally applicable among the Santals, a tribal people living north-west of Calcutta. The area comprised 'a thousand square miles of forest, rough roads and no roads, to be covered by bicycle, bullock-cart, and foot, through monsoon mud and swollen rivers, under the searing summer sun.'[8] When they were first mentioned in the report from the Bengal District in 1883, it was with regret – they spoke no Bengali and the missionaries no Santali. Twenty years later, Methodism had a foothold in six villages and there were 200 converts; ten years after that, 830. A Santal school was opened, with positive results. It grew into a Middle School, from which successful students in turn became teachers, some in the little schools which the mission continued to open, some at independently-run schools in other villages.

Not all Dalit people lived in villages. The Doms of Benares city were just as downtrodden. They lived by scavenging – the manual removal and disposal of excrement – by prostitution or by theft. They were loathed and feared in equal measure; Phillips Cape said, 'A dozen Doms could empty the streets of Benares more quickly than a British regiment'.[9] Cape was appointed to the city on the banks of the Ganges in 1903; after twenty years of Wesleyan presence he found just twenty-eight members. His contact with the Doms in the city and its environs produced many changed lives in the next five years. The number of Doms in prison for theft fell noticeably, and Cape reported:

[7]   Balasunderam, quoted in Haslam, p. 24.

[8]   J.P. Hastings, superintendent of the Santal Mission Circuit 1952–1957, quoted in N.B. Mitra (ed.), *Methodist in Bengal* (Kolkata, Shantigriha, 2007), p. 75.

[9]   The Missionary Review of the World, vol. 40 (1917): p. 924.

A big demand for soap and coconut oil has arisen, and the cleaner clothes and persons of our Christians are matters for congratulation. In one hamlet, at first most filthy and hopeless, we now find not only clean-swept thresholds, but an attempt at a flower garden, planted, we were informed, 'for its beauty's sake.'[10]

On ground that to all appearances was absolutely unpromising, the seed of the gospel flourished.

China

Sam Pollard[11] reached Yunnan in 1888. Twelve years later the Boxer terror forced the Bible Christian missionaries to leave, but after only a few months he was back in the small walled city of Zhaotong. Anti-foreign feeling had diminished sufficiently for him to take the risk, and before long, faced with new opportunities, he was taking more. Yunnan was the home of many ethnic groups with their own languages, customs and dress, such as the Nosu, the Lisu and the Hmong, or Miao.[12] Hitherto the Bible Christians had worked primarily among the Chinese population, having put great effort into learning Mandarin. But Pollard considered the time right to extend his ministry to the Nosu. Their heartland was at the time self-governing: the chiefs owned the land, serfs farmed it in return for protection, and other peasants, some of them Chinese captured in border raids but primarily Miao, were their slaves. Forbidden by the Chinese authorities to cross the upper reaches of the Yangtze into Nosuland, Pollard ignored the ban and set out on one of his long preaching tours, with an interpreter and his magic lantern. This, he wrote, evoked 'cries of pleasure, roars of laughter, exclamations of surprise, shrinking fear, shouts of wonder (which) succeeded each other for an hour'.[13] He hoped to keep the tour secret but inevitably his whereabouts became known; not for the first time he was the object of plots to be rid of him. However he survived, and was planning a second visit to the area when his attention was turned from the Nosu to the Miao.

---

[10]   Ibid.

[11]   See W.A. Grist, *Samuel Pollard, Pioneer Missionary in China* (London, Cassell, 1920) and R.E. Kendall, *Beyond the Clouds* (London, Cargate Press, 1948). Pollard's *Tight Corners in China* (c. 1910), *The Story of the Miao* (1919) and *In Unknown China* (1922) were republished as E. Pollard (ed.), *The Sam Pollard Omnibus* (Pennsylvania, Woodburn Press, n.d.) and his diary was edited by Kendall as *Eyes of the Earth* (London, Cargate Press,1954). See above, pp. 8–9.

[12]   The Nosu are known in Mandarin Chinese as the Yi people and the Hmong – some of whom live in Laos, Vietnam and Thailand - as the Miao, the name commonly used in China.

[13]   Pollard, *Tight Corners in China,* in *Omnibus* p. 312.

There are several Miao sub-groups and it was four Hua Miao[14] – otherwise known as Flowery Miao – from the hills who on 12 July 1904 arrived in Zhaotong wanting to learn more about Jesus. Their rudimentary knowledge of the gospel had come from James Adam of the China Inland Mission; he directed them to Pollard, since they lived only two days' journey from Zhaotong whereas Adam's station was much further away. Pollard received the four visitors kindly and let them use a room in the mission compound. Their Chinese was by no means as good as his, but for four days he put aside other tasks to talk with them. The Hua Miao were desperately poor, cruelly exploited by landlords, but up in the hills, at an altitude of 8,000 feet, there were thousands of them who had vaguely heard of Jesus and wanted to know more. The delegation was barely literate and they wanted Pollard to teach them to read. But after four days their food ran out and they left. Then, less than a week later, five more Miao arrived, followed by another thirteen the next day; by the end of the year no fewer than 4,000 had come to Zhaotong to sit with the missionary for a few days and learn about the faith. Their comings and goings aroused the suspicion of the authorities, and more particularly of Nosu landlords who supposed the foreigner was inciting a Miao revolt. Pollard was well known to the Chinese magistrates and could dispel their suspicions, but many of his visitors were brutally maltreated by their landlords. He succeeded in obtaining an injunction to the effect that people who became Christians were entitled to the same protection that missionaries received and in November set out on a three week journey from village to village, encouraging the Miao to be steadfast in their faith and fearlessly confronting their persecutors. He later wrote:

> If any one had to choose a people to teach and train, surely he would pass by these Hwa Miao, and select a people whose outlook seemed more promising. So we think. So does not God think. He often does a startling thing, a new thing. The serfs in the dirty villages, the poor in the homes of poverty, the ignorant in the grip of the wicked medicine men: these appealed to the love and sympathy and chivalry of the great God. He treated them as he did the serfs in Egypt. He heard their groaning.[15]

In 1905 Pollard was relieved of his other work to focus on a ministry to the Miao. One of the Nosu landlords was persuaded to give the mission a ten-acre plot at Shimenkan, twenty-five miles from Zhaotong. This village became well-known to Bible Christians everywhere by its English translation, 'Stone Gateway'. There the new Christians themselves put up a cob-walled, thatch-roofed chapel, unpretentious but with floor space for 350 people. It doubled as a school, which opened that November. The celebrations coincided with the first Miao baptisms. 2,000 people gathered: a hundred of them were publicly examined, and all but a handful found worthy – not only by Pollard but by the elders whom the people

---

[14] Recent ethnographers prefer the name A-Hmao.

[15] Pollard, *The Story of the Miao*, in *Omnibus*, p. 127.

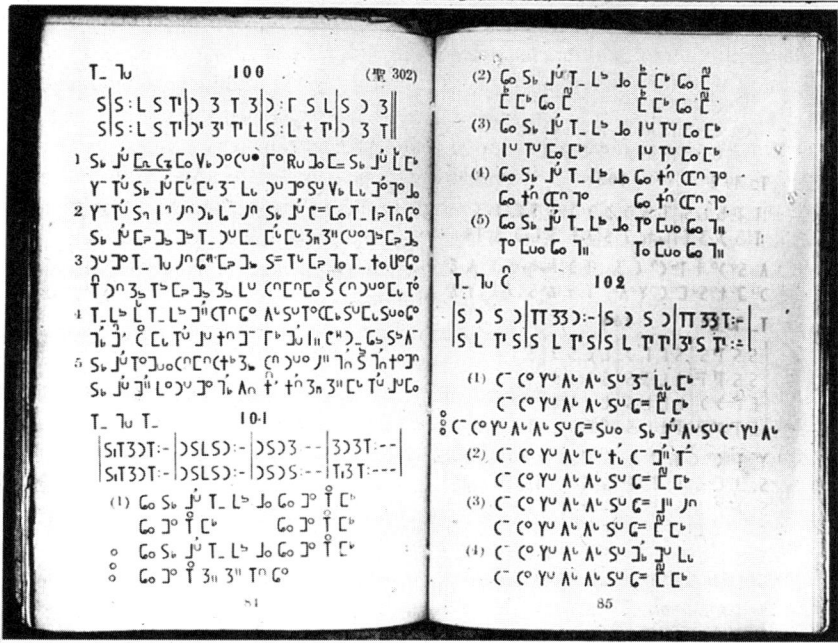

Figure 6.1　Miao Bible in Pollard script

had appointed. After that the chapel was packed every Sunday with three or four successive congregations. Many would walk for two days or more to be there. The villagers also helped Pollard build a three-roomed 'manse' which he named the 'Five Pound House' since that was what it cost. The rear wall was the bank of earth against which it was built, and it was very damp, but it did boast glass in all three front windows. Sam and Emma Pollard and their two children moved in, to be joined in 1906 by the newly-wed Harry and Edith Parsons.

The Miao were notorious throughout the region for the laxity of their morals. Every village had its brothel hut where married and unmarried alike would meet.[16] Wherever Pollard was invited to a village, he made it plain that the hut had to be torn down first. He also tackled head-on the customary Feast of Flowers, Hua-chang, held every year on the fifth day of the fifth month of the Chinese calendar, when people from numerous villages came together to indulge in drunkenness and debauchery. He wasted no time in instituting an alternative festival with feasts and watchnight services. 1,500 came to Shimenkan for the first in June 1905. 'In recording the story of the Miao,' wrote a later missionary, 'we should not do

---

[16]　Ibid.

justice to the immense change that has come over their entire way of life if we did not include the transformation of their moral life.'[17]

Pollard and Parsons studied the Miao language assiduously and made rapid progress. It was not a written language and from the time of the first contacts Pollard had made his notes in the Roman alphabet. He was determined that the Miao should have the Bible in their own tongue and he needed to find a simple means of writing it in a way that an illiterate person could pick up in a few days. Neither Chinese nor Roman alphabets were suitable for the purpose, so he experimented with phonetic characters that would represent the syllables and tones of the language, as had James Evans for the Cree of Winnipeg long before.[18] By the time he returned from furlough in 1908 he had devised what rapidly became known as the Pollard Script, and he set about translating the gospels.

Sam Pollard died of typhoid in 1915.[19] By then thousands of men and women were reading the gospel story for themselves, and singing the hymns he translated for them; 'Jesus loves me, this I know' was a favourite of his and of theirs. They sang too about their changed lives in their own words:

> We wash our faces now, we didn't then.
> We wash our clothes now, we didn't then.
> We wash our bodies now, we didn't then.
> We don't drink wine now, we did then.

and added to another popular hymn the lines 'Take my pipe and let me be / clean and wholly sweet for thee'.[20]

The number of Methodist members recorded in South-West China had risen from three when Pollard arrived (all of them missionaries' wives[21]) to 5,458 when he died, with 12,000 more under instruction. Frank Dymond, who had travelled to China with him in 1886 and survived a near-fatal illness in Zhaotong in 1888 thanks only to Pollard's unskilled but devoted attentions, preached at his funeral and continued to work in Yunnan until 1931. William Hudspeth, who recovered from typhoid just as Pollard succumbed, served in the region from 1909 to 1937, and remained in China working for the Bible Society until 1948. Harry Parsons, Pollard's first colleague at Shimenkan, served from 1902 to 1928. Under their leadership the number of Miao Christians continued to grow until the mid-1930s, but there was a downturn as China became more and more unsettled, with brigands roving the area; the attack on the school at Shimenkan which resulted

---

17 Kendall, *Beyond the Clouds*, p. 96.

18 Pritchard, *Methodists and their Missionary Societies 1760–1900*, p. 38.

19 Kendall, *Beyond the Clouds*, pp. 131–5.

20 A.G. Nicholls in the periodical *China's Millions* (Melbourne) 48 (December 1922): p. 182.

21 Ministers were recorded separately.

in Heber Goldsworthy's death[22] was a devastating blow. Parsons' twin sons, born in 1916, followed in their father's footsteps, both returning in wartime to work among the Miao until all the missionary corps began to leave China in 1949. The last recorded statistics for the South-West China District date from 1946 when there were 4,080 members and a total community of nearly 18,000. The one figure which steadily rose through the years was the number of Chinese ministers, who were already holding the church together when the last two missionaries, Vernon Stones and Elliott Kendall left.

From most parts of China missionaries had already been obliged to depart by February 1951, when Stones and the few women missionaries in Zhaotong accepted that the time had come to withdraw and left to join Kendall in Kunming. But on the outskirts of Zhaotong they were stopped and their papers examined; Stones was detained and the rest told to leave. He spent the next nineteen weeks in solitary confinement in a tiny cell which he only left for interrogation. Kendall refused to depart without him, whatever the cost. In July, after persistent but fruitless attempts to gain access to his colleague, he was summoned to the Security Police and told that Stones had confessed to 'illegal behaviour and spying'. Kendall vigorously refuted the charge, and eventually

> the door opened and Stones entered, looking pale and worn. The spokesman then took an official looking document from his pocket and pronounced the verdict that Stones was to be 'deported along with his accomplice Kendall'! On 5 July they were marched to the railway station …[23]

That was the last the Miao were to see of foreigners for forty years. In the so-called Cultural Revolution of 1966–1975 the Christians suffered terribly. The notorious Red Guards targeted Stone Gateway, calling it the 'Second Hong Kong', because it had been a centre of Christian education. The graves of Pollard and Goldsworthy were desecrated. Bibles, hymnals and anything else written in the Miao script were burnt – a Miao New Testament somehow rescued from the flames, its edges scorched, was many years later put on display at the Bible Translation Museum in Kunming. But the Miao in their thousands kept the faith; visitors to Shimenkan and other centres in the 1990s were overwhelmed by the welcome they received, the size and sound of the colourful choirs that entertained them and the high proportion of young people in the church.

The conversion of the Hua Miao was the first mass movement in China. Elsewhere men and women turned to Christ in much smaller numbers. The Districts of Wesleyan origin counted only 3,000 members by the time the church became self-supporting and the missionaries withdrew; the former MNC and UMFC Districts, a similar number. Other missionary societies reported gradual,

---

[22] p. 37.

[23] G.R. Senior, *The China Experience* (Peterborough, Methodist Publishing House, 1994), p. 65.

but never spectacular, growth. Under the oppressive atheistic regime of Mao Zedong, the number of those confessing their faith openly began to decline. No membership statistics for the 1950s exist, but the number of Protestant churches of any denomination still open for worship in 1960 had dwindled to a few hundred. In Beijing sixty-five churches were reduced to four, in Shanghai the number fell from 200 to twenty-three.[24] From 1966 all religious practices of any faith were banned. The churches were closed, their buildings used as factories and warehouses. Bibles were burned. Church workers had to find secular employment; many were deported to rural areas to live and labour in the harsh conditions that the peasants endured. Some were imprisoned for years, spending much if not all of the time in solitary confinement. Beatings by the Red Guards were the order of the day, Christians foremost among their victims.

In 1972 their plight eased and here and there house meetings were begun. In 1979, well after Mao's death, church buildings began to re-open. What happened next was a mass movement of incredible proportions, as Chinese, enjoying a measure of both freedom and stability they had never known in their lives, flocked to the churches. Some of them remembered the missionary era; the great majority were new to the faith. Both from the Han majority and from minorities like the Miao, they clamoured for pastors and teachers. Theological seminaries, revived as quickly as possible but themselves short of theologians, could not train a fraction of the leadership called for by such a massive groundswell of Christian commitment. Throughout the 1980s and 1990s, Protestant churches and meeting-points under the umbrella of the China Christian Council opened or re-opened at the phenomenal rate of six every day, and large numbers of independent house churches thrived. Whereas the Protestant community in China was estimated at a million or less in 1950, at the turn of the millennium there were 20 million at the very least. Not only self-governing and self-supporting, the church which emerged from the years of turmoil and trial was fervently self-propagating.

Africa

One of the most extraordinary instances of spontaneous lay pioneering was the ministry of the Liberian William Harris in the Ivory Coast, a French colony situated on the west coast of Africa between Liberia and the Gold Coast. Although Methodists and others were working in these neighbouring territories, the Ivory Coast remained unevangelized. Indeed, the French West African possessions had 'a combined population of about fifteen million' (according to William Platt in 1921) and 'to all these people there are only two [Protestant] missionaries' – one in Dakar and Platt himself in Dahomey.[25] The Roman Catholic presence was, in the main, chaplaincy to the French; RC statistics for 1913 tell of just 1,100 baptized

24   R. Whyte, *Unfinished Encounter* (London, Collins Fount, 1988), p. 267.
25   *The Foreign Field*, June 1921: p. 172.

Figure 6.2   William Wadé Harris, 1914

Africans in the Ivory Coast. There were a few small Methodist congregations of migrant Fantis from the Gold Coast. Then Harris came.

He had been born around 1860 and brought up just across the Liberian frontier. In his teens he lived in the home and attended the school of his maternal uncle, a Methodist pastor-schoolmaster, who baptized him, though it was some years later that he was converted. In 1888 he was confirmed in the Episcopal Church, for which he worked as a teacher and preacher as well as serving as an official government interpreter. There was at this time much tension between the indigenous African peoples of Liberia and the immigrant Americanized blacks who ran the country. Harris vigorously opposed the régime, was involved in a failed coup d'état in 1909, and was twice imprisoned. Some time in 1910 he had a vision in which the angel Gabriel promised he would be released. 'You will be a prophet,' he was told. He was indeed amnestied;

> He described himself as being commissioned like the watchman in Ezekiel 33, and when he was released, he went about preaching, 'Prepare ye, prepare ye,

Jesus Christ is at hand. Repent ye... I say to all men, black or white, to repent and believe in Jesus Christ. I am the last prophet.'[26]

Preaching in his home area had little effect, so in 1913 he went east. He made his way along the coast, with different companions at different times, staying longer in some places – notably the lagoon area around Grand Lahou – than others. He eventually reached the frontier with the Gold Coast and entered Apollonia, the frontier region of the British colony, where he was known as Professor Harris. He stayed for three months before re-entering the Ivory Coast. He preached to all who would listen, most of whom had never heard Christian preaching before, and attracted crowds of hearers. The word spread that 'Here is a man who talks about God'. From up to 100 miles inland, people made their way south on narrow bush paths to listen to him. It was said that he baptized over 100,000 people. Undoubtedly some of the baptisms were performed by associates, notably A.E.M. Brown, a clerk from Saltpond in the Gold Coast, and an Ivoirian known as Papa.

Harris was reputed to be a miracle-worker and rain-maker. The latter derived from an occasion when the crowd asking for baptism was too large for him to baptize in his customary manner with calabash and Bible. It began to rain, and Harris had a brainwave: asking them all to kneel, he pronounced the words of baptism as water from heaven fell on their heads.[27] Both he and Papa subsequently repeated this ingenious if unorthodox practice.

For a while he met with the approval of the French authorities, for under his influence people were drinking less and working harder. But in late 1914 some of his followers incurred the wrath of Marc Simon, a French administrator whose porters one day declined to proceed on their *tournée*, on the grounds that 'Harris says we should not work on Sundays'. Simon had no difficulty getting Harris expelled from French territory – an alien drawing vast crowds was unwelcome in a country at war.[28] Harris returned to Liberia, and later went preaching in Sierra Leone, but every attempt to return to the Ivory Coast – he tried eight times – was blocked by the colonial authorities.

The fruits of his work were immediately visible in the Gold Coast. When Charles Armstrong heard that more than 2,000 people, baptized by Harris, were clamouring to join the church, he went at once to Axim – and found 8,000. A circuit of nine churches was within a few months holding services in fifty-two villages. William Goudie, the ex-India missionary familiar with mass movements and now Africa Secretary, visited the region and saw for himself the great opportunity. From village after village they came requesting catechists and schools, seeking baptism. In the six years after 1914 there were 36,000 Methodist adult baptisms in the area. But with war raging in Europe no additional missionaries could be sent, nor were there

---

26   G.M. Haliburton, *The Prophet Harris* (London, Longman, 1971), p. 35.

27   A. Roux, *L'Evangile dans la forêt* (Paris, Les Editions du Cerf, 1971), p. 25

28   M. Simon, *Souvenirs de Brousse 1905–1918* (Paris, Nouvelles Editions Latines, 1965), pp. 170–175.

sufficient trained Africans to rise to the challenge. It proved a lost opportunity. The converts became discouraged, the little churches they had built were deserted and fell into ruins, while one of Harris's Ghanaian converts, John Nackabah, founded 'The Church of the Twelve Apostles' around 1922 and many joined him.

It was different in the Ivory Coast. Already in his annual report for 1914, the Roman Catholic vicar apostolic, Monsignor Moury, was reporting that 'a whole people, having destroyed its fetishes, invades our churches *en masse*, requesting Holy Baptism.'[29] Yet the vast majority of those who heard Harris preach did not in the end join the Roman Catholic Church. Either they had travelled great distances from villages where there was no RC activity; or, having been baptized by Harris or by one of his associates, they resented the requirement of Catholic baptism; or else they recalled Harris's injunction to pray for a missionary to come and teach them to read the Bible, which was not a feature of the RC mission at that time. Instead they formed their own congregations and built their own little pole-and-dagga chapels. In a few places they were joined by Fanti Methodists, who taught them hymns. They rehearsed what they could remember of Harris's teaching. They suffered persecution. If a village was forced to send labourers to work on the new railway line the Harris Christians would be picked on. In some places their churches were repeatedly burned down.

In 1919 the Protocol of Saint Germain, regulating various aspects of the European presence in Africa, was signed. It provided for freedom of conscience and of all forms of religion, including the rights of missionaries, limited only by what was 'necessary for the maintenance of public security and order, or as may result from the enforcement of the constitutional law of any of the Powers exercising authority in African territory'. The French authorities used this clause to decree in 1922 that only French, Latin or a local vernacular might be used at religious services in the Ivory Coast. The effect on the few Methodist congregations, which used either English or one of the Ghanaian languages, was to close them for sixteen months, until William Platt, a young but already experienced Wesleyan minister (later to be General Secretary of the BFBS) was sent from Dahomey to meet the Governor and reach a compromise. In the course of this visit Platt was told about the Harris movement: tens of thousands in hundreds of villages all along the lagoons and inland who were praying for a teacher but were not connected with any Missionary Society. Benjamin Dickson, the minister of the Gold Coast District who was stationed in Grand Bassam, then the territory's principal port, apparently knew nothing of them. Platt was authorised by the WMMS to return in April 1924 and investigate more thoroughly.

On the evening of Easter Sunday he sat down to write to his parents, doubtless by the light of a Tilley lamp. He had just completed a twelve-day trek with a full day in Bassam. He would shortly be compiling his official report, but his letter home was his first, excited account of his experiences:

[29] Archives of the Société des Missions Africaines, Rome.

I never had such crowds in my life. We started along the lagoons to Abidjan which is the future capital of the Colony. Two hundred people came to meet me. The same day went up the railway line to a place called Anyama and there were 200 people on the Rly Station awaiting my arrival. Some of them had walked 10 miles to meet me. I walked 2 miles out to the first village and there must have been 300 or 400 people in the Church there. I had lunch and then started off on a 10 mile walk over hill and dale through the most thickly wooded country I have ever seen. There was a good road – good enough for walking – cut through, but for miles the bush was 12 or 15 yards high. Great, huge trees ... I found a village (Akoupé) almost all protestants – 600 or more in a good church. The R.C. priest has persecuted them in his periodic visits, but they've stuck tight. Returning the following day, after being up till midnight talking various 'palavers', I went to a village where 400 people awaited me.

Returning to Abidjan I went a two hours run in a Ford and got to Dabou and there slept the night. Around Dabou are <u>dozens</u> of villages, every one with its tiny Roman church and its large Protestant church. ... Village after village flocked in to ask me, please to visit them. They had no teaching. Many of them are wholly illiterate, no Hymn Books, no Bible, no printed word at all. All they do is done by memory. All their hymns are learned by heart. Many of them have not seen a paid agent of the mission or a pastor at all – and <u>never</u> a white protestant missionary.[30]

Platt's report came to the WMMS General Committee in September 1924, at a time when a serious financial shortfall was also on the agenda. In spite of the deficit – or perhaps because the committee was not only greatly touched by Platt's account, but shrewdly recognized that it would appeal to Methodist hearts and pockets – it was agreed that he and a team of evangelists from Dahomey, soon to be joined by French missionaries, should set up work in the Ivory Coast to build on Harris's foundations. They rapidly organized the Harris Christians into a Methodist Church, though by no means all accepted the direction of foreigners. A French minister, Pierre Bénoit, was sent to Liberia to track down the aging Harris. Bénoit returned with letters from Harris telling his followers to become Methodists and not Roman Catholics, to accept Platt as his successor, to shun fetishes, to read the Bible and to observe the Ten Commandments and the word of Jesus Christ.

The letters, and a photograph of Bénoit with Harris which was printed and widely circulated, secured the result Platt intended. The future of Ivoirian Methodism was assured. But not everyone was convinced. Two years later an Ivoirian, Jonas Ahui, followed in Bénoit's footsteps and found Harris shortly before he died. Ahui brought back the prophet's cross and Bible and his last written message, and in 1931 founded the *Eglise Harriste*, which as a wholly African Church was to be influential during and beyond the struggle for political independence. Taking into

---

[30]   Photocopy of the original given to the author by Platt.

account the rapid advance of Roman Catholicism after 1914, Harris's all-too-brief evangelistic campaign – 'the most extraordinarily successful one man evangelical crusade that Africa has ever known'[31] – can thus be said to have been the making of three Churches in the territory.

The story of Harris enthused generations. Platt captivated his audiences wherever he spoke. A whole generation of missionaries discovered their vocation as a result of hearing him. Several popular accounts were published.[32] Dahomey and Togo were detached from the Lagos District and joined to the Ivory Coast in a new French West Africa District, initially with Platt as Chairman. No time was wasted in beginning to train Ivoirians as catechists. A Bible School was started. One of the students was rebuked in January 1930 for arriving late for the new term, yet again. He apologized, saying that he could not come without his clothes. It transpired that in his vacation he had been in a village which had not yet seen a catechist, preaching and teaching – and so keen were they to hear more that, to stop him leaving, they had confiscated his clothes. After a few years some of the catechists were sent to Porto Novo in Dahomey for ministerial training, and Martin Mel and Lambert Dé began their ministry in 1941.[33] In 1963, the fiftieth anniversary of Harris's arrival in the country, the first African Chairman of the District was installed.

A less widespread but still significant movement began in the Gold Coast in 1920, when Samson Oppong, or Opon, an Ashanti with a reputation as a sorcerer and a criminal record for misappropriation, received a vision.[34] He was commanded to burn his magic apparatus and to proclaim God's wrath on all 'fetishism'. Then in his mid-thirties, he was baptized by an African Methodist Episcopal Zion (AMEZ) minister, Ofosuhene. Afterwards he made a cross of bamboo sticks, dressed in a long black robe which had a large cross in the centre and a red cross on each shoulder, and, with his hair falling down to his shoulders, began to tour the region. His zeal and fiery preaching touched off a mass spiritual awakening in Ashanti. He won converts by using appeals to fear and pity, with threats of hell fire, promises of heaven, wildly emotional oratory, and hymn singing. Stories reached the Wesleyan Synod of the results:

---

31   A. Hastings, *African Christianity* (New York, Seabury Press, 1976), p. 10.

32   J. Bianquis. *Le Prophète Harris* (Paris, Société des Missions Evangéliques, 1924); F.D. Walker, *The Story of the Ivory Coast* (London, Cargate Press, 1926); W.J. Platt, *An African Prophet* (London, Student Christian Movement Press 1934); D.S. Ching, *Old Man Union Jack* (London, Cargate Press 1946); M. Musson, *Prophet Harris* (London, Religious Education Press, 1950); T.F. Fenton, *Black Harvest* (London, Cargate Press, 1956).

33   Dé subsequently resigned and after independence became the Ivory Coast ambassador in London.

34   H.W. Debrunner, *The Story of Sampson Opong, The Prophet* (Accra, Waterville Publishing House, 1965).

'whole communities assembling themselves together on Sundays, waiting, waiting, waiting for someone to come along' who would tell them 'the meaning of the new aspirations and strong desires' which possessed their hearts.[35]

Garfield Waterworth, the superintendent of the Ashanti mission, encouraged Oppong. He calculated that a Methodist community of 32,000 in Ashanti in 1915 had become 105,000 by 1922. Certainly some 10,000 people were baptized in less than two years. Mindful of the lost opportunity in Apollonia a few years earlier, it was decided to open Wesley College for the training of teachers and catechists in Kumasi, instead of in the south as had originally been the intention.[36] In his later years Oppong became a drunkard and lost his prophetic powers, as well as his alleged ability to read the Bible; he was excluded from the church. But before his death in around 1960 he returned and settled down as a local preacher in his home town near the Ivory Coast border.

Another African of note, Simon Kimbangu of the Belgian Congo, came out of the Baptist mission. After a ministry of only five months in 1921 he was arrested for disturbing the peace; sentence of death was commuted by King Albert of Belgium to life imprisonment, and he died in prison in 1951. The movement he started was ultimately far more successful, in numerical terms, than Harris's; it had close ties, as did many other independent African-instituted Churches, to the liberation struggle. The Belgians were much the least benevolent of the colonial powers. The thousands who, in five short months, had come to believe that Kimbangu was a prophet sent by God, were sent into internal exile in remote parts of the vast Congolese territory. Groups of these Kimbanguists met in secret but had little contact with one another. However in 1959, six months before Congo became independent, the 'Church of Jesus Christ on Earth through the Prophet Simon Kimbangu', under the leadership of his son Joseph Diangienda, was legally recognized. As the movement was gradually unified, it became clear that there were now several million Kimbanguists. The Church became a member of the WCC in 1977. In 1976 Bena Silu, one of its young leaders, studied in Selly Oak, living part of the year in Kingsmead College. This resulted in an invitation to Albert Mosley, then Principal of Kingsmead, to visit the Kimbanguists, which he did in 1981 as General Secretary of MCOD. The Church leaders made clear that they did not want ongoing financial support from British Methodism, but at that time they were desperately short of hard currency to buy medical supplies for their hospitals and MCOD made a grant to help with that. They also asked for the prayers of British Methodists and their concerns, along with those of other Churches in Zaire (as the country was named at the time), were included in the Prayer Manuals of 1981–1985.

---

[35]   F.L. Bartels, *The Roots of Ghana Methodism* (Cambridge, Cambridge University Press, 1965), p. 188.

[36]   p. 106.

Manyano – the Red Blouse Movement

A mass movement of a different kind took shape in South Africa early in the twentieth century. Well before it settled on a name women were meeting informally for prayer together in many places. In earlier days missionaries had organized weekly sewing classes; women who were preparing for baptism came to make clothes so that they could be dressed in the western fashion that was deemed proper. Christian women came together in these classes in a way that men never did; but the spiritual hunger that had led them to Christian faith was not satisfied there. So they began to meet in homes and under trees. Although some had attended mission schools, most were unlettered. The Manyano movement, first documented in Natal in 1905, freed them to pray not only in their own language but in their own style, volubly and emotionally. Their meetings included exhortation and preaching, and there were many who discovered gifts of eloquence which stirred their sisters. They encouraged one another to be better home-makers and to evangelize their unbelieving neighbours. They denounced the destructive effects of African beer, and total abstinence became one of Manyano's features. Although it remained essentially a prayer union, Manyanos were not self-absorbed. The 'oldest, largest and most enduring and cohesive' of all South Africa's women's organizations,[37] they made their presence felt, for example, in anti-pass demonstrations in Bloemfontein in 1913 and in the Natal beer protests of the 1920s.

By then their existence could not be ignored on Thursday afternoons, the only slot in the week when domestic servants had time off. Since many Manyano women were in service, this became their regular meeting date. They were highly visible because of the uniform they wore, an innovation in the early years which became general and official when the movement was formally recognized by the Conference in 1926. Worn only on Thursdays and special Sundays, it resembled neither traditional African dress nor the European clothing their grandmothers had been taught to sew:

> A black skirt denotes sin, a red blouse – more like a belted jacket – represents the redeeming blood of Christ, the number of buttonholes his wounds, and a deep white collar and a small round hat cleansing from sin through Christ, or holiness.[38]

By Europeans Manyano was known as the 'Red Blouse Movement'. Membership was open only to married women, normally mothers. In time a Young Women's Manyano was organized for the unmarried. There was a six month probationary period, during which a woman had to demonstrate both her knowledge of the Bible and an upright life. After that came a joyful robing

---

[37]   M. Brandel-Syrier, *Black Woman in Search of God* (London, Lutterworth Press, 1962), p. 97

[38]   P.Attwell (ed.), *Take Our Hands: The Methodist Women's Auxiliary of Southern Africa 1916–1996* (Cape Town, Salty Print, 1997), p. 139.

ceremony. No rule excluded white or 'coloured' women, but very few ever joined – white women had their Women's Auxiliary and coloured women, from 1947, their Women's Association. The exceptions were the District Chairmen's wives, who were robed *ex officio*. It was the invariable practice that the minister's wife, irrespective of her abilities, was the President of the local branch; the beginnings of Manyano coincided with an increase in the number of black ministers after the Boer War, and it was assumed that their wives would have an active role alongside the husbands.

Transvaal and Swaziland formed a District of the British Conference until 1931, while the South African Conference operated in the rest of the territory and there was a small PM mission in the Orange Free State and Aliwal North. For the Prayer Unions, these distinctions were of no account, and from 1908 Manyano women organized well-attended conventions, where they slept on a church floor and brought their own food.[39] They became a popular feature of Manyano life, and sometimes they went on for a week. One held in Swaziland in 1915 dispersed for two days to preach in the countryside to 'heathen women in the kraals'.

When the three branches of South African Methodism united, the Rules and Regulations of the united Manyano movement began 'The Women's Manyano … is the Methodist Women's Prayer and Service Union and stands for holiness in life, purity of speech and conduct, temperance, and service to the glory of God and for the extension of His Kingdom'.[40] The emphasis of the movement continued to be on personal life and home life: on industry, cleanliness, honesty and moral improvement. Many women in domestic service saw little of their children, who were left in the care of their grandmothers; but for mothers and grandmothers alike, the physical, moral and spiritual nurture of children was at the forefront of their prayers and one of the matters on which they counselled and exhorted one another.

Manyano grew and spread: by 1940, there were more than 45,000 members. Then came the bleak years of full-fledged apartheid. Their solidarity in the face of its multiple injustices was a notable contribution to the struggle for freedom. They encouraged each other to stand firm in their faith and not lose hope, praying for a new South Africa. And when it came to pass, their number had risen to 100,000.

The Ruwadzano-Manyano in Zimbabwe (Ruwadzano being the Shona term) and the Runyumfwano in Zambia were off-shoots that took root and flourished independently. The wives of the South African evangelists who helped to establish Methodism in Rhodesia laid the foundations well before the turn of the century. Women and girls were the first to respond to the gospel in numbers and they were gathered together for teaching, prayers, encouragement and fellowship. As the Women's Prayer Group, it was first formally recognized by the Rhodesia District Synod in 1920 when Emma White, the Chairman's wife, was its President.

---

[39]   D. Gaitskell, 'Power in Prayer and Service' in *Christianity in South Africa,* ed. R Elphick and R Davenport (Cape Town, David Philip, 1997), p. 265.

[40]   [40]MCSA *Laws and Discipline,* 1997: p. 181, quoted in U. Theilen, *Gender, race, power, and religion* (Frankfurt am Main, Peter Lang, 2005), p.265.

Figure 6.3   Ruwadzano Manyano members celebrating the delivery of a mobile clinic, 1988

From 1926 the movement held annual gatherings, the first a national assembly at Nenguwo and thereafter, because the distances made travel costly and for many impossible, at circuit level. Wesleyan work in Zambia was part of the Rhodesia District until 1932; Douglas Gray's wife Louie, at Chipembi, composed a prayer that was used (generally in vernacular translation) every week in both countries. In 1943 Muriel Platten, a deaconess who spent twenty-five years in Zimbabwe, was set aside at the movement's request to run Bible schools for women; the appointment was agreed by the Society on condition that Ruwadzano funded it. By no means wealthy, the women met the challenge; furthermore, in 1949 they sent a donation to Britain to assist the rebuilding of bombed churches. Literacy classes and skills training were organized and Ruwadzano/Manyano played its part in working for the emancipation of Zimbabwean women. Its activities were disrupted during the liberation struggle when many churches had to close down and in rural areas the church went underground, but at independence in 1980 the movement sprang to life again. The newly established Ministry of Community Development and Women's Affairs co-operated with the training programme, and the movement worked collaboratively with other non-governmental organizations in post-war reconstruction.

Chapter 7
Mens sana in corpore sano

Methodist medical work began on mission house verandas, and gradually expanded into dispensaries, clinics and hospitals. It was of the essence of Methodism: John Wesley had founded the first free medical dispensary in England in 1746, and published his treatise on *Primitive Physic: or, an easy and natural method of curing most diseases* in 1747.[1] Yet, although the WMMS began formal medical work in 1864, with Porter Smith's appointment to central China, and the Bible Christians, MNC and UMFC also started work in China in the nineteenth century, at the start of the twentieth most of these institutions were still small. From small beginnings, however, some impressive facilities were developed.

Institutions and Issues

The larger institutions were of three main kinds. There were *General Hospitals*, especially in China and later in Africa. In the British West Indies the Colonial Medical Service was well organized; the Society supported small clinics in Panama and Haiti, but embarked on no other medical work in the Caribbean. In India, similarly, the Indian Medical Service was the main provider. But Indian women could not be persuaded into mixed-sex facilities, or to be treated by male doctors. *Women's Hospitals* were the answer; most of the medical work set up by Methodists, as by other missions in India, was devoted to women and children, and serviced by female staff. A third distinct area was the treatment of *leprosy* and the care of its victims.

The issues that faced medical workers were much the same everywhere. They went with a two-fold sense of responsibility: to share both the gospel, with the value it set on every human life, and the skill and resources of western medicine. But the attitude of the people to western medicine was ambivalent. They were glad of a bandage for an injury or a tablet for a headache, but for more serious problems many preferred to resort in the first instance to traditional treatments. Traditional concepts of sickness and health did not encourage them to make use of the 'alternative medicine' practised at the mission station. Or if they did, it might be for a surprising and mistaken reason, as in Central Africa in the 1890s. Early PM missionaries were supplied with 'the best medical outfit procurable' and 'a small library of medical works', and one of the pioneer party wrote:

---

[1]   J. Wesley, *Primitive Physic* (London, J. Paramore, 1747).

There was no need to put out a sign or issue an announcement that we were
prepared to treat cases ... Patients came from far and near with all manner of
afflictions ... There was at the outset a tremendous run on eye lotion. Children
especially suffered. They were never washed, their eyes became inflamed, and
the flies and other noxious insects were allowed to feast on the corruption that
formed ... But what puzzled us most for a time was the large number of men that
came for eye lotion with no sign of disease ... one day we discovered the cause.
It had been noised abroad somehow that this was the secret of our being able
to shoot. We put this medicine in our eyes, and it enabled us to send the bullets
straight, and so kill our game.[2]

Disease, on the other hand, was seen as unnatural, a punishment from some
malevolent supernatural power. To identify the human agent of the supernatural
tormentor, a diviner would be consulted. If a mother died in childbirth, as
happened all too often, no diviner was needed: clearly the infant was the evil
one and could be left to the fate that awaited a motherless child. In many places
twins were regarded as monstrosities and abandoned. Diviners would employ a
variety of methods to determine both the cause of a sickness and its remedy. Some
remedies, using local plants and herbs, were well-tried and effective. Many had no
rational basis and could easily make a patient worse. Missionary frustration at the
persistence of such practices was usual. Yet in one respect the traditional world-
view and Christian faith were agreed. The interpenetration of the material and the
spiritual world were for each a basic premise. So at mission hospitals, spiritual
ministration accompanied material medicine. Prayer, though given more attention
by some practitioners than others, played its part.

A second issue was whether to attempt surgery with inadequate equipment
in unsterile conditions. Young missionary doctors routinely performed operations
which at home would have been the preserve of a senior consultant. Those who had
the benefit of X-rays to guide them were uncommonly fortunate. But from time to
time they would be faced with an emergency, or with a patient too far gone to give
any hope. Sometimes – it is impossible to say how frequently – they concluded
that while surgery might well kill the patient, to do nothing meant certain death;
and they operated. If the patient survived, the reputation of hospital and doctor was
enhanced, and people saw the wisdom of coming sooner rather than later. But if
the patient's life was lost, not at home but on the operating table, the doctor would
be blamed – which was why the doctor hesitated in the first place. Letters home
told of both scenarios. A success story came from Sierra Leone on the very day
the new hospital at Segbwema was opened in December 1930. The previous night,
Dr John Kearney was summoned to an emergency nine miles away. There was no
motor road from Segbwema to Daru; there was the railway, but no train was due
for days. However, a railway trolley was procured, and with four men pumping

---

[2]   Baldwin, pp. 68–9.

The Medical Missions of the W.M.M.S.

DISTRICT.	STATION.	REMARKS.
CEYLON AND INDIA		
NORTH CEYLON.	PUTTUR	Work done by Wesley Deaconesses.
MADRAS	TINNANUR	Work being done by Indian assistant.
NEGAPATAM	MANNARGUDI	Under the Rev. Elias Daniel, who has received training up to the standard known in India as "sub-assistant-surgeon." No European doctor since 1899.
HAIDARABAD	ARMUR	Much valuable honorary work has been done by Dr. Isabel Kerr (1907). whose husband, the Rev. G. M. Kerr, is Superintendent of Circuit. On furlough; the work is at a standstill.
	ALER	
	MEDAK	
	PAPANNAPETT	These five places are supplied by Indian workers. This development calls for adequate European oversight.
	ASAFABAD	
	NIRMAL	
BENGAL	SARENGA	Dr. Caleb Davies (1914). Furlough due; hospital must be left for twelve months in the hands of Indian assistants.
	DEOLI	An outlying dispensary visited from Sarenga.
BOMBAY	SANGANNAR	Indian worker only.
BURMA	KALAW	Burmese worker only.
CHINA		
SOUTH CHINA	FATSHAN	Dr. Webb Anderson (1900), now on furlough, has worked alone since 1915. Dr. Hooker is supplying until Dr. Early (1913) can arrive.
	SHIUCHOW	Dr. Hooker (1906) transferred to Fatshan. His furlough is due; hospital must be closed until Dr. Vickers (1910) arrives in autumn.
WUCHANG	WUCHOW	Chinese assistant only since 1916.
	HANKOW	Dr. P. K. Hill (1912), the only doctor, and Sister Alice Shackleton (1910), the only English nurse.
	TEIAN	Dr. Morley (1886) the only doctor.
	TAYEH	Dr. Chiang, our Chinese doctor, alone.
	ANLU (Men's)	Dr. Cundell (1906), Sister G. Stevenson (1915) matron.
	ANLU (Women's)	Dr. Ethel Rowley (1895) [honorary] alone.
	SUICHOW	Dr. Thomas (1909), whose husband, Rev. G. M. Thomas, is Superintendent of Circuit. Supplying district as large as Yorkshire and Lancashire combined.
	WUSUEH	Visited from Hankow, 120 miles away.
HUNAN	PINGKIANG	Dr. W. G. Clayton Grosvenor (1913) on furlough.
	YUNGCHOWFU	Dr. Helen Hadden (1905), carrying on while her husband, Dr. Geo. Hadden (1906) is doing Red Cross work in Siberia.
	PAOKINGFU	Hospital closed since 1912.
AFRICA		
LAGOS	ILESHA	Closed since 1917, doctor urgently needed.

Where hospitals exist, black capitals are used—in all other cases either there is a dispensary or the work is being done with practically no equipment at all in the way of buildings.
Dates indicate the year in which the doctor or nurse went to the mission field.

130

Figure 7.1   WMMS Medical Missions, 1918

the levers he got there in the darkness, operated successfully by lamplight and returned by trolley in time for the opening ceremony.[3]

These were issues which even the best-staffed hospitals encountered. But the Methodist hospitals were rarely well-staffed. When a doctor went on furlough, services were drastically curtailed. In a 1916 paper Dr Percy Wigfield, the WMMS medical secretary, deplored the fact that in West Africa, where furlough was taken every second year because of the climate, a hospital might be effectively shut for 25 per cent of the time. He argued for 'the abolition of single-staffed hospitals'; he calculated that that would entail an increase in the number of missionary doctors from nineteen to thirty-three and the appointment of twelve new nursing superintendents. But it was wartime and he was realistic about the prospects for his proposal:

> One of the effects of the war will in all probability be to create a shortage of young men of the kind we might reasonably have hoped to receive as candidates.[4]

On the other hand he recognized that if the overseas churches were to become self-governing, self-supporting and self-propagating, they would need to recruit indigenous senior staff for their institutions. 'They must increase,' he wrote, 'we must decrease.'

In India

The WMMS operation was more extensive in India than anywhere else, and so was its medical work. In mid-twentieth century there were – excluding clinics with fewer than twenty beds – fourteen hospitals in India compared with nine in China and just six in Africa. Besides these there were several clinics and dispensaries, with a few beds and a visiting doctor who came as frequently as hospital duties and distance allowed. The European staff were fully supported by the Society, but local staff costs and all other expenses were found mainly through fees, local church support and, sometimes, government grants, with limited grant support from Society budgets. In 1972, twenty-five years after the CSI was formed and two years after union in North India, the MMS still had five doctors, eleven nurses and four other hospital staff working at thirteen institutions – nine of them originally Methodist and four founded by others of the uniting Churches – while in the whole of Africa there were five missionary doctors, eighteen nurses and three others.

Of the two hospitals in north India one, at Azamgarh in Uttar Pradesh, was run by the Australian MMS. The other began in 1914 under a banyan tree at Sarenga in the Santal country of West Bengal. Dr Caleb Davies lived initially in a tent, until he was able to take over an indigo-planter's bungalow. In 1916 he reported that he had treated 9,000 patients, many of them in their homes and

---

3   D.S. Ching, *They Do Likewise* (London, Cargate Press, 1951), p. 11.

4   MCH: 'The future policy of the WMMS in relation to medical missions', restricted circulation.

others at the dispensary, despite a dearth of buildings and equipment. By 1918 the first buildings were completed, and there was a great celebration meal; 'the food,' he said, 'was given almost entirely by Hindus, though caste restrictions prevented them from partaking'. From then on WMMS annual reports would refer to Sarenga as 'our most important medical mission in India' or even 'our only hospital', because all the others were founded, funded and separately reported by the Women's Auxiliary.

The Holdsworth Memorial Hospital in Mysore was established in 1905 for women and children – at the time, there was only one other hospital in Mysore, staffed exclusively by male doctors. The Holdsworth's first local recruits were illiterate village girls. Over the years new buildings were added. Above the main entrance, carved in stone, was the name 'The Home of Mercy' in Kannada. It became a mixed facility only in 1950, when the Indian Nurses' Training Authority decreed that all hospitals with nursing schools to State Registered Nurse level must provide experience in nursing both men and women, including surgical cases. Frank Tovey, re-assigned after forced departure from China, was the first male doctor.[5] In 1956 a separate Children's Hospital was opened on an adjoining site. The government hospital was still at that stage the only other hospital in Mysore; half a century later more than twenty private hospitals had opened, providing a wide range of medical services but at a price that only the wealthiest citizens of Mysore could afford. The Holdsworth continued to provide medical care at an affordable cost to a large number of poorer people and the School of Nursing was known throughout southern India for its high standards of training.

At Ikkadu, in Tamil Nadu, north-west of Madras, where a dispensary opened in 1889, the WA found benefactors who sponsored steady enlargement over the years; when the CSI took over it had 98 beds. In the early days William Goudie visited the hospital every morning; he was also a persistent advocate of public health services. He wrote to the Deputy Collector of Tiruvallur, after a cholera outbreak:

I regard the following as most necessary:-

(a) That the place be cleared of unhealthy rubbish, all dry stuff being consumed by fire and all moist refuse carried to a distance and buried;

(b) That the place be fumigated by the burning of tar and sulphur;

(c) That the roofs of the affected huts be stripped and burned and new leaves supplied gratis to the people who are totally destitute;

(d) That the two small wells in the village be thoroughly cleansed, repaired and secured against the percolation of surface water.

---

[5] Tovey, *Cor Blimey!* includes two chapters and an appendix of particular interest to medical professionals, where Frank describes the wide spectrum of the hospital's work.

It is true that these sanitary measures will involve a small outlay, but surely the need is sufficient to justify the expenditure, without scruple and without delay.[6]

In Mylapore, a district which at the end of the nineteenth century was becoming the commercial and cultural hub of Madras City, a hospital was presented to the Society in 1909 by Subramanyam Iyer, a prominent Brahman citizen who had been converted as a youth at the Wesleyan School in Negapatam. Named Kalyani Hospital in memory of his mother, it too expanded in time: fifty-seven beds in 1930 became 160 twenty years later, when 1,064 confinements were recorded. The hospital in Medak, founded by Charles Posnett and his sister Emilie, had eighty beds by the time they left India, and 110 in 1950; but it later declined and eventually closed.

Vellore, an ancient city midway between Madras and Bangalore, became known around the world for the Christian Medical College and Hospital which in 1900 was a one-bed clinic and at the end of the century counted 5,500 outpatients, 2,500 inpatients, 75 surgical procedures, 22 clinics, and about 30 births every day. It was never a Methodist hospital, nor a CSI one; its overseas staff came from many different countries and societies, and its Indian staff from a variety of Indian churches. Among those sent to Vellore by the MMS was Eirene James, a pharmacist (1946–1956). She lectured to the medical students as well as running a department which made its own pills and ointments which were often dispensed on a banana leaf. Her dispensers, she said, were able to tell by patients' clothes how much they were able to pay – until the hospital acquired a huge stock of army surplus supplies. By the 1990s all the staff were Indian, and former staff on return visits lost their way through the jungle of new buildings.

In China

China had its own long history of medical practice, but Chinese traditional medicine was usually ignored and often despised by practitioners with western qualifications. Medical missionaries were the standard-bearers of western medicine prior to the 1912 revolution. Under the Republic the formal healthcare field was thoroughly westernized and traditional practitioners lost their standing. Paradoxically it was then that a number of missionary doctors, particularly in the medical schools of Christian universities, began to take a serious interest in Chinese pharmacology and published more sympathetic accounts. Later generations of missionaries, learning to approach indigenous culture with respect rather than scorn, shed the negative attitudes of the nineteenth century, though they understood the principles of Chinese medicine too little to embed it in hospital life.

The hospitals, like all institutions in China, came under state control when the communist regime came to power. Expatriates were obliged to leave but most of the Chinese staff remained in post, and some survived to greet foreign visitors

---

[6]   J. Lewis, *William Goudie* (London, WMMS, 1923), p. 78.

Figure 7.2   Ruth Kendall and a Miao co-worker vaccinating children against smallpox, Yunnan, c. 1942

when the bamboo curtain was drawn back almost forty years later. When contact was terminated there were nine Methodist hospitals. In Hankou in central China, one of the three cities on the Yangtze which today make up the conurbation of Wuhan, the original Hospital of Universal Love begun by Porter Smith in 1864 was restarted after a period of closure and relocated with the help of David Hill's personal funds. Next door a separate women's hospital was opened in 1887. The two later came under a common administration and there was a proposal to unite with the London Missionary Society (LMS) hospital, keeping the two sites. This

Figure 7.3   The Hospital of Universal Love (Methodist General Hospital), Hankou, c. 1937

did not materialize, but in 1928 a United School of Nursing was formed under the direction of Sister Gladys Stephenson,[7] while the LMS hospital became a joint venture, Union Hospital, and the Methodist Hospital was again rebuilt in 1932. Dr Edward Cundall, whose long career in central China began in 1907, worked in each at different periods, and came back out of retirement to Hankou in 1946 for two years. Both hospitals had survived the Japanese invasion and the civil war. After the enforced departure of the last missionary personnel, they were nationalised but the Chinese staff, many of them Christians, remained. The Methodist General Hospital was renamed 'The Workers' Hospital' but its original name was not forgotten and when the repression of Christianity was relaxed the Chinese characters for Universal Love were reinstated on the gateway.

There were three hospitals in Hunan Province. Dr George Pearson, who arrived in Shaoyang in 1920, found a couple of derelict rooms and a dozen cast-iron bedsteads. He planned and supervised the building of a hospital of mud bricks, which disintegrated in the floods of 1924; he built again, using more substantial bricks. He stayed at his post until forced to leave in 1951. Throughout his time the hospital had no running water yet major surgery including caesarean sections, laparotomies and removal of cataracts was carried out successfully. He was renowned too for his violin, with which he loved to accompany hymns. Another of the Hunan hospitals, at Pingjiang, made a pact with the Provincial Health Bureau in 1935, setting up a 'County Health Station' which served a population of

---

[7]   pp. 25–6

300,000 and had a special emphasis on public health in schools. But its buildings were destroyed by the Japanese in 1939 and the scheme came to an end.

In south China a hospital was begun in Foshan, a few miles from Guangzhou, in 1881.[8] From the first it was a big institution. The building was rented through the generosity of an English businessman, and was converted into a main ward of eighty beds, a women's ward with sixteen and a further twelve beds specifically for opium addicts, together with an outpatient department, operating theatre, laboratory and chapel. Charles Wenyon, who had no skilled help, performed fifty operations in the first three months. Wenyon treated indigent patients for nothing, but charged fees to those who could afford them, which enabled the hospital to become self-supporting. He was followed in 1896 by Dr Webb Anderson, who was in charge until 1924, overseeing the move to a new building on a new site in 1904. Shortly after Anderson left hospital life was disrupted by anti-British, anti-Christian demonstrations, which forced a temporary closure. By then, however, there was a contingent of trained Chinese staff who re-opened it. There were soon several Chinese doctors, including two women. But in 1938 the city was taken by Japanese troops. Amid the chaos and destruction, the various churches organized refugee camps, the hospital was filled with casualties, and the children's ward took in a score of baby girls abandoned at the gates. The hospital was allowed to work on under Chinese leadership when the European staff were interned, but in war conditions it was easier to care for patients than for buildings and they deteriorated badly. There was no opportunity to renovate them before Mao's Liberation Army took control.

In the north the Japanese took a harsher line. While Foshan was allowed to keep going, Laoling hospital, opened by the MNC in 1878, was burned down on Christmas Day 1939 in retaliation for treating wounded Chinese soldiers. It was never rebuilt – the North China District was too enfeebled and restricted to recover its vitality between the defeat of Japan and the victory of the Red Army.

The UMFC hospital in Wenzhou was opened in 1897, and was much improved with the help of Henry Blyth of Great Yarmouth, who in 1900 funded three buildings: men's and women's wards, and a third with a consulting room and dispensary and an upper floor for European patients. To build it was one thing; to staff it, as with many a mission hospital, was another. According to the *China Medical Journal* in 1919, Wenzhou's one doctor that year, Dr Edward Stedeford, saw 1,418 in-patients and 24,130 out-patients, compared with an average load in China of 213 in-patients and 5,864 out-patients per doctor. Stedeford worked at Wenzhou from 1914 to 1950; his long-time colleague Bessie Petrie Smith, the hospital matron, died in China in 1940.

In Africa

The year 1913 was a momentous one in the annals of medical missions. It was the year that the renowned theologian, philosopher and organist Albert Schweitzer

---

[8]   J.R. Rose, *A Church Born to Suffer* (London, Cargate Press, 1951), pp. 56–66.

began his new career at Lambaréné in Gabon, and dramatically raised the profile of the missionary doctor. In the same year the WMMS appointed Dr Sydney Osborn to Kwenda in Mashonaland where he initiated medical work in Rhodesia with a little hospital of eighteen beds, and Dr John Stephens arrived at Ilesha in the Yoruba territory of Nigeria.[9] The Wesley Guild movement had decided to support a medical mission in Africa, and the Society had fixed on Nigeria, where medical services were in their infancy – there were just eight hospitals in the entire country. Stephens was selected as the first 'Guild Doctor'. The way had been opened by John Bond, a Joyful News evangelist in Nigeria from 1890 who, after a short course in basic health care, returned in 1905 to start a clinic in Igbo-Ora, another Yoruba town. John Stephens and his wife were based there when they first arrived in 1912; in six months he treated 1,700 people in the dispensary and cycled over 700 miles along bush paths to assess the needs of villagers round about. But Ilesha was a more suitable location for a proper hospital; it was chosen because the local king was a Christian, the church there was strong, and the town had better transport links than most.

Several times the embryonic hospital had to close for lack of funds or staff, but a more reliable service developed thanks especially to Sister Stella Liony, a black British nurse who spent the years from 1923 to 1947 at Ilesha and pioneered female nurse training in Nigeria. She was not the only missionary to give long service. Her colleague, Sister Elsie Ludlow, was there from 1929 until 1960 and Dr Andrew Pearson, who had followed in his father's footsteps in China for five years, transferred to Nigeria as medical superintendent for the years 1953–1975. The hospital was relocated and greatly enlarged in 1954. It became internationally renowned for its research into patterns of child health and mortality, and the success of the Under Fives Welfare Clinic which resulted and was widely copied. The all-important weight charts devised and piloted by Dr David Morley and Sister Margaret Woodland in the village of Imesi-Ile, twenty-five miles from Ilesha, came to be used worldwide.

The Guild's continuing support supplied only a fraction of the running costs; at times when government grants fell into arrears the survival of the hospital was precarious. With significant co-funding from ICCO, a Dutch Christian aid organisation, it was again expanded in 1972, with 197 beds and around 230 staff. But the hospital's success was becoming a liability. 85 per cent of out-patient attendances and 54 per cent of the in-patients were under eighteen and therefore receiving free treatment. This was not only a long-standing, principled policy: it was a condition of the government grant. Then the rate of inflation prompted the government to demand a huge increase in salaries without increasing its grant. Nurses went on strike and the management had reached an impasse. After a military coup in 1975 the hospital was expropriated by the Nigerian Federal Government.

---

[9]   C.A. Pearson, *Front-Line Hospital* (Cambridge, FSG Communications, 1996); for how Methodism reached Ilesha, see F.D. Walker, *A Hundred Years in Nigeria* (London, Cargate Press, 1942), pp. 108–112.

PM medical work began in Kasenga, in central Africa, where Dr Herbert Gerrard ran a small hospital from 1915 to 1934 and became a legend for his work among the Ila people. In Eastern Nigeria, the PM mission had various medical posts and one, Ituk Mbang, became another major hospital. Founded in 1931, it provided a wide range of services, besides a midwifery training school. Harry Haigh, medical superintendent from 1940 was reputed to do up to thirty hernia repairs in a day, starting at 6 am, and to run the hospital on the proceeds. Ituk Mbang was highly regarded, but was a victim of the Nigerian Civil War (1967–1970) when the hospital was looted and vandalised, and staff fled for their lives. The church did not have the resources to re-establish the work and eventually the state took over; the state proved just as incapable.

Another victim of the civil war was the Queen Elizabeth Hospital in Umuahia, for a time the capital of Biafra. An enlightened regional government had built the hospital and asked the Anglican, Methodist and Presbyterian churches to run it, on condition that they did so jointly. Among the staff was an Irish obstetrician, Edgar Ritchie, and when the war turned the hospital into a major centre for relief work he was joined by Maureen Neill-Watson, a social worker with twenty years' service in the region. She was on furlough in Dublin when the situation deteriorated and she chose to return to the war zone. She organized the distribution of emergency food supplies, living frugally and dangerously, and witnessed many harrowing scenes. Both Ritchie and Neill-Watson, exhausted and malnourished like all around them, were eventually persuaded to return to Ireland to recuperate. He had to be admitted to hospital at once; she collapsed and died shortly after reaching London.[10]

Two hospitals opened in 1930. One was at Segbwema in the interior of Sierra Leone, where a clinic had been started by Alice Medd, a missionary wife with District Nurse experience, ten years before. It too had some Wesley Guild support, but it was fortunate to have the interest of John Nixon of Newcastle-on-Tyne who contributed substantially to the expansion of the facilities between 1949 and 1971. When he died, at the age of 96, it became the Nixon Memorial Hospital. In the 1950s a School of Nursing was properly established and a Community Health programme set up, and following the outbreak of Lassa fever in 1976 it was designated for research into the disease. Dr Aniru Conteh, the medical director from 1980, became a leading authority on Lassa. The hospital tried to remain open when civil war broke out in 1991, but Segbwema was in the heart of the war zone. More than once the hospital had to be evacuated until in 1999 it was completely trashed by the rebels. Conteh was one of the thousands left homeless and starving, but he survived when many did not and in the midst of the fighting re-established the only Lassa fever isolation ward in the world at the Kenema government hospital. Amid the ruins of Segbwema a day clinic opened in 2003, with one doctor, one nurse and one cleaner.

---

[10]   N.W. Taggart, *Irish Methodism and World Mission in the Twentieth Century*, unpublished monograph, 2012.

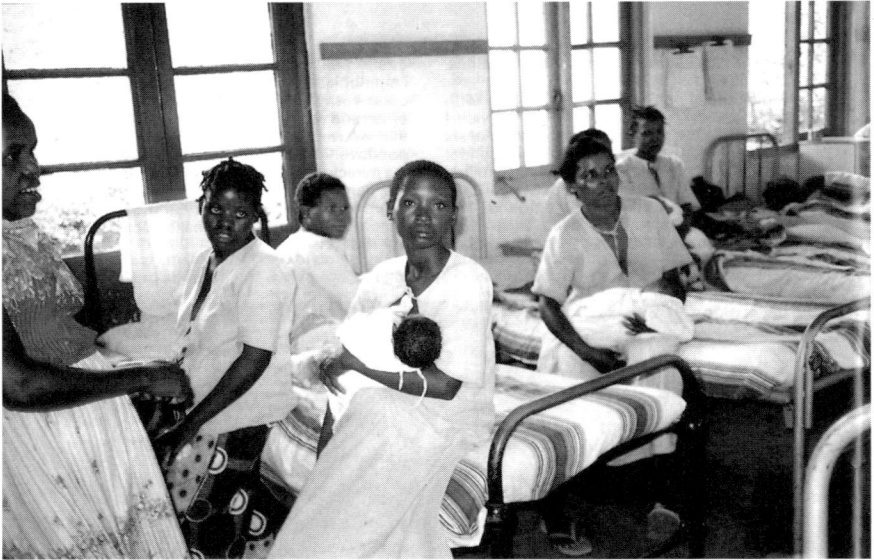

Figure 7.4   Maternity Ward, Maua Hospital, Kenya

In Kenya, the UM missionary committee appointed Dr Harry Brassington to open a hospital in Meru, with the help of a government grant of £500. The original site was not satisfactory and in 1929 the decision was taken to build at Maua. A donation in memory of a young man who had hoped to be a medical missionary but died at the age of 22 led to the name Berresford Memorial Hospital. It opened in July 1930 with Brassington's wife and sister serving as nurses. After six months he wrote that outpatient attendances 'mean at least 1,580 people have been brought in touch with practical Christianity'.[11] Money was not in common use in the Meru district in those days and payment for outpatient treatment was by food, which in turn was fed to the inpatients. Under the leadership of Stanley Bell from 1940 to 1950 a nursing school was established, and tuberculosis, children's and maternity wards were added. By the 1980s there were 3,000 deliveries a year. Another important development was the community nursing and primary health care project which began in 1976. Community health workers and traditional birth attendants as well as nurses were trained and in 1988 training was given for community-based distribution agents for oral contraceptives. A dental clinic opened in 1991 was an instant success, and with the prevalence of AIDS on the increase a palliative clinic was started in 1995. It drew national attention and became one of a select number of clinics partially subsidized by the Kenyan government.

Elsewhere in Kenya another hospital was opened in 1950 at Ngao on the Tana River, assisted by a floating dispensary with such a shallow draft that in the dry

---

[11]   *How Many Loaves Have Ye?* 1931 Report of the UMC Missions, p.72.

season it could sail on 14 inches of water. In Ghana, a hospital was established in 1952 at Wenchi. The local people valued the little Methodist dressing station but any other medical attention necessitated a fifty-mile journey to Sunyani, so a block of the Methodist School was converted into a ward to facilitate the birth of the hospital. In Zimbabwe, the hospital at Kwenda never thrived: the Shona were reluctant to come for treatment and it was closed at the end of 1917. Ten years later a new start was made at the Waddilove Institution, with a small hospital where nurses were trained and orphans were cared for. It was enlarged with a bequest from John White in 1937, but in 1964, when the government raised the training requirements, it was closed and the nurses in training departed.

Leprosy

A particular impetus to leprosy work arose from the numerous biblical references to leprosy and the accounts of Jesus's ministry of loving touch – although the modern and biblical diseases stem from different bacilli. Lepers everywhere, often horribly disfigured, despised and rejected, were driven from their homes for fear of contamination; the very word reflected the cruel stigmatization to which they were subjected, and it was eventually discarded by well-wishers. Leprosy work was thoroughly altruistic. Victims were in no position to pay fees for their care. No material advantage accrued to those who reached out to them. And while other medical work could produce visible results with much more immediacy than either preaching or education, this was not true of leprosy work even after effective drugs were found.

The first active Methodist encounter with leprosy came in Burma. It was only after Upper Burma was annexed by the British in 1886 that the WMMS opened work in the country; within four years the first ward of an 'Asylum for Lepers' was in operation in Mandalay, with patients collected in a bullock cart from the alleys and bazaars. At first there was a rumour that they were being brought together so that they could be poisoned, but such suspicions were soon dispelled and more wards were filled as fast as they could be built. It grew to 250 beds. In the early days there was little that could be offered in the way of treatment but much in terms of tender loving care. Before long settlements for leprosy victims were opened in Bengal, where they could live in dignity, work in the gardens and make use of the chapel, and in 1905 Roderick Macdonald[12] bought an island in the river at Wuzhou in south China where a group of sufferers could live and earn their livelihood by fishing and growing vegetables, among them a Christian farmer who helped to organize the colony and preached to them.

Not only among Methodists but among all who took a special interest in leprosy, the outstanding names were Dichpalli and Uzuakoli. The centre at Dichpalli, in Hyderabad, grew out of work begun in 1908 by Dr Isabel Kerr, who lived nearby

---

[12]   Pritchard, *Methodists and their Missionary Societies 1760–1900*, pp. 265–6.

at Nizamabad where her husband was the minister. She was spurred to action when she realized from his clawed hands that the man who sold her daily bread was smitten. She persuaded the Nizam's government to cede fifty acres of land for a settlement. At first, Dr Kerr could only treat her patients' sores, but the advent of chaulmoogra injections held out hope of effective treatment and soon Dichpalli became not just a home but the Victoria Leprosy Hospital. With the assistance of philanthropic Indian subscribers and of the Mission to Lepers, it opened in 1915. It expanded as more land was given or bought, and George Kerr was in charge of administration, building, and cultivation. When Dr John Lowe joined the staff in 1924 the complex accommodated 800 patients, but there were six times as many applicants as places, so non-infective cases were not admitted. Occupational therapy in the form of cottage industries was developed for the residents: gardening and farming, making water pumps. Staff worked on the principle of 'Faith, Oil and Work – and the greatest of these is Work'. By 1932, when Dr Kerr died and Dr Lowe resigned to work with British Empire Leprosy Relief Association, the quality of Dichpalli was recognized throughout India; it became a training centre for Indian doctors and physiotherapists, and its research department was a world leader. Norman Cockett, who joined the staff in 1954, developed a procedure for reconstructing diseased noses which became known worldwide as 'Cockett's op'.

Uzuakoli was one of the last and greatest PM initiatives before Methodist Union. With the encouragement of the colonial government, the Eastern Nigeria Synod of 1931 deputed Dr Kinnear Brown, newly arrived medical missionary, to identify and negotiate for a suitable site. He recounted:

> Looking for land with fertile soil, water, timber, building materials, and all the things one needs to establish a large, self-contained community, was as difficult as the pessimists feared and the objectors hoped.[13]

After many a 'not in our backyard' response from local chiefs, a plot three miles from Uzuakoli was obtained, and

> Gradually the settlement took shape – two villages, one either side of a pleasant valley, with all the main buildings on the crest of the ridge. One village was for the women, and one for the men ... We started night school for all adults and they were only exempt when they had learned to read. They were then presented with a Bible ... It was interesting to walk around in the evenings and see little groups of adults reading by hurricane lamps, and being taught by school children ... The first thing we did was to put a patient into a house and tell him to clean it and make it attractive. Often there was a refusal which went on for days or even weeks until the impact of others taking an interest in their house began to awaken interest. When a patient saw a man from a neighbouring village decorating his

---

[13]   Fox, p. 104.

house or planting his garden, the competitive spirit was stimulated. If that man could do it, so could he …[14]

Brown's account went on to mention

the first communion; the opening of the unaffected children's ward; the installation of electric light; the building of the new church and its opening in 1936 … the farm and plantations … the citrus orchard … the first paper published from Uzuakoli (on Leprosy and Diet), the result of many months of laborious investigations … our first Discharge Service.

In 1936 Brown was succeeded by Frank Davey, both minister and doctor, whose name and that of Uzuakoli soon became renowned in the world of leprology. He knew little of leprosy and nothing of the local Igbo language but soon put both shortcomings to rights, taking his MD on his first furlough. On his arrival he found 800 resident patients, but there were tens of thousands in the region with leprosy. In collaboration with the authorities Davey trained leprosy control officers and organized voluntary 'segregated villages' where sufferers could be monitored and treated. In the 1940s he was joined by John Lowe and they worked together on dapsone treatment, much more effective than chaulmoogra injections. They initiated mass treatment with the new drugs. Uzuakoli became the foremost leprosy research centre in Africa, if not in the world. By 1959, when Davey returned to London as the MMS Medical Secretary, some 20,000 patients had been discharged as symptom free.

Then came the Biafran war. Five battles were fought across the settlement between 1966 and 1970. All expatriate staff were evacuated, everyone else departed, the buildings were left in ruins. But Uzuakoli rose from the ashes; the Welfare Department, the responsibility of Methodist Church Nigeria, took on a new lease of life under the visionary inspiration first of Margaret Snell and then of Ros Colwill. A 1988 report described three 'Grainger villages' (named after their original British sponsor, Lila Grainger), a variety of rehab workshops, the elementary school, the farm, a printing press, a 2.5 hectare rubber plantation being tapped daily, and an oil-mill processing home-grown oil palm.[15]

When Frank Davey, in the course of his Medical Secretary duties, visited Dichpalli he found morale there low, obvious mismanagement and corruption, the hospital nearly bankrupt. He was challenged to save the place from closure and so in 1968, after nine strenuous years at headquarters, and at the age of sixty, he resumed his leprosy work. Providentially a retired Indian Army Officer, Laurie Ponnayia, took on the post of administrator and instilled discipline into the organization, leaving Davey free to concentrate on the medical work and tackle the

---

[14]   Ibid., pp. 108–9.

[15]   MCH: J.R. Pritchard, report circulated within MCOD of the Africa Secretary's Visit to Nigeria, April 1988.

entrenched fear and stigma that still surrounded leprosy. He realized what progress had been made when other cricket teams wanted to play the Dichpalli eleven.[16]

The objectives of leprosy work were six-fold: to treat victims at the earliest possible stage, arrest the progress of the disease, and achieve a cure wherever possible; to provide a home for victims forced from their village homes; to empower them through education and training, leading to a means of livelihood; to care for those who, because of the advanced stage of the disease or through advancing years, were unable to care for themselves, and cut off from family care because of their leprosy; to confront the beliefs and attitudes that treat victims as outcasts, with education about the realities of contagion and demonstrable rehabilitation; and to restore broken relationships and reconcile families estranged because of leprosy. The motives of leprosy work included compassion for people in weakness, isolation and distress; contributing to the global campaign against leprosy; and an opportunity to proclaim the Christian gospel of God's saving grace in Jesus, to demonstrate it in practice and to lead people to Christ. The individuals and organizations at work did not all give equal weight to each.

In London

In view of the growing number of hospitals, the WMMS established the post of Medical Secretary in 1907. The appointment also carried responsibility for all matters concerning the health of missionaries. The duties were codified in 1927. They embraced all medical examinations of candidates and missionaries, and the authorization of any special payment in the event of medical need; advising on the suitability of candidates for medical work, and guiding prospective candidates in their medical studies; the general oversight of the Society's medical work, including presenting grant applications; and home propaganda. This was a wide brief, but it did not trespass on the domain of the WA, which operated independently until the 1960s. Frank Davey, on his appointment, discovered that he had responsibility for seven hospitals in Africa and three in Asia, while WW was concerned with seventeen in Asia and two in Africa – and there was no medical specialist among the WW Secretaries. WW and the parent body were fully integrated, health care included, only in 1966.

Davey complained of the small proportion of the Society's turnover allocated to medical work. It was time, he said, for a re-appraisal. He advanced three reasons for much greater commitment. In the first place, Jesus was a healer – he put the gospel he preached into action. Secondly, every effort was going into building up the young churches – without a holistic ministry their witness was inadequate and ineffective. Lastly, a great evangelistic opportunity was being missed – hospitals

---

[16]   G.R. Senior, *Thomas Frank Davey* (Peterborough, Foundery Press, 1996), p. 28.

provided the context for 'friendly outreach to thousands'.[17] He proposed that the Society should open one new institution a year for the next five years.

It was not an achievable objective, but a number of significant projects followed. In 1983 a substantial bequest was received from John Wightman of Bournemouth, out of which £300,000 was earmarked for medical work;[18] it enabled support for a few hospitals, managed by autonomous sister Churches, to continue at a relatively high level. In 1992 the Committee adopted a policy statement on the Healing Ministry which recognized that

> It is the state's responsibility to elaborate and co-ordinate an overall policy covering the entire population and to implement it either directly (that is, government-run institutions and programmes) or indirectly (that is, in cooperation with voluntary bodies such as the church)...

> There is a prophetic task for the church in undertaking innovative thinking and engaging in constructive dialogue with the government, the medical profession and community leaders about approaches to health and healing ... the church may become involved practically in pioneering aspects of health care as yet beyond the scope of government's activity – for example hospices, mental health units, leprosy rehabilitation, health education, nutrition programmes – as formerly it pioneered general health posts in places remote from government institutions.[19]

The ability of national governments to meet their responsibilities was affected by the harsh conditions imposed by bankers in return for debt relief; many were obliged to slash their health and education budgets. But Churches, with encouragement and sometimes assistance from MCOD, had in many instances taken the pioneering role to heart.

Later Initiatives

Frank Davey's 1961 proposal was ambitious and could not be realized; there was, however, one significant result. Dabou Hospital in the Ivory Coast was a joint project with MAYC, marking the centenary of the Society's medical work and twenty-one years of MAYC. MAYC raised £180,000 and provided skilled volunteers who worked with local villagers on the construction, completed by a British engineer. Training of nurses and technical staff was started. The first patients were received

---

[17]   MCH: T.F. Davey, 'Medical Missions – Challenge to Expand', discussion paper, February 1961.

[18]   Wightman left almost £1.1 million, expressing an interest in 'medical building overseas' but without creating a binding trust.

[19]   Central Committee papers, 22 March 1992.

in April 1968. The initial staff consisted of eleven expatriates – missionaries and volunteers – and over a hundred Africans. The hospital quickly acquired a high reputation, and some patients came more than 600 miles. With two doctors and five qualified nurses the hospital carried out over 1,000 consultations each week – 2,000 by 1975. The emphasis was on out-patient services and outreach, and only twenty-one beds were initially opened. A team visited surrounding villages, each of which formed a health committee and provided health workers. Prevention – including immunization and nutrition – was always a priority. The number of doctors gradually grew from two to seven, and the beds to 106 (more than half for children). African staff progressively replaced expatriates, the last of whom left in 1996.[20]

In 1978 the World Health Organization published its Alma-Ata declaration on primary health care, with a programme calling for 'Health for all by the year 2000'. One of its planks declared 'The people have the right and duty to participate individually and collectively in the planning and implementation of their health care'. At Maua in Kenya, the principle of Community Based Health Care, that health problems and priorities should be identified by local communities rather than in remote capital cities, was already being put into practice. From 1967 nurse training was extended by a full year to include community nursing as well as ward nursing and midwifery. Simultaneously hospital staff began to encourage the formation of local health committees, at first in a handful of villages where they had for some time held clinics and were known and trusted. Involving traditional leaders, government officials, church representatives and local businesses, the first committees were formed in the vicinity of Maua; later the scheme was extended to more areas where the Methodist Church was strong and took the lead role. Among other outcomes, traditional birth attendants were helped to improve their standards of hygiene and to recognize obstetric problems needing medical attention, and local circumcisers were encouraged to use a spare hospital building to mark the rites of passage in a hygienic environment. A disability programme was started and gradually parents came to see the point of giving disabled children the educational and social opportunities formerly denied them. When AIDS became a major concern, education and prevention, HIV+ treatment and the support of those who became guardians of orphans were all introduced at Maua. In time local prostitutes began to come for treatment. Maua was taking Health for All seriously.

Two further initiatives were developed in Nigeria. In 1988 Ros Colwill, then the Welfare Officer at Uzuakoli, shared with Nigerian Methodist leaders and with the Secretaries in London a vision of a centre for people with severe mental disorders. The leprosy victims with whom she was then working were outcasts, as they were in Jesus's day. An important part of her work was combating the notion that leprosy is a defilement rather than a disease. But here was another group of

[20]   P.H. Snell (Medical Superintendent 1967–1982) in *Dictionary of Methodism in Britain and Ireland (DMBI)*, http://dmbi.wesleyhistoricalsociety.org.uk (accessed 1 March 2013).

outcasts, so deranged that their families could no longer care for them, unable to say where their home once was. Some of them, as in New Testament times, were chained, abused, even forced to go around begging in gangs. Colwill's ambition was to provide a home for them, where they might receive care and treatment and be helped back to at least some degree of mental health.

So it was that Amaudo – meaning Village of Peace – came into being: a complex with a chapel in the middle of a circle of buildings – accommodation for fifty to sixty residents, workshops, dining room, common room. Only those who had lost all contact with their families were admitted. The Amaudo régime was a mixture of conventional drug treatment, traditional African herbal remedies, occupational therapy, rehabilitation through a variety of craft activities and the simple experience of living in community, with prayer in the chapel at the heart of it all. Many of those who were collected from the street because they had nowhere else were, after two years at Amaudo, restored to such a degree of health that they were able to recall where they came from, meet their families again and even return to their village where, with regular support from the community care team, some could live a relatively normal life.

Later, a community psychiatric programme was set up in collaboration with the Ministry of Health to provide mental health services to ex-residents and other mentally ill people. People were treated in their own homes and advice and support given to the family by psychiatric nurses employed by the state and managed by the tiny Amaudo staff team. Another dedicated worker concentrated on cases of human rights abuse. One achievement was to break up a begging gang controlled by a man who forced destitute, mentally ill people to chant and beg in the market place wearing chains, and drugged them to keep them awake. Amaudo got the ringleader arrested and treated the victims.

Amaudo was one of the projects supported by the Nigeria Health Care Project set up by the Wesley Guild. No longer able to be of use to a much-altered Ilesha hospital, which was now half of the Obafemi Awolowo University Teaching Hospitals Complex, the Guild embarked on a fresh challenge in the run-up to its centenary which was due in 1996. At first it focused on fund-raising to support three places – the Uzuakoli Leprosy Centre, Amaudo, and Bethesda Hospital further north which had been pioneered by Dutch missionaries and inherited by Methodist Church Nigeria. By the year 2010 the Project had raised a million pounds and was assisting thirteen hospitals, clinics and health centres, three centres for mentally ill homeless people, a leprosy centre, an eye clinic, a motherless babies' home and an orphanage. Many of these establishments were started in areas where no other medical facilities existed; to be self-sustaining was a seemingly unattainable aim.

Chapter 8
Life-Long Learning

To list every Methodist school overseas is no more possible than to list every Methodist church. The churches ranged from cathedral complexes to precarious wattle-and-daub structures needing extensive repair after every rainy season. The institutions were almost as varied: elementary schools, secondary schools, middle schools and colleges (the terms carried varied meanings), and teacher-training institutions. In a few places special schools were opened, for people with sensory or physical impairments. Although all these institutions were designed to educate the young, it often happened that because of late starting, years out for family reasons or inability to meet the fees, and repeat years after failing the grade, even those who persevered were much older than European students at a comparable stage. Adult literacy programmes for those – especially women – who had never had the chance of schooling, or made little progress, were neither common nor well-resourced.

The nineteenth-century debates about the fundamental purpose of church schools were never wholly resolved. On the one hand were those who argued that the object of missions was to make Christians, not citizens or scholars, and criticized the sums invested in education. On the other were those who pointed to the injunction, 'Go into all the world and *teach* all nations'. The curriculum was not confined to basic Christian teaching, literacy, Bible and catechism: science, liberal arts, vocational courses were a natural extension of elementary schooling, introduced wherever the government could be persuaded to give grants-in-aid. This was to be expected; it was the educational system which missionaries knew, and which their educated local counterparts and successors inherited. Besides, a ministry devoted to human development was, like the ministry of healing, part and parcel of a holistic gospel. Yet it was easy to confuse human development and social control, a civilizing mission with an imperialist agenda. And without doubt many beneficiaries of mission schooling were attracted solely by the material advantage that accrued, not in the least by the religious teaching.

The first Bishop of Calcutta, T.F. Middleton, had written in 1818:

> One great instrument of the success of Christianity will be the diffusion of European knowledge: it seems almost impossible that they, who in childhood shall have been accustomed to use their minds, can ever afterwards be capable of adopting the absurdities and reverencing the abominations now proposed to them as truth …[1]

---

[1]   Letter to the Society for the Propagation of the Gospel (SPG), 16 November 1818, quoted in M.A.C. Warren, *Social History and Christian Mission* (London, SCM Press,

His thesis was not borne out by events; but education remained a prominent element in the missionary project. Methodists were in a tradition which gave it the highest importance. The agenda of Wesley's first Conference in 1744 opened with the questions 'What to teach?' and 'How to teach?' and Kingswood School 'was a project, as Wesley himself recorded, on which he spent more time and thought and patience than on any other'.[2]

Formal Education

The majority of the elementary schools began small – as small as a single classroom with one teacher and a handful of pupils – and many expanded in time to provide a complete course of primary education. They were built, and any specialist contractors paid for, by the people they served. Very few grants came from Britain, though sometimes well-wishers sent money. The extent to which government grants paid for buildings was variable; salaries were more commonly subsidised by government, but even the better-funded schools needed to charge school fees to make ends meet. Only staff with teaching qualifications would be eligible for government money, and there were rarely enough to staff every class. Handling a school's finances was no small matter; managing a dozen or more in a circuit made heavy demands. Some Districts might have scores of schools in their care, and occasionally a Director of Education – an ordained or lay missionary – was appointed. Whatever pedagogical expectations appeared in the job description, the reality was that their time was spent on recruiting staff, negotiating with government, keeping accounts and balancing budgets. In-service teacher-training, if it could be arranged, was squeezed in. Such missionary appointments were infrequent, and it was rare, before a District became autonomous, for a national to be made Director of Education; generally school management was left to the local minister or superintendent.

Lack of supervision meant many shortcomings in the educational system. Few Districts had the benefit of a William Balmer, Sierra Leone's Education Secretary (as well as Principal of Richmond College, Freetown) from 1903 to 1907, who was asked to visit and review all the Wesleyan day schools in West Africa in 1907–1908.

> I used to find registers left unmarked for weeks at a time. As they must be marked up for Government returns, this means that they are afterwards filled in with no regard to the truth. Not only so, but as the Government grants are assessed on attendance, these unmarked registers are filled in so as to show full attendance on the part of every child.[3]

1967), p. 86.
　[2]　F.C. Pritchard, 'Education', in Davies, George and Rupp (eds), vol 3, p. 279.
　[3]　Report on the West African Schools, 12 May 1908, p. 1, quoted by H.E. Thomas, *W.T. Balmer* (unpublished monograph, 1979).

Figure 8.1   William Balmer, sleeping on a camp bed in a schoolroom, Sierra Leone, 1909

He found that the scripture syllabus he had prepared at the Synod's request was neglected because it earned no government grant. So much for what was supposed to be the prime *raison d'être* of mission schools.

There were far fewer secondary schools, but some of them acquired an outstanding reputation, despite the ill-equipped, shabby premises in which they generally began, increasingly cramped and inadequate as the number of pupils grew. In climates where moth and rust corrupt rapidly, and with no surplus available for maintenance, they became increasingly dilapidated. Some eventually closed; that others continued to produce good results in such conditions spoke volumes for the quality of the teaching and the determination of the taught. Sooner or later came the point where a major building project, perhaps involving relocation, had to be undertaken, with funds raised both locally and worldwide. Alumni who prospered, like John Mensah Sarbah,[4] the first African to be called to the bar in London, were

4   http://www.dacb.org/stories/ghana/sarbah_john.html, accessed 1 March 2013.

foremost among the benefactors. The driving force behind modernization, until well into the twentieth century, was generally a missionary principal; the principal was most commonly a minister, with any lay missionary in a supporting role. The time came when nationals took over headships – in the 1940s in some places, as late as the 1980s in others. The church's target for indigenization was sometimes overtaken by the political independence movement. The new rulers were rarely as abrupt and thoroughgoing as communist China in dispensing with expatriate personnel and eliminating all trace of religious affiliation from the education system, but tighter regulation of grant-aided schools was common and outright nationalization was not unknown.

Indispensable to the educational task was training teachers. Training institutions often ran courses for lay agents, evangelists, or catechists – names meaning much the same thing – as well, and some of them trained men for the ordained ministry. Despite the very basic qualification level, both Euclid and Greek were on the timetable in Ibadan in 1913.

William Balmer entered the ministry from a school headship and was dispatched immediately to circuit work, before answering an appeal to open 'the Richmond College of West Africa' in Freetown in 1901. It was intended to be a theological college serving all the Districts along the coast, and the fact that Balmer had no academic theological training did not handicap his appointment or his work – while still a probationer himself he was made the examiner of the probationers in Sierra Leone. But the college never had more than eight students and Ghanaians and Nigerians took exception to sending their ministerial candidates to Freetown; indeed leading Methodists in Sierra Leone wanted their ministers trained at the 'real' Richmond in England. After his visitation of the other Districts Balmer, who endeared himself to Ghanaians by preaching in Fante three weeks after he arrived, was transferred in 1908 to Cape Coast. He was to take over a school with a complicated history, restarted in 1905 by John Mensah Sarbah, one of its original ten pupils. Sarbah renamed it *Mfantsipim* – Fante for 'Soul of the people', for a school intended to respect and develop indigenous culture. Balmer arrived to find it had failed yet again; there was no teacher left. Yet, to his amazement, eight boys were still doggedly trying to study together. He christened them 'The Faithful Eight' and viewed this as a promising situation rather than the converse. Furthermore Cape Coast was geographically better placed than Freetown to serve the three Districts. His proposal to transfer the 'Richmond of West Africa' to Mfantsipim was endorsed by the Gold Coast Synod but once again the other Districts were not interested in a centralized institution. Mfantsipim thrived, but after Balmer left in 1910 no courses for church workers were run until in 1924 a large training college for teachers, evangelists and ministers was opened on the outskirts of Kumasi, with accommodation for 150 residents. The imposing buildings of Wesley College cost £22,500. One third was provided by the Society, the rest by Gold Coast Methodists, Ashanti, Fanti and Ga all contributing, ancient feuds forgotten.

Figure 8.2   Mfantsipim School, Cape Coast, Ghana, 1926

Figure 8.3   Opening of Wesley College, Kumasi, Ghana, 3 March 1923

Mfantsipim moved to a new site on which a well-equipped school was built which gained an enviable reputation. Influenced by the results of the 1929 Civil Service examinations, in which Mfantsipim boys took the first five places, the Governor promised a grant of £13,000 towards an extension costing £40,000. But the grant never arrived. Richard Lockhart, who was in charge when the Governor reneged on his promise, was furious, and said so in the press in no uncertain terms. His persistent and intemperate criticisms, against the advice of the District Chairman, were counter-productive: the grant was not reinstated, nor was duty on the building materials waived. However, Lockhart's prudent administration enabled the new buildings to open in 1933, and his emphasis on academic standards enabled him to announce that in the Cambridge School Certificate examinations in 1934 Mfantsipim's pass rate was 85 per cent – compared with an average of 61 per cent at schools in England. Lockhart was criticized for his emphasis on academic success, but, given the ascent of fascism in those years, he recognized how vital it was, in the words of the historian and old boy, Adu Boahen, to prove

> to that ignominious racist pseudo-scientific School of Anthropology ... so influential in the 1930s and 1940s, that the African was not racially inferior and could be intellectually as good ... given the same opportunities and conditions despite his so-called cephalic index![5]

From Lockhart's time on, the best testimonial an old boy could have was the name of his school, and the old boys were the best publicity for Mfantsipim: not least Alex Quaison-Sackey, the senior prefect in 1945, who was the first African to preside over the General Assembly of the United Nations, and Kofi Annan (1954–1957), seventh Secretary-General of the UN. Annan, who credited the school with teaching him 'that suffering anywhere concerns people everywhere', once led the student body in a successful hunger strike to get better food in the school cafeteria.

Wesley Girls' High School, nearby, enjoyed a comparable reputation. It grew from the little establishment run by Elizabeth Waldron and later by Clara Ellis[6] to a school for 1,200 girls, built on a new site in 1954. Wesley Deaconesses played an important part in building up the Girls' High Schools in Freetown, Cape Coast, Accra and Lagos early in the century.[7] When another Girls' Boarding School was opened in Segbwema in 1924, it was one of the Mende chiefs who said

> We all know that when we roast a banana, we roast one side and then turn it over and roast the other side. In like manner we have given our boys to the Mission to

---

[5]   A.A. Boahen, *Mfantsipim and the making of Ghana: a centenary history, 1876–1976* (Accra, Sankofa, 1996), p. 309.

[6]   Pritchard, *Methodists and their Missionary Societies 1760–1900*, pp. 140, 246.

[7]   p. 24.

learn God's book; but they are only one side of our country, and today we come to give our girls also, because we want our country to be like a banana well roasted.[8]

Like Cape Coast, Galle in Ceylon could boast two prestigious Methodist schools: Richmond College for boys, founded in 1882, and Southlands College for girls, lying within the ramparts of the sixteenth century fort, which dated from 1884. It was named in 1922 to honour Mabel Westlake, headmistress from 1907 to 1918, who had been trained at Southlands Methodist College in Battersea. Among Richmond's pre-1962 alumni were Wijeyananda Dahanayake, Prime Minister in 1959–1960, and Mahinda Rajapakse who became President of Sri Lanka in 2005. In 1962 the government took over all mission schools. The last expatriate heads had already departed and subsequent heads were appointed without reference to their faith allegiance. Bo-trees and statues of the Buddha came to adorn school grounds in much of Sri Lanka.

In central China, Wuchang on the Yangtze's south bank was an important seat of learning, one of the centres to which thousands flocked for the triennial civil service examinations. Here David Hill established a high school in 1888; it moved to a larger site with better facilities, outside the city wall, in 1907, taking the name Wesley College. A normal (teacher-training) school and a theological institution shared the site. On the opposite bank of the river, in Hanyang, a girls' school was opened in 1896 and named after Hill who died that year. It began with eight pupils in an ancestral temple – many such buildings were being used for educational purposes. Before long a permanent site was acquired and a three-storey building erected, comprising classrooms, bedrooms and a dining hall. It expanded steadily and by 1925 there were primary, middle and 'normal' departments. The school handbook declared

- Foot binding is not allowed in the school.
- Extravagance in dress or in personal expenditure is forbidden. The wearing of jewellery is strictly forbidden.
- All letters sent or received must pass through the Principal's hands.
- Christians are asked to bring their hymn-books and Bibles.[9]

In the South China District Haigh College was built in 1914 close by the hospital in Foshan, on land which had formerly been the town's execution ground. It was for years the only middle school in the province outside Guangzhou city. The name of Henry Haigh, a WMMS Secretary whose missionary service was in India, meant little to the Chinese and it soon became known as the *Wa Ying* (meaning Chinese-English) Middle School. The Wa Ying girls' school was built on the same compound. Both schools were moved to Hong Kong when the Sino-

---

[8]   F.D. Walker, *The Day of Harvest in the White Fields of West Africa* (London, Cargate Press, 1925), p. 68.

[9]   SOAS, MMSL CH250, David Hill Girls' School Hanyang, Prospectus, n.d.

Japanese war broke out. When they moved back to Foshan in 1945 they decided to remain a co-educational school and took the name Wa Ying College, but in 1951 it was confiscated, like all mission schools in China. Many alumni were among the hundreds of thousands who escaped to Hong Kong over the next few years, and they initiated a project to restart Wa Ying there. In 1971 it opened in brand new premises and its reputation became such that there were soon fourteen applicants for every place.

Methodism arrived in Zimbabwe much later, and brought with it the experience of running educational institutions in South Africa. No time was lost in starting village schools and soon there were several centres where both the three Rs and industrial skills were taught. One of these was at Nenguwo in Mashonaland, which developed rapidly after 1915 thanks to the generosity of Sir Joshua Waddilove of Bradford. Renamed the Waddilove institution, it became a centre of excellence that attracted students from all over the country and further afield. Until 1928 there was a rule that only English might be spoken between 6 am and 6 pm; after it was relaxed, students' spoken English improved markedly. Ndabaningi Sithole, who became one of the leaders of the struggle for black majority rule, went to Waddilove in 1939 and later wrote:

> Our professional teacher in the Teacher Training Department was William Tregidgo. We all admired him. He was strict and thorough, fair and firm, and demanded the same from us. By his own example he taught us to be punctual ... The principal ... [the Revd George] Pluke was opposed to any form of corporal punishment, and he taught us not to use it. We did not agree with him ... we secretly thrashed the children we taught during our practical teaching periods.[10]

But times changed, as did pedagogical principles and methods. A secondary school was eventually started at Waddilove in 1966 with an African headmaster, Heyi Malaba. Two years later he became principal of the whole institution – primary and secondary schools, teacher training and the school farm. The demand for academic success did not please a lot of white Rhodesians who ranted that it only added arrogance to ignorance, but the Church stuck to its last. Teacher training closed in 1981, for the Church was unable to afford the cost of enlarging and upgrading its facilities to meet the higher standards demanded by the new government following Zimbabwe's independence. The ethos of Waddilove began to change: recruiting staff of the right calibre became harder in the face of civil service and private sector competition, government assumed responsibility for staffing, and religious activities were practically confined to Sundays.

Foremost among the other Methodist schools in Zimbabwe was Tegwani, in Matabeleland.[11] Here an 'industrial institution' was begun in 1897. It became a

---

        [10]   N. Sithole, *African Nationalism,* (London, Oxford University Press, 1968 edition), pp. 16–17.
        [11]   Or Thekwane, the official name from 1980.

boarding school for boys in 1924. The students made their own bricks and, working under an African bricklayer, put up new buildings. Together with an African carpenter they did all the woodwork. The report in the 1929 Rhodesia District Handbook stated that in two years they had done all the carpentry for two new classrooms, four dormitories and three teachers' houses, and they had made – for themselves and for sale – doors, windows, blackboards, tables, cupboards, desks, seats and imphala boxes (in which their clothes and books were kept). A teacher-training department was introduced in 1929 by Will Tregidgo; he ran it for ten years before transferring to Waddilove where he worked for another twenty-five. Girls were admitted to Tegwani in 1934. As well as the primary classes and post-primary teacher training, the institution ran courses in agriculture, building and carpentry and, for the girls, homecraft. Then in 1951 the secondary school opened. It was one of the first in the land for Africans; previously the only possibility was to go and study in South Africa. Teacher training, and the building department, ceased in 1971 in order to concentrate resources on the newly opened sixth form. The school reported excellent results until 1978, when the liberation war intensified. After the war Canaan Banana, a former pupil and subsequently the school chaplain, became the first President of Zimbabwe.[12] The thrill of independence was shattered in 1985 when headteacher Luke Kumalo was murdered along with his missionary wife.[13]

Across the Atlantic in the Bahamas, Queen's College in Nassau, founded in 1890, became an élite co-educational school, priding itself on its academic excellence and producing many leading citizens. The last two missionary principals, Geoffrey Litherland (1959–1964) and Neville Stewart (1964–1970) oversaw the school's enlargement from 360 to 1,800 pupils with a massive building programme on a new site, including a hostel for boarders from the 'out islands'. Under Litherland the proportion of black children rose to half, though the teachers were almost all white; 'QC' relied on staff recruited on the principal's annual visits to London until the 1980s. By the end of the century, with an enrolment of over 2,000, it comprised an Early Learning Centre, Primary School and High School.

Excelsior School, in Jamaica, had a very different history.[14] It was founded not by a missionary but by a Jamaican, Wesley Powell, who, despite his forename, hailed from a Seventh Day Adventist family. Secondary education had to be paid for in the 1920s and the Powells made many sacrifices so that he could qualify as a teacher. He was troubled by the knowledge that many Jamaican children, as intelligent as himself, were prevented by the cost from studying beyond primary classes, and he resolved to dedicate his teaching career to them. The school he started on his parents' veranda expanded swiftly, moving to a succession of ever

---

[12]   Zvogbo, 'An overview', pp. 16–34 records the history of Waddilove and Thekwane in some detail.

[13]   pp. 39–40.

[14]   A.W. Powell, *The Excelsior-EXED story* (Kingston, Jamaica, Methodist Church in the Caribbean and the Americas, Jamaica District, 1989); Davey, *Changing Places,* pp. 106–8.

Figure 8.4   Excelsior School students, Kingston, Jamaica

bigger rented premises, before he acquired a fifteen-acre site in East Kingston on which he planned to build. But his funds ran out and developments stalled until in 1951 Methodists came to the rescue, and for a consideration of £40,000 Excelsior School became a Methodist foundation, with Powell as a very successful head teacher. He went on to turn the complex into a community school committed to life-long learning, which came to be known as 'EXED'. It was typical of his way of working that planning this development involved thirty sub-committees with some 240 members. EXED opened in 1972, its range of provision extended at both ends, with an infant school, a sixth form and adult literacy classes; both a teaching course and a nursing course were afterwards officially recognized. As well as offering courses tailored to the disadvantaged community of East Kingston, the quality of EXED's programmes attracted students from less deprived areas too.

To highlight a handful of the more successful schools is not to discount all the others. Their pupils may not have become cabinet ministers, diplomats or lawyers, but numerous lives were enriched, and many life-long Christians were formed. Teachers were not all up to the job, but there were many heroes who struggled with oversized classes, dilapidated buildings and meagre salaries, with an energy and a dedication that changed whole communities.

Methodists in the British tradition did not attempt to run post-sixth form education abroad, other than ministerial training. American Methodists had a different tradition, and were determined to found Methodist universities overseas as they had done so successfully in the United States. They chose to set up the 'Africa University' in Zimbabwe, where both traditions had founded Methodist

Churches. It opened in 1992. Inspired by this project, Lawi Imathiu, the Presiding Bishop of the Methodist Church in Kenya launched an appeal for a Kenya Methodist University. A property near Kaaga, in Meru, acquired in 1954 for a Rural Training Centre, with a ministerial Training Institute built later, would be its nucleus. Imathiu was Chairman of the World Methodist Council (WMC) and had many international contacts. He was a persuasive advocate, but it took years to turn the vision into reality. However, with careful planning in consultation with the Higher Education Commission and experienced Kenyan educationists, with encouragement from Britain, with a great deal of financial support from the USA and with Korean help, it was inaugurated in 1998. From eleven pioneer students – three in theology and eight in business administration – it grew over the next dozen years to number 4,000 students in nineteen departments with 300 staff and received its official charter in 2006.

Church Institutions and State Services

A National Christian Conference in Shanghai in 1922 heard that 'opportunities for religious education in our Christian schools are practically unlimited, for nowhere is there any serious prejudice against it.'[15] It was a serious misjudgement. The 'Restore Educational Rights Movement' of 1924, a manifestation of the swelling tide of nationalism, was directed against Christian schools and colleges. By 1927 the Guomindang was in the ascendant and its capture of Beijing in 1928 obliged the western powers to acknowledge its rule. Fiercely anti-Communist, but fiercely nationalist, one of its decrees required all private schools in the territories under its control to register; all principals had to be Chinese citizens; religious instruction could not be made a compulsory subject. For the UMFC-founded Wenzhou District and the College it had started in 1903, the first two demands were acceptable but the third compelled them to consider their position, and in 1929 the College closed. Thomas Chapman, the District Chairman, wrote:

> Our very raison d'être as a missionary college has been taken away if we are not allowed to teach the Christian religion. It is not our duty to supply this country with a secular education, and when a missionary college ceases to be a very definite factor as a Christian influence, our position is untenable.[16]

The Guomindang leader, Chiang Kai-shek, was converted soon afterwards and became a Methodist. This did not bring about any relaxation of Nationalist policy, although the extent to which it was implemented during the turmoil of the next twenty years varied from province to province. Communist policy left no room at

---

[15]   F.J. Rawlinson (ed), *The Chinese Church as Revealed in the National Christian Conference* (Shanghai, Helen Thoburn, 1922), p. 117.

[16]   UM Annual Report 1930, p. 53.

all for church institutions. When Mao Zedong came to power in 1949, all schools and hospitals were soon taken over by the state, as they were in Burma in the wake of Ne Win's 1962 coup.

The view that the state should shoulder its responsibility for the nation's health and its children's education was laudable and was shared by governments elsewhere which did not necessarily hold the virulent anti-foreign attitudes of red China and Burma. Few were quite as benign as the colonial government in Northern Rhodesia, which offered to provide full funding for buildings, staff, and students if the missions would give up their separate teacher-training courses and unite. The men's course at Kafue, started by the PMAMS in 1915, and the women's course begun later at the WM station in Chipembi, came together with four others, all ranging in size from twenty to fifty students, in the ecumenical David Livingstone Teacher Training College which opened in 1959. The college was soon making an impact on primary education throughout the country, influencing the syllabus, producing text books and supporting teachers through national radio; and the successful co-operative venture was a factor in helping bring to birth the United Church of Zambia in 1964.

For newly independent governments, there were two ways of asserting their authority in the education and health sectors. The full take-over of funding and management responsibilities was one: it did not necessarily entail a change of staff, but any expatriates were usually replaced within a short space. Alternatively, government might recognize the significant role being played by institutions in the charitable sector and provide grant aid, perhaps on a per capita (pupil or patient) basis or even help with capital costs. If the second way were chosen, there would be sundry conditions, more or less rigorous in their requirements and more or less strictly monitored from place to place, to ensure that the shape and quality of the school's curriculum, or a hospital's care, conformed to national policy.

There was much opposition from Christians, especially to wholesale nationalization. That the church did not perish when it ceased to manage primary schools was a lesson learned. But Churches were proud of their great secondary institutions, however costly they were to run; loss of control severely dented their pride. Where the institutions had proved themselves an effective plank in their strategy of evangelization, the Churches were particularly aggrieved. What made matters worse was the tendency, not invariable but widespread, for standards to fall. Buildings and equipment were poorly maintained. Books and blackboards were in short supply. Staff were less willing to burn the midnight oil or forgo their days off. Wherever the institution had enjoyed a good reputation before the take-over – which was not always the case – the local population came to yearn for the good old days.

The root of the problem lay in the deteriorating economic climate. Even where the Churches – almost all now autonomous – retained responsibility for their institutions they had difficulty in maintaining standards. By the 1980s many countries found themselves having to spend more and more on servicing their debts. Less and less was available for their education and health budgets. Where the International Monetary Fund imposed conditions in connection with a debt relief package, these inevitably included cutting back on social welfare programmes. Where church-run institutions had been in receipt of government grants, these were reduced to a fraction of their earlier purchasing power, if not phased out altogether. Where the institutions had been wholly taken over, some severely indebted governments were suddenly keen to hand them back. The Roman Catholic Church somehow found the resources to accept the offer and restart colleges and hospitals, and other Churches, anxious not to be outdone, tried to follow suit. But even if they had formerly been able to provide high quality services to all-comers, many could now meet only modest standards, and that only by charging fees beyond the reach of the poorest. By this time the funds being raised annually by British and Irish Methodists had long since become inadequate to bail them out. The schools that prospered in spite of difficulties were those with successful alumni who, like Mensah Sarbah, acknowledged tangibly their debt to their education.

Special Schools

In 1888 David Hill opened a school for blind boys in Hankou. Blind children in China – the 'forlorn castaways of an indifferent Confucianism'[17] – were quite commonly left to die in infancy, and those who survived became beggars with a very low quality of life. But in Hankou, thanks to an ingenious adaptation of Braille in the local dialect devised at the school, the boys learned to read as well as acquiring the techniques of some useful trade. There was instruction in hammock-making, basketry and knitting, and the school developed a strong musical tradition.

At the time of Ghana's independence in 1957, the national Director of Education was an English Methodist, Bernard Carman. That year he visited Wa, the base of Methodism's new Northern Ghana Mission, and approved proposals for a school for the blind. The first school of the kind in Ghana, a joint Presbyterian–Methodist venture, had been established at Akropong in 1945. Ben Awumee was an experienced teacher at Akropong and was appointed headmaster at Wa. The school opened in temporary accommodation in 1958 and was replaced by a large, purpose-built building in 1976. Awumee served the school faithfully until 1981, when he returned to Akropong as head. A steady stream of the most able progressed to the Methodist Secondary School in Wenchi to study alongside sighted students, and some went on to obtain degrees.

At Waddilove an experimental scheme for teaching blind pupils alongside their sighted schoolmates was introduced in the Primary School in the mid-1960s. It was successful enough for some students to progress to the Secondary School, and

---

[17]   W.T.A. Barber, 'Methodist Foreign Missionary Enterprise: The Work of British Societies', in G. Eayrs, W.J. Townsend, H.B. Workman, (eds), *A New History of Methodism* (2 vols, London, Hodder & Stoughton, 1909), vol. 2, p. 330.

Figure 8.5   The David Hill School for the Blind, Hankou, c. 1937

one, Pearson Nherera, went on to a law degree at Cambridge and a lectureship at the University of Zimbabwe.

In Kenya, the Kaaga School for Deaf Children started in 1966 with six boys. For a while it shared a classroom in a *Harambee*[18] secondary school, but in 1971 it moved into purpose-built premises with classrooms, dormitories for four to six children per 'family', a treatment and testing room, kitchen and common room. It was not easy to persuade parents to bring their children, and pay boarding fees, when the children were still young enough to get the maximum benefit. But by the late 1980s there were 150 residents, from the nursery class through eight years of primary school to vocational classes in carpentry and dress-making.

In 1965 nine children arrived by minibus at a church hall in Mombasa for their first day at school. All victims of polio, they would never have made it to the schools their sisters and brothers attended; they could only crawl around. Eighteen months later the project, with a staff consisting of two teachers and an odd-job man, had thirty pupils and a waiting list. It needed its own buildings, with a boarding hostel; the Lands Department granted a ninety-nine year lease on five acres in the Port Reitz neighbourhood of the city, opposite the Round Table's Polio Clinic which the children were attending regularly. Funds came from *Brot für die welt* in Germany and other agencies. The buildings were erected, and numbers

---

18   *Harambee* is Kiswahili for 'All pull together' and is the official motto of Kenya; the name was given to community schools built and maintained largely by local fundraising.

grew to 100, including children with spina bifida and cerebral palsy. But day-to-day running costs were a constant worry until Methodist Young Wives' groups in Britain made the school a three-year project and raised £10,000. Corporate donations too helped the Port Reitz School for the Handicapped to develop further and by 1990 there were 175 pupils, all boarders, gaining excellent exam results and winning awards for music and drama.[19] The Methodist Church remained well represented on the management committee, while the Kenyan government supplied and paid the ten teachers and twenty-five other staff.

'Special' in a quite different way were the centres set up for girls no longer in formal education, whose future would revolve around marriage and family rather than a professional career. The primary purpose was to prepare the fiancées of ministers, theological students and evangelists for life in the manse: the courses covered all aspects of housecraft, further literacy and Christian formation. One such centre at Dabou in the Ivory Coast, staffed by WW missionaries, acquired a fine reputation, as a result of which there were always well-to-do men queuing up to send their wives or fiancées to board for a year or two. A modern building, opened in 1964, proved the ideal place to train girls who had been brought up in the bush to adapt to life in a town house or apartment. Similar centres were established at Savé in Benin, Kwadaso in Ghana and Sandringham in Zimbabwe.

Literature and Literacy

In 1858 four British missionary societies – BMS, CMS, LMS and WMMS – set up the Christian Vernacular Education Society for India, designed not to compete with

> existing educational establishments which employ the English language and literature and which are chiefly attractive to the higher classes of Hindu youth .. but rather to reach the village populations, and the masses of the lower orders in towns throughout the country, exclusively through the vernacular of each district.[20]

After several changes of name and scope it became the United Society for Christian Literature (USCL) in 1935. Methodist involvement in literature work was reflected in the secondment of a number of missionaries: among others, Joseph Passmore to the Christian Literature Society (CLS) in Madras (1908–1927), Albert Clayton to the Board of Tamil Literature (1907–1938), Arthur Cornaby to the CLS in Shanghai (1904–1912). Later, Leslie Wallace in Sierra Leone was Director of the Christian Council Literature Bureau and Bunumbu

---

[19] Margaret Beetham (née Bridgwater), the first head, wrote about some of the pupils in *NOW*, March 1991, pp. 4–6.

[20] First Annual Report of the Society, 1859: SOAS, CWML B.3/7.

Printing Press (1956–1967), and in the 1960s John Hastings was seconded to the Bengal Christian Council for literacy work.

1922 saw the advent of a new department of the WMMS, the West Africa Literature Society. The concept was Edgar Thompson's; its aim, to provide and distribute literature for day schools and Sunday schools, and – as the founding memorandum stated – for 'the nurture and building of a Christian nation'. He asked William Balmer, now back in England, to take on the task. Balmer returned to the Gold Coast on an exploratory visit. His remarkable abilities were noted by Harry Webster, the District Chairman, who wrote about the Synod meeting in Accra:

> Balmer soon tired of the routine of Synod and ... sat at work on the Ga Language. Patiently he worked by my side while debate and argument and the return of schedules proceeded. He scarcely ever raised his eyes from his Ga Bible and text book. The next day he made a request. Could I lend him a young minister for a few hours? ... I missed him that day and the next altogether ... On the following Sunday, within ten days of his arrival in the Ga language area, he read the New Testament lesson almost as if it was his native language.[21]

Vernacular literature, however, would have to wait. Balmer's priority was to produce English texts for schools across the region, to replace schoolbooks written in and for a land and culture remote from Africa. The schools were an obvious market and it was hoped that the books would make a profit that would subsidize the subsequent production of specifically Christian literature and of vernacular texts. They would be published, Balmer decided, under the imprint of the 'Atlantis Press' and the series would be entitled 'Atlantis Readers'. He wrote two Primers and eight Readers, all published between 1924 and 1926. In the same period he wrote up some lesson notes he had prepared years earlier at Mfantsipim, published as *A History of the Akan Peoples,* and put his mind to a series of catechetical books. *A Catechism of Christian Experience,* first published in 1924, was eventually translated into a dozen West African languages and into Shona.

The West African Literature Society was supposed to have a branch committee in each territory, to make suggestions about publications, to promote them and distribute them, and to recommend how any profit should be used. The Gold Coast Committee was much the most active; it embraced the work of the Book Depot established in Cape Coast in 1883. In 1924 Leonard Pickard, a lay missionary, was sent to be the Book Steward. Webster called him a young man in a hurry; he was impatient with the pace at which Atlantis titles appeared, and was wont to overspend his credit. But his initiative and business sense built up a successful operation and brought in a steady income which the District earmarked for theological education. Vernacular texts were held up by disputes about orthography, which led Balmer to consult Dietrich Westermann, the world's leading authority on African languages, in Berlin. Westermann approved Balmer's suggestions, but then produced even

---

[21]   *The Foreign Field,* September 1928: pp. 235–6.

more radical proposals which the Gold Coast government adopted. With his former Mfantsipim pupil Francis Grant (later to be the first President of the autonomous Ghana Conference), who spent six months in England for the purpose, Balmer proceeded to compile *A Grammar of the Fante-Akan Language.*

From the mid-1920s developments in the Ivory Coast[22] increasingly claimed Balmer's attention. Gospel and catechism translations in three Ivoirian languages were drafted by missionaries and converts on the spot, but he needed to resolve inconsistencies of orthography before they could be published. Typically, he made himself familiar with the rudiments of grammar and vocabulary of all three as well. He paid two extended visits to the territory and in the course of the second, in 1928, he became ill. Fortuitously Edgar Thompson was there on a Secretarial visit; they sailed home together. Within weeks Balmer died; the post-mortem revealed a brain tumour.

Arthur Southon was released by Conference to take Balmer's place, and served the Society for five years. He was not replaced, though an Overseas Literature Committee continued to meet until 1971. From 1945 to 1967 Fred Pearson at the Home Organization Department dealt not only with Atlantis publications but with a variety of publications commissioned from the overseas districts. Most were for the Cape Coast Book Depot along with books in Kimeru for Kenya and a Mukuni hymnbook for Northern Rhodesia. Atlantis's last vernacular publication was an Efik Grammar delivered to Nigeria in 1963. In 1964 MMS was a founding partner in Joint Action for Christian Literature Overseas, eventually to be known by the less unwieldy name *Feed the Minds* (FTM). The existence of an ecumenical organization specifically devoted to the promotion of literacy and literature made the MMS Committee redundant; grants for literature work hitherto made by the Society – for example regular support for the Bo Press and Bookshop in Sierra Leone – were thereafter channelled through FTM. At the final meeting of the Overseas Literature Committee in 1971 there was a last reference to the Atlantis Press, making an interest-free loan of £1,000 from its residual funds for the publication of 5,000 Ogoni hymn-books following the Biafran war; the balance of the cost came from a Nigeria Rehabilitation Fund. Henceforward the MMS made an annual grant to FTM and over the years many of its Secretaries were co-opted by FTM as advisors.

Leslie Wallace had studied typography and graphic arts in Belfast and was employed in the printing trade before entering the ministry. Within a year of his arrival in Sierra Leone in 1955 he was appointed to manage the Christian Council's Literature Bureau and Press at Bo. The Press supplied materials to schools, printed vernacular Christian materials and co-operated with the Bible Society in translation and publishing work. Wallace became responsible for a national literacy campaign producing literacy material including primers and follow-up readers in various vernacular languages.

---

[22]   pp. 75–7.

Figure 8.6   Methodist Bookshop, Cape Coast

Many of the early Methodist preachers abroad were illiterate. Even a book of ready-made sermons was of no use to them unless they had someone to read it to them. The Bible itself was only accessible aurally. One way to tackle the problem was for a minister or evangelist to meet the preachers and prepare

Sunday's sermon together, relating the Bible passage to local circumstances, and memorize it before dispersing. In parts of the Ivory Coast, for example, preachers were known to spend most of Thursday walking to the meeting place and much of Saturday returning to their village, going through their sermon again and again as they made their way home. The following week it might be another preacher's turn, but some made the journey week after week, greeting everybody they passed and sharing their faith, as well as their news, on the way.

The practice had much to commend it, but preachers and congregations alike longed to read for themselves. In North China, George Candlin had reported in 1889 that

> Mrs Chang Hsiu Ling learns her New Testament while weaving cloth, plodding her way laboriously through the hard characters. She … makes her husband tell her the words she does not know, and as he knows very little himself, he sometimes tells her wrong; of course, he gets into trouble when she catches him at this. Mrs Chang would make a capital Biblewoman if she could be got up to a sufficient standard of education.[23]

She persevered and from 1905 took over the work of her mentor, the veteran Mrs Hu.[24] Thousands of new Christians made the same effort; the prospect of reading the gospels for themselves, in their mother-tongue, was all the incentive they needed. For Frank Laubach, an American Methodist missionary in the Philippines, however, this did not go far enough; a structured approach to illiteracy was called for. With the slogan 'Each One Teach One' he pioneered mass literacy campaigns from the 1930s onwards.

One man who caught Laubach's vision and came to see mass literacy as a mission priority was the Irishman Ormond McConnell, who worked in Haiti from 1933 to 1970. He made the first translation of the Bible into Haitian Creole and adapted the Laubach method so that Creole speakers could use it.

> We found it frustrating preaching, singing and carrying on almost all the work of the Church in French though the vast majority of the people only spoke Creole. When I talked of the possibility of writing Creole simply so that the 'masses' could learn to read and write in Creole, people laughed me to scorn. The idea came, why not write Creole phonetically? (I had studied the International Phonetic System.) I had read about the Laubach method of teaching illiterates to read … Laubach's *Toward a Literate World* … gave us exactly what we wanted. The phonetic orthography was finalised.[25]

---

[23] Quoted by Hedley, pp. 98–9.
[24] Pritchard, *Methodists and their Missionary Societies 1760–1900*, p. 183.
[25] H.O. McConnell, unpublished memoir, 1986.

Laubach visited Haiti in 1943, was received by the President and gave a broadcast lecture. The President decided to start a weekly newspaper in Creole and nominated a committee to pursue the Adult Literacy Campaign with McConnell as secretary. McConnell also chaired a committee, representing fourteen Protestant churches and missions, which published booklets in Creole on such varied topics as Hygiene, Agriculture, Arithmetic and Marriage as well as on the Christian faith. One year, on the day he left for furlough,

> Thirty pages of a book on the Old Testament we had prepared and printed in French still remained to be translated into Creole. I got up at 2 am and worked without a break until I had finished the job at 4 pm so that the book could be printed while we were away. When we returned after furlough, the printing was not even begun ...[26]

Another literacy pioneer was John Hastings, whose work in Bengal and Bihar had involved writing, translating, publishing and distributing Christian literature. In Bihar he travelled miles in his van adorned with the logo *Susamachar Bahok,* 'Carrier of the Good News', which was sometimes mistaken for an ambulance. But literature was useless without literacy. Literacy, he realized, was the key to better health, increased skills, better economic prospects, a lower birth rate and above all greater self-respect. It had the power to break the chains of oppression and poverty. He established several adult literacy schemes and then, after a period in Britain which included six frenetic years with the Methodist Relief Fund (MRF), he was invited back to north India. When he was not granted a visa, he went instead to Bangladesh where he could still use his fluent Bengali to serve and motivate some of the world's poorest communities. He worked out a low cost method of self-education which would be more efficient at enabling people to become literate and more effective at enabling them to escape the downward spiral of deprivation and exploitation. Central to his methodology was the belief that people and communities have the knowledge and resources to help themselves. A pilot programme in 250 villages made 12,000 adults literate and set up 100 village libraries. In retirement the Hastings returned again to Bangladesh and, disappointed by the government's failure to adopt a mass literacy programme, started a grass-roots movement, *Nijera Shikhi* (meaning 'Let's Teach Ourselves'). It was evident that with a population rising by two million every year, the number of illiterates was not falling but was constantly on the increase. Hastings's gigantic vision was to recruit 700,000 helpers – he eschewed the label 'teachers' – to make 61 million Bangladeshis literate. An impressive start was made with as many as 20,000 volunteers but after his death in 1998 changes of government and policy obliged *Nijera Shikhi* to shift focus and pursue, with continued vigour, other UN Millennium Development Goals.[27]

---

[26]   Ibid.

[27]   Andy Cawthera, evaluation of Nijeri Shikhi 2003, http://www.eldis.org/fulltext/ nijerashikhi.pdf, accessed 1 March 2013.

Chapter 9
Vocation, Selection, Preparation

In common with other Societies, Methodists commissioned increasing numbers of missionaries, lay and ordained, in the first half of the century; their number declined thereafter as younger churches came of age and the Christian world's centre of gravity moved south. Some of them spent a lifetime of service in the same remote place; some took up new challenges, like the couple who met in Papua New Guinea in 1975 and later worked in Portugal, Mozambique and Sierra Leone. Others returned to their homeland after a few years with a global vision which informed and inspired their life and witness in an unbelieving society, as well as a lifelong concern for the unprivileged world.

There were always Christians who heard a call and went abroad on their own account. But Methodist missionaries were 'sent'; they were under the discipline of the Society and the Conference. Before they were sent they were, in theory if not always in practice, given some training; before they were trained, their call was tested.

Vocation

The call to overseas service made itself heard in many ways – the best documented are the public meetings and the missionary literature. It would be interesting, but impossible, to calculate how many candidates had once been JMA collectors. Through JMA, children were helped to see from an early age that they were part of the missionary enterprise, and while many soon lost their enthusiasm, in others the ground was prepared and a seed was sown which gradually took root and matured. Popular accounts of missionary adventures were given as Sunday School attendance prizes. The Girls' League with its policy of appointing young District Secretaries, the smaller Young Laymen's League with its annual treks, YMA (which merged the two) with its residential conferences each helped to lead some from prayerful support to personal service; the Girls' League kept a record of those of its members who went overseas.

Not all who responded were cradle Methodists. By the 1960s, optimistically designated by the UN as the 'Decade of Development', there were candidates, both from Methodist families and from unchurched backgrounds, who wanted to use their newly-acquired qualifications – in education, medicine, agriculture – abroad, if only for a few years while in their prime. They were challenged by the cause of world development as much as by missionary sermons, and were more likely to read the *New Internationalist* than *The Kingdom Overseas*; but the MMS was a channel through which their response could be matched with a situation of need. Not all were sufficiently convinced, or able in their particular circumstances, to answer the call immediately, but later in life, when circumstances changed, some heard it again. Others gave it thought for the first time in middle age, inspired perhaps by a conversation with someone who recognized their potential, or by an advertisement for a specific post at a point where they were contemplating a career change. For some, improvements in health care and in transport as the century advanced made it more feasible to contemplate a spell abroad.

In a series of tape-recorded interviews with retired missionaries conducted in 1970, the first question asked was 'Why did you become a missionary?'

> The answers were varied and sometimes complex. Some, though not a large proportion, were conscious of a sudden, even dramatic call: 'I heard God saying to me, Child this is what I want for you.' Others spoke in more mundane terms of overseas work as 'a vocation which every Christian ought to look at', or of an offer for overseas work as the culmination of 'three years of prayer and enquiry'. A large proportion of missionaries interviewed were children of the manse, had missionary relatives, had been brought up abroad, or had parents who had wished to become missionaries themselves. 'My call,' said the daughter of one missionary couple, 'came from a Chinese bible woman who asked me to come back and be a missionary when I grew up.' ... Negative factors in the home environment were sometimes mentioned: two missionaries confessed to going abroad in order to escape the frustrations of their work at home, and a woman missionary felt herself *de trop* when her father remarried.[1]

Tom Beetham (1906–1992) wrote:

> When I was seven I had a Juvenile Missionary Collecting Book, with a penny a week from parents, neighbours and members of the church. A children's missionary magazine told that the money was for missionaries who preached, taught in schools, or worked in hospitals in China, India and Africa ... So I learned a sense of responsibility to share the Gospel with people across the world, but it was in an 'us' to 'them' relationship, a call to enlighten darkness in others, heightened by missionary biographies that spelled out the adventure and sacrifice of those who went to serve in foreign lands ... Half-way through my university course I went one Saturday evening to a Young Methodists' Missionary Meeting ... to hear the Rev W J Platt ...That night I knew I must respond to a call.[2]

Winnie Tovey was not a Methodist but grew up in a Christian family and was confirmed at the age of fifteen in the Moravian Church. A youthful ambition to be

[1] MCH: P. Ellingworth, report on a Missionary Records Project, 3 January 1971.
[2] *International Bulletin of Missionary Research* 1990, p. 167.

a missionary nurse was shattered at the age of twenty in 1938 when an infected fingernail made her unsuitable to continue training. After the war she worked as a medical secretary and met Frank Tovey, a young doctor. Then at last an opportunity to go to Tibet with the Moravian Mission arrived; the prospect prompted Tovey to propose. Shortly afterwards he obtained his FRCS and notified the MMS that he was now available to the Society. 'Can you sail for China in two weeks' time?' was the immediate response and he replied 'Yes, provided I can get married and sail with my wife'. The whirlwind activity of the next fortnight is reminiscent of some early nineteenth century marriages: 11 December 1947 wedding in Bedford, 15 December valedictory service in Bath, 17 December sailed from Glasgow.[3] Not all missionary wives began their courtship with that sense of vocation; many were motivated wholly by their love for their partner and a determination to go wherever he went.

Betty Hares (1921–1999) in her autobiography wrote:

> the wish I had had since childhood to be a missionary overseas crystallised to the point of my knowing that it must be put to the test. Was it only a wish, an ambition even, or was it a real vocation? Many things contribute to the birth and growth of one's calling. It may begin as an attraction to a person, or to a story, or to an idea … or it may be a subtle desire to do something different or something heroic, to be something or somebody. But that first blurred vision is confirmed or unconfirmed by the light that faith sheds on it as we pass along the road, and by the people and events we encounter on the journey. It is stimulated by an awareness of the world and of our neighbours. It is nourished or dies within the community of faith. There is a 'hunch' quality about vocation, an inner compulsion to explore a certain track, a sense of the fitness of things, which has to be tested.[4]

Selection

Winnie Tovey's call was taken on trust. It was debatable, and from time to time debated, whether a candidate's wife should even be interviewed. It was not normal in the secular world; and in the church, if circuit stewards made a minister's wife's lifestyle a factor in determining whether or not to extend an invitation, there came a time when they faced censure should their reasons become known. But life overseas made particular demands not just on the missionary but on the spouse. To live far from family and old friends, out of telephone contact (for most of the century) and with (in many places) an unreliable postal service to compound the sense of remoteness; to live, perhaps, without water on tap, with electricity

---

[3]   W.E. Tovey, *Strangers in Chaotung* (Northampton, Little Knoll Press, 2010), pp. 45–52.

[4]   G.B. Hares, *Journeying into Openness* (Bristol, Shoreline, 1991), pp. 25–6.

erratic at best and with only rudimentary kitchen equipment; to wage war daily on ants, cockroaches and rats; to struggle with a new language; to shop in crowded, pungent markets where stall-holders had little or no English: all this required a degree of resilience. The committees were all too aware, as well, of the infant and maternal mortality rates of the nineteenth century. Health checks for both men and women were mandatory. So the Toveys were untypical – and even they had to fit the medicals into that packed fortnight. Wives or fiancées were generally interviewed, not primarily about their faith and their understanding of mission but with probing questions on 'Have you thought about…?' lines.

Men, and single women, could expect a more thorough exploration of their vocation. There were forms to fill in, summaries of their Christian experience and call to overseas service to write, references to obtain, and normally at least two interviews before the decision was made. The pre-1932 WA form began with the questions, later deemed inappropriate, 'Are your parents living? What is your father's occupation? Is your offer made with the knowledge and consent of your parents or guardians?' It continued, 'What are your reasons for wishing to become a missionary? What special preparation for missionary work have you made? Have you made a study of any special missionary problem or mission field?' Then came questions about the candidate's understanding of the 'general qualifications' for missionary work and the 'trials and temptations' that might arise. Muriel Stennett (1905–1987) wrote in 1929:

> I should suggest that the first and foremost [qualification] is a convincing knowledge and experience of the power of God unto Salvation – but that alone is not enough: a love of humanity that can transcend racial difference; a power of sympathetic understanding that can enter into another man's feelings; and a faith that can 'keep on keeping on' and give God the glory. Perhaps these are Christian rather than 'general' [missionary] qualifications? Health (and a reserve of it), steady nerves and a sense of humour should be added to the list…

About the temptations, she confessed

> A desire to dominate rather than to serve – that is perhaps a bit of the teacher in me, which among those of a different race, with widely different traditions and conceptions, might prove fatal and certainly damaging … I don't think despondency or the almost unmasterable sense of repulsion towards customs so different from our own, which are sometimes quoted as the great foes of a missionary, are failings of mine.[5]

This was a very thorough testing of a candidate's suitability. The PM system was less rigorous. In February 1919 Emily Godfrey heard from Joseph Barkby, the Primitive Methodist Missionary Secretary, in reply to her expression of interest:

---

5   MCH: Candidates' papers, Stennett.

I am delighted to have your letter and to find that you are so much interested in our great Missionary enterprise. It would be to me personally a great pleasure to have you on our staff and I am sure you would be able to render us real service. Unfortunately at the moment we have no vacancy for a person like yourself … If you would like to apply I suggest that you do so, giving all information about yourself, stating what Christian work you have done and what qualifications you have for Missionary work and also why you desire to be a Missionary…

I note that you are 34 years of age; our limit is 30, except in exceptional circumstances.[6]

Undeterred, Emily made her application and in June was informed:

We had our Executive meeting today and I am very glad to say that it was unanimously decided to accept you for work in Nigeria … We have, as you will know, wonderful openings in this country, & we anticipate for you & all our Lady Missionaries a period of great usefulness.[7]

The normal practice of the post-union MMS continued to involve forms, references and interviews, though the interview sometimes amounted to no more than a meeting with one of the Secretaries – in the case of ministers, at their theological college (Mission House staff visited the theological colleges each year to challenge ministers-in-training to consider an overseas posting). But there were occasions when the process was short-circuited. Colin Morris was doing research at Oxford when Tom Beetham, now the Africa Secretary, made contact about a key appointment on the Copperbelt in Northern Rhodesia. Within months he was on a boat to Cape Town. His only visit to the Mission House was for a medical examination. Usually, however, candidates or couples would meet with a panel, either at the Mission House or occasionally at Kingsmead College. The practice changed in the mid-1970s. A new Overseas Service Committee started work in 1968, bringing together the MMS and WW candidates' committees. The new committee felt it desirable to include an interview with a psychologist in the process, and at that point it became the custom to hold a residential weekend of interviews, where several candidates were examined: the psychologist could not possibly make an assessment on the basis of a short meeting, nor should other panel members. By then one of the considerations was previous experience of living, or travelling, outside the United Kingdom, whereas right up to the 1960s it was common for a candidate who had not done military service to have no passport until accepted.

---

[6]   F.C. Godfrey, *Emily the Relentless Nurse* (Loughborough, Teamprint, 1999), pp. 18–19.

[7]   Ibid.

Preparation

Lay candidates – Godfrey, Stennett, Hares, Tovey, were typical – were required to obtain professional qualifications, just as ministers had to complete their initial training, before their offers were acceptable. But professional skills alone were not enough. The report of the 1910 World Missionary Conference argued that missionaries needed to be competent in their professional field, equipped with practical skills for daily living, sufficiently versed in mission history and anthropology to avoid repeating others' mistakes, knowledgeable about the other faiths they would encounter, trained in pedagogy because much of any missionary's work entailed teaching, capable of mastering a foreign language, and – above all – spiritually robust. Yet, in the case of Methodist ministers, it was assumed well into the twentieth century that their college course was sufficient. Richmond in particular had been intended to prepare missionaries and students going overseas were traditionally honoured with a joyous 'Rolling Off' ceremony when they left college followed by a solemn 'Warble' (*sic*) when they were known to be at sea.[8] At Handsworth in the 1930s the principal, Dr Lofthouse, influenced many of his students towards work abroad. William Goudie, as Secretary of the WMMS Centenary Committee, wrote in 1910:

> If I could work towards an unpaid or possibly a paid chair of World Missions for the four colleges, and leave that as one of the permanent gains of the Centenary Movement I should be glad. But there are many obstacles ...[9]

The obstacles were not overcome; whichever college they came from, ministers went off with no further ado. Their orientation to a different world took place *in situ*. In many places that entailed intensive language study, and as they immersed themselves in a foreign tongue they familiarized themselves with the foreign culture. Their missionary probation – distinct from, though often concurrent with, ministerial probation – was treated seriously by their senior colleagues. In India, from 1894 onwards, articles regularly appeared in *The Harvest Field* debating how best to prepare new arrivals, and whether it were best done in Europe or India. Henry Haigh started the debate with a lengthy article in which he argued:

> To decline to give men just beginning their work the advantages of a sufficient period of training on the ground of expense or on the plea that it is well to let a zealous young man get into the thick of the battle at once is false economy and bad generalship ... Considering the numbers of missionaries now being sent out, the time is coming when the great Societies should unite in forming training colleges... There is one place at least, Bangalore, where the three great

---

[8]   F.H. Cumbers, *Richmond College 1843-1943* (London, Epworth Press, 1944), pp. 18–19.

[9]   Letter to C.H. Monahan, 4 February 1910, quoted in Lewis, p. 134.

languages of South India are all in constant use. Why then should not certain Societies combine to establish in Bangalore such a college…?[10]

In 1910 the 'United Theological College of South India and Ceylon' (UTC) was established in Bangalore by the LMS, the WMMS, the United Free Church of Scotland and others as 'a Christian College where students may obtain a sound theological education'. It did not do all that Haigh advocated, but it was common for Methodist probationers to spend an initial period there. Pre-departure training for ministers, however, was still in the future.

PM policy recognized that some medical knowledge would be invaluable and from 1897 began to send candidates to Livingstone College in London, which specialised in training missionaries in tropical medicine.[11] The 1908 PM report claimed that all Hartley College students were taking a medical course. A later PM candidate, Frank Davey, who already had an MSc in organic chemistry when he was called to the ministry, was encouraged to study medicine rather than theology. He spent the six years of his course living at Hartley College, on the strength of which he was ordained when he qualified – and had a distinguished ministry, both medical and pastoral.[12] When the UM minister William Hudspeth, who went to south-west China in 1909, was asked what special training he had received after his theological course, he replied:

> Except for two-and-a-half months of training in a London hospital in rudimentary medicine and dentistry there was no missionary training, but [that was] very useful because … I pulled out hundreds of teeth.[13]

Whereupon the interviewer, Elliott Kendall, who went to the same area thirty years later, remarked that he had the same training and was likewise an amateur dentist.

The practice for deaconesses resembled that for ministers, but for other women the picture was different. From the start of the century the Auxiliaries recognized the value of pre-departure preparation, however well qualified a teacher, nurse or doctor might be. Kingsmead College in Selly Oak, Birmingham, became the normal location for such training. In 1903 Woodbrooke, the first of several colleges in Selly Oak, situated not far from the Cadbury chocolate factory and the Bournville model village, was opened by George Cadbury, a Quaker, in what had been his family home. He then offered the Friends' Foreign Missionary Association the use of a neighbouring property which was renamed Kingsmead. At first it was primarily for Quaker women, but in 1915 UM and in 1916 WM

---

[10]   *The Harvest Field,* March 1894, pp. 329–30.

[11]   R. Johnson, 'Colonial Mission and Imperial Tropical Medicine: Livingstone College, London, 1893–1914', *Social History of Medicine* 23/3 (2010): pp.549–566; Young, p. 15.

[12]   Senior, *Davey,* p. 2.

[13]   MCH: Interview recorded November 1969.

candidates came to the college, and from 1918 only the promise of an annual grant from the Wesleyan WA saved it from closure. The Methodist involvement and influence increased steadily. In 1921 the United Methodists presented the college with a house and the Wesleyans paid for its adaptation and extension.

Other colleges were opened in the vicinity, including two more for preparing women missionaries (Carey Hall and the College of the Ascension), and in 1918 a Selly Oak Council was formed to be responsible for a central staff of lecturers and all matters affecting the life of the whole community of colleges. Sydney Cave, the first lecturer to be appointed, was, significantly, a specialist in comparative religion. More buildings to serve the whole Selly Oak Federation (as it was designated in 1922) were built: all owed much to Cadbury munificence, as did the establishment in 1936 of 'a Department of Missions with a professor, research fellowships and resources that would provide an opportunity for research into missionary problems and practice'.

> It was the genius of Edward Cadbury that he saw the need for an ecumenical approach to mission that would stir the missionary societies out of their narrowness and make them face the missionary situation as it really was … This department was meant to serve the missionary societies and to encourage them, but also to give them something which they would not or could not provide for themselves, namely to bring together missionary theology and missionary practice in an ecumenical setting where there were educational resources of books and news-sheets and experienced missionaries and competent theologians, and all this in a Christian community that provided fellowship and discussion and worship.[14]

Godfrey Philips from the LMS was the first professor; he was succeeded in 1944 by the erstwhile Primitive Methodist, C.P. Groves, who had been on the Kingsmead staff from 1926. Groves' *magnum opus,* the four-volume *Planting of Christianity in Africa,* was published 'under the auspices of the Department of Mission' between 1946 and 1958. In 1937 John Foster from China was appointed to the Colleges' chair in Church History.

Kingsmead was bought by the MMS in 1945, and until 1970 successive wardens – Stanley Beaty, Alec Spooner, Basil Clutterbuck and Tom Beetham – were ex-missionary ministers in their last appointment before retirement. The resources of the Federation were considerable, but Methodist women students had many of their classes in Kingsmead itself. Some said Kingsmead, in order to prepare single women for the restrictions of life to which they were going, was 'run like an Indian girls' boarding school'. Students were already professionally qualified, and Betty Hares was restless:

> The year at Selly Oak was a real endurance test. I missed the activity of hospital life; and I found irksome what I felt to be petty discipline. It was not that I was

---

[14]   D. Mole, *A History of the Selly Oak Colleges*, unpublished monograph.

unused to discipline; there had been plenty of it in hospital; but here we were –
all of us having had considerable responsibility – being treated as schoolgirls.
And I resented the constant probing into my inner life.[15]

Besides their work as teachers, nurses or administrators they were going to
be leaders of worship and of bible study groups, class leaders and, in one way or
another, evangelists. So they had courses in Old and New Testament studies, church
history and Christian doctrine. A limited amount of anthropology was covered but
missiology was not on the syllabus until the 1970s. There was some introduction
to life in the country for which the student was designated, but designation often
came late in the day. Hares wrote:

> The Missionary Society had a curious way of training and appointing people in
> those days, and it seemed to happen too often not to be deliberate. In my first
> interview with the Warden at Kingsmead, he asked me which area of the world I
> was interested in. I replied, 'India,' and was allotted Indian religions among the
> other subjects we studied … It was all very theoretical, with hardly any practical
> work of any kind. Then came the time for appointments to be made and, to my
> horror, I was listed to go to China as a nurse/evangelist. The nurse/evangelist
> part was fine – but China! I was inconsolable! It was a conversation with the
> Islamics Professor that changed things. When I told him what had happened, he
> put his arm round my shoulders and said, 'Never mind, my dear, nothing you
> learn is ever wasted.'[16]

It was not all study and devotions, and not all irksome. There were outings, end-
of-term entertainments, and the college magazine carried amusing pieces as well
as thoughtful contributions. But only when Kingsmead became a mixed college in
1966, under the visionary leadership of Tom Beetham, was the régime transformed.

From the mid-1920s the Selly Oak Colleges had tried unsuccessfully to interest
the missionary societies in a course for candidates coming out of theological
colleges. The MMS was less half-hearted about the idea than other societies, but
war intervened and the project was shelved. Then in 1948 St Andrew's College
was founded to accommodate Baptist, Congregationalist, Methodist and English
Presbyterian men and couples preparing for overseas work. This brought a new
dimension to the pre-departure training of ministers. Some ministers spent the final
year of their college course, or an extra term, at St Andrew's. In the 1950s language
study at SOAS was provided for some; driving lessons became important too. Yet
there were always those whose preparation consisted of 'one day at Selly Oak',
'four days at Farnham Castle', 'a two-day course in double-entry book-keeping

---

[15]   Hares, p. 36.
[16]   Ibid., pp. 36–7.

and administration at 25 Marylebone Road' and for some 'I had no training or preparation for missionary service'.[17]

In 1966 the MMS left St Andrew's and concentrated training at Kingsmead, which was modernized and extended. In both colleges the experience was mixed. For an accountant, the bible and doctrine courses were an opportunity to supplement his Christian knowledge and he regretted that it only lasted a term because he was urgently needed in Nigeria. Wives also valued that aspect; not so a minister with a degree in theology who was expected to do the basic New Testament Introduction course. For him, it was 'a waste of time' and for another 'totally inadequate'. The best thing about a term or two at St Andrew's or Kingsmead was, for many, the time to read, reflect and meet students from other traditions. On the other hand, one described his two terms as 'an excellent foundation in theology of mission'; and others were grateful for the instruction in car maintenance and in hair-cutting.[18]

Bigger changes now shaped the pattern of missionary preparation: the end of the colonial era and the advent of autonomous Churches raised serious questions about the role of expatriates. An emphasis on adaptability and sensitivity was at the heart of the Selly Oak programme. Living together in a very varied college community was a key element. From the 1970s Kingsmead was no longer solely a missionary training college but a home for people of all faiths and none. Alongside Methodists lived men and women from continental mission societies preparing to work in Anglophone countries, church leaders or potential leaders on sabbatical from overseas churches, people on the child care or development studies courses run by other departments of the Selly Oak Federation, and from the mid-1970s a regular throughput of Namibian exiles from the South West Africa People's Organization (SWAPO). There might be people of up to twenty different nationalities in residence at the same time, and there were well over eighty nationalities in the space of twenty years, including Muslims, Hindus, Buddhists, people of no faith and Christians of very diverse traditions. There were inevitable tensions, not least between the Methodists: on occasions when it was Kingsmead's turn to lead the weekly joint worship for all the colleges there might be disagreement between Africans who wanted a traditional form and British students arguing for something more contemporary or experimental. In one instance it ended up with British students only leading the service, and it took weeks to work through the resulting discontent.

Gordon Shaw, a 1962 student, recalled that

> the intention was partly to help us to know ourselves better, partly to share information with us about what it is like to live in a totally different cultural, religious and economic context, and partly to prepare us for that experience. Effort was put into reminding us that what we were engaging in was an on-going historical and therefore imperfect process which required theological

---

[17]   Responses to a questionnaire, provided to the author in January 2011.
[18]   Ibid.

investigation and understanding, and at Kingsmead there was a real desire to inculcate respect for the new things we would encounter, and for the colleagues we would work with.

I am not sure this was a feasible undertaking … As for those who had the unenviable task of trying to prepare us, their social and administrative formation had taken place in the context of the unchallenged assumptions that had moulded the whole colonial enterprise, and what the post-colonial situation would be like was, I think, beyond the imaginations of nearly all of us.[19]

David Winwood said that Kingsmead and Selly Oak in 1988 offered

an overview of the missionary movement through the years and the way in which the vision, style and understanding of mission has been changed by the end of colonialism, a more liberal understanding of Christian Theology, deeper insight into the breadth of mission embraced by NT teaching, a shift in the centres of power in the world church and diminishing resources available from the Western Churches…[20]

He learned about inculturalization and African culture, and was able to reflect on the role, responsibilities and accountability of a mission partner, and gain some insight into the adjustments they would need to make in order to relate creatively to the people of Zimbabwe and avoid imposing inappropriate expectations and ways of working in the new situation. In the same year two couples were returning to West Africa after a long interval in Britain. One 'benefited from a personal choice of study', focusing on Islam in Africa and African preaching; the other resented a standard course, 'as if we were new recruits'.[21]

Those who for whatever reason did not have a spell at Selly Oak (and some of those who spent time at Kingsmead) usually benefited from a short course at the Overseas Service College at Farnham Castle, a briefing centre for civil servants, business people and others going abroad. Its overall briefing and its country-specific induction were highly appreciated. But others had even less preparation, including future Presidents of the Conference – Colin Morris, Donald English, John Newton and Brian Beck – whose abilities were recognized early by the Mission House talent-spotters.

The generalization of air travel led to shorter tours of duty and some missionaries then began to argue that they would benefit more from a course during their first furlough, when they had experienced the context in which they were to work, than from pre-departure preparation. The idea was not adopted as policy, though there were one or two who did a term at William Temple College before taking up a ministry in industry and a minister who spent three months studying tropical

---

[19]   Ibid.
[20]   Ibid.
[21]   Ibid.

medicine at the Royal Homeopathic Hospital in order to do some 'bush medicine' on return. The request to defer their studies was understandable but based on a mistaken idea of what preparation was intended to do. It did not claim to turn out fully-trained missionaries. The accent continued to be on adaptability and flexibility, in an age of rapid social change and unpredictable shifts of emphasis as overseas church leaders tried to keep pace with it.

In 1992 the costs of Kingsmead were seen to consume a disproportionate percentage of the MCOD budget, and the decision was taken to pool resources with the USPG's College of the Ascension. To the chagrin of the staff, of many former students and of well-wishers, Kingsmead was sold, and in 1996 the partnership formally became the United College of the Ascension (UCA). The change was not an easy one, especially in respect of college worship: Methodists and high Anglicans did not have the same liturgical expectations. But George Mulrain from the Methodist Church of the Caribbean and the Americas (MCCA), the principal of Kingsmead who became vice-principal of UCA, did sterling work to make the integration a success. However Selly Oak was as much affected by rapid change as the global south, and over the next decade preparation for work abroad – with many fewer departures – was reshaped and moved elsewhere; UCA and most of the other college properties in Selly Oak were sold to Birmingham University. It was the end of an era.

Chapter 10
Methodist Union

The reunion of the several Churches which traced their origins to John Wesley had been discussed repeatedly over many years.[1] In Canada, Australia and New Zealand it was already accomplished. There were no theological reasons to remain separate, and sound practical reasons to unite. Others set the example. In Canada, Methodists, Congregationalists and Presbyterians formed the United Church in 1925; the Church of Christ in China, a Presbyterian-Congregationalist-Baptist-Brethren union, was formed in 1927; in Scotland the Kirk and the United Free Church reunited in 1929; and the Methodist Church of South Africa (MCSA), the WM Transvaal District and the PM Church came together on 1 January 1931. In Britain, the necessary compromises were agreed by 1930 and the union of Wesleyans, Primitive Methodists and the United Methodist Church became effective in 1932. Each had its missions overseas, and they became overseas Districts of the newly constituted British Conference, while the headquarters administration and home support combined as the Methodist Missionary Society, to which all Methodist members belonged. The alignment of Church membership and MMS membership was clarified 'for the purpose of resolving any doubts' by a Conference resolution in 1942, applying to the MMS what George Findlay had written at the start of the WMMS History:

> The WMMS is no 'Society' distinct from the 'Society of People called Methodists' but to all intents and purposes that same Society in its missionary character; it is simply Methodism organized for missionary service.[2]

Facts and Figures

The Wesleyans had many more members than the other uniting bodies, overseas as in Britain, with settled church structures and missionaries serving in China, India, Ceylon and Burma, in the West Indies, in France, Italy, Spain and Portugal, in seven West African colonies and in Rhodesia (both Zimbabwean and Zambian territory). Nearly 60,000 members in the Transvaal District, by far the biggest of the overseas Districts, were now attached to the MCSA; the growth of Wesleyan

---

[1] R.N. Wycherley, *The Pageantry of Methodist Union* (London, Epworth Press, 1936); R.E. Davies, *Methodism* (London, Epworth Press, rev. 1976), pp. 159–60; A. Turberfield, *John Scott Lidgett* (London, Epworth Press, 2003), pp. 307–321.

[2] Findlay & Holdsworth, vol 1, p. 60.

Methodism in South Africa had been such that it counted more members and 'probationers' (adult catechumens, baptized but not yet admitted to membership) than in all the overseas Districts of the British Conference together. Statistics can only be approximate, but the Minutes of the 1932 WM Conference reported 517,551 Wesleyans in Britain, 30,057 in Ireland, 1,411 in France, 303,148 in South Africa and in all the other Districts together 289,221.

The WMMS was supporting 358 men (most of them ordained) or couples and 215 women missionaries.[3] There were sixty-four PM missionaries, including nineteen single women, and 23,000 members or probationers in eastern Nigeria, Fernando Po and Northern Rhodesia. There were forty-eight UM missionaries, sixteen of them women, and 35,000 members or probationers in the four China Districts, Kenya and Sierra Leone. The churches in the Freetown area who had affiliated with the UMFC in 1859 opted out in 1934, unwilling to consummate union with the more numerous Wesleyans, and formed the West African Methodist Church.

Uniting the three took more effort in Britain than abroad. When Edgar Thompson asked for a copy of the constitution of the United Methodist Missionary Society he received the terse reply that there was no such constitution because there was no such society. The only references to a UMMS are found in the Wesleyan literature of the time, and in the early numbers of the new monthly, *The Kingdom Overseas*. Already in 1930 the UM minister William Grist, who had served in China with the Bible Christians, was appointed, with the consent of the UM and PM Conferences, as the WM China Secretary; and George Ayre, Secretary of the PM Foreign Missionary Committee, joined the team of Secretaries in 1932. To mark the occasion, the Cargate Press published a survey of the history and state of the Methodist missions by Fred Pratt Green,[4] who much later became the only Methodist hymn-writer to bear comparison with Charles Wesley. The first issues of *The Kingdom Overseas* were largely devoted to introducing the work and personnel of the uniting Societies to one another. Consolidating the three sets of accounts was a complicated and protracted business; although the WMMS accounts were closed at the end of 1932, it was another year before the UM and PM accounts were wound up. The PM headquarters at Holborn Hall became one of the offices of the MMS and there was some relocation of staff. Secretaries and treasurers for overseas missions continued to serve in their local churches, while Districts and circuits were not short of enthusiasts to fill new appointments.

Overseas, the only country where all three uniting Churches were at work was China; only in Nigeria, Sierra Leone and Zambia (then Northern Rhodesia) were there two.

---

[3]   The figure excludes the thirty-one ministers and any others who had put down roots in South Africa and transferred their allegiance to the MCSA.

[4]   F.P. Green, *Methodism and the Mountain Summit* (London, Cargate Press, 1932).

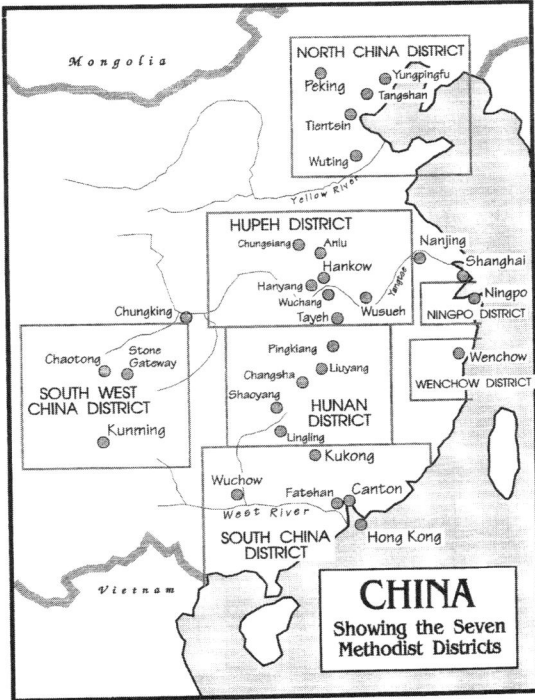

Map 10.1   China

China

The seven China Districts did not overlap and the day-to-day life of the churches was scarcely affected by the union. But their new relationship was marked by the first All-China Methodist Conference, held in Ningbo in October 1933. It reported that 'the Methodist Church (British affiliation)' had 100 missionaries, 324 churches, 224 preaching place, 21,000 full members, 11,000 on trial, and a community of about 50,000 persons under its supervision. For some reason that summary made no mention of the twenty-nine Chinese ministers and innumerable lay workers who were at the heart of the operation and would soon begin to exercise leadership. The following year the Hubei District led the way when a Chinese Chairman, Shen Wen Ch'ing, was appointed to succeed Harold Rattenbury who was returning to England after thirty-two years' service in China. Shen was the first national Chairman of an overseas District anywhere (other than the brief tenure of Charles Knight in Sierra Leone, 1874–1877), yet in comparison with some other Churches in China, Methodism was slow off the mark. The advent of Chinese leaders was in part due to a considerable decline in the number of Protestant missionaries from 1926, as a result of the unrest throughout the country, the activities of lawless warlords, and an anti-Christian movement in which

Students and schoolboys led mass attacks on Christian churches, educational institutions, and even medical missions. By organising labour unions and strikes, they withdrew Chinese nurses and servants from hospitals, and created a very serious boycott of 'foreigners' and everyone connected with them. Missionaries were compelled to retire to places of safety, mission property was seized, and great anti-Christian gatherings and processions took place.[5]

Many North American missionaries, and a number from Britain, departed. Most Methodists returned to their work as soon as it was safe to do so, but there was a growing sense of insecurity; they had offered for a lifetime of service in China but there was now a strong possibility that that service would be cut short. It became imperative to transfer authority to Chinese leadership. The process was hastened by a government decree that heads of all educational institutions must be Chinese, and all boards of control must have a Chinese majority. The 1934 report declared:

> Today, our missionaries are in China, not as masters and rulers, but as brethren and as servants of the Chinese Church. Our colleges have Chinese Principals, our hospitals Chinese Superintendents ... [though the latter was not everywhere the case][6]

Chinese Christians bore the brunt of banditry and civil war – in 1927 one devoted and capable worker in Hunan was hauled out of church and beheaded in the street – yet their passion for evangelism was not diminished by adversity. When Japan occupied north-east China in 1931, the North China District, begun by the MNC, was directly affected. In 1933 the Japanese and their puppet Manchukuo allies advanced again and Tangshan, where there was a Boys' College with over 300 students, was cut off. Fred Heslop wrote of how the town filled with retreating soldiers and refugees. Some fifty terrified women and children refugees, fleeing with nothing after being 'looted by their own soldiers', sheltered in the mission compound. Manchukuo officials arrived and annexed the town. Heslop wrote, 'It looks like having to begin again right from the beginning when peace does come – when!'[7] It never did. The Japanese offensive led to a full-scale invasion in 1937. For the Chinese and for the missionaries, yet greater trials lay ahead.

Nigeria

The PM and WM areas were far apart, but there were Methodists who migrated between them for one reason or another, and some Yoruba people who had moved to the east early in the century requested the services of WM ministers. The first

---

[5]   MMS Annual Report on 1934 (published June 1935), p. 46.

[6]   Ibid., p. 47.

[7]   20 May 1933, published in *The Kingdom Overseas,* September 1933: pp. 209–11.

was sent in 1914, and others, both African and European, followed. Two circuits were formed, but they were so far from Lagos, and communications were so poor, that it was decided to transfer them to PM supervision in 1929 and the ministers were lent to the PM Mission. After union the PM work was formally constituted as the Eastern Nigeria District – a term not previously used for PM missions – while the old Lagos District, shorn of its francophone work from 1925, became the Western Nigeria District. It was not just the Districts that served different language groups; moving from circuit to circuit often entailed using a new language. The church in Opobo, on the Niger delta, recorded around this time Ghanaian and Sierra Leonean Society Stewards, Poor Stewards from Calabar and Gold Coast, Yoruba, Igbo and Fanti sidesmen, and Yoruba, Igbo, Efik, Ghanaian and Sierra Leonean class leaders.

Oliver Griffin, who arrived in Nigeria in 1897 and remained until 1928, was the WM Chairman for twenty-one of those thirty-one years. From start to finish he was devoted to the Yoruba Interior Mission, principally among the Ijesha branch of the Yoruba people. He lived at Oyo, thirty-four miles from the city of Ibadan, which in his early years was a seven-day journey from the nearest doctor, in Lagos. The railway to Ibadan eventually reduced the journey time to one day. Griffin declined to be carried on a hammock when he travelled the rough forest paths, preferring to go by bicycle although it had to be pushed as much as ridden. Seventy miles from Oyo lay the town of Ilesha where the Owa, or king, was attracted to Christianity; he refused to live in the royal palace because of its associations with pagan worship. Griffin and his Nigerian colleague Atundaolu extended Methodist work to the town, and soon secured a site there for a hospital. In twenty-one years as Chairman, when his duties often required him to be in Lagos, Griffin still managed to spend half of each year in Oyo, opening numerous outposts and building up the local leadership.

Fred Dodds likewise spent thirty years in the country, latterly as Chairman of the Eastern District before returning to the Mission House as Africa Secretary in 1939. He too made long journeys on forest paths, by bicycle or on foot, to make contact with Igbo villages which proved very receptive to the gospel message. The PM field of activity spread steadily northwards until it covered an area half the size of England. One of Dodds's long-serving colleagues was Ernest Pritchard, working mainly among the Efik people between 1912 and 1932, when he was invalided home. His Efik Grammar, completed in retirement, was published by Atlantis in 1963. He laid the foundations of Ituk Mbang hospital, which opened in 1931. But perhaps the most visionary and far-reaching achievement of the PM mission, also in 1931 on the eve of union, was the establishment of the Leprosy Settlement at Uzuakoli in the heart of Igboland.[8]

Methodist union affected the missionary staff who now belonged, and would one day return, to a Church much altered from the one they had left. African Christians had a broader concern. In 1923 began a series of conferences of 'Senior

---

[8] p. 96.

African Agents', who were ashamed of, and impatient with, the divisions and disunity exported from Europe. In 1931 they were already arguing for a central church in each town, a common name, a common catechism and an interchangeable ministry. They declared:

> In view of the great Commission we have received from our Lord, of His express desire that His people should be one, and of the desirability of presenting a united front to the world in the evangelization of our people, we, the African delegates representing the Churches of the Eastern Regional Committee of the Christian Council of Nigeria, deprecate the existence of divisions among us as a source of weakness and strongly urge that steps be taken to the consolidation of Union among Churches.[9]

In this spirit the CMS ceded to the Methodist mission its Uzuakoli Institute (a short distance from the new Leprosy centre) in 1931 and in 1932 five churches further north in Idoma territory.

In the west, one of Griffin's colleagues was Bill Mellor, who from 1921 to 1953 worked among the Ijebu, a Yoruba group centred on the town of Sagamu, midway between Lagos and Ibadan. Perhaps the most memorable event in all those years was when the new *Akarigbo* of Remo announced that his coronation would be a Christian ceremony. He wrote to the young missionary:

> I have totally refused to be crowned by the heathen chiefs, and have determined to be crowned by the ministers of the Ijebu circuit. I have received the consent of my chiefs about the matter, and you are respectfully invited to preside in laying the crown on my head.[10]

It would be a complete break with tradition and aroused fierce opposition among those who wanted him to comply with the old customs, but the *Akarigbo* could not be dissuaded. The church prospered in Sagamu, with thriving Boys' Brigade and Girl Guide companies, a dispensary and a Girls' Boarding School. Mellor was awarded the Royal African Society medal 'for dedicated service to Africa' in 1966 and the citation read:

> Mr Mellor has been described (by a Missionary not of the Methodist denomination) as probably the outstanding missionary in West Africa since the end of the first World War.[11]

---

[9]   M. Marioghae and J. Ferguson, *Nigeria under the Cross* (London, Highway Press, 1965), p. 47.

[10]   F.D. Walker, *A Hundred Years in Nigeria* (London, Cargate Press, 1942), p. 130.

[11]   J.A. Olusola, *Baba Mellor, Frontline Missionary in Nigeria* (Ibadan, Daystar Press, 1973), p. v.

Map 10.2   Sierra Leone

Sierra Leone

In the Freetown area and in Mende country both Wesleyans and United Methodists were active, and a special Synod was held in February 1933 to celebrate the union. In both areas African ministers outnumbered missionaries. Of the thirteen missionaries in the country at the time, three had gone out as UMs; one of them, Albert Dymond, became the District Chairman and remained until 1946. While a majority of the Krio UM ministers and members went to the West African Methodist Church in 1934, others preferred to remain in the newly-integrated District. Up-country, the railway (a narrow gauge track built between 1897 and 1907) enabled advance eastwards. A towering figure in Mendeland was J.R.S. Law who arrived in 1917 to assist W.T. Balmer at the Wesleyan Boys' High School in Freetown. In addition to his school work Balmer, with his linguistic proficiency, was conducting regular Mende services; on Law's first Sunday in the country, he was taken to one. Before long he was transferred to Jojoima where he remained until his retirement in 1959, the year he finished translating the Bible into Mende.[12]

A feature of Mende culture was the importance of two secret societies, secret not in the sense that their existence was kept hidden – in fact they were known to everyone – but in that what went on in them was known only to the initiate.[13] Poro for the men and Sande for the women, as well as others less well known, had as one function – probably their primary function – preparing 'young men and women for manhood and womanhood within the framework of Mende law,

---

[12]   After his wife died in 1968, Law returned to Jojoima until his own death in 1971.

[13]   The use of the past tense does not imply that the societies later became defunct.

custom and tradition'.[14] They were the foundation of Mende society; no man could expect to marry in Mendeland unless he was initiated into Poro. Their hold on members was absolute. When a society meeting was called, other commitments had to be ignored – to miss church was regrettable, to miss Sande or Poro was unthinkable. The conflict of loyalties raised hard questions for Mende Christians, and in different ways for the European missionaries and the Krio ministers who worked among them. They adopted three general principles. They needed to expound the gospel in such a way that their hearers could distinguish good from evil, rites and activities compatible with Christian discipleship from those that were incompatible. Secondly, they must avoid uninformed criticism. Thirdly, they had to trust the judgement of Mende Christians and the work of the Holy Spirit in their hearts and minds. Missionaries did not find this an easy course, and there were some whose outspoken condemnation was unhelpful. Krio ministers hesitated before accepting an appointment in the interior, not just because of family ties in Freetown or because of the language, but also because their mindset could not cope with Mende attitudes and practices. The differences between the colony and the protectorate loomed much larger than those between WM and UM.

Zambia

The components of the Northern Rhodesia District were the PM mission stations – they were never styled circuits – and the WM Rhodesia District's work north of the Zambezi, a single circuit covering an area three times the size of Wales and centred on Chipembi. Consolidating the union was no easy task, since the respective fields of work were widely separated, but Douglas Gray, who had been based at Chipembi since 1913, lost no time in moving to the former PM station at Nambala. The local congregations were barely affected by the change; the PM missionaries, on the other hand, were faced with a new situation and new expectations. They had been operating quite independently, each corresponding directly with Holborn Hall. They submitted a quarterly return on a single sheet of foolscap with income and expenditure on one side and a report of their work on the other. At their infrequent get-togethers for mutual encouragement, they would appoint one of their number as chairman of the meeting and he would write to headquarters about such matters as stipends and allowances, but he had no continuing duties. Now, however, they were being required to submit annual returns on five separate forms which demanded a great deal of detail. Even more irksome was the fact that they were now under the authority of a General Superintendent who was more than a chairman though Chairman was in his title, a man who had the official responsibility of ensuring that Conference and MMS directives were observed. It was a masterstroke to appoint Graham Soulsby as the first General Superintendent. It was his first overseas posting but he had thirty-

---

[14]   E. Wright, *Behind the Lion Mountains* (London, Cargate Press, 1962), p. 28.

one years' experience in the PM ministry. Under his leadership, disenchantment evaporated and a sense of unity and colleagueship took root. He described his work at Kabwe (known then as Broken Hill), where Scots members were plentiful, as an ex-PM minister in an ex-WM church serving an ex-Presbyterian congregation.

The District now comprised nine circuits. One was centred on Lusaka, which became the capital of the colony in 1931, but the main Methodist centres were at Kafue and Chipembi. At Kafue the PMs had bought a large tract of land in 1916 with a gift from Charles and Martha Clixby of Gainsborough. Of the 'Native Training Institute' set up there in 1918 to prepare teachers and evangelists, Edwin Smith said that it 'made more educational impact on Northern Rhodesia than twenty little mission stations each running half a dozen outschools'.[15] A dispensary, bookshop and printing press followed. A delegation from Britain in 1929 reported that Kafue was now running vocational classes in typing, carpentry and printing as well as academic courses, while every student was engaged in bricklaying for new buildings. It reported too that the missionaries' hesitation over the readiness of Africans for ministerial training had been overcome, and four candidates were accepted at that year's Synod.

The expansion of the Chipembi complex also dated from 1918, when Gray returned from war service. Here the school included a girls' department, promoted by his able wife, Louie. By the time she died, still young, in 1930 it had developed to the point where a full-time Domestic Science teacher was justified, and before long Chipembi Girls' School was known throughout the colony. In 1946 it became the first secondary school for girls in Northern Rhodesia. Alongside it there grew up a training institution for evangelists and teachers, and later a Farm School for boys, which supported itself from its produce, receiving no school fees, no government grant and no grant from the Society.

The Paris Missionary Society (PMS) had worked in western Zambia since 1885 but in 1932, short-staffed, raised the possibility of handing over some of its work to the MMS. The MMS then suggested taking on the whole of the PMS's Zambezi mission field, and handing to PMS its work in the French colonies of Dahomey and the Ivory Coast. The scheme was carefully considered, but abandoned in 1934 because the Ivory Coast missionaries, who would need to stay on for some years to effect the transition, were unwilling to submit to PMS conditions.

Elsewhere

In the Districts not directly affected by Methodist Union, life carried an as normal – though normal was anything but humdrum. Despite having no one to unite with locally, in *Kenya* the United Methodists held services of thanksgiving in Mombasa and Nairobi – the one in the Anglican cathedral, the other in the Church of Scotland's commodious church. It was good to have something to celebrate at a

---

[15]   Young, p. 52

time of heated debate, when Methodist membership in Meru had suddenly fallen from seventy to six. The controversy was over female initiation. Missionaries were in no doubt as to the permanent physical injury and suffering that genital mutilation could cause, and in 1930 they minuted a resolution to the effect that:

> ... in common with the other Allied Missions, we declare our attitude towards this degrading and barbarous custom to be one of uncompromising opposition, that the promise to take no part in it be made part of catechumenal and baptism vows at Meru, and that we require all our Church members to fall in with this law, breaches of which will be disciplined.[16]

Reg Worthington, the General Superintendent, was not prepared to see his life's work undermined and 'uncompromising opposition' became blind eye. Several factors, apart from the loss of members, tempered the opposition. It was not clear why female circumcision should be condemned but not boys' – and the traditional rites of initiation to manhood were manifestly sacrosanct. And to interfere with an age-old tradition on which the Bible speaks no authoritative word was questionable. Arthur Hopkins, Worthington's successor in the Chair, claimed in 1936 that:

> It is a dangerous misunderstanding of the significance of the custom that Europeans should allow their natural repugnance to the ugly features of this rite to mislead them into the view that a campaign for its abolition is to be regarded as rescuing African girls from an indignity to which they reluctantly submit. Nothing is further from the truth. It is the simple fact that girls in Meru look to this rite as a dignity which gives them a standing in the tribe, which otherwise they would not possess.[17]

A third issue concerned the wisdom of Europeans laying down the conditions under which African believers might be admitted to membership and ministry in the church. The colonial government, resisting pressure to enact legislation which could never be enforced and would foment and unite African hostility, advised missionaries to use education rather than regulation. Methodists took the advice. Hopkins recognized the significance of the controversy. In words which would find an echo more than two decades later in the first novels of Achebe of Nigeria and Ngugi the Kenyan, he wrote:

> ... the bands of the old order are loosening everywhere; the anxiety of a lost spiritual heritage has entered the soul of Africa. The most dangerous phase of

---

16   Z.J. Nthamburi, *A History of the Methodist Church in Kenya* (Nairobi, Uzima Press, 1982), p. 72.
17   Ibid., p. 73.

a people's spiritual history, when the old has lost its grip and the new is not in sight, is everywhere today the challenge of Africa to Christendom.[18]

Haiti caused much heart-searching to the WMMS in the years prior to Methodist union. The country was occupied by American marines in 1915, the latest in a line of acquisitions in the region to secure the economic interests of the United States. After a long period of civil unrest, the occupation was at first welcomed with relief by the missionaries and in London; the ageing Thomas Picot, Chairman of the District, wrote:

> It is the Lord's doing, and it is marvellous in my eyes ... Never again will our work cease, our schools close, our properties be burned down, our new converts be rushed away ... No more horrible massacres and atrocities in the capital, no more burning in the villages and pillaging of plantations, and annihilating of populations, as has obtained since 1804.[19]

But there was widespread opposition among Haitians, especially the mulatto élite, and in the north guerrilla resistance was reported for several years. Methodists were rapidly disenchanted with the exploitation and racism practised by the new overlords. Auguste Albert, a minister who had taken early retirement, was an outspoken critic, and became the editor of *L'Opinion Nationale*, a paper founded in 1921 in the defence of the people's rights and interests. By that time the Secretaries in London had changed their view of the occupation. The Americans eventually withdrew in 1934.

The church in the capital, Port-au-Prince, the largest and best educated congregation in the tiny District, seceded in 1916, following a clash between its minister, Parkinson Turnbull, and his college contemporary, Henry Arnett. Both were recalled to London after some unsavoury and unsubstantiated allegations and an unhappy Synod which exonerated Arnett and censured Turnbull.[20] It was Picot's last Synod after thirty-seven years as Chairman; he had been ill and was quite unable to handle the situation. Turnbull, who was married to a Haitian, refused to leave and with his supporters constituted the Free Methodist Church. Possession of the property was disputed; the loss of the Society's grant and Turnbull's stipend left the independents struggling financially; the breach was healed in 1928. Turnbull was reinstated by the Conference and at his death in 1954 had spent fifty-four years in Haiti.

All these trials had prompted the Society to consider abandoning its work in Haiti. Edgar Thompson paid a Secretarial visit in 1929. He found that there was no body to which the work could be handed on, and observed signs of

---

[18]   *Women's Work* Magazine, July 1936, p. 355.

[19]   SOAS, WMMS/West Indies/Correspondence/Haiti/FBN43, Picot to Andrews, 26 November 1915.

[20]   Griffiths, p. 214.

increasing interest which before long was marked by the appearance of fledgling congregations meeting under bamboo and banana leaf shelters. Although the two circuits in the Dominican Republic were handed over to the Board for Christian Work in Santo Domingo (an alliance of Methodist Episcopal, Presbyterian and United Brethren missions from USA), Thompson's report ensured that Methodism in Haiti took on a new lease of life, administered for the next three decades – until the advent of the autonomous MCCA – as a section of the Jamaica District.

Another section of the District was *Panama* where a young missionary, Ephraim Alphonse, was working. Not a missionary from Britain, but a self-taught Panamanian who was acquiring a reputation as a scholar, poet, writer, teacher, preacher and linguist *extraordinaire*. He had volunteered in 1917, at the age of twenty, to go and live among the 10,000 Guaymi Amerindians of the Valiente peninsula as an evangelist. He knew nothing of them except that they lived scattered through the forest, practically untouched by civilization; and he knew not a word of their tongue. He settled at a hamlet called Cusapin and tried to teach such children as could be persuaded to come, using English and Spanish; but he met at first with indifference and hostility. Then, at a watchnight service he held at the end of 1918, forty-five people decided to be Christians. They built a chapel, and gradually Cusapin grew into a village around it. Alphonse travelled by foot, on horseback or along the creeks and lagoons in a motor launch funded by Jamaica. He reckoned it took him thirteen years to become proficient in Guaymi. But well before that, he had heard an inward voice saying 'Write a hymn' and in due course he produced a Guaymi hymn-book, as well as translating some books of the New Testament. He was at first at a loss to translate the name of God, which was shrouded in mystery. He was taken to the secret shrine of an old medicine woman deep in the forest, who went into a trance and pronounced the sacred name: 'These men are talking about *Ngobo*, the God of heaven and earth. Listen to them!'[21] Alphonse was sent to Kingston for ministerial training and returned to the peninsula in 1926. In 1937, twenty years after he began his life's work, the Guaymi were still practically unknown and despised outside Valiente and it was a coup when he was presented to the President of Panama and persuaded him to send four teachers to the peninsula. Later on, he taught the Guaymi language at the University of Panama, produced a trilingual dictionary (Guaymi, Spanish, English), and received many honours, unsought but richly deserved.

In *India,* the long ministry of the redoubtable Charles Posnett had another six years to run. He, his sister Emilie and her friend Sarah Harris all arrived in 1896 and would all retire in 1939. They had arrived at a time of famine in Hyderabad, and had endured several more great droughts and associated epidemics. In June 1919 a student sitting an examination in the compound in Medak fell ill with cholera, died within two hours and was buried half-an-hour later. As a precaution

---

21   E.A. Nida, *God's Word in Man's Language* (New York, Harper, 1952), p. 38.

it was imperative for the rest of the students to be sent home to their famine-stricken villages. But Posnett was able to turn adversity to some advantage. Men who could no longer till the cracked earth were offered food-for-work. They dug wells, made bricks, put up new buildings on the compound including a bungalow for women missionaries and built two 'Homes of Blessing' for medical work in nearby villages. Supervising the work-teams, distributing food, getting hold of medical supplies took its toll. In May 1921 Posnett wrote in his diary:

> I am utterly sick of this famine work and to do it under the present conditions with a temperature 115° in the shade is a harder job than I have ever tackled before. I am exhausted every evening and am longing for the time to come when the rain will fall to relieve this terrible distress.

And then, on 4 July: 'Thank God, rain at last.'[22]

He did not trouble to seek permission or request a grant for his building projects; he reported to the Synod 'costs met by private funds' and managed to attract the help of enough well-wishers to balance the books. Medak became renowned throughout the Nizam's dominions. Towering over the compound was the gothic church seating nearly five thousand, built of white granite.[23] Begun in 1914, it was opened on Christmas Day 1924. The imposing tower with its four pinnacles would have been taller still had not the Nizam, when granting planning permission, insisted that it should not exceed the height of the fabulous sixteenth century Charminar mosque ninety miles away in Hyderabad. Besides the church, Posnett oversaw the erection of an orphanage, a hospital, a girls' school and a theological college.

Growing the church naturally took precedence over building churches. Posnett was able to report in 1933 that when he first went to Hyderabad there were 'just a few scattered Christian families' but there were now over 88,000 Christians. Many of these were from tribal or outcaste groups. In 1914 he had started the 'South India Methodist Missionary Society' and its evangelistic work had borne fruit. He remembered how, when he had first crossed the Godavari river in 1917, he was boycotted by all; yet in 1919 he found 1,000 people waiting at the river bank to welcome him. In Hyderabad conversions were not confined to outcaste communities. In 1925 he organized a summer school for caste Hindu enquirers. Soon their numbers began to grow, and by 1933 thousands of them were being prepared for baptism, many from villages where in the outcaste quarter there was already a baptized, worshipping congregation.

Each of the thirty-three overseas Districts had its own issues, but some experiences and challenges were common to each. A report to the 1929 *Rhodesia* Synod included elements that would have been familiar to many.

---

22   F.C. Sackett, *Posnett of Medak* (London, Cargate Press, 1951), p. 136.
23   In 1947 it became the CSI's Medak Cathedral.

Sickness, economic problems, removals, shortage of staff have conspired together ... In Matabeleland two years of drought have brought the native people into serious straits; cattle have died in large numbers, people have been short of food, whilst others have had to remove or send their children with cattle to distant grazing grounds. This has meant a dislocation of many established schools, with resulting financial difficulties. In Bulawayo during the year there was an outbreak of smallpox ... In Selukwe difficulties were experienced owing to the resignation of one worker who tried to stir up trouble. At Sinoia the economic conditions were severely felt by the farmers engaged in tobacco growing; and to this was added the closing of the Copper Queen Mine and the slump of the mica fields.[24]

The next year's report was quite different in tone but again typical of experiences elsewhere:

We have reached the stage at which expansion could not be stayed even if we wished it. We could give example after example of a school and church being opened in some new village. Within a short time another village, a few miles away, has been awakened, either by the people having seen the work or by the preaching of the evangelist, and then the call comes for a teacher for that village also. This call being answered, the same process is repeated in some other adjoining village, until the whole Reserve is reached ... the European ministers direct the lines of advance, but the African ministers, evangelists, local preachers and members prepare the way of the Lord.[25]

1932 was not only the year of Methodist union, it was the year when the controversial report of a study commissioned by John D. Rockefeller was published. Rockefeller was the foremost supporter of foreign missions in America. The 'Laymen's Inquiry' into the foreign missionary enterprise, undertaken not by mission boards but under the auspices of the Rockefeller-sponsored Institute of Social and Religious Research, concentrated on India, Burma, China and Japan. Thirty research workers carried out a fact-finding exercise and a group of fifteen academics, businessmen and church people formed a Commission of Appraisal, led by William Hocking, Professor of Philosophy at Yale. The report *Re-Thinking Missions* (1932), was a challenge to all missionary societies and a grave offence to conservative evangelicals.[26] Widely circulated and read, the debate which it provoked reflected the widening gulf between fundamentalists and 'modernists'. For some, the paramount aim of world mission remained to save as many as possible from eternal punishment. But the Great War had caused many to rethink:

---

[24]   Cited in C. Thorpe, *Limpopo to Zambesi* (London, Cargate Press, 1951), p. 85.

[25]   WMMS Annual Report 1930, p. 76.

[26]   W.E. Hocking (ed.), *Re-Thinking Missions, A Laymen's Inquiry after One Hundred Years* (New York, Harper, 1932).

the idea that a loving God could impose eternal punishment on men who, through no fault of their own, had suffered the hell of Flanders, was unacceptable. The message of salvation was based not on a threat but an invitation.

The report called for new thinking in two particularly sensitive areas. Its appreciative attitude towards the truths to be found in other religions provoked the reproach that the 'enquirers' had abandoned the idea of conquest in favour of coexistence, and sabotaged the missionary impetus. Secondly, it deplored the cult of institutions. Hospitals and schools, it argued, should not be used as tools for attracting and retaining an audience for preaching. Those on the receiving end of educational and medical work were in a temporary situation of dependence, and to take advantage of that dependence was contrary to the spirit of Christ.[27]

Although it attracted much attention on both sides of the Atlantic at the time, the influence of the Laymen's Inquiry was limited. The primary aim of missionaries and their national counterparts everywhere was unchanged: to lead men and women to faith in the God who loved the world so much that he sent his Son, and to gather them into the fellowship of Christ's disciples. In the wake of Methodist Union, the size of the MMS task force grew apace.

---

[27] S. Neill, G. Anderson, J. Goodwin (eds), *Concise Dictionary of the Christian World Mission* (London, Lutterworth Press, 1970), pp, 339–40.

Chapter 11
Wider Union: Achievements and Failures

Methodist union was an important (and overdue) achievement in Britain, but only a beginning. Abroad, it made no sense for a variety of denominations to evangelize side by side: wasteful duplication for the Societies and the bewilderment of the evangelized were the inescapable outcome. The World Missionary Conference in Edinburgh in 1910 was a pivotal moment in ecumenical affairs. Yet in the same year, John Griffiths reported how the United Methodist work in Kenya was extended to the Meru area:

> I chose a site about three miles from the Government station ... If I went too far in my action without the Committee's authority, I hope they will forgive me; I was compelled to take this course by the action and competition of other societies.[1]

The principle of comity[2] – each Society confining its activity to agreed geographical areas, and non-interference in one another's affairs – had been much discussed from 1888 onwards.[3] Indeed the first recorded agreement was made between the LMS and the WMMS in the 1830s, defining Tonga and Fiji as Methodist spheres and Samoa as an LMS field.[4] But comity was only sporadically and partially implemented, as often by undocumented understandings as by formal memoranda. Even where agreements of either sort were put in place, they were undone by urbanization. Migrants to the cities brought their own traditions and patterns with them and were unwilling to exchange them for unfamiliar ways.

As part of a comprehensive policy statement adopted in 1914, the WMMS declared:

> As to the complete union of the Churches on any field, the Society recognizes such union as the only right aim – ultimately – of all our work; and has no desire on any field to perpetuate the unhappy divisions by which Western Christianity is rent asunder and enfeebled. On the other hand, hurried union might well lead to hurried and grievous disruption, while a more gradual approach ... might secure ultimately a more intelligent and stable basis of union. It is, moreover, of

---

[1] *Missionary Echo* 1910, p. 123.

[2] R.P. Beaver, *Ecumenical beginnings in Protestant world mission: a history of comity* (New York, Thomas Nelson & Sons, 1962).

[3] At the 1888 'Centenary Conference' in London, with almost 1600 participants, comity was high on the agenda.

[4] Pritchard, *Methodists and their Missionary Societies 1760–1900*, pp. 82–3.

great importance to the young growing Churches of the Mission Field that they should for some time to come maintain their connexion with the Churches that under God have given them birth and nurture, and that they should cherish in perpetuity the consciousness of a Catholic rather than a national Christianity.[5]

This was much too timid for far-sighted church leaders such as the Anglican bishop Azariah of Dornakal, who had made a great impact as a young delegate at Edinburgh. In a sermon at the World Conference on Faith and Order in Lausanne in 1927 he said:

The divisions of Christendom do not appeal to the Christians in these lands. Christians in India, for instance, did not have a share in creating them...

Unity may be theoretically a desirable ideal in Europe and America, but it is vital to the life of the Church in the mission field. The divisions of Christendom may be a source of weakness in Christian countries, but in non-Christian lands they are a sin and a scandal.[6]

India

Twenty years after Azariah's Lausanne sermon the Church of South India, the most comprehensive union scheme of the twentieth century, was born. The road to unity had been long. There were local ecumenical partnerships such as the prestigious Madras Christian College and the Women's Christian College in Madras whose main function was to produce graduates to teach in Girls' High Schools, but also inspired educated women to go into the slums and help very poor families. On the regional level, Presbyterians and Congregationalists joined in 1910 to form the South India United Church (SIUC), and lost no time in making overtures to the Wesleyans. These did not immediately find favour, especially among the Indian ministers, and when a gathering of Indian clergy in Tranquebar in 1919 – a milestone in the prehistory of the CSI – resulted in a joint Manifesto of the SIUC and Anglican representatives and then a formal Joint Committee of the two bodies, the Wesleyans were for a while no more than interested observers. They began to attend the SIUC–Anglican Committee on a consultative basis in 1924 and became fully party to the negotiations in 1928. In North India too, where a much larger number of mission agencies was working across a far larger area, conversations about uniting began. Here again Congregationalists and Presbyterians led the way, coming together in the United Church of North India (UCNI) in 1924. They lost no time in circulating others with a proposal to investigate ways towards a wider

---

    5   The 100th Report of the WMMS, 1914: p. xv..

    6   H.N. Bate (ed.), *Faith and Order: Proceedings of the World Conference* (London, SCM Press, 1927), p. 495.

unity, and here the WMMS was the first to respond. Wesleyans and UCNI held talks about talks in 1927, and Round Table Conferences involving representatives of eight Churches and Missions began in Lucknow in 1929.

Anglican commitment owed most to Azariah. He was at the 1920 Lambeth Conference which issued the *Appeal to All Christian People* to work for visible unity:

> We do not ask that any one Communion should consent to be absorbed into another. We do ask that all should unite in a new and great endeavour to recover and to manifest to the world the unity of the Body of Christ for which he prayed.[7]

In proposing 'a form of commission or recognition which would commend our ministry' to the congregations of other denominations and hoping 'that the same motive would lead ministers who have not received it to accept a commission through episcopal ordination' (a proposal which re-emerged in the Anglican-Methodist conversations of the 1960s in England and again caused passionate debate), the Appeal argued:

> In so acting no one of us could possibly be taken to repudiate his past ministry. God forbid that any man should repudiate a past experience rich in spiritual blessings for himself and others. Nor would any of us be dishonouring the Holy Spirit of God, whose call led us all to our several ministries, and whose power enabled us to perform them. We shall be publicly and formally seeking additional recognition of a new call to wider service in a reunited Church, and imploring for ourselves God's grace and strength to fulfil the same.[8]

For Wesleyans, any scheme of union would need the approval of the Conference in Britain; whereas the Church of India Burma and Ceylon was autonomous and could, theoretically, act without any reference to authorities outside India. But it was never likely to proceed unless continued communion with the rest of the Anglican world was assured, and Azariah was again pleading the case at the next Lambeth Conference in 1930: 'In India we wonder if you have sufficiently contemplated the grievous sin of perpetuating your divisions and denominational bitterness in these your daughter churches.'

His 'we' did not include all Indian Christians. Daniel Napoleon, at the WM Provincial Synod of that same year, took the opposite view, arguing vehemently against the scheme and ending, in unaccustomed English, with the resounding peroration: 'If union come, Methodism go to dog, India go to dog, world go to dog!'[9]

---

[7]   Conference of Bishops of the Anglican Communion: Encyclical Letter with the Resolutions and Reports (London, SPCK, 1920), Resolution 9: Reunion of Christendom, p. 29.

[8]   Ibid.

[9]   B. Sundkler *Church of South India* (London, Lutterworth Press, 1954), p. 227.

Methodists, however, now became major players on the Joint Committee in the South. They took a mediating role between Anglican and Congregational positions. The Committee invariably met at the Methodist headquarters in Royapettah, Madras, which eventually became the headquarters of the CSI. Henry Gulliford and Charles Monahan were successive chairmen of the Committee and from 1934 its Secretary was J.S.M. Hooper, General Secretary of the BFBS in India, Burma and Ceylon and a late convert to the cause of union. Charles Wesley also played a part. In 1935, as the Committee struggled to find an acceptable route to the mutual recognition of their ministries, one delegate quoted his line: 'thy undistinguishing regard'.[10] Stephen Neill, a young Anglican delegate, broke in:

> 'That's your formula for the Scheme', and into the scheme it went. 'The uniting churches recognize that Christ has bestowed His grace with undistinguishing regard on all their ministries and has used them all greatly to His glory. All are therefore real ministries of the Word and Sacraments in Christ's Church, nor can any church say that the Sacraments and other ministrations or ministries which He has blessed are invalid.' The sweeping generosity in Charles Wesley's hymn was quoted in order to reconcile differing views. It was also taken to be a factual statement of the relationship between the ministries.[11]

The scheme provided that the basic organizational structure of the CSI would consist of congregation–diocese–Synod (Synod being the governing body). 'The historic episcopate, locally adapted' was always the *sine qua non* of Anglican participation in the scheme, but it was only in 1941 that a form of words was, after much debate, finalized:

> All the uniting churches are agreed that, as episcopacy has been accepted in the Church from early times, it may in this sense fitly be called historic, and that it is needed for the shepherding and extension of the Church in South India.[12]

Confirmation by a bishop was not a constitutional requirement, though it became the general practice. Episcopal ordination was to be invariable in the CSI once it came into existence, but there would be many presbyters who had not been so ordained and any rite that could be construed as re-ordination was eschewed. There would therefore be a 'double ministry' for the initial period. Another stumbling block was the issue of lay celebration of the Eucharist, practised by the SIUC and adamantly opposed by the Anglicans. In mass movement areas there were far too few ordained ministers. The solution was to ordain 'assistant ministers' who would celebrate the sacraments but would not have independent

---

[10]   C. Wesley, from the hymn 'Father, whose everlasting love' in *Hymns on God's Everlasting Love* (London, W. Strahan, 1741).

[11]   Sundkler, p. 269.

[12]   Ibid., p. 299.

Map 11.1   The Church of South India

care of pastorates. The Joint Committee had now done its job. One by one the governing bodies of the negotiating Churches gave their assent, though one of the two Anglican societies, the high church Society for the Propagation of the Gospel (SPG) could not swallow the plan and a rump of 'continuing Anglicans' in Dornakal, Azariah's diocese, went its own way. Azariah himself died in 1945; like Moses, he was only able to gaze on the Promised Land from afar.

The CSI, with a million members from four language areas – Tamil, Telugu, Kannada and Malayalam – was inaugurated in Madras in September 1947, six weeks after political independence. Meanwhile to the north, amid continuous bloodshed and rampant disease, millions of refugees, Hindu, Muslim, Sikh, were streaming across the frontiers between two newborn nations in one direction or the other. Hooper preached at the inaugural service:

The reconciliation between our divergent elements ... enables us with fresh conviction and force to proclaim the Gospel of reconciliation to all the clashing elements in this nation's life.[13]

At the first Synod of the CSI in 1948 the women's organizations of the uniting Churches were authorized to combine in one Women's Fellowship. It took off in both town and rural areas, and by 1952 there were nearly a thousand branches. In Bangalore that year a religious Order for Women was inaugurated, with active members, committed to full time service in pastoral, evangelistic, medical or educational spheres, and associate members. Women were first admitted to the CSI diaconate in 1970 and to the presbyterate in 1982.

In North India progress was slower. Participation at the Round Table Conferences fluctuated until 1941, at which point it consisted of the Church of India Burma and Ceylon, the UCNI, the Methodist Church of Southern Asia (MCSA: a 'Central Conference' of US-related Methodists) and the Districts of the British Conference. A formal Negotiating Committee began work in 1951, and Baptists, Brethren and the Disciples of Christ subsequently rejoined negotiations. In 1957 it was decided to work towards two Churches with similar constitutions, for North India and for Pakistan.

The Lambeth Conference of 1948 had given general approval to the tentative North India proposals, as well as a more advanced scheme for Ceylon, but Lambeth 1958 raised objections. It accepted that 'admission to communicant status with a form which includes prayer for the gift of the Holy Spirit and the laying on of hands by a Bishop or a presbyter authorized by the bishop' is equivalent to confirmation; but the manner in which the unification of ministries might be achieved was a sticking point. The scheme did not require all ministers to be ordained in accordance with the Anglican understanding of the apostolic succession, nor was there to be a 'double ministry' for an interim period. The place of bishops with no claim to be in the succession – the MCSA bishops – made the process still more complicated. The negotiating Churches had a choice – to go ahead anyway, or to pause. They chose to go back to the drawing board. Yet in some situations, churches could not go on waiting. Kenyon Wright described his experience in Bengal:

> I had to drive regularly ... on the Grand Trunk Road (past) a small village by the roadside surrounded by jungle ... By 1957 it became clear that this area was to become a major steel plant. Within a few years, what had been a tiny village was part of a growing town of some 300,000 people ... Approaches (were) made separately by people from various Churches to Mr K C Shivaramakrishnan, at that time Director of the Durgapur Development Authority to ask for land to build churches. He asked us all to come back to see him together, and challenged us with words like these: 'In this place, I have to build a united community out

---

[13]   Ibid., p. 339.

NORTH INDIA AND BANGLADESH
with Diocesan Boundaries of CNI

AMRITSAR

CHANDIGARH

Delhi

AGRA

RAJASTHAN

Lucknow

Azamgarh

Allahabad

PATNA

Darjeeling

SIKKIM

ASSAM

GUJARAT

Ahmadabad

BHOPAL

CHOTA-NAGPUR

Purulia

Dhaka

Howrah

Calcutta

JABALPUR

SAMBALPUR

Nagpur

CUTTACK

DURGAPUR

BANGLADESH

Chittagong

NASIK

BOMBAY

KOLHAPUR

0 Miles 500

0 Km 500

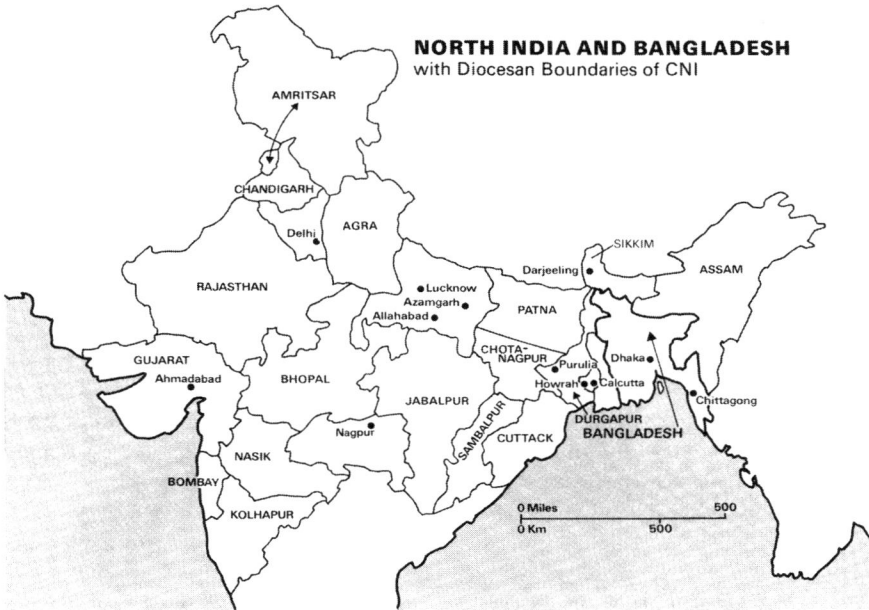

Map 11.2　　The Church of North India

of people from all over India and the world. Go away, and come back when you are ready to be part of the answer, not the problem.' – and the Durgapur United Church was the result.[14]

It was another ten years before a Plan that met Anglican objections was finally devised. It involved the laying on of hands by senior leaders of all Churches together and the 'unified' presbyters making the affirmation: 'Believing myself to have been lawfully ordained in the [Methodist] Church, I now ask for whatever gifts the Spirit offers for my new ministry in the CNI'. This provided the apostolic imprimatur without denying the validity of previous ordination. The stage was set for unification in 1970. Again a Methodist headed up the preparations, but this time it was an Indian Methodist – Christa Chara Pande, Chairman of the Bengal District and affectionately known as Shanu Babu, moved to Delhi as Secretary of the Negotiating Committee in 1967. Then, at the last minute, the MCSA, by far the largest of the negotiating Churches, pulled out.

---

[14]　K.E. Wright, 'A Personal View of the Methodist Bengal District from 1955 to 1970' in Mitra, p. 31.

In 1968 the General Conference of the United Methodist Church (UMC)[15] passed an Enabling Act permitting the MCSA to join if the vote in India was favourable. It was: a two-thirds majority was easily obtained. But then the church leadership requested a postponement, because the question of the MCSA's endowments had not, in their view, been adequately addressed. The other Churches considered forty years of talking was long enough, and could wait no longer. A disgruntled South Asia Central Conference voted, in August 1970, to reject the Plan. Three months later, on All Saints' Day, the Church of North India, its projected size reduced by half, was inaugurated. The Church of Pakistan, inaugurated simultaneously, did include the MCSA; British Methodists were not present there.

Within months, East and West Pakistan were at war and in 1974 East Pakistan became a separate nation, Bangladesh. In 1974 the Synod of the Church of Pakistan recognized the autonomy of the Church of Bangladesh. It consisted only of former Anglican and Presbyterian churches, but established relations with MCOD and from 1982 mission partners began to be sent, most appointed jointly with other British agencies and working with the Social Development Programme.

Once the united Churches were set up, the mission agencies related not only to those areas where they had historically worked but to the CSI and to the CNI as a whole. Missionaries, now under Indian discipline, might be sent to any diocese, though ministers were not imposed on congregations with definite reservations about their orders, and in practice there was a great deal of continuity. Henceforth the MMS's common practice was to station probationers destined for India in a British circuit for a year or two, and then send them to be ordained in the united Church. This had a happy effect when they eventually returned to Britain: having been episcopally ordained, their ministry was recognized by the Church of England. One, Ken Gill, who eventually became the Bishop of Mysore Central diocese, then returned to be the Assistant Bishop of Newcastle, and Kenyon Wright became a canon of Coventry Cathedral.

Another sensitive area was finance. Grants-in-aid continued to be sent, but the autonomy and maturity of the young Churches had to be respected, not least in budget-setting. Partnership in mission had to be cultivated, and, in both South and North India, Related Missions Committees were formed, in which representatives of the overseas agencies met, more or less annually, with the church leaders.

The advent of the united Churches did not produce an undivided Christian presence on the sub-continent. Roman Catholics and the ancient Churches of Kerala were not involved; Lutherans only participated in Pakistan; the Methodist Church in India (as it became) went its own way; the Mar Thoma Church engaged with CSI and CNI to consider ways of affirming and demonstrating their common faith, but remained apart; meanwhile, all manner of independent, Pentecostal and evangelical bodies appeared, in India as they did around the world. Yet the accomplishment of unions to which Anglicans were party, and the formation

---

[15]   The Methodist Episcopal Church joined with the Evangelical United Brethren in 1968 as the United Methodist Church.

of Churches which were members of both the Anglican Communion and the World Methodist Council, was no mean feat and one achieved nowhere else. The commitment of Methodists to work positively and creatively to help produce acceptable schemes was an important contribution. But it is clear that without Bishop Azariah's unwavering dedication to the cause success would never have been realized. The rest of the world lacked Azariahs.

Zambia

At a General Missionary Conference of Northern Rhodesia at Kafue in 1922, attended by representatives of ten different missions, Douglas Gray presented a paper on 'Unoccupied Areas and Limitation of Spheres' and a resolution was passed:

> This Conference, while recognizing that Spheres of Influence may only be temporary, yet holds strongly that at this early stage in the development of mission work, there is ample room for missions to occupy distinct areas, and it would therefore remind all the Missionary Societies of the waste and friction that result from overlapping and urge them to avoid this evil wherever possible.[16]

The last three words contrived to combine strong condemnation and feeble qualification. By no means all the Societies went with comity thereafter, but several agreed to confine their work to specified parts the territory. The General Missionary Conference continued to meet every four or five years, until 1944, when it became the Christian Council of Northern Rhodesia.

In the late 1920s copper was found in what had been no-one's land and mining began to attract both technical and managerial staff from Europe, and migrant African workers from all over the territory. The Societies who had co-operated over comity felt it wrong to perpetuate their divisions in the new industrial zones, and the United Missions in the Copperbelt (UMCB) were begun in 1936. While the young Methodist District supported the venture and Graham Soulsby, the Chairman, obtained a grant from the Society towards the costs, Methodists did not join the United Missions officially. The Society's goal was a more comprehensive union including Anglicans, along the lines devised in India. A few years later, when the Church of Central Africa in Rhodesia (CCAR) was formed in 1945, uniting the LMS work with the UMCB, both Methodists and Anglicans again remained apart. For Methodists, the successful completion of the CSI scheme encouraged the hope of a similar outcome in Zambia; they were slow to see that the high church Anglicans of the Universities' Mission to Central Africa (UMCA) would not compromise their position.

---

[16]   *Proceedings of the General Missionary Conference of Northern Rhodesia 1922* (Livingstonia, Mission Press, 1923), p. 13.

Map 11.3   Zambia

A turning point came when Tom Beetham, the MMS Africa Secretary, revisited the District in 1951. He recognized the intransigence of the Anglicans; he saw that an earlier fear that the CCAR would be an African church, leaving out the European congregations, was unfounded; and he realized that the Copperbelt would have a critical role to play in the burgeoning movement for Zambian independence. Back in England he recruited a dynamic young minister, Colin Morris, who was appointed to the Chingola Free Church on the Copperbelt and soon became known for his outspoken opposition to any form of racism – both he and Merfyn Temple, Douglas Gray's son-in-law, formed a close bond with Kenneth Kaunda, the leader of the United National Independence Party (UNIP).

In 1958 a group of European congregations on the Copperbelt joined the CCAR, which promptly elected Morris its President. In the same year the Mindolo Ecumenical Foundation was established near Kitwe under the leadership of a charismatic Australian, Peter Matthews, as a Copperbelt-wide educational base with an international dimension; from the start it was planned to be the great all-Africa training centre it became. The Church of Barotseland (planted by the PMS) was collaborating with the MMS and others in the David Livingstone Teacher Training College in Livingstone. There was thus a long history of co-operation between many of the Protestant missions and Churches, and the Methodist Synod's request to enter negotiations about organic union was a logical, soundly-based consequence.

The District needed the approval of Conference and the details of the scheme, to which the UMCA was not party, were put to the Faith and Order Committee.

The Committee had a lot of reservations; it was at the same time considering a scheme in Nigeria which included Anglicans and which in British eyes was the preferred model. By 1964 all other parties were ready to proceed, but Faith and Order demanded another year to resolve some aspects of the proposals. In Zambia, however, there was insistence that the union should not be further delayed. Political independence was to be realized in October and it was unthinkable that the participating Churches should continue to be under foreign tutelage any longer. An infuriated Synod raised the funds to send Morris – who had been at the Lancaster House talks which achieved Zambian independence – to England again to argue the case at the Conference, where he won the day. The United Church of Zambia (UCZ) was duly inaugurated on 1 January 1965, with Morris as its first President. But the leadership was essentially Zambian: Doyce Musunsa, another ex-Methodist, was as Synod Clerk the chief executive officer, and Jackson Mwape, richly experienced, succeeded Morris as President in 1968.[17]

The hesitation of some members of the British Conference was tied up with the delicate Anglican-Methodist conversations under way in England. Their concern was aggravated by the application of Peggy Hiscock, a Wesley Deaconess serving in Zambia from 1958, to be ordained as a UCZ minister. There was nothing in the UCZ constitution to deter either her or the church authorities, but in Britain the day of women ministers had not yet arrived. Until it did, she accepted that she would be known as 'Revd' in Zambia and 'Sister' at home, and she was ordained in 1968.

Other Non-episcopal Unions

In several predominantly Roman Catholic countries in Europe, the Protestant Churches saw the wisdom of coming together and pooling their resources. The *France* Conference, the first to become autonomous after the United States, was the second, after Canada, to sacrifice its identity for the sake of effective mission. It never grew to be more than a collection of small, scattered, largely rural congregations; if the man in the Parisian street had heard of Methodism at all, he probably regarded it as an outlandish sect and did not realise how much it had in common with the French Reformed Church, the largest Protestant body in the country. In fact, French and British Methodists and French Reformed missionaries worked together in French West Africa, where the Paris Missionary Society collaborated with the WMMS. Discussions on the reorganization of French Protestantism began in 1935 and the Reformed and Methodist Churches and two other small evangelical unions came together in 1939.

In 1955 Methodism in *Spain* united with the Spanish Evangelical Church, itself an amalgam of several tiny protestant bodies. George Bell, who had served

---

[17]   E.G. Nightingale, *A history of Methodism in Northern Rhodesia*, privately printed and circulated, 1965

in the Spanish colony of Fernando Po from 1916 to 1936 and in Barcelona from 1948, was instrumental in bringing about a union first mooted in 1906.

In *Italy* the two branches of Methodism (of American and British origin) joined together as the Evangelical Methodist Church in 1946. Three years earlier, 'driven by the hard necessity' of wartime, the British branch had asked permission to unite with the Waldensian Church in north-west Italy, which traced its history to the twelfth century and, after centuries of persecution, was legally recognized in 1848. The Conference agreed but the union did not materialize. Instead the amalgamated Methodist body remained a district of the British conference until it became autonomous in 1962. Then in 1975 it entered into a covenant with the Waldensians, forming a united Church with one synod and a common presbyterate and diaconate, and shared training at the Waldensian Faculty in Rome, though the two parts maintained their individual identities, international relationships, finance and administration. Ecumene, a youth centre near Rome built in 1954 under Methodist auspices with the cooperation of young volunteers from all over the world and from different Christian denominations, sought – despite the ever-present tensions in Italy between Catholics and Protestants – to be a symbol of the unity of the church and a witness to reconciliation, justice and peace.

On the other side of the world, the Australian MMS began to work in *Papua New Guinea and the Solomon Islands* at the end of the nineteenth century, with support from the New Zealand Conference. In 1968 Methodists, LMS and others formed the United Church in Papua New Guinea and the Solomon Islands, with 100,000 communicant members at its inception. Its polity and terminology were Methodist: a local church meeting and leaders' meeting, a circuit, a regional Synod and an overall Assembly. In 1996 the United Church divided, but on territorial not confessional lines, to serve the two independent nations.

Aborted Schemes

CSI aspired to be 'the piece of grit in the ecumenical oyster without which the pearl of unity will not form'.[18] By 1970 almost sixty schemes of union had come to fruition in twenty-eight countries involving 169 Churches, and another thirty-three were under consideration in twenty-seven countries, involving 120 Churches; but several schemes in which Methodists – both national church leaders and missionaries – invested a lot of time, enthusiasm, meticulous attention to detail and stubborn determination, failed to materialize. In some instances there were theological issues, where 'my sacred convictions' and 'your stubborn prejudices' were in irreconcilable conflict. In others the stumbling block was the transfer of property and other worldly assets to which churches clung jealously.

---

[18]   A.M. Ward, *The Pilgrim Church* (London, Epworth Press, 1953), p. 191.

The *Sri Lanka[19]* scheme was built on foundations laid in 1912, when John Mott visited Ceylon in the course of his post-Edinburgh travels and a National Council of Churches was formed. In the 1930s, as a South India scheme took shape, impatience with the divisions separating Ceylonese Christians gathered momentum. Two names recur constantly in the record: Daniel Niles and Basil Jackson. Jackson devoted his entire ministry to Ceylon, for a few years as Chairman of the South Ceylon District but mostly in ecumenical institutions. He founded and directed the National Council of Churches' Study Centre for Religion and Society from 1951 to 1962 and from 1963 until he retired in 1967 was the first principal of the Theological College of Lanka, which was not only denominationally inclusive, but also the earliest Protestant institution to teach in both Sinhala and Tamil. The first steps towards a project of union were taken at a Teachers' Conference in Kandy in 1934 where Jackson 'almost single handed ... bullied a few other people to join me to form the Friends of Reunion'.[20] In 1940 he proposed that the Ceylon Provincial Methodist Synod should invite other Churches to form a Joint Committee 'to study, discuss and report upon the possibility of forming a scheme of Reunion for the Christian Churches of Ceylon'. With remarkable speed the Anglicans, Baptists, Presbyterians and the Jaffna area of the SIUC (as it still was) accepted the invitation and the Joint Committee on Church Union held its first meeting that November.

The scheme had a long gestation period. In 1951, on his return from furlough, Jackson was elected to chair the Committee – though he recorded in his diary that:

> 'as a matter of fact it is DT [Niles] who runs the meeting, with everyone's consent.' Jackson was a good and sympathetic chair of a meeting. He could always see both sides of a question; he was always at pains to ensure that everyone was able to say what they wanted to and he was never accused of using such a position to further his own purposes. D T Niles was, and was known to be, single-minded in the pursuit of Church Union. He would not have wanted to chair such a committee; it would have made it more difficult for him to get the committee to agree to what he wanted. He could be much more ruthless than Basil in trying to do that. Although in some ways it would have seemed right to have had a Sinhalese or Tamil minister as the chair, it was generally agreed that Basil was probably the only one who could stand up to D T Niles without disrupting the committee.[21]

It was 1969 before the Methodist Conference (autonomous only from 1964) voted on the scheme, and then it did not achieved the required majority of 75 per cent; but in successive votes in 1970 and 1971 it did, as did all the other

---

[19]   Ceylon's name was officially changed to Sri Lanka in 1972.

[20]   G.B. Jackson, 1971 diary entry, in 'Basil', unpublished memoir by his son G.C. Jackson.

[21]   Ibid.

participating Churches. With relief and thanksgiving, services of intercommunion with concelebration were held in twenty centres throughout the island. Advent Sunday 1972 was fixed as the date of inauguration. There was still much work to be done: an enabling Bill would have to go to Parliament, the financial structure of the united Church needed finalising, the first bishops had to be elected. But dissension within Anglican ranks brought the project to a sudden halt. Three members of the Church of Sri Lanka challenged in a court of law the legitimacy of the Anglican vote and an interim injunction was issued restraining the Bishop of Colombo and the Council from acting upon the resolution. There was no point in going on drafting measures; everyone could see that the plan was dead.

The movement for visible unity in *Nigeria* began in the East. A conference in Calabar in 1905 had begun to map out comity arrangements; in 1931 a gathering of 'Senior African Agents', who had been conferring regularly called for a central church in each town, and a common name, liturgy and catechism. They went on to

> deprecate the existence of divisions among us as a source of weakness and strongly urge that steps be taken to the consolidation of Union among Churches.[22]

A Conference at Onitsha in 1947 laid the foundations of a scheme that eventually embraced Methodists, Anglicans and Presbyterians. There was action as well as talk. The three began joint ministerial training in the East in 1948 and established Trinity College in Umuahia in 1950. In Umuahia too a women's teacher training college and the Queen Elizabeth Hospital were joint undertakings. In the West, teacher training was being done jointly and Immanuel College in Ibadan training Anglican and Methodist ministers – there were hardly any Presbyterians in the West – opened in 1958.

In 1950 a Nigeria Church Union Committee was formed; it met annually, and devised its own scheme which went through three drafts from 1957 to 1960. Its secretary was William Wood, originally a Primitive Methodist, who became General Secretary of the Christian Council of Nigeria (CCN). In 1963 a target date for union was set: December 1965. At this point the diocese of the North, one of seven Anglican dioceses, withdrew, citing the 'unique problems and difficulties' of work in the North. The Province of West Africa as a whole, however, encouraged the scheme, and gave assurances that the 'residual Province', including the diocese of the North, would be in full communion with the united Church (though the position of the Anglican Communion in general was that, as with the CSI, a decision about relations with the new Church would be taken only after its inauguration). Methodists too had their reservations, but secured satisfactory amendments to the proposed Constitution, providing better lay representation on the governing bodies at every level, and the appointment of a Lay President. The new Church would have nineteen dioceses; eleven of the designated bishops were Anglicans, six were Methodists and two Presbyterians; one of them would

---

[22]   Marioghae and Ferguson, p. 47.

be known, as in India, as the Moderator. From 1964 Wood's Committee gave way to an Inaugural Committee, which not only dealt with unresolved constitutional issues and practical arrangements, but had a 'Life and Mission Group' set up to inspire Nigerians with a vision of what the new Church might achieve. Its booklet, *The Way Forward,* published by CCN's Daystar Press, stressed in the Introduction that the purpose of union was not 'in order to have a larger organization or to get more worldly power. We want unity because it is God's will for us.'[23]

At the Methodist Conference of January 1965 in Uzuakoli, both the pastoral and representative sessions voted overwhelmingly in favour of the scheme. Beneath the surface, however, there was unhappiness in the Methodist ranks. It emanated from two sources, distinct but allied. There were some members of Lagos congregations whose fears arose from the likelihood that Archbishop Patterson would be the first Moderator of the Church of Nigeria and that the Methodist offices on the Marina of Lagos Island would become the new Church's headquarters. In their eyes this was an Anglican takeover. At the same time there was a dispute between two eminent Methodists on the staff of Ibadan University: Egemba Igwe, the Secretary of Conference and a member of the 'Life and Mission Group', and Bolaji Idowu, a scholar whose recent book on *God in Yoruba Belief* (1962)[24] was justly acclaimed, and who would later prove at once the most original thinker and the most divisive figure in the history of Nigerian Methodism. It is not irrelevant to note that Igwe was an Igbo from the East and Idowu a Yoruba from the West. The two exchanged lengthy letters in August 1965, Idowu claiming that

> The Anglican Church in Nigeria wants and is demanding that Church Union should subserve her own domineering purpose and convenience ... It is they who have set up the cult of personalities within the Church of Christ and are, like Nebuchadnezzar, commanding us to worship at the shrine or be thrown into the fiery furnace of their wrath.[25]

Later events would reveal the irony of Idowu complaining about a cult of personality.[26]

In view of the rumblings Joseph Soremekun, the President of Conference, issued a pastoral address to the Methodist people in October, consisting of a series of questions and reassurances about the scheme and re-affirming 11 December as the date for the inaugurations – though some complained they had only voted on a tentative date and the leadership had railroaded it through as definitive. It was disingenuous of the Lagos laymen, well educated, to say they had not been

---

[23]   Church of Nigeria Inaugural Committee, Life and Mission Group, *The Way Forward: the Church of Nigeria* (Ibadan, Daystar Press, 1965), p. 3.

[24]   E.B. Idowu, *Olodumarè: God in Yoruba Belief* (Lagos, Longman Nigeria, 1962).

[25]   O.U. Kalu, *Divided people of God: Church union movement in Nigeria, 1875–1966* (New York, Nok, 1978), pp. 88–90.

[26]   pp. 212–13.

adequately informed despite the constitutional and liturgical texts, the informal manual *The Way Forward*, and the Bible study aids on Ephesians that had been produced, and the occasional publication of *Church Union News*. They were influenced by material from the 'Voice of Methodism', an organization in Britain adamantly opposed to reunion with the Church of England, and its arguments bolstered their own. They now effectively torpedoed the scheme with lawsuits against the Conference leadership, suggesting that the new Church would subscribe to doctrinal standards different from those in the MCN Deed of Foundation. On 3 November, Idowu wrote to the Inaugural Committee calling for a postponement. The language of the letter was intemperate, especially in regard to Willliam Wood. The Committee expressed its full confidence in Wood and moved on.

Idowu wanted a year's postponement; a compromise of three months was put to an emergency meeting of the Methodist executive. But the representatives from the East, where support for the scheme was always strongest, were impatient and the motion to proceed in December was carried. In vain: at the end of November all three participating Churches resigned themselves to postponement. In Patterson's judgment, no-one should 'think that theological or ecclesiastical interests are involved. It is all a clash of personalities and fears about property.'[27] The postponement was prolonged by the Biafran War and the Inaugural Committee was dissolved in 1971. At Immanuel College the Eucharist was long afterwards still usually celebrated using the order proposed for the united Church, though students no longer expected to minister in a Church where it would be duly authorized.

A twenty-eight year quest for church union in *Ghana* began in 1957, with a Committee chaired by the Presbyterian, Professor Christian Baeta. Laurence Creedy, a Methodist lay missionary who had been in Ghana since 1934 was its secretary. Both men served throughout the Committee's lifetime. A statement of its aims and principles, *Our Approach to Church Unity,* was published in 1960. By 1963 *Proposals for Church Union in Ghana: The Inauguration and Constitution of the United Church* was circulated; it was revised two years later in the light of responses from the Anglican, Methodist and two Presbyterian Churches. It was decided to consult every congregation and ask each to sign up to a declaration that

> We, the congregation [name to be inserted], solemnly declare that when our Synod/Conference has decided, after full consultation throughout the church, that the Constitution of the United Church and arrangements for its inauguration are acceptable, we, for our part, will GLADLY GO INTO UNION, and that accordingly during the period before union we will in every possible way CO-OPERATE WITH OUR BRETHREN IN THE CHURCHES CONCERNED.[28]

---

[27] Kalu, p. 68.

[28] Quoted in C.B. Essamuah, *Genuinely Ghanaian* (Trenton, New Jersey, Africa World Press, 2010), p. 145.

A helpful pamphlet entitled *Church Union in Ghana: Questions and Answers* was translated into Ewe, Fante, Ga and Twi, and some 100,000 copies were sold. By late 1972 almost all had signed and in 1973 a formal act of worship was held in Accra to initiate the final phase of negotiations. It was still a protracted business. In 1977 the leaders of the negotiating Churches toured Ghana together, answering questions and encouraging local congregations to work and plan together. In 1978–1979 a resolution 'The Church agrees to unite with all the other Churches which also agree on Union, in accordance with the proposals ...' was passed overwhelmingly by Methodists and Presbyterians; but, shortly after the Anglican Consultative Council had pronounced its support for the proposals, the diocese suddenly withdrew – according to John Pobee, himself a Ghanaian canon, who chaired the liturgical and indigenization subcommittee, because in many eyes

> to go into union in Ghana was to fall out of communion with the mother Church in England. Crudely put, the African Anglicans were afraid to lose access to the resources of SPG.[29]

In 1983 the two Presbyterian Churches also decided to proceed no further, leaving Methodists jilted at the altar.

Ecumenical history in *Kenya* went back to United Missionary Conferences in Nairobi in 1909 and Kikuyu in 1913. These were missionary gatherings, and although 'one united native church' was the chief item on the agenda at Kikuyu, not a single African delegate was present. The 1913 conference proposed a Federation of Missions, with intercommunion on the horizon. This incensed the UMCA missionary Bishop Weston of Zanzibar, who accused the CMS missionary bishops of Mombasa and Uganda 'of promoting heresy and schism, appealed to the Archbishop of Canterbury and immediately rushed his views into print.'[30] No federation ensued, but once the furore in Anglican circles had evaporated an 'Alliance' was formed in 1918 by the Church of Scotland Mission, the Church of the Province of Kenya, the Africa Inland Mission (AIM) and the UM Mission; the Kenya Missionary Council, with a broader membership but no greater influence, was set up in 1924. AIM, much the strongest protestant body in the colony, laid down the basis on which it would participate in the Alliance. It

> did not see how there can be a real and workable union ... unless the other Societies in the Alliance agree to send out to Kenya as missionaries those only who hold the conservative evangelical position.[31]

---

[29]   J.S. Pobee, 'The Anglican Church in Ghana and the SPG' in D. O'Connor (ed.), *Three Centuries of Mission* (London, Continuum, 2000), p. 420.

[30]   A. Porter, *Religion versus empire?* (Manchester, Manchester University Press, 2004), p. 312.

[31]   M.G. Capon, *Towards Unity in Kenya* (Nairobi, Christian Council of Kenya, 1962), p. 28.

At the time the Representative Council of the Alliance agreed to this condition, which allowed the Alliance High School to open in 1926. The school became the most prestigious in the country, and outlived the Alliance itself.[32]

AIM and CMS were uneasy bedfellows; their contrasting theologies and stances made further progress unlikely – AIM wanted to rebaptize any Anglicans who moved into their area, and wanted non-teetotallers excluded from full membership of any United Church. For Africans differences between the missions on issues of discipline relating to alcohol, smoking, male and female circumcision and methods of contracting marriage were more confusing than matters of doctrine and liturgical practice. However, developments in India prompted discussions from which a 1932 document, based on the South India scheme, emerged: *Church Union in East Africa: Proposed Basis of Union*. The Methodist Synod was lukewarm about it, reporting it to the MMS Committee without comment.[33] It was shelved; and when in 1944, as Kenyan Christians began to take a more active part alongside western missionaries, the Missionary Council set up the Christian Council of Kenya, the CCK was inaugurated only after Arthur Hopkins gave an assurance from the chair that the new body would 'never be used to promote Church Union'. Any talk of organic unity would have to be held in another context, and the Africa Inland Church, as it became, would not be involved.

Kenya was under a state of Emergency during the years of the Mau Mau uprising, 1952–1959, and Kenyans had other concerns to deal with. A negotiating committee of Anglicans, Methodists, Presbyterians, Lutherans and Moravians was formed in 1962. It produced an Interim Basis of Union in 1965, abandoned it in 1967 because it was not acceptable to the Lutherans and Moravians, and disappeared into thin air after its 1969 meeting. Meanwhile Kenya had become an independent nation in 1963 and the Methodist Church autonomous in 1967. A last attempt by Methodists, the Anglican Province of Kenya and the Presbyterian Church of East Africa to revive negotiations and involve African indigenous Churches was made in 1975–1976, but once again the talks foundered. Johana Mbogori, who at one time chaired the Negotiations Committee (and was later the Presiding Bishop of Methodist Church Kenya), blamed non-theological factors:

> Personal prejudices, pride of the past, ambition for positions of responsibility, these are the things which keep the ministries of the Church divided; apathy, lack of understanding and knowledge, and sentiment, these are the obstacles which confront the laity.[34]

---

[32]   Over half of President Kenyatta's first cabinet were former Alliance HS students.

[33]   Nthamburi, p. 123.

[34]   E.K. Cole, *A History of Church Co-operation in Kenya* (Limuru, St. Paul's College Press, 1975), p. 15.

Donald M'Timkulu from Natal, the first General Secretary of the All Africa Conference of Churches (AACC), had another explanation for the failure of these African schemes:

> The social ties binding the African Christian to his extended family and clan have always been stronger than the forces of separation that arise from membership in different denominations. The important family occasions like births, marriages, funerals and clan festivals bring together in one place of worship relatives with different confessional backgrounds. On these occasions they not only share in common acts of worship with gay disregard of denominational differences, but they also take part in symbolic acts of family and clan unity that have their roots in the traditional past.[35]

China

As far back as 1877 a Missionary Conference which attracted missionaries from all over China 'expressed a desire and a hope for unity and even pleaded that Western denominationalism be disregarded as irrelevant for China',[36] while in 1907, John Campbell Gibson in his opening statement to the Centenary Missionary Conference in Shanghai, said

> Let us recognize that Chinese Christianity is bound to seek two things and to regard them as intimately related, namely independence of the control of foreign Churches and union among their own.[37]

He referred to 'the time honoured' three-self formula adumbrated by CMS Secretary Henry Venn and the American Rufus Anderson half a century earlier: the objective of a self-supporting, self-governing, self-propagating church. But progress towards that end was halting at best. Once again Presbyterians and Congregationalists led the way; the Church of Christ in China, which held its first General Assembly in 1927, brought together sixteen denominational groups representing between a quarter and a third of Chinese Protestants. The Chinese resisted including 'united' in the Church's name because that would be a reminder of the foreign denominational origins they were anxious to leave behind.

The majority of Chinese Christians and foreign missionaries had had no direct contact with communists before 1949, and few knew what to expect when the Red

---

[35]   D.G.S. M'Timkulu, *Beyond Independence: The Face of New Africa* (New York, Friendship Press, 1971), p. 22.

[36]   W. Merwin, *Adventure in Unity, The Church of Christ in China* (Grand Rapids, Eerdmans, 1994), pp. 21–2.

[37]   *China Centenary Missionary Conference Records* (New York, American Tract Society, 1907), p. 3.

Armies came to liberate them. It gradually became clear that Sinofication would entail not only the departure of foreign missionaries and a ban on foreign funding, but the abolition of foreign denominational labels. The new government had no avowed intention of enforcing atheism, but did prescribe the parameters within which Christian leadership had to function. The Three Self Patriotic Movement (TSPM) was set up in 1951 by Chinese Christian leaders, to encourage Protestant Christians to balance love for the motherland (*aiguo*) and love for the church (*aijiao*); a comparable Catholic Patriotic Association was established in 1957. They were seen by many as the price to be paid for tolerance by the government. The TSPM's constitution did not envisage merger: it stated that it would 'respect the creeds, organizations and rituals of the various churches, and encourage each church in the same spirit of mutual respect'.

Under the auspices of the TSPM, the 'First National Christian Conference'[38] met in 1954 – the National Council of Churches, established in the missionary era, had passed into oblivion. The Conference issued a 'Letter to Christians Throughout China' reiterating that:

> The goal of self-propagation is not the unification or modification of belief, but the thoroughgoing eradication of vestiges of imperialist thought … We should have mutual respect for the differences that exist among the churches in creed, organization and ritual.[39]

But Christians fell foul of the Anti-Rightist movement of 1957; many were denounced, on the flimsiest of grounds, as 'imperialist running dogs' and penalized by being dismissed from their posts, dispatched to manual labour in the countryside, or imprisoned. A movement suddenly emerged in 1958, supervised by the TSPM, to unify churches through the closure of many and the amalgamation of congregations of different backgrounds.[40] Christians still met together, but increasingly in homes rather than public places. Denominations were of no account and disappeared. It was a shotgun union.

The 'Great Proletarian Cultural Revolution' of 1966–76 saw the last churches closed, Bibles burned, all religious assemblies prohibited for years. When persecution came to an end, and Christianity emerged from the shadows, it was soon apparent that there were now more believers than ever. A Third National Christian Conference in 1980 set up the China Christian Council (CCC) as the umbrella body, alongside the TSPM, of what was proclaimed – justifiably but not altogether accurately – to be a post-denominational Protestant church. (The CCC accepted the autonomy of the Little Flock, True Jesus Church, Jesus Family, and those practising Adventists traditions.) Among CCC and TSPM leaders at

---

[38]   'Christian' in the Chinese context implies Protestant – Chinese has a different word for Catholics.

[39]   Quoted in Whyte, p. 233.

[40]   p. 219.

provincial, county and city level were numerous ex-Methodists, proud of their Methodist past but even more proud of the 'ex'.

Inorganic unity

The high hopes engendered in India for visible unity evaporated. But Methodists, disappointed in England as well as abroad, were eager to engage in other forms of ecumenical witness. In the CBMS, BCC and WCC they played a prominent part, as they did in many national Christian Councils and in the regional Councils which sprang up one by one. Besides these individual contributions to the ecumenical cause, the Society itself, in its later years, developed new relationships not confined to the Methodist family. The Presbyterian Church in Cameroon (PCC), offspring of Baptist work begun in 1858 and the Basel Mission which arrived in 1886, became autonomous in 1957. At the time the area where the PCC was established was a UN Trust Territory, administered by Britain as an autonomous region of Nigeria, and English was the *lingua franca* of church and state. The people voted in 1961 to become part of newly independent Cameroon. MCOD established links with the anglophone PCC in 1979, a time when Methodist–Presbyterian union along the coast in Ghana was anticipated. In the years that followed the links were reflected in a succession of mission partners, a number of scholarships and funding for Nationals in Mission Appointments.[41] It was a relationship established with little fuss, perhaps because a much-publicized Latin American venture a few years earlier had disappointed expectations.

AMPLA

Conversations between the Church of England and the Methodist Church, begun in 1955, produced proposals for a two-stage reunion which were overwhelmingly adopted by the Conference but failed to reach the required majority in the General Synod in 1969 and 1972.[42] Relations between the Missionary Societies, however, did not depend on the success or failure of the conversations, and in 1970 an unprecedented joint meeting of the MMS Central Committee and the Council of the United Society for the Propagation of the Gospel (USPG) was arranged to consider how they might co-operate in a shared venture in mission. Given the historic reticence about union schemes of USPG's ancestors, the SPG in India and the UMCA in Zambia, it seemed to some an unlikely overture; the CMS would surely be a more natural bedfellow. But it was not so; at Selly Oak, where the Societies rubbed shoulders constantly, the Methodists at Kingsmead felt much

---

[41]   p. 235.

[42]   J.M. Turner, Conflict and Reconciliation (London, Epworth Press, 1985), pp. 194–214.

closer to the College of Ascension (USPG), in spite of its higher churchmanship, than to Crowther Hall (CMS).

Two successive Lambeth Conferences had appealed for greater Anglican involvement in South America; USPG, now ready to respond, considered ecumenical rather than denominational action to be the right course. In the context of the ongoing conversations, it was natural to turn to MMS. Eric Trapp, the General Secretary, wrote to his Methodist counterpart Geoffrey Eddy, to enquire

> whether there was any possibility of our working together ... regardless of whether our respective churches decide to move forward into Stage 1 – though of course, if they do so decide, a joint enterprise of our two Societies (and maybe others) in some part of the world would be a splendid way of marking the event.[43]

The Anglican-Methodist Project in Latin America (AMPLA) was not conceived as a new mission on virgin soil, or as competition with others serving God there. It would only materialize if an invitation came. When Harry Morton and Betty Hares, with two USPG representatives, visited several countries in 1971, they met serious reservations from Latin Americans, who suspected disguised colonialism and feared it would undermine indigenization. Despite these misgivings, there was enough interest in Argentina for a start to be made in Buenos Aires, with invitations from both Methodist and Anglican Churches and an assurance from the Roman Catholic bishops that the ecumenical department 'is very keen to collaborate with this team' from the outset. A local Advisory Group was set up to liaise with the Societies in London. It would be a small project: two or three people from Britain with a couple of Latin Americans were envisaged. Their role, prior to departure, was described in two ways. It was to work with local churches, ranging from Catholics to Pentecostals, and help

> to stimulate training programmes, to share in building bridges of understanding between churches, to enter into the vigorous and often revolutionary student life, to get alongside the intellectuals and the desperately poor who flood into the towns, to help churches in Britain understand how the Gospel is related to the tensions which so easily lead to revolution in South America.[44]

That was an enormous and impossibly demanding agenda. Harry Morton had a more simple vision: 'the team is called to be something rather than to do something.' But that too was demanding: being rather than doing is not quantifiable. In the event, the team never settled into either mode. USPG was unable to find a suitable and willing candidate. In 1974 MMS sent two couples nevertheless, but they received little pastoral care or practical help. Before long they became highly critical of the project. John Roberts wrote that 'AMPLA at present is like a Christmas Tree,

---

43   O'Connor, p. 189.
44   *NOW*, December 1972, p. 32.

ornamental and superficially admirable but it has no roots and is incapable of growing or producing seeds of life' and John Hopkin asked 'How can we avoid the charge of theological imperialism in bringing the ideas, the money and personnel from outside?'[45]

By the end of the year both resigned. Loudly trumpeted at the outset, the Project was quietly buried.

---

[45] O.Connor, p. 192.

Chapter 12
Christian Mission and the Faith of Others

The attitude of John Wesley to men and women of other faiths was not as clear-cut as his sermon on *The General Spread of the Gospel* might suggest. There he condemned Muslims as

> 'utter strangers to all true religion … as void of mercy as lions and tigers; as much given up to brutal lusts as bulls or goats'.[1]

In his sermon on *The Catholic Spirit*, however, Wesley argued:

> While he is steadily fixed in his religious principles, in what he believes to be the truth as it is in Jesus; while he firmly adheres to that worship of God which he judges to be the most acceptable in His sight, and while he is united in the tenderest and closest ties to one particular congregation; his heart is enlarged toward all mankind, those he knows and those he does not; he embraces with strong and cordial affection neighbours and strangers, friends and enemies.[2]

and in the sermon on *Living Without God*:

> I have no authority from the word of God 'to judge those that are without'. Nor do I conceive that any man living has a right to sentence all the heathen and Mahometan world to damnation. It is far better to leave them to Him that made them … who is the God of the heathens as well as the Christians, and who hateth nothing that he hath made.[3]

These and kindred texts were explored and expounded in the late twentieth century by Methodist theologians and inter-faith practitioners, notably Kenneth Cracknell and Elizabeth Harris.[4] In John Wesley's day, and for a century and more afterwards, it was the apparently damning texts that carried weight. Bishop

---

[1]   A.C. Outler (ed.), *Works of John Wesley*, Bicentennial Edition, vol. 2 (Nashville, Abingdon Press, 1985), p. 486.

[2]   Ibid., p. 94.

[3]   Outler, *Works*, vol. 4 (1987), p. 174.

[4]   K.R. Cracknell, *Towards a New Relationship* (London, Epworth Press, 1986), pp. 12–16; E.J. Harris, 'Wesleyan Witness in an Interreligious Context' in P.R. Meadows (ed.), *Windows on Wesley* (Oxford, Applied Theology Press, 1997), pp. 53–85.

Heber's notorious 'The heathen in his blindness / Bows down to wood and stone' echoes Wesley's sermon on *Original Sin*:

> We do not, like the idolatrous Heathens, worship molten or graven images. We do not bow done to the stock of a tree, to the work of our own hands.[5]

For John Wesley, the 'heathen' were those outside the Abrahamic faiths (he used the phrase 'Heathens, Mahommetans and Jews'). But this sermon was directed at Christians, not at others; Christians, Wesley emphasized, were idolaters too:

> We 'have set up our idols in our heart'; and to these we bow down, and worship them. We worship ourselves, when we pay that honour to ourselves which is due to God only.[6]

Some later Methodists displayed a much less 'catholic spirit', influenced less by John Wesley's nuanced tones than by his brother Charles's lines blatantly calling Muhammed

> 'that Impostor ... The Arab-thief, as Satan bold / Who quite destroy'd thy Asian fold.'[7]

William Moister, in the mid-nineteenth century, wrote:

> ... wherever the Moors succeeded in establishing their authority, they required all, by the powerful arguments of fire and sword, to submit to the dogmas of the false prophet.[8]

and of Hindus:

> They build splendid temples to the honour of their numerous gods, in which are set up idols ... of the most hideous and repulsive forms ...But it is on the occasions of the great festivals, when the people congregate to the number of tens of thousands, that the sin and folly of these miserable idolaters are most apparent.[9]

while George Clayton wrote in 1906:

---

[5]   R. Heber, 'From Greenland's icy mountains', hymn first published in the *Evangelical Magazine*, 1822; Outler, *Works*, vol. 2, p. 179.

[6]   Ibid.

[7]   The hymn 'Sun of unclouded Righteousness', first published 1758 – see Cracknell, *Towards a New Relationship*, p. 298.

[8]   W. Moister *Conversations on the Rise, Progress and Present State of Wesleyan Missions in Various Parts of the World* (London, Hamilton Adams & Co, 1869), p. 420.

[9]   Ibid., p. 421.

Buddha's conquest has not been over Christianity, nor over the power of sin, but over all that is noble and pure, all that is honest and of good report. As his worship has spread in this land [*ie* China], purity has been vanquished, and in his train have come immorality, lust, murder, suicide, cruelty.[10]

Methodists throughout the first half of the century, and even as late as the 1970s, were still singing with gusto of 'lands where Islam's sway Darkly broods o'er home and hearth' and 'O'er heathen lands afar Thick darkness broodeth yet.'[11] The antipathy such lines embodied and inculcated was mutual. Converts to Christianity could be shunned by their family and community, physically maltreated, sometimes killed.[12] But hostility was not general. It became less common in those Christian circles where convictions about the final destiny of the unconverted became less dogmatic. Many missionaries living at close quarters among people of different faiths saw that a negative assessment of other belief-systems and religious practices did not preclude approaching their adherents with sympathy and understanding, courtesy and love.

In the course of the twentieth century many new factors affected the way Christians perceived and engaged with people of other faiths. Paving the way was the 1893 'Parliament of Religions', when 'the Christian organizers magnanimously invited to Chicago representatives from all the great religions'.[13] Whatever the motives of the organizers, those who accepted the invitation ensured that inter-faith issues were recognized as being about human relationships and not just philosophical discussions of comparative religion. A big set-piece event was not the place for a fruitful dialogue, but for many it was a wake-up call: no longer could important questions, however threatening, be ignored. The questions were still being asked a century later, at a conference on world mission and evangelism in Salvador, Brazil:

> To what extent may other religions be acknowledged as being expressions of God's mercy and grace found in Christ? At what points do these expressions appear to run counter to God's fullness, life and love in Christ? Some do not doubt that people of other faiths experience decisive moments of deliverance, integration and communion which come to them as gift, not achievement, and that these experiences are akin to what Christians experience as salvation in Jesus Christ. Others question whether such experiences attest to the fruits of the Spirit, the presence and grace of God in them.[14]

---

[10]   G.A. Clayton, *Methodism in Central China* (London, Wesleyan Book Room 1906), p. 128.

[11]   From the hymns 'Let the song go round the earth' by Sarah Stock (1838–1898) and 'Thy kingdom come, O God' by Lewis Hensley (1824–1905).

[12]   See for example Lewis, *Goudie*, pp. 55–6.

[13]   D.J. Bosch, *Transforming Mission* (New York, Orbis Books, 1991), p. 479.

[14]   Duraisingh, p. 33.

Diatribe and Dialogue: from Edinburgh to Salvador

One of the eight Commissions that prepared for the World Missionary Conference in 1910 studied 'The Missionary Message in relation to non-Christian Religions'. Its report was based on responses to a questionnaire sent to several hundred serving missionaries about their attitudes to other faiths. The replies were varied; one wrote that there was 'much to be said for the old system of indiscriminate disapproval. It is understood by the convert.'[15] This was not a typical response; the majority, while not abandoning the Christian claim to finality and absoluteness, emphasized the need to treat other religions with respect. Among Methodist respondents, Henry Gulliford in Mysore wrote of 'intelligent sympathy … sympathetic and well-informed criticism will be most helpful. Such criticism should come from a true knowledge of the people.' William Balmer, writing from the African perspective, used the same word: 'sympathetic, striving earnestly to understand the native conception of things'; and from a Chinese perspective Arthur Cornaby pointed out that 'the ancient writing of China … contains many a passage on the majesty, righteousness and goodness of God' and laid stress on doing 'fullest justice to Chinese religious thought'.[16] None of the PM or UM missionaries was consulted – or if invited, none responded – but Henry Chapman, home from China (and President of the 1910 UM Conference), was a member of the Commission. One day of the Edinburgh Conference was devoted to the Commission's report, and Charles Monahan from Mysore contributed to the debate, not dissenting from the case for good will, yet warning that Christian tolerance must not overlook 'the ugly aspects of Hinduism … in the endeavour to bring out its better features.'[17] There was another side to that coin, however: the pitfall of comparing the best in one religious tradition with the worst in another. Christianity too had its 'ugly aspects', and it would soon become apparent just how ugly they could be. A very ugly war between so-called Christian nations was only four years away.

One problematic area was syncretism, defined as the amalgamation of the Christian gospel with the ideas and customs which previously shaped the life and thought of converts. Some of these were cultural practices which could be absorbed without compromising the gospel, and should have been recognized as welcome elements in the indigenization of Christianity. Some, it was held, were intimately related to a religious system incompatible with the gospel. James Hope Moulton, another of the Wesleyans in Edinburgh, did not make so sharp a distinction. He believed that:

---

[15]   Cracknell, *Justice, Courtesy and Love*, p. 238.

[16]   Ibid., pp. 199–202, 206.

[17]   Ibid., p. 276; Monahan's account of the debate and his subsequent reflections appeared in *The Foreign Field*, August 1910: pp. 350–2.

> Once a sure foundation had been laid ... stones from widely distant quarries could be brought and fitted into a superstructure which must shelter the whole world.[18]

For some decades to come, missionary policy ignored Moulton's case. The use of certain musical instruments, such as African drums, was rejected as 'pagan' and 'superstitious', as was 'the profound need of many peoples to include the living presence of their ancestors in an organic and holistic vision of reality'.[19] As a result evangelization continued to be handicapped by the perception of Christianity as a western, ethnocentric religion.

The uniqueness of Christ was not in dispute, but while some talked of a radical discontinuity implicit in conversion, others spoke of Christianity as fulfilment, not just of the Hebrew prophecies but of the aspirations of other religious teachers. Fulfilment theology was prominent in the responses to the Edinburgh questionnaire, and dominant at the next world conference, organized by the International Missionary Council (IMC) at Jerusalem in 1928.[20] The official statement from Jerusalem affirmed:

> We recognize as part of the one Truth that sense of the Majesty of God and the consequent reverence in worship, which are conspicuous in Islam; the deep sympathy for the world's sorrow and unselfish search for the way of escape, which are at the heart of Buddhism; the desire for contact with ultimate reality conceived as spiritual, which is prominent in Hinduism; the belief in a moral order of the universe and consequent insistence on moral conduct, which are inculcated by Confucianism.[21]

Not included in that litany was a mention of African religion. There was still a paucity of literature on the subject, though Edwin Smith had been writing about it since 1907. He used the traditional beliefs of the Ila people among whom he was working in central Africa as stepping-stones to Christian faith; for example, he used their praise names for God in his preaching. True, there was not one African religion but many (though the same might be said of Hindu religions, which were commonly treated as one). Smith recognized in Bantu religion a *praeparatio evangelica*:

> Jesus put his stamp of authority upon much of the teaching of the prophets ... He equally puts his stamp of approval on much that Africans have said about the Highest Being.[22]

---

[18]   Moulton, pp. 84-6, quoted in Cracknell, *Justice, Courtesy and Love*, p. 274.

[19]   Duraisingh, p. 69.

[20]   The IMC, conceived by the Edinburgh continuation committee, was set up in 1921.

[21]   *Report of the Jerusalem meeting of the International Missionary Council* (3 vols, London, Oxford University Press, 1928), vol. 1, p. 491.

[22]   E.W. Smith, *African Beliefs and Christian Faith* (London, USCL, 1936), p. 155, quoted in Young, p. 151.

Periodical conferences on world mission themes continued to be held, organized by the IMC until 1961 and then, after its merger with the World Council of Churches, by the WCC. In 1928 and 1938 the dominant concern was how to replace other religions by Christianity. The question of how to relate the living faith of Christians to the living faiths of others in a pluralistic world was not yet articulated. The idea that a close encounter with other forms of faith and spirituality might be mutually enriching was not voiced. Conferences, however, rarely shape attitudes; they reflect them; attitudes are shaped by events and experiences. In the 1940s the Shoah led to a re-appraisal of Jewish-Christian relationships; the Council of Christians and Jews, the oldest inter-faith organization in Britain, was founded in 1942. In India in 1948, Christians were greatly exercised by invitations to participate in memorial services for Gandhi. His ashes were committed to the water in several places, and memorial meetings were held everywhere. In some places, Christians refused to read their scripture in a multi-faith gathering; Ruth Anstey would not read the Bible at the service on the riverbank in Trichinopoly, because the Bhagavad Gita and Qu'ran were to be read as well. In Bangalore, on the other hand, where passages from the same scriptures were read, Harold Moulton of UTC (J.H. Moulton's son) read Psalm 23 and extracts from John 14 and Matthew 5. Some of the students at the Missionary Language School expressed their concern at an action which seemed to them to set Christianity on a par with Hinduism and Islam although Marcus Ward, another Methodist on the UTC staff, commented that no-one could miss the contrast between the Bible passages and the other readings.[23] In other places, the assumption that Christians would participate was taken as a matter of course.

In the 1960s the exploration of common religious experience in dialogue began to be promoted as the most fruitful mode of encounter between faith communities, but the concept called into question traditional understandings of key theological terms: evangelism, conversion, salvation and witness. To some the very idea of dialogue was a denial of everything they understood by those words. The new unit formed by the WCC-IMC merger in 1961 had to be named the Commission on World Mission *and Evangelism* (CWME), in order to affirm unequivocally that while mission had many facets, including education, healing, and working for justice and peace, it was incomplete without telling the story of Jesus and calling people to accept him as their Saviour. The MMS reported in 1958:

> A minister in Western Nigeria tells how he was bidden to come quickly to a new church some distance away to baptize five new young converts. 'But I can't be with you for four weeks,' he replied, looking over the vast itinerary before him. 'You must come now,' said the young man. 'I am entering college next week, and I do not want to go with my Muslim name. Having decided for Christ now,

---

[23]   Ruth Anstey and Margaret James, personal communications.

I want His mark on me, and a Christian name, so that all the students will know that I belong to Him.'[24]

The argument that both evangelism and dialogue were authentic forms of witness satisfied some of the critics, but the tension was never resolved. Proponents of dialogue were accused of a defective understanding of repentance and conversion. If converts did not completely abandon their old beliefs, customs, traditions and rituals – in some circumstances even their family and community – their motivation was suspect. But many Asian and African Christians had indeed taken the path of rejection, or their ancestors had, and yet could not condemn out of hand everything in their people's long quest for religious truth. There was still a place for dialogue, listening and learning.

In the light of such considerations the WCC, now with a Methodist, Philip Potter, at the helm, set up a Sub-Unit on Dialogue with People of Living Faiths and Ideologies in 1971, and chose the theme Salvation Today for its next conference on world mission and evangelism, held in Bangkok in 1972. There people from sixty different nations offered definitions of the word used to translate 'salvation' in their own tongues. In religious discourse, 'salvation from sin' was not to be seen only as referring to one's own selfishness, impurity and breaches of the ten commandments, but as salvation from the sin perpetrated by oppressors, warmongers, unethical businesses and land-grabbers. It was a conclusion that echoed J. Hope Moulton sixty years earlier, writing of the 'enthronement of righteousness'[25] which was at the heart of Jesus' preaching, praying and ministering, as the ultimate end of religion.

The different Christian attitudes to other faiths which had by now taken shape came to be classified under three heads: exclusive, inclusive and pluralist.[26] For the exclusivists, there was no worth in other religions, no salvation outside the Christian faith; 'No-one comes to the Father but by me' (John 14:6) and 'No other name by which we may be saved' (Acts 4:12) were their mantra.[27] Inclusivists recognized that other religions were not totally false but had insights and values which found their fulfilment in the gospel; whatever is good, true and beautiful in any culture or religion belongs to Christ. Pluralists believed that more than one religious teacher or system could mediate salvation or liberation. For exclusivists, dialogue was anathema; at the opposite extreme, evangelism was held to be an affront to the religious sensibilities of others. At issue was whether the prayer 'Your kingdom come, your will be done' could be answered only by all becoming Christians, and all other religions passing into history along with the worship of Zeus, Isis and Thor, or accomplished rather with the achievement of freedom of belief, conscience, expression and association, freedom from persecution on religious or any other grounds, freedom from poverty and fear.

---

[24]   *The Kingdom Overseas,* July-August 1958: pp. 18–19.
[25]   Moulton, p. 211.
[26]   A. Race, *Christians and Religious Pluralism* (London, SCM Press, 1983).
[27]   Cracknell, *Towards a New Relationship*, pp. 69–109.

In 1979 the WCC adopted a set of Guidelines on Dialogue which emerged from the Sub-Unit's work. They included affirmations such as:

> Dialogue can be welcomed as a way of obedience to the commandment 'You shall not bear false witness against your neighbour' ... The relationship of dialogue gives opportunity for authentic witness ... We feel able with integrity to commend the way of dialogue as one in which Jesus Christ can be confessed in our world today; at the same time we feel able with integrity to assure our partners in dialogue that we come not as manipulators but as genuine fellow-pilgrims ... To enter into dialogue requires an opening of the mind and heart to others. It is an undertaking which requires risk as well as a deep sense of vocation. It is impossible without sensitivity to the richly varied life of humankind.[28]

In 1981 a Sri Lankan Methodist, Wesley Ariarajah, succeeded the Indian theologian Stanley Samartha as Director of the WCC Sub-Unit on Dialogue. Kenneth Cracknell's account of its work recorded a perpetual ambivalence between 'two diverse sets of values, the one quite negative and exclusive, the other open to dialogue and co-operation'.[29] His headings included words that demonstrated his frustration: slowness, grudging, marginalization. Then came the 1991 WCC Assembly in Canberra, and a huge controversy sparked in the opening session by a Korean theologian, Chung Hyun Kyung, whose address, accompanied by Korean and aboriginal Australian dancers and drummers, invoked the spirits of the departed martyrs of many different cultures and histories. Pauline Webb, a former Vice-Moderator of the WCC Central Committee, wrote: 'Her presentation was received by some with rapturous applause, and by others in stunned silence.' In the debate that followed Chung was charged with syncretism and 'the question was raised as to what limits there are to theological diversity. How far is the Church called to Christianize the cultures among which the gospel is preached and how far is Christ to be presented as one who is relevant to all cultures?'[30] The sequel, Cracknell contended, was 'the virtual abandonment of the theological achievements and trajectories undertaken by the Dialogue sub-unit'.

The 1996 world mission conference in Salvador (where this account ends) disappointed those who had been privileged to sit down regularly with people of other creeds, and explore together the nature of their differences and their common convictions. Yet its statements were by no means anodyne:

> To dialogue is to witness to the love of God revealed in Christ. This requires mutual respect and openness to learn from others. It is wrong for Christians to

---

[28]   *Guidelines on Dialogue with People of Living Faiths and Ideologies* (Geneva, World Council of Churches Publications, 1979), p. 22.

[29]   K.R. Cracknell, *In Good and Generous Faith* (London, Epworth Press, 2005), p. 181.

[30]   Webb, *World-Wide Webb*, pp. 198–9.

pass judgment on partners in dialogue – just as they cannot impose conversion, which is the work of the Holy Spirit…

It is important to reaffirm … that 'we cannot point to any other way of salvation than Jesus Christ; at the same time we cannot set limits to the saving power of God.'…

On the journey of dialogue, Christians – as well as their partners from other religions – may be surprised, for Christ may encounter them where they would never have expected him…[31]

These affirmations, plainly in tune with John Wesley's Catholic Spirit, were far from universally endorsed, even within WCC circles. The murderous attack on New York and Washington in 2001 by Islamic extremists was a serious setback for inter-religious dialogue, yet had there never been such dialogue the atmosphere of hostility and suspicion would arguably have been even more extreme.

Methodist contributors to Faith Awareness

Cracknell and Harris were eminent figures in a succession of Methodist scholars, going back to William Goudie and James Hope Moulton in the early 1900s, via Edwin Smith and Geoffrey Parrinder. Some of the overseas Churches produced scholars and practitioners of equal eminence: Ariarajah, for example, acknowledged his debt to his fellow Sri Lankan Methodists, Daniel Niles and Lynn de Silva.

Voices from Asia

Sri Lanka has formed a striking number of Christian thinkers about faith relationships; it is a small island with Buddhist, Hindu, Muslim and Christian communities of long standing, and its history has been shaped by the relationship between them. Methodists, from Daniel Gogerly and Spence Hardy in the nineteenth century to Basil Jackson in the twentieth, were profoundly marked by their study of Buddhism, while Daniel Niles was one of the first Asian figures to stride the ecumenical stage: Executive Secretary in the WCC Department of Evangelism 1953–1959 and the first Secretary of the East Asia Christian Conference 1959–1968 as well as the second President of the autonomous Sri Lanka Methodist Conference in 1964. One of his major contributions was *Upon the Earth,* written in 1962 at the WCC's request. He set out the various Christian positions he discerned, ranging from the view that Christianity must supplant all other religions because they are purely human constructs, to one which held that:

---

[31]   Duraisingh, pp. 61–2.

the motive of Christian witness should be not one of seeking to make Christians of adherents of other religions, but of so presenting Jesus Christ to them that He Himself will become for them the point of reconception with respect to their own religion.[32]

Niles himself took the inclusivist position that the gospel addresses men and women to whom God is no stranger, though at times they rejoice in God and at other times they rebel against God. He helped Christians in the younger churches

to make greater sense of their own relation to the non-Christian world, which was no longer a world 'out there', 'to be occupied', but one they had inherited and where, together with persons of other faiths, they had to build communities.[33]

Lynn de Silva was one who rose to the challenge. For twenty years he directed the Study Centre for Religion and Society in Colombo, founded by Methodists in 1951, and made it an internationally recognized Ecumenical Institute for Study and Dialogue. He addressed the WCC assembly in Nairobi in 1975, when the problem of syncretism was raised again. Dialogue, he said, is 'a safeguard against syncretism rather than a means of temptation'; an essential route to discovering 'the Asian face of Jesus Christ, and for the church to be set free from institutional self-interest and play the role of a servant in building community.'[34]

Ariarajah in turn became an ardent advocate and practitioner of dialogue, convinced that

'religious pluralism is here to stay, and we will need to find theological bases and spiritual resources to accept and affirm the whole realm of human life as the area of God's love and activity'. [35] '

Of course,' he wrote,

in one sense I cannot say whether there is 'salvation' in Hinduism or not. My experience of God is rooted in Christ. But at the same time, I can no longer ignore the witness of my Hindu or Muslim neighbour to a life in God that has become profoundly meaningful to them. Since I believe in one God who is the source and sustenance of all life, the Hindu and Muslim witness has to

---

[32]   D.T. Niles, *Upon the Earth: The Mission of God and the Missionary Enterprise of the Churches* (London, Lutterworth Press, 1962), p. 229.

[33]   S.W. Ariarajah, *Hindus and Christians: A Century of Protestant Ecumenical Thought* (Grand Rapids, Eerdmans, 1991), p. 112.

[34]   Cracknell, *Justice, Courtesy and Love*, p. 195.

[35]   S.W. Ariarajah, *The Bible and People of Other Faiths* (Geneva, World Council of Churches Publications, 1985), p. 71.

become a part of my theological data. Without it I cannot think theologically in a pluralistic world.[36]

In 1986 Elizabeth Harris went to Colombo, not as a mission partner but to study at the Ecumenical Institute. Buddhism's emphasis on non-violence[37] and meditation appealed to her and although she acquired her doctorate in 1993 her primary interest was not in academic work but in experiencing Buddhism from the inside. She took the risk of 'passing over and coming back' – or perhaps not coming back. She worked with the Jesuit, Aloysius Pieris, a colleague of de Silva; she made Buddhist friends; she learned to meditate in the Buddhist manner; she joined in pilgrimages. She lived among people who valued silence, and learned that the 'detachment' taught by the Buddha is freedom from lust and greed, and has nothing to do with passive indifference to human suffering. She was confirmed in the conviction that Buddhism is blessed by God: wherever there is love and compassion and spiritual awareness, God is there. She was not primarily engaged in dialogue; she was not there to articulate the Christian faith. Her sharing in multi-religious initiatives for peace in a troubled land was as a woman of faith with no denominational label. After ten years she came back, her faith in Christ tested, shaken but intact, her spiritual awareness heightened, deepened and broadened. She was for a time the Methodist Church's Secretary for Inter Faith Relations. She enjoyed quoting:

> … it is better to honour other religions for this reason. By so doing, one's own religion benefits, and so do other religions, while doing otherwise harms one's own religion and the religions of others. Whoever praises his own religion, due to excessive devotion, and condemns others with the thought 'Let me glorify my own religion,' only harms his own religion. Therefore contact between religions (sometimes translated as 'concord' between religions) is good.[38]

The words, she would reveal, were those of King Asoka in India in the third century BCE.

Among missionaries to *India*, similarly, a wealth of scholarship was to be found. William Goudie, an officer of the WMMS from 1909 to 1922, cut his teeth in Tamil Nadu, where he ministered from 1882 to 1906. He made a special study of the Saiva Siddhanta, a Hindu revivalist movement, and spoke frequently at meetings in Madras for educated Hindus. In a paper read to the Madras Missionary Conference in 1900 he said:

---

[36] S.W. Ariarajah, *Not without my Neighbour* (Geneva, World Council of Churches Publications, 1999), p. 123.

[37] E.J. Harris, *Buddhism for a Violent World: A Christian Reflection* (London, Epworth Press, 2010).

[38] Peter Bell Memorial Lecture, March 2010.

... a knowledge of those things to which the [Hindu] mind has already attained ... will bring to us sympathy, and not seldom inspiration; and it is only by the sympathetic touch between mind and mind that we may hope to lead men from the entanglements of error and half truths into the light and freedom of perfect truth and wisdom.[39]

He was cautious, however, about the direction in which Edinburgh seemed to be pointing, 'very much afraid lest the new attitude should be supposed to involve too high an estimate of the elements of truth to be found in non-Christian systems'.[40] He made a reasoned case, but it would be foolish to suppose he was not influenced by the rough treatment he received in the course of his first tour in India, where he was pelted with stones more than once: 'With these stones,' he would say, 'God will build his Church.'

For forty years after Edinburgh, the attentions of South Indian church leaders were focused on their relationships with one another. J.S.M. Hooper, for example, was remembered for his role in the theological and diplomatic discussions which led to the CSI[41] rather than his important 1929 translation from ancient Tamil of selections of the *Hymns of the Alvars*. But in the 1960s there were, among the Methodists who were ordained as presbyters of the CSI, some who made the relationship of Christianity and Hinduism their special interest.

Eric Lott, who spent most of his ministry in theological education in India, made a close study of the *bhakti* tradition of Hinduism. He said that it was the hymns of Charles Wesley which predisposed him to study *bhakti*; in an essay entitled *All Loves Excelling* (2000) he described them as 'devotional love songs' and compared them with the writings of *bhakti* poets for whom 'the soul's sharing in divine love is the highest goal of the human journey'.[42] He wrote that God's grace is to be found not only in Christianity; the *bhakti* tradition rejoices in the experience of God's compassion and forgiveness. His work went

> beyond the trading of texts across traditions. Rather, he offers a springboard, built on Methodist tradition, from where we can dive into 'the other' on its own terms.[43]

Roy Pape was a systematic theologian and insisted that 'other religion' was, like experience, revelation, scripture, tradition and reason, a formative factor in theology; it could not simply be subsumed under 'culture'. He was excited by the Hindu analogy between the relation of the human personality and mind to the

[39] Lewis, pp. 120–1.

[40] Moulton, p. 93, quoted in Cracknell, *Justice, Courtesy and* Love, p. 277.

[41] pp. 154–6.

[42] E.J. Lott, 'All Loves Excelling: A Methodist Reflection on Hindu Faith' in M. Forward & others (eds), *A Great Commission: Christian Hope and Religious Diversity* (Bern, Peter Lang, 2000), p. 246, quoted by E.J. Harris in *Epworth Review* July 2008: p. 73.

[43] Harris, ibid.

human body they inhabit, and the relation of God to the universe: our personality is incarnate – made flesh – in the physical body through which we express ourselves, and similarly God communicates and operates through the medium of God's creation. 'To describe God ... as Being, Intelligence and Joy is in no way to depersonalize God. Rather it is to conceive of him/her/it as beyond our profoundest thoughts, yet as having a real affinity with our personal reality'. To say that God is incarnate in creation does not, he argued, 'call into question the uniqueness of God's incarnation in Christ'. Like Lott, he was attracted by the *bhakti* approach to God 'in total self-surrender ... with no attempt to justify oneself by one's own good works.'[44]

Two missionaries to North India made significant contributions to faith relationships, one as a scholar and one as a practitioner. Frank Whaling spent four years, 1962–1966, in Varanasi and went on to a distinguished academic career in Edinburgh; *An Approach to Dialogue: Hinduism and Christianity,* the first of his many books, was published in India.[45] John Hastings went to Bengal in 1951 and stayed for twenty years.[46] His practical engagement with men and women of other faiths, in India, in Britain and in Bangladesh, was outstanding. When ten million refugees, Hindu and Muslim, crossed into India in 1971 at the time of the Bangladesh independence war, he was at the forefront of the United Relief Service, as well as supporting the Volunteer Service Corps of 2,000 refugee teachers who maintained morale in the camps and prepared for the return to a free Bangladesh. In 1985 he was instrumental in setting up the Bangladesh Inter-Religious Council for Peace and Justice, and such was the respect in which he was held that when he returned once again in retirement it was at the invitation of a Muslim organization, the Dhaka Ahsania Mission. Relieving suffering and liberating the poor are tasks for people of all religious persuasions, calling for concerted action in mutual trust.

India produced its own outstanding scholars in the field. Israel Selvanayagam was a missionary in reverse. A CSI presbyter, he was sent to England in 1996 under the auspices of the World Church in Britain Partnership[47] to teach at Wesley College in Bristol and was later Principal of the United College of the Ascension. He took the view that neither evangelism nor dialogue can be authentic without the other and wrote that

> dialogue need not compromise the Christian's conviction that the Gospel has universal relevance. Rather, it can deepen faith, purifying it of false claims and enhancing its communication ... In a multi-religious context it is not wrong to believe that we have a right to be understood, to try to remove others'

44   K.R. Cracknell and C. Lamb, *Theology on Full Alert,* (London, British Council of Churches, 1984), pp. 40–42.

45   F. Whaling, *An Approach to Dialogue with Hinduism* (Lucknow, Lucknow Publishing House, 1966).

46   p. 122.

47   p. 265.

misunderstanding of us. At the same time, we have a responsibility to attempt to understand others as they understand themselves. We will allow them to remove our misunderstandings about them.[48]

Among the mid-century *China* missionaries, Jack Chamberlayne, though his service there was cut off after a mere three years, had a life-long interest in its multiple religious traditions and practices. He had virtually no opportunity after 1948 to engage with Chinese people in an exploration of their beliefs, but he was an assiduous scholar and familiar with the literature, from the *Analects* of Confucius to *Researches into Chinese Superstitions.*[49]

Voices from Africa

Edwin Smith, one of the PM pioneers in Zambia, was the first serious student of African religion and the only missionary to be elected President of the Royal Anthropological Institute. An early book, *The Religion of Lower Races,* came out in 1923. The title was not his own; he apologized for it in a subsequent work and refused to sign a copy in New York twenty years later. In the Hartley Lecture, *The Golden Stool,* which he delivered at the PM Conference of 1926, he suggested that African baptismal names, dances, drama, indigenous music, and the Christianization of initiation and marriage ceremonies would help Christianity in Africa to be more rooted in African experience. It was essential, he wrote, 'to purge our missionary enterprise of all taint of cultural imperialism.'

Geoffrey Parrinder began his ministry in Dahomey (now Bénin) and the Ivory Coast, and was enthralled by the religion of West Africa. He spent the years from 1933 to 1946 there, with interruptions due to the war. In 1949, the year of his first book, *West African Religion,*[50] he took up a post in Ibadan where he lectured in Religious Studies. His DD thesis on *Religion in an African City* (1953)[51] was perhaps the best of his numerous books. From 1958 until his retirement in 1977 he taught at King's College London. It was a period when immigration from Asia was becoming a significant factor in the religious demography of Britain, and he devoted his attention increasingly to Asian faiths. His work on Indian religions, Islam and comparative themes, most notably *Avatar and Incarnation* (1970),[52]

---

[48]   I. Selvanayagam, *Evangelism and Inter-Faith Dialogue* (Birmingham, Selly Oak Colleges, 1993), p. 23.

[49]   J.H. Chamberlayne, *China and its Religious Inheritance* (London, Janus Publishing, 1993).

[50]   E.G. Parrinder, *West African Religion* (London, Epworth Press, 1949).

[51]   E.G. Parrinder, *Religion in an African City* (London, Oxford University Press, 1953).

[52]   E.G. Parrinder, *Avatar and Incarnation* (London, Faber & Faber, 1970).

appealed to a wide reading public and helped to promote better understanding and closer collaboration between people of different faiths in a multi-cultural society.[53]

Parrinder's *African Traditional Religion* (1962)[54] was followed in 1973 by another work with the same title, written by his successor at Ibadan, Bolaji Idowu. Idowu was the continent's leading Methodist authority on the subject, though both Kwesi Dickson of Ghana and Gabriel Setiloane of South Africa were well-versed in it and included important chapters in their books on theology in Africa.[55] (Idowu was later President of the Nigerian Conference and precipitated a radical 'Africanization' of its structures which divided the Church.[56]) Like Parrinder, Idowu struggled to find a general term for primal African beliefs, which for the most part include both a supreme God and other divinities too.[57] He rejected 'animism' and 'fetishism' along with paganism and heathenism; his preferred expression was 'diffused monotheism'. 'I do not know of any place in Africa where the ultimacy is not accorded to God,' he wrote.[58] But alongside the supreme God or creator, most Africans traditionally worshipped other gods or spirits, often associated with some local tree, rock or river, and communed with their departed ancestors, a few of whom were deified. Another general feature was the use of charms, amulets and traditional medicine which, Idowu wrote, neither modernization nor evangelization would change. Resorting to, and even smuggling into hospital, medication prepared and consecrated in the traditional manner, was commonplace. In matters pertaining to the passages and crises of life, most Africans, although outwardly professing faith in Christianity or Islam, would, he held, continue to turn to the beliefs and practices of their ancestors for succour. Religion is by nature dynamic and syncretistic, and 'It does not yet appear what we shall be'.

Islam demanded every bit as much attention as the primal religions of Africa. In 1952 MMS and CMS jointly commissioned Spencer Trimingham, who had been a missionary in the Sudan and Egypt, to spend a year surveying the impact of Islam in West Africa. His forthright conclusions referred to 'the tragic history' of the relationship of Christianity and Islam and the need for 'penitence first and foremost'.

> We need the humility to acknowledge and honour the genuine seeker after the truth whatever religion he belongs to. We need to remember that the attitude of Christians towards Islam largely determines the attitude of Muslims towards Christians. Christians and Muslims, neighbours on the material plane, strangers on the spiritual plane, have yet to learn the things that belong unto their peace…

---

[53] M.H.F. Forward, *A Bag of Needments* (Bern, Peter Lang, 1998).

[54] E.G.S. Parrinder, *African Traditional Religion* (London, Hutchinson, 1954).

[55] K.A. Dickson, *Theology in Africa* (London, Darton Longman & Todd, 1984); G.M. Setiloane, *African Theology* (Johannesburg, Skotaville Publishers, 1986).

[56] See pp. 212–13.

[57] Parrinder, *Religion in an African City,* p. 11.

[58] E.B. Idowu, *African Traditional Religion* (London, SCM Press, 1973), p. 135.

Westerners are indebted to Christianity for a realization of the infinite worth of the individual, and that may be our gift to Africa, but our misdirected emphasis on purely personal salvation has contributed to the chaos within African society. Africa has to teach us that salvation is only possible for the individual-in-community.[59]

In 1959, a year after the All Africa Conference of Churches first met, the Islam in Africa Project was formed. Ten years later the AACC Assembly in Abidjan was urging that

If we want *true* dialogue, we have to be prepared for our own knowledge of God to be deepened by our encounter with Muslims. We believe that Christ is at work in this deepening of the faith of Muslims and Christians, although we must not minimise the fundamental differences between Muslim and Christian ideas of God and although we still hope that they may one day confess Jesus Christ as Lord.[60]

The Project was later renamed, to avoid misunderstandings, the Programme for Christian-Muslim Relations in Africa (PROCMURA). With headquarters in Nairobi, it built a network of regional and country advisers in both East and West Africa, funded by grants from European agencies including MMS. One of the first was the British Methodist, John Crossley, in Nigeria.[61] Crossley wrote:

Islam denies the most precious truths of our faith in Christ ... but this must not prevent us from appreciating the piety and goodness of the devout Muslim ... Our approach to him is not 'Listen to me, I've got a monopoly of the truth, I've come to convert you', but rather 'Let us listen to one another, and may God lead us both to deeper knowledge of His truth.' Such an approach is not a compromise, for we are convinced that the truth is Christ; but it makes all the difference to the impression of Christianity ... the Muslim receives from us.[62]

PROCMURA's work was based on the belief that there was no contradiction between faithful Christian witness in an interfaith environment, which is an integral aspect of Christian identity, and constructive engagement between Christians and

---

[59]   J.S. Trimingham, *The Christian Church and Islam in West Africa* (London, SCM Press, 1955), pp. 40, 53.

[60]   *Engagement:* the Second AACC Assembly, 1969 (Nairobi, All Africa Conference of Churches, 1970), p. 117.

[61]   In the 1990s first Cokkie van't Leven and then Martha Frederiks, both Dutch ministers, were based in Banjul and hosted by The Gambia District – though Frederiks complained that Methodist Synod reports consistently failed to include any reflection on Christian-Muslim relations or on witness to Muslims.

[62]   *The Kingdom Overseas*, April 1965: pp.18–21.

Muslims in building the bridges of mutual understanding that enable and underpin peaceful co-existence.

In 1962, two young missionaries arrived in Eastern Nigeria. Both Donald English, who taught for three years at Trinity College, Umuahia, and Kenneth Cracknell, whose missionary service was cut short by the Biafran war in 1968, were to have worldwide influence within and beyond Methodism, English as an evangelist and apologist and Cracknell as an inter-faith specialist. Both acknowledged their debt to all that their years in Africa taught them. Engaging with people of other faith became Cracknell's life-long passion. An ardent advocate and skilful practitioner of dialogue, he pioneered the work of the BCC on inter-faith relations and adumbrated four principles, which were enshrined in the BCC's Guidelines in 1981, encapsulating more economically the 1979 WCC guidelines:

> Dialogue begins when people meet each other.
> Dialogue depends upon mutual understanding and mutual trust.
> Dialogue makes it possible to share in service to the community.
> Dialogue becomes the medium of authentic witness.[63]

He dealt skilfully with the verses in John 14 and Acts 4 that led some to demand a total condemnation of other religions and the conversion of their followers. His familiarity with the Biblical languages often disarmed his critics. He explored how Christians may engage in dialogue, mutual support and practical co-operation with devout believers of other creeds without being unfaithful to Jesus Christ or betraying the missionary message. In Ariarajah's words, 'without denying any of the positive aspects of mission,' Cracknell challenged Christians to re-think their attitudes to others free from 'prejudices stemming from the assumption of cultural superiority'.[64] He concluded that:

> It is not only perfectly proper for [Christians] to bear witness to their Christian faith among people of other faiths; it is imperative that they do; otherwise they are not contributing anything to the conversation. Indeed if they are silent or diffident this will be profoundly disappointing to their partners, who characteristically expect Christians to be as genuine and as committed as they themselves are. Because there is a conversation, Christians must expect to hear the witness of people of different faith and ... be blessed by being able also to listen to the good news that they have to share. This is the way Christians become fellow-pilgrims and not 'manipulators' ... Such is mission in bold humility, and it makes friends across the faith-barriers.[65]

---

[63]   *Relations with People of other Faiths: Guidelines for Dialogue in Britain* (London, British Council of Churches, 1981).

[64]   Ariarajah, *Hindus and Christians*, p. 191 citing Cracknell, *Towards a New Relationship*, p. 9.

[65]   Cracknell, *In Good and Generous Faith*, pp.177–8.

A striking example of this approach is to be found in the story of the Kenyan minister, Elijah Shimbira. For the first twenty years of his life his name was Muhammed Ali. Brought up in the Muslim part of his village, he had been befriended by his cousin, a Methodist Local Preacher. This man did not preach to him but procured a Swahili version of the Qur'an and studied it carefully. He could then, from time to time, talk to Muhammed Ali about Jesus, the honoured prophet Isa, on the basis of the Qur'an. On one occasion Muhammed Ali flew into a rage and asked him to go away and stay away. The next day came a message and a gift to ask forgiveness for causing his anger. So they remained friends, continued to converse, and eventually Muhammed Ali was baptized Elijah. Later, ordained, he took a leading role in the Kenya Methodist Church's mission among the Maasai and its outreach into Tanzania.

The Impact in Britain

Christians and Jews had for long lived alongside each other, if not exactly together, but the arrival of Asians and their various religions made the indigenous British, in places where the newcomers settled, take notice. There were many parts of Britain where there were none of these strangers to notice, but in the cities and industrial towns, there were at least passing contacts. Entering one another's homes was a rare event, except for small numbers of women who undertook to help Asian women with their English. But there were new, difficult and inescapable questions to face. How should religion be approached in a school where children came from homes in which different faiths were practised? What happened to the 'civic service' tradition when the next mayor was a Sikh? Where there was a redundant church building and a Muslim community without a mosque, was it possible to promote good community relations without sacrificing Christian convictions? What should happen when people with different faith-commitments fell in love? The questions became more insistent with the advent of mosques, gurdwaras and temples. Here and there local inter-faith groups were formed; it was often people who had worked abroad who were the prime movers. But such groups were small. While there were Methodists who had strong convictions, both for and against such contacts, most remained bemused.

The evangelical tendency saw Donald English as their spokesman and respected his views. What he had to say carried weight. In 1989 he summarized the range of Christian attitudes to other faiths, and indicated what he felt to be 'nearest to the teaching of Jesus, by word and deed, as we have it in the New Testament':

> Jesus himself was constantly surprising people by the way in which he declared the most unlikely people to be acceptable, when those who expected to be praised by him often got strong criticism … It is easy to dismiss people whom we do not know. The test is, as Jesus himself said, that you know the tree by its fruit. Whatever else we affirm or deny about other faiths and their members, we

do well to see that it accords with what can be seen to be the case in their lives ... we must be on guard against comparing the best in our faith with the worst in others ... the major factor is what God chooses to do with our relating or not relating, our doing or speaking, our concerns and our sensitivities.[66]

If ignorance and misunderstanding were to be dispelled, the subject had to be included in the formation of ministers. Cracknell initiated the Association for Ministerial Training in a Multifaith Society, which arranged conferences for student ministers and for those in service whose courses, years before, had taken little or no account of other religions. Changing the way systematic theology was taught in Methodist colleges was not accomplished overnight, but his work and that of his successor, Martin Forward, at Wesley House in Cambridge, and the appointment of Selvanayagam to Wesley College in Bristol, were influential.

The most delicate and divisive question, in Britain and Ireland as well as far-away lands where Christians were in a small minority, was 'Can we pray together?' Living together, working together and studying together were forms of encounter which were less threatening. Participating in the spiritual and liturgical practices of other religious traditions was another matter. Most inter-faith groups settled for a period of silence, perhaps around a lighted candle; sometimes events were arranged at which participants read from their own scriptures. To enter more fully into the formal worship of a particular faith community was for most, whatever their affiliation, a step too far. A hybrid marriage service, for example, was as unthinkable as a Catholic–Protestant wedding prior to (and in many places long after) Vatican II.

Methodists, like other Christians who were enthusiastic supporters of mission and missionaries overseas, were faced with the problem of how to translate their arm's length enthusiasm for the missionary enterprise in relation to the new arrivals on the doorstep. Some became prominent in inter-faith activity locally or nationally. But many were perplexed. They could see how inappropriate and unproductive aggressive evangelism would be in the British context, and wondered what missionaries had been doing abroad. They recognized that it was the right of other people to cherish their beliefs, to publicize their activities and to have their own sacred places. What went for Britain went for foreign lands too. Consequently enthusiasm for the overseas missionary enterprise waned, and in local churches and circuits it was sometimes hard to find younger people to promote it when older folk relinquished the role. Generous in their support for relief and human need, their support for world mission funds declined. It would be some time before a re-visioned theology of mission for a globalized and pluralistic world emerged.

---

[66]   M.H.F. Forward (ed.), *God of all Faith* (London, Methodist Church Home Mission Division, 1989), pp. 85–7.

Chapter 13

The World at War

More than three times as many people perished in the Second World War as in the 1914–1918 conflict. It was, far more than the 'Great War', a global conflict, though it affected some areas of the world more severely than others. The report of the Upper Burma District for 1940 spoke of being remote from the theatre of war and unaffected by the hostilities – no blackouts, no rationing: a short-lived calm, as it soon turned out. Other countries had been plunged into war well before 1939: the Spanish Civil War, the Italian wars of aggression in Ethiopia and Libya, the Japanese invasion of China, had already taken a terrible toll.

When Barcelona, a Republican stronghold, fell to Franco in January 1939, the Methodist churches were forcibly closed. Franco was bent on ridding Spain of the 'Protestant heresy'. The four Spanish ministers took refuge in France. Subsequently two of them went to South America as missionaries under the Methodist Episcopal Church while the Capo brothers were eventually able to return. The valiant English deaconess Isabel Adam, remained at her post, with a small congregation on the outskirts of Barcelona, right through WW2.

Italy entered the war in June 1940. The Chairman and sole missionary, Charles Armstrong, left and communication was severed. The Italian congregations were thinly dispersed from the Alps to Sicily; moreover many Italian Methodists were scattered far and wide and unable to attend worship. Before the war the church had devised a way of keeping in touch with them, in the form of a cyclostyled order of service with a short sermon, which by 1939 had a circulation of 2,500. The contents of this *Culto per Isolati* were contributed by a different church each week, and used in its Sunday worship. A soldier in Libya wrote:

> It is a great joy to receive the Culto per Isolati, which enables me to feel myself spiritually united with my brethren in the faith during the hour of common prayer and meditation. Here in this land of Africa, burnt by the sun, living in a tent, one feels God very near during this hour of Fellowship.[1]

War brought this ministry to an end; Italian Methodism was hard-pressed to survive, and one of the few communications that got through to London was a request to throw in its lot with the Waldensians, though that came to nothing.[2]

---

[1] This translation was included in the MMS Annual Report for 1939.

[2] p. 162.

Fred Rea, an Irish minister serving in Rhodesia, saw front-line action in the Italian campaign as a chaplain with the Rhodesian troops, part of the South African forces. After a year's training in Egypt, he and his men reached Italy in April 1944:

> A dozen shells fell all around us. We dropped flat, another lad and I, side by side. Suddenly he cried out, 'I've had it!' He had been shot through the lungs.[3]

Rea survived, was awarded an MBE and returned to Rhodesia where he had an influential ministry for another forty years.

In China, the Japanese invasion became full-scale war in 1937. Major cities like Guangzhou, Shanghai and Nanjing fell by the end of the year. People fled in their thousands as the Japanese armies approached. During 1939 there was a mass migration westward, to Chongqing, the provisional capital of free China, and the provinces of Guizhou and Yunnan. Universities, businesses, industries were relocated. But only the well-to-do could make such long journeys. Most Chinese could only melt into the surrounding countryside, and often had to move back into occupied zones when their meagre resources ran out. The Japanese allowed crossing points through the battle lines, so that people could move to free China, because this reduced the number of mouths to be fed in the occupied areas. Famine was rife during the war years.

A 1945 report gives a flavour of what life was like for Christians under the occupation.

> During the past eight years the whole of the Hupeh District lay within the Japanese area of occupation, the country circuits being on the unfortunate fringe of their influence where incessant guerrilla warfare made steady work and even settled life impossible ... For all it was a time of intense nervous strain, and ministers, scattered in lonely country stations in an atmosphere of depression and terrorism, cut off from fellowship with one another, and preoccupied with the economic struggle, became spiritually exhausted. The hospitals of the District proved to be a rallying-point for the Christian workers. Here several groups were able to express their Christianity in non-partisan service for their fellow countrymen, while maintaining the fellowship ... they did this heroically.[4]

In contrast the North China District, in Japanese hands from an early stage, was able to carry on much of its work with little disruption, and when news came of the London blitz the District arranged a collection and sent £15 for the 'relief of bombed fellow-Christians'. The destruction of the Laoling hospital was a devastating blow: it was burnt down by Japanese troops on Christmas Day 1939 as punishment for treating wounded Chinese irregulars.

---

[3]   K. Rea, *The Best is Yet to Be: Fifty Years in Zimbabwe with Fred and Kathleen Rea* (Harare, Munn Publishing, 1992), p. 41.

[4]   Quoted by Senior, *The China Experience,* p. 36.

The South-West China District lay some 2,000 miles from the battlefields. For a while it was unusually well-staffed, because missionaries returning from furlough, unable to reach their old stations, were redeployed there. The Central China Christian College, driven from its spacious compound in Wuchang by the Japanese advance, was evacuated first to Guilin, a forty-six day trek. But soon Guilin too was threatened and envoys were sent to Kunming to scout for suitable premises near the Burma border. They were told of a rich landlord who wanted to improve his village and had offered the use of a temple to one of the migrant universities. The university had no use for it, but the College snapped it up. Moving everyone there was a difficult and protracted operation. The Guangzhou United Theological College also took up residence there.

Missionaries in the occupied zones were at first placed under house arrest and were still able to communicate freely with their Chinese colleagues and get special passes for pastoral purposes. Later the Japanese decided to banish them and they were removed to Shanghai, to be shipped to Mozambique. Shipping was scarce and only a few sailed before the policy changed again. Seventy missionaries, with twenty children, were interned in Civil Assembly Centres for the rest of the war. Camp life had irritations of every sort but conditions were better than many anticipated and among the guards there were some, at least, who were described by internees as capable and considerate.[5]

In Burma, few took preparations for war at all seriously until the attack on Pearl Harbor. Florence Cleaver was taken aback by a letter from WW Secretary Hilda Porter warning her at all costs to avoid being interned by the Japanese – the thought had never entered her head. But Mandalay was bombed in February 1942, only a day after Clement Chapman, the Chairman, had circulated evacuation instructions to all missionaries. Most were able to fly out to Chittagong on army transport planes in the following weeks. They were limited to 16lb of luggage so, despite the heat, wore as many clothes as they could. From Chittagong they were taken to Calcutta by truck. Florence Cleaver and Sister Elsie Bush were taking a break in the Chin Hills and their host, hearing of the fall of Rangoon, led them out over remote mountain passes. The last few men also left overland to a railhead in India; Chapman's journey remains shrouded in mystery.[6] Behind a bamboo curtain, Burmese Methodism fragmented.

> Responsibility rested on the shoulders of unknown and hitherto untried local church leaders … They had no precedents to follow, so had to extemporize, bend, ignore and break the rules.[7]

---

[5] Ibid., p. 50.

[6] M.D. Leigh, *Conflict, politics and proselytism* (Manchester, Manchester University Press, 2011), pp. 110–123.

[7] Ibid., p. 129.

They suffered more at the hands of the Burmese Independence Army, which regarded Christians as traitors, than from the Japanese. Wesley Church in Mandalay was totally bomb-damaged and the mission house and girls' school were requisitioned in 1942; Mahazayabon, a prosperous suburb of Mandalay, became a gathering point, and almost every Sunday to the war's end services were held, morning and evening, in private villas.

In north India the ministerial missionaries all had duties as chaplains to the forces, which occupied much of their time. The vernacular work was largely left to their Indian colleagues. The Indian ministers grew in stature; they gained confidence, won respect, and the church progressed all the more rapidly towards maturity. Missionaries escaping from China and Burma landed on Indian doorsteps, some deeply traumatized, all in need of rest and recuperation, before they could be redeployed or repatriated.

Until 1943 the territories of Dahomey, Togo and the Ivory Coast, which made up the French West Africa District, were controlled by the Vichy government. The French missionaries were all called up for military service; but after two months they were released and permitted to continue their church work. Their main difficulty was financial, for it was impossible to send money drafts from Britain.

Naval warfare featured prominently in the Caribbean ever since the days of pirates and privateers and Nelson's later sea-battles with the French. Submarine warfare arrived in 1941, when a U-boat blew up the oil refinery on Aruba. Thereafter inter-island traffic was severely affected. But published reports during the war years were more concerned with the Jamaica earthquake in 1941, the large numbers emigrating from the region and the rise of fanatical, emotional sects in the Virgin Islands.

At the outbreak of the war, many missionaries about to go on or return from furlough had to put their plans on hold as ships were requisitioned. Farewells said, cases packed, they waited, some for months, for a passage. 'Brides-elect', as the Society's 1940 report quaintly called them, had to await their opportunity. Somehow news of their sailing got through to their fiancés and somehow the men, forsaking all other duties, got to the docks in time to welcome them. At least one was greeted in Bombay with the words, 'Do you want to get married tomorrow or this afternoon?' – and opted for the afternoon. A report from the Gold Coast said that:

> The African ministers and people have been most anxious about the safety
> of missionaries and (appreciate their) willingness to face the dangers of sea
> voyages in order to return to the work.[8]

Between the declaration of war and 15 April 1941, the Society recorded a total of 589 persons – men, women, children – sailing to or from Britain, and reaching their destinations safely. But that day claimed the lives of Alec Fenby and Herbert

---

8   MMS Report 1940, p. 36.

Williams when their convoy was attacked and their ship sunk.[9] Thereafter sailings were curtailed to a minimum, and family separations were prolonged. Securing a passage was hard, and one or two India-bound brides were advised to masquerade as nurses travelling out to tend the troops. John Barker in Barrackpore, after a seven-year engagement, discovered that his Win, unable to wear her ring, had been assiduously courted by a young sergeant for three weeks while waiting for an onward passage through Suez. But the nurse-fiction enabled her to escape his attentions and soon there was another ring on her finger ...[10]

In Britain paper rationing restricted the production of Prayer Manuals and other literature. Work on the new Mission House in Marylebone Road was halted, and the BBC occupied the completed lower floors. It was from 25 Marylebone Road that King Haakon broadcast to the people of Norway; it is said that when he arrived the commissionaire asked his name, and then rang upstairs to announce 'a Mr King from Norway'. Despite repeated air-raid warnings the work at headquarters got done, as it did across the capital. The Secretaries were concerned to maintain the morale of missionaries who were not only contending with diverse privations themselves but were desperately concerned for their families and friends in Britain. Harold Rattenbury

> was a master of spin – the blitz was 'badly aimed bombs' and England was unfazed by invasion threats. Rattenbury remonstrated with the *Methodist Recorder* for publishing photographs of bombed-out churches and urged the missionaries to take no notice of them. His letters concluded with rip-roaring phrases like 'our people are so optimistic' and the 'Church and Nation are in good heart'.[11]

But it was a world war, and took its terrible toll around the globe. At home and abroad, lives were scarred by loss and grief, by separation and privation, and – even for those who were spared the worst – by tension and weariness, frustration and perplexity. Methodism was familiar with all these moods and emotions, but at least it did not fall prey to paralysis and stagnation. Far from it. The MMS report on 1943 was entitled *Only the Scaffolding.*

> In the building of the Churches overseas, the Missionary Societies are the scaffolding, indispensable for a time, but only a temporary expedient. As the rising Churches of China, of India, of Ceylon, of Africa, of the West Indies approach completion, the scaffolding must be removed. It is then that the quality of our work, the grandeur of the design, will be revealed.

---

[9]   p. 38.
[10]   J.H. Barker, privately circulated memoir.
[11]   Leigh, p. 110, quoting letters to Vincent Shepherd in the last quarter of 1940.

The last thirty years have witnessed startling progress in the growth and development of the 'Younger Churches' overseas. National Christians of different lands are rising up to take over the responsibility of leadership, to be masters in their own house. They must increase; we must decrease...

And, wonderful as it may seem, the mighty upheavals in the Far East have contributed more to this than anything else has done – or could have done. The war is of necessity throwing more responsibility upon the Churches. The Nationalist movements are developing the truly national instincts; and we look for these to influence the life of the Churches – the Indian sense of worship and the African love of song and rhythm, the Chinese powers of organisation, and – may we not add? – the Japanese delight in art and courtesy...

Year by year, piece by piece, the scaffolding is being taken down, the spirit of devolution is prevailing everywhere...

And the resounding conclusion: the MMS

must begin afresh in new places, lay new foundations and erect new scaffoldings for new Churches; and in this we can count on the eager co-operation of our brethren of the 'Younger Churches'.[12]

---

[12]   MMS Annual Report 1943 (published July 1944), p. 2.

Chapter 14
Autonomy and Indigenization

The Churches which set up their own Conferences in the nineteenth century were all under white leadership and with a considerable emigrant European membership (except in the case of France, where emigration was not a factor). The 'three-self' ideals – self-government, self-support and self-propagation – advanced by Rufus Anderson and Henry Venn from the middle of the century were widely shared in principle, but the day of self-government for Christians not of European stock was still remote. Susannah Wesley's hero Ziegenbalg in Tranquebar, whose avowed aim was an Indian church with an Indian ministry, and who ordained a Hindu convert in 1733, was far ahead of his time. The WMMS centenary history, contrasting the failure of the first West Indian Conference with the Canadian, Australasian and South African Conferences, concluded:

> Each of those other countries was occupied by numerous and prosperous British communities, amongst which Methodism had rooted itself with the prospects of large development, supplying the basis for independent Church institutions and aggressive missionary work. In the West Indies these favouring conditions, indispensable for the success of the project in hand, were wanting, and laymen competent for Church business and assistance in counsel were few and far between.[1]

It was evidently the common view that for autonomy to work 'prosperous British communities' were required, and so the transfer of authority to Africans and Asians had to wait. The desirability of training an indigenous ministry was not in question. The debates, over many years, were about how soon it was practicable, about the criteria by which to judge a person's suitability, about the sort of training and probation that were required, about whether they should be under close supervision or allowed to minister in remote appointments, about how many native pastors could be effectively supervised, about what should be entrusted to them and expected of them in the missionary's absence – and just possibly about how soon an indigenous circuit superintendent or District Chairman could be contemplated.

But the British Conference did none the less regard autonomy as the natural and logical outcome of church growth and maturity. A Conference commission on 'The missionary obligation of the Church' affirmed in its report in 1955 that autonomy rather than a world-wide Conference was the goal. In this respect British Methodism may be distinguished from American Methodism, which saw itself as

---

[1]   Findlay and Holdsworth, vol. 2, p. 450.

a 'global communion', incorporating under the General Conference the Central and Annual Conferences in Africa, Asia and Europe as well as in the Americas. Immediately after Union, the 1933 Minutes of Conference listed 36 Overseas Districts. By 1996 there were two – Togo became autonomous in the year 2000 and The Gambia in 2009. It might then be supposed that, just as political agitation brought new nations into being, beginning with India and Pakistan in 1947 and continuing through the 1950s and 1960s until Zimbabwe in turn achieved its goal in 1980, so a parallel clamour for independence eventually – and more tardily – brought about the transfer of authority from the British Conference to newly autonomous Churches. Whereas in the United States, a nation untrammelled by any Empire of which to divest itself but wedded to its spheres of influence, the UMC was not plagued by pangs of colonial conscience and took a different stance: one in which the American influence continued to dominate.

The picture is in fact less simple. It was during a period of colonial expansion, not decolonization, that Venn wrote of the 'euthanasia of the mission' – by which he meant not an end to foreign missionary service, but an end to foreign missionary control of indigenous churches. And Anderson, who likewise favoured devolution, was an American. Lecturing at Andover Seminary in 1866, he commended 'the apostolic example':

> When [Paul] formed local churches, he did not hesitate to ordain presbyters over them, the best he could find; and then to throw upon the churches, thus officered, the responsibilities of self-government, self-support and self-propagation; ... [thus our] grand object is to plant and multiply self-reliant, efficient churches, composed wholly of native converts, each church complete, with its pastors of the same race with the people.[2]

Hesitant Initiatives

No-one present at the Centenary Conference in Shanghai in 1907, where these ideals were proclaimed,[3] could foresee how they would be, at least partially, achieved through the xenophobic policies of that unlikely latter-day Cyrus, Mao Zedong. But by 1927, with Mao already flexing his muscles, Arthur Bray, later on Chairman of the South China District, was writing:

> How is Christ to be preached? The Chinese Christian Community, the Foreign Missionaries, and the Home Church must all work together to give Christ to China. Leadership has got to pass to the Chinese ... and the same process will

---

[2]   R. Anderson, *Foreign Missions* (New York, Charles Scribner, 1870), pp. 110, 115.

[3]   pp. 19, 169.

yet be repeated in Africa and China ... The new Christian leaders ... have a ... tremendous intellectual and spiritual task before them.[4]

China took note: the first indigenous Chairmen of Overseas Districts of the British Conference were Shen Wen Ching in Hubei in 1935 and Tao Vuh Sa in Wenzhou in 1936. In contrast, when nominating Harold Burdess as Chairman of the Italy District in 1932, MMS Secretary Walter Noble commented, 'It is still considered necessary to appoint an English Chairman, but it is hoped that in a few years' time the development of the District will justify the appointment of an Italian Chairman.'[5] War intervened before that time arrived. Charles Armstrong, the Chairman and only missionary then stationed in Italy, had perforce to return to Britain, but it was only in 1946 that Emanuele Sbaffi, who had held the reins throughout the war, was formally appointed.

If national Chairmen were seen as stepping stones to autonomy, that was not in the 1930s an immediate prospect. Regulations were needed. There would have to be a missionary with the responsibility of 'committee representative' to oversee all financial matters involving MMS funds. There should be a limit to the Chairman's term of office. After consulting the overseas Districts, regulations were approved by the Conference in 1939, 'to be brought into operation only when in the judgement of the Synod and of the Committee the District is ready for this degree of devolution.' The limit of five years was promptly exceeded in the Trichinopoly District.

Other stepping stones included giving Synods a voice in deciding whether a missionary should return after furlough, ceding responsibility for supervising probationers – indigenous and expatriate – and determining their suitability for ordination, and phasing out the missionaries' meeting except as a gathering for fellowship. There was no rule of thumb by which these changes were introduced

With the appointment of Chu Shui Kang in South West China in 1949, all seven Chinese Districts had Chinese leadership.[6] Shortly afterwards Mao had all foreign missionaries expelled, all communication was severed, and shotgun autonomy was in place by September 1951 – the Chinese Districts were last listed in the 1951 Minutes of Conference.[7] Elsewhere the process was more systematic.

---

[4]   *Irish Christian Advocate*, 19 August 1927: p. 1043.

[5]   WMMS Western Committee minutes, 19 May 1932.

[6]   Senior, *The China Experience*, pp. 27–29.

[7]   The list is prefaced by the note 'Owing to special circumstances now obtaining in China, it has not been possible to embody any changes of appointments made later than the Conference of 1950. Those appointments, so far as they refer to Chinese Ministers and Probationers, are here reprinted.' The names of British ministers, other than those in the Hong Kong Circuit of the South China District, are noted as 'visiting England'. In 1952 the Chinese Districts disappeared and the Hong Kong District first appeared.

Grasping the nettle in Ghana

In West Africa an Inter-District Conference in 1939 considered a proposal to establish a Provincial Synod like the South Indian one, an intermediate body between the Districts and the Conference. There was no strong case – travel between the West African Districts was far more difficult than in India with its extensive rail network – and the idea was shelved. However at the next Inter-District Conference, at Ibadan in 1954 there was a complete change of attitude. The meeting had been prepared meticulously by Tom Beetham, MMS Africa Secretary from 1950; and both the Missionary Committee in London and the District delegations (each led by a missionary Chairman) were persuaded that the time had come to set up, not now a Provincial Synod, but a separate Conference of the Methodist Church in West Africa. The Ibadan proposals were approved unanimously in The Gambia, Western Nigeria and Eastern Nigeria Synods, and by substantial majorities in Sierra Leone and Ghana. A drafting committee set to work on 'The Constitutional Practice and Discipline of the Methodist Church in West Africa' which went back to the Synods, with remarkable speed, by January 1956. But in the space of a year there had been another change of heart. Influential Ghana Methodists saw drawbacks in a West African scheme and wanted a

> Methodist Church in Ghana as an autonomous Methodist Church which is a legal entity, with full control over its finance and property; but with such constitutional relationship with the Methodist Church in Britain as would maintain and strengthen the fraternal relations between the two Churches, and leave the door open for the help and guidance of the Mother Church continue to be available...[8]

Nevertheless work on the proposed Conference proceeded, and revised drafts tried to reconcile divergent viewpoints. An immense amount of energy was expended on the scheme, by Beetham in London and by the two secretaries of the West African Conference (African) Committee, Koomson of Ghana and Wallace of Sierra Leone. But it became clear that while The Gambia, Sierra Leone and now the Ivory Coast and Dahomey–Togo Districts too wished to be part of a larger entity, there was no real enthusiasm in either Nigeria or Ghana. By 1958 Beetham and Geoffrey Eddy, the last missionary chairman of the Gold Coast/Ghana District, who had each been wholehearted proponents of a regional scheme, accepted that it was doomed and gave their full support to new proposals for an autonomous Ghana Conference which they saw through.[9]

The stage was therefore set for autonomy nation by nation, beginning with Ghana in 1961, when the British Conference set the precedent of transferring its

---

    [8]   Working papers for the West African Conference (African Committee) meeting, 2–8 May 1956, quoted in Bartels, p. 303.

    [9]   For a fuller account see Bartels, pp. 293–323.

Map 14.1   Ghana

authority by standing vote. A little earlier in the year a momentous gathering took place in Skegness: a 'Connexional Overseas Consultation', with some hundred participants from 28 countries, representing Britain and Ireland, the overseas Districts, and the five CSI dioceses with historic Methodist links. The objectives of this Consultation were described by Douglas Thompson, the MMS General Secretary, as

> to reach a common knowledge of the whole of our resources and the whole of our opportunity; to plan our line of progress; to facilitate exchanges between parts of the Church; to devise means of continued service, mutually organized, through autonomous Churches; to make the resources of the Missionary Society an evangelical tool of each and all the Churches.[10]

Reporting on the Consultation, Thompson wrote:

> The different nature of the Church when compared with nations is demonstrated by the disparity between the reasons for which a Church seeks independence and the world's nationalist slogans. Nations wish for freedom for reasons which could be corporately described as 'negative'; they wish to be free because they do not wish to be bound. They wish to escape domination because they dislike domination. The Churches on the other hand desire autonomy for positive reasons which can be summarized under four heads.

---

[10]   D.W. Thompson, *Beginning at Skegness* (London, Cargate Press, 1962), pp. 13–14.

[1] ... the Church wishes to be in the right position to speak to its own nation... to be of the nation within the nation is the best way to achieve what is our common goal.

[2] In these days the Church – which has always been deeply committed – in Imperial days as now – in social and cultural life does best if it is a self-governing unit within its own people... a 'national' Church 'without strings' fits best into a nation with national power and afraid of strings.

[3: in the WCC and other bodies] it is inefficient to have growing Churches without an identity of their own but simply 'lumped into' the Mother Church.

[4] ... one of the weaknesses of Christianity as a world Faith is that it is for historical reasons a predominantly Western Faith. It is often attacked as 'the White-man's Faith' and its truth or validity are challenged for this reason on prejudiced grounds. It is essential in the modern world to have the universal Faith obviously expressed in as many regional forms as possible.

So, he went on,

The granting of autonomy to any Methodist District overseas is really the next step necessary in a process of adaptation [he might have written 'indigenization'] which has been going on for years. [11]

Meeting the Challenges

As the Districts one by one began to move forward on this trajectory, a whole raft of issues had to be taken into account. Some were formal, technical and legal in character. Others, at least equally important, were human and spiritual. Constitutions had to be drafted, property legally transferred. But equally leadership had to be nurtured, not just at senior ecclesiastical level but for medical and educational institutions. The ongoing financial provision for these had to be considered, and it was vital to disentangle financial support from control.

The formation of those who would carry significant responsibility in church life was given a high priority in the Society's budgets year on year, out of recurrent income and also from the proceeds of sale of Richmond College. In addition there was an Overseas Training Fund (OTF), initially set up in 1937 to provide senior ministers with exposure to British church life and subsequently with courses in Church Management at Westhill College, Selly Oak. Later it became the Scholarship Fund which supported a wider range of courses, including doctoral studies. Many who went on to lead their churches spent time in Britain under this

---

[11]   Ibid., pp. 59–62.

programme. A prime task for missionaries was to train local counterparts to whom they would then hand over – in colleges, hospitals and administrative offices. There was added urgency because of the declining number of mission partners. Doctors, pharmacists, teachers and lecturers were not easy to replace after British employers unwisely became less ready to appoint people whose CVs showed years out of the British system.

Then there was the vexed question of pensions for church personnel. In societies where the social security system was rudimentary at best, the norm for most people was to work as long as they could and then to rely on the care of children and the extended family. Frank Davey, the Medical Secretary, visited several countries and spent long days giving medicals to the local ministers in preparation for establishing Ministers' Retirement Funds. In such instances the Society contributed a capital start-up sum, but circuits had trouble keeping up with contributions – meeting stipend commitments was hard enough.

The whole question of financial ability was an enormous headache, and the reason for strenuous resistance on the part of some to cutting the 'mother church's' apron-strings. A church might have the ability to be self-governing, and assuredly had the demonstrable ability to be self-propagating, but it could hardly be self-financing in the context of an economy undermined by unfair terms of trade, exploitative transnational corporations and global economic injustice – and/or by nepotism, corruption and ethnic conflict. It could hardly be expected to assume responsibility, overnight, for institutions set up in the missionary era and funded for decades by MMS grants. It was hard to recruit indigenous doctors, pharmacists, midwifery tutors, when they could command better salaries in government hospitals. In some situations such problems were resolved by government takeovers of schools, colleges and hospitals – a solution that was generally unwelcome.

Clearly financial independence would be a long time coming. In any case independence was seen to be an inappropriate objective for churches, a theologically flawed concept. The Christian church was called to be interdependent, to share its resources, human, financial and intangible, in mutual support. Emerging nations prized their independence, even if in reality many of them relied heavily on external aid. Methodist churches in those nations were more realistic. They prized their autonomy, but rejoiced in a relationship of interdependence with the British Conference. In each case MMS made a commitment to continue its annual grants: self-government was not to be accompanied by the withdrawal of funds. This commitment was qualified in two ways. Firstly, those grants were as far as possible to be general grants with no strings attached, so that the autonomous Church could determine its own priorities and allocate its resources – both home-grown and contributed from overseas – accordingly. And second, it was hoped that the amount of the general grant would reduce gradually over a period of years, as the Church grew in numbers and in its financial capacity. For this was in the years dubbed by the United Nations as 'decades of development' when it was taken for granted that the emerging nations would become increasingly prosperous and the

Churches therefore increasingly able to meet their budgets. For instance there was an agreement with the MCCA that its large general grant would reduce by 2½ per cent each year. But the terms of the agreement included the rider 'adjusted for inflation', which effectively meant that for many years the grant grew rather than decreased. In the long-term, however, the financial security of the overseas Churches depended – insofar as security could be considered a laudable aim – on their becoming self-supporting, if not fully then to a much greater degree. Various initiatives were taken to underpin the income derived from the year-on-year giving of the faithful with reliable income-generating investments. While the primary motive for agricultural projects was to improve the quality of rural life, there was often pressure on their managers to show a profit, and mixed motives generally meant that neither objective was satisfactorily achieved. Property investments were also explored – a substantial one-off grant to Methodist Church Kenya made possible the acquisition of a block of flats for letting, which Lawi Imathiu spoke of in terms of a gift to a Church that had 'come of age'.

The most protracted and indeed notorious of these schemes was the development of one of the compounds on the Plateau in Abidjan, an astute acquisition in the 1920s by Bill Platt as Chairman of the French West Africa District. It was a large, leafy site in the heart of the Ivoirian capital, a prime piece of real estate, and all around it multi-storeyed government buildings were going up. The government demanded that it be redeveloped in keeping with its environment, on pain of appropriation, and endless efforts were made to find a source of co-financing. It was intended that the District[12] should contribute the land, MMS a substantial capital sum, and the business partner a far larger sum, in order to build two towers of up to twenty floors, a few for immediate church use and the rest to revert to the church after twenty years. This would have brought a reasonable income immediately on completion, and far greater returns in due course. In fact it took twenty years, scheme after revised scheme, before a much more modest project was realized. It was enough finally to remove the threat of compulsory purchase, and enough to provide, after management, maintenance and depreciation costs, a return well in excess of the Society's annual grant at that date. On completion of the project the annual grant ceased, as stipulated long before, given the Society's capital input to the scheme of £200,000.

The quest for additional sources of income in order to achieve a fuller measure of self-support was pursued independently of autonomy. Another expensive investment was made by Methodist Church Kenya with the enlargement and upgrading of its Guest House in Nairobi. In this instance MCOD did not make a capital contribution but several loans recouped over the years by withholding the annual grant. The Guest House somehow combined the imperative of showing a financial return with its availability for church use, to accommodate visitors to Nairobi from upcountry and from overseas, and for Conferences and committees.

---

[12]   Known in the Ivory Coast as the Eglise Protestante Méthodiste en Côte d'Ivoire.

None of these matters were directly related to the constitutional transfer of authority. They were part and parcel of the growth and maturity of the overseas Churches and the consolidation of the pioneer work of missionaries and the early converts. But autonomy carried legal implications. One critical area was the title deeds to the properties, which had to be transferred to local ownership – or rather local trusteeship, a concept not understood in the same way in every legal system. Time and again lawyers proved dilatory, as is their wont, and the matter progressed sluggishly. There were special problems for the MCCA, working in numerous different national territories each with its own legal framework.[13] The other legal issue was how precisely the authority of the British Conference was to be transferred to a self-governing overseas jurisdiction. Reporting on the 1961 Skegness Consultation, Thompson wrote:

> ... nothing so well-worth doing could be easy, and freeing Churches into autonomy is not so simple as just saying, 'Go, and God bless you.' ... It would be illegal ... for the Conference to use money or property given to it in good faith for something that should not be done (or taught) in the name of Methodism. It follows that the new Church which is set up in any place must – if it is to take over the assets given to the British Conference – satisfy not only the British Conference but British law that it is in fact the spiritual and ethical succession to its Mother-Church. It must (be) a recognisable kindred Church of which the British Church can declare in legal terms that it honestly and in all conscience can say, 'this new Church will do in this particular place what I did there before – and nothing, ever, which will contradict the values for which the assets I surrender were given.'[14]

So the doctrinal clauses of the 1932 Deed of Union, supposedly enshrining the essence of Methodism, had to be echoed in the foundation documents of autonomous Methodist Churches. The method which was adopted consisted in two Deeds, the text of which was negotiated between the Transfer of Authority Committee of the Conference and a local committee in the territory concerned. A Foundation Deed, to be signed by representatives appointed by the British Conference and those appointed by the Synod, declared that authority was duly transferred. The second, a Deed of Church Order, comprised the basic constitutional provisions. 'Its clauses could be changed, but only by a slow and deliberate procedure; they thus formed a ... firm foundation for the more mutable structure of Standing Orders.'[15] The presumption was that in this way Methodist doctrine was guaranteed and recognizably Methodist practice assured.

---

[13]   The Leeward Islands District alone included ex-British, American, Dutch and French territories.

[14]   Thompson, *Beginning at Skegness,* pp. 64, 66.

[15]   Bartels, p. 311.

Autonomy for Italy and Nigeria was approved by the Conference in 1962, Ceylon's and Upper Burma's in 1964, Kenya, Sierra Leone and the Caribbean and the Americas in 1966; Rhodesia (Zimbabwe) became autonomous in 1977, following a Conference vote back in 1967 endorsed in 1975, while in Zambia the Northern Rhodesia District became part of the UCZ at its inauguration, just three months after political independence, in 1965.[16]

Smaller Churches

One by one the larger overseas Districts moved forward into autonomy. But the Skegness Consultation had recognized that autonomy for smaller Districts was problematic. Surely there had to be a minimum number of members, and of theologically trained ministers, to avoid the danger of domination by a strong individual or clique, with possibly heterodox beliefs, a sufficient number to ensure that no individual or congregation became the object of a vendetta occasioned by a clash of personalities, a number large enough to allow, in the unhappy event of complaints and disciplinary cases, for a hearing before a competent panel of folk not already embroiled in the case. Surely the smaller Districts would have to engage energetically in self-propagation before they could achieve self-government. (The smallest Districts, The Gambia and Togo, had signally failed in this regard, since for most of their history they had largely confined their activity to the Aku community of Banjul and to the coastal Mina people of Togo.)

There was still a France District, comprising one church for English-speakers at rue Roquépine in Paris; it closed in 1977.[17] The Bahamas District, having remained separate at first, took its place in the MCCA in 1969, though it remained an uneasy relationship and degenerated into schism in the 1990s. The two Hong Kong Districts (Chinese and English) merged with the American Methodist *Wei Li Kung Hui* in 1975 and 1987 respectively. By 1978, the other surviving Districts were Portugal, then with six ministers; The Gambia, with four; and the three francophone Districts, Togo[18] with four ministers, Bénin with nineteen and the Ivory Coast with twenty-five.

The French West African Districts were wary of 'autonomy' – in the history of France's African colonies 'autonomy' had been one short-lived phase of partial independence. In addition, Harry Henry, the long-serving Chairman of the Dahomey District (the Bénin District from 1975 when the country was renamed), saw no reason for change, since he rightly perceived that none of the policies and decisions he steered through locally were likely to be over-ruled in London.

---

[16]   pp. 160–61.

[17]   C.J. Davey, *Rue Roquépine* (London, Methodist Church Overseas Division, 1977).

[18]   Togo became a separate District in 1978. It had previously been one circuit of the Dahomey-Togo District (and before that, along with the Ivory Coast, the French West Africa District).

The process was further complicated by the need not only to produce the legal documents in French but to adapt them in conformity with a different juridical system. Portugal presented the same challenge. There was thus a significant interval between the Zimbabwe votes and the transfer of authority to the Ivory Coast in 1984, Bénin – despite Henry's reluctance – in 1992, Portugal in 1995 and Togo in 2000.

Inculturation

Legal and financial provisions could not of themselves create an authentically African, Asian or Caribbean church. There had to be another ingredient: self-expression. In reaction to the association of Christian mission with westernization, there was a conscious effort to discern in what ways the gospel affirmed or contested traditional cultural values and practices, and to express the gospel, live the faith and organize the church in ways which harmonized with the cultural context. Russell Chandran of the CSI asserted that

> Genuine indigenization takes place whenever and wherever the Church is alive to her mission of proclaiming the Gospel in the contemporary language of the people. It is not a technique for evangelism but a necessary witness to the Incarnation of the Word of God.[19]

Indigenization denoted relating the gospel to local cultures: 'culture' meaning all those non-material traits – language, beliefs, customs, ethical codes, recipes, proverbs, etc – which are transmitted from one generation to another not by genes but by society. From the 1970s the term contextualization was increasingly used, denoting the gospel's relationship to cultures that were constantly interacting and undergoing rapid social change. For Christians in the emerging churches the interaction of cultures was not just inescapable but desirable. Chinese Christians, having been forcibly cut off from the rest of the world from the early 1950s to the late 1970s, were categorical: 'Three-self but not self-isolation!' Paul's teaching about the Body of Christ was plain: one member cannot live apart from the rest. What they resented was being patronized. Azariah's barbed jest made the point: 'You missionaries are too generous. You insist on doing everything for us. You even make our mistakes for us.'[20] Well into the era of autonomy churches in the global south were all too often depicted in the north as the objects of charity and the targets of mission. This was a source of irritation to church leaders who wished to be seen not as receivers only, but as senders and givers themselves. An editorial in the *South India Churchman* complained that CSI was

---

[19]   In *Student World*, 51 (1958): p. 427.

[20]   Quoted by G.C. Oosthuizen, *Theological Battleground in Asia and Africa* (London, C. Hurst, 1972), p. 67.

not only foreign in its personnel; it is foreign in its ethos; it is foreign in its administrative machinery; it is foreign in its theology; and, above all, it is foreign in its material resources.[21]

In consequence there were some, both indigenous leaders and missionaries, who were led to advocate a moratorium on overseas missions.[22] Its protagonists were not seeking to sever all ties with the sending Churches and agencies, but they were challenging the nature of those ties.

Contextualized, indigenized self-expression materialized fitfully. The liturgies, music, art and architecture of the churches betrayed the extent to which they were still under western influence long after they became formally autonomous. Innumerable Methodist congregations continued to use the 1933 Methodist Hymn Book – or rather a repertoire of fifty or sixty hymns from it – long after it had been replaced in Britain. Local liturgies were viewed with suspicion. The use of instruments such as African drums which early missionaries condemned as pagan was only slowly rehabilitated. Churches were built in the same shape as in Europe, even – where Swiss missionaries had been active – with steeply pitched roofs so that the equatorial snow could slide off. But other influences were at work. The beautiful Cathedral of the Epiphany at Dornakal in India, dedicated in 1939, with its Muslim-style minarets and Hindu motifs, was a striking piece of Indian self-expression. Local instruments and local rhythms gradually took their place in worship alongside, or even instead of western tunes and keyboards. The graceful, unhurried movement of a Ghanaian congregation dancing to the front of the church with their thank-offerings became a high point of the liturgy.

Polity did not so readily find self-expression. Although self-governing, the Churches were governed according to inherited constitutions. They were fearful of tampering, just as independent nations were fearful of tampering with colonial boundaries, because any change would probably be in someone's self-interest at the expense of another's. However, a spectacularly bold and self-conscious constitutional reform was made by the Methodist Church Nigeria in 1976. The architect of the new church order was Bolaji Idowu, who became President of the Nigerian Conference in 1973. In 1961, when a lecturer but not yet a professor at the University of Ibadan, he had delivered three broadcast talks on *The Problem of the Indigenization of the Church in Nigeria*, based on the premise that 'The time is now overdue for the Church in Nigeria to look at herself; to examine her soul.' Methodist autonomy was still a year away and in other Churches too, he affirmed, authority

appears too much to reside with the European or American overlords who supply European or American staff, prefabricated traditions for the guidance of her life, and money for her maintenance. The result is the detrimental fact that

---

[21]   Ward, p. 158.

[22]   pp. 263–4.

it is these over-lords and not the Lord of the Church who is 'pre-eminent' over the Church in Nigeria.[23]

His talk reviewed some of the areas where indigenization was urgently called for, including language, theology, liturgy, dress and vestments. He did not address questions of church order, except to say that 'the European structure of the Church has, to a large extent, made for spiritual sterility in her life'.[24] His fertile mind continued to turn these ideas over for a decade and more, a decade which saw the prospect of a united Nigerian Church (for which he had argued strongly in the last of his lectures) evaporate, in part due to his own interventions,[25] and the unity of the Nigerian nation rent by civil war. With his election to the Presidency, the opportunity came to translate his theories into practice. In the face of outraged opposition, he devised and pushed through a new constitution, declaring the Church to be autocephalous and endowing it with priests and presbyters – conceived, unscripturally, as different ranks of ministry – bishops, archbishops and a life patriarch. To this office at the pinnacle of the hierarchy Idowu was himself inducted in a five-hour ceremony at which he was presented with two golden keys, the symbol of his authority. The patriarch was to be addressed as Your Pre-eminence, notwithstanding his repudiation of such language in his 1961 lecture. Sumptuous robes were designed for each order of ministry, which ensured work for the Methodist Tailoring Factory in Yaba.

Obvious questions were raised about the extent to which all this represented Africanization. If in part it reflected the social order of Yoruba chiefdoms, it did not appeal to the more democratic Eastern tribal groups. A sizeable minority of circuits, mainly in the East, seceded and formed 'Methodist Church Nigeria (1962 Foundation Constitution)', and a fourteen-year schism ensued with ugly disputes over property. Throughout the period MCOD was continually lobbied, particularly by former missionaries in the East, to take unequivocal sides in the dispute, but steadfastly refrained. Only under Idowu's successor, Sunday Mbang, was reconciliation achieved (and a few congregations in Umuahia and Owerri remained apart until 2011).

Most of the other autonomous Churches, with the notable exception of the MCCA, opted to amend the Deed of Church Order and adopt a functional episcopate. In Kenya this happened because of a decree that no-one should hold the title President other than the President of the country; the President of the Church became the Presiding Bishop, and other bishops were appointed subsequently. These constitutional changes were made in accordance with the stipulations of the founding Deeds, although in Bénin the President, clearly contravening those safeguards

---

[23]   E.B. Idowu, *Towards an Indigenous Church* (London, Oxford University Press, 1965), p. 13.

[24]   Ibid., p. 15.

[25]   pp. 165–6.

and precautions in a bid for life tenure, precipitated another painful schism which reconciliation missions from Britain and Nigeria were unable to resolve.

Indigenous Theology

Besides all this there was a fundamental theological issue: how did the African, Asian or Caribbean heritage and context affect the lens through which God was perceived and the manner in which the gospel was proclaimed? Most theologizing was done informally, orally and in the vernacular, particularly in the course of bearing witness to others in conversations on the street and at the market, Christians telling others the Christian story as they remembered and understood it. Somewhat more formally, it was done by preachers planning and preaching their sermons, by the congregations who listened and absorbed them – selectively, as hearers are bound to – and by musicians responding with spontaneous lyrics and praise-songs or composing them for their choirs. Out of such oral and liturgical theology came fresh insights and rich veins of reflection, opening western as well as southern eyes to the new things God was doing. The Gambian Lamin Sanneh, whose pilgrimage from Islam to Catholicism was via Methodist baptism and who repeatedly acknowledged Tom Beetham as a father in God,[26] saw the gospel's 'translatability (as) the taproot of Christian expansion'. As Andrew Walls pointed out, 'Christian faith rests on a divine act of translation: the Word became flesh, and dwelt among us.'[27] Missionaries set great store by translating the scriptures and, wrote Sanneh,

> It began to dawn on African populations that the missionary adoption of vernacular categories for the Scriptures was in effect a written sanction for the indigenous religious vocation. The God of the ancestors was accordingly assimilated into the Yahweh of ancient Israel and 'the God and Father of our Lord Jesus Christ.' But there was a profound difference. The 'God' of missionary preaching was a jealous God who forbade worship of other gods, a jealousy that in the religious history of the West often manifested itself in wars and other forms of intolerance. In Africa, however, God was a hospitable deity who was approached through the mediation of lesser deities. The exclusive notion of Western Christianity was replaced with the inclusive rule of African religions...[28]

---

[26] 'Of those most knowledgable about Christianity in the new Africa, few can rival [Beetham] in the depth and sympathy of his grasp or the scope of his view. During many years of friendship he has impressed me with his utter humility and sagacity.' – L. Sanneh, *Translating the Message* (New York, Orbis Books, 1989), p. xiv.

[27] A.F. Walls, *The Missionary Movement in Christian History* (New York, Orbis Books, 1996), p. 26, in an essay first published in 1990 on 'The Translation Principle in Christian History'.

[28] Sanneh, pp. 159–60.

Kwesi Dickson of Ghana, Zablon Nthamburi of Kenya and Gabriel Setiloane of Botswana all contributed significantly to the development of African theology, as did Mercy Amba Oduyoye, daughter of a President of the Ghana Conference. 'African Christian theologians,' she wrote,

> have a duty to ... incorporate the authentic African idiom into Christian theology. Utilizing African religious beliefs in Christian theology is not an attempt to assist Christianity to capture and domesticate the African spirit; rather it is an attempt to ensure that the African spirit revolutionizes Christianity to the benefit of all who adhere to it.[29]

The theologians wrote in the context of a massive expansion of Christianity in Africa, seeking to understand its causes and envisage its consequences. In the course of the twentieth century the number of African Christians grew from a few thousand to 350 million, as 'the Lord added to the number of those being saved every day'.[30] Throughout the non-western world Christianity experienced steady and sometimes spectacular growth. In the fifty years following the inauguration of the CSI, the younger Churches both celebrated their autonomy and demonstrated their confidence and courage. The largest Christian communities on the planet were now to be found in Africa, Latin America and China.

It was not easy for Europeans and North Americans to adjust to this shift. In all other respects they retained power. Their wealth, above all, reflected the inequalities of the global economy. Their weaponry, if the stakes were high enough, could call the shots in international politics. Their calendar, with its Christian base-line, formed the framework of the world's business and was built in to every computer. One of their languages, English, had become the primary tool for international communication. It was hard not to assume that their theology and spirituality, honed over the centuries, were normative for Christians everywhere. A letter in the *Methodist Recorder* claimed in 1997:

> There is no such thing as BLACK theology. The word 'theology' admits of no adjectival qualification. The Word of God is for all and the colour of a person's skin is irrelevant.[31]

Yet this 'shift in the centre of gravity of the Christian world' was but the latest in a 2000-year-long series. Originally a Jewish faith, then predominantly a Hellenistic faith, Christianity became, with the rise of Islam in other Christian

---

[29]   M.A. Oduyoye, 'The Value of African Religious Beliefs and Practices for Christian Theology' in K. Appiah-Kubi and S. Torres (eds), *African Theology en Route* (New York, Orbis Books, 1979), p. 116.

[30]   Acts 2:47.

[31]   Letter from K.R. Brown, *Methodist Recorder,* 20 March 1997.

heartlands, a European faith – Europe and Christendom were one and the same. 'Each phase of Christian history,' Andrew Walls pointed out in 1982,

> has seen a transformation of Christianity as it has entered and penetrated another culture … Once more the Christian faith is penetrating new cultures – those of Africa and the Pacific and parts of Asia … the present indicators are that these southern expressions of Christianity are becoming the dominant forms of the faith.[32]

Within Methodism and in the 'missionary-sending' churches in general, this shift was variously appreciated, ignored, resented, resisted or welcomed. But the essential interdependence of the Methodist family was a given, and continued to be expressed not only by the transfer of funds and the exchange of mission partners but through sharing one another's concerns, campaigns, projects, prayers and theological insights.

---

[32]   Walls, pp. 22, 24.

Chapter 15
Forced Withdrawals and New Beginnings

The second half of the twentieth century was marked, even more than earlier decades, by rapid social change.[1] Churches and mission agencies were affected and challenged like every part of society. The MMS made many changes, even to the name by which it was known in Methodism. Clifford Cook, retiring as Chairman of the Hong Kong District in 1954 after twenty-five years in China, wrote:

> The staff of the Chinese Methodist Church in Hong Kong no longer use the word 'missionary' or the term 'Missionary Committee Representative'. I was called the Representative of the Conference of the English Methodist Church. A letter that I brought to Mr Childe from the Hong Kong Circuit was not addressed to the Missionary Society but to the 'Department of Overseas Evangelism of the English Methodist Church'. These new terms are deliberate. As a young, progressive Church leader said, 'For us, the missionary era is over.'[2]

Hong Kong's terminology did not find favour. But the new name eventually adopted by the MMS in 1973, Methodist Church Overseas Division, reflected the change in relationship and attitude Cook had reported, now widely shared both in Britain and around the world.

Some of the changes in priorities and programmes – notably the withdrawals from China by 1951 and Burma in 1962 – were forced by circumstances. Others were new ventures and partnerships.

China

The Chinese had good reason to resent foreigners, both westerners because of the opium wars and the unequal treaties, and the Japanese on account of numerous atrocities during the invasion and occupation. Chinese Christians had an ambiguous attitude to their foreign friends. They were grateful to the missionaries who had brought them the gospel, built schools and hospitals, and run them capably; they were unhappy that their faith was everywhere regarded as a foreign religion,

---

[1]   In 1955 the World Council of Churches commissioned a study on issues arising from rapid social change which resulted in two major reports: P. Abrecht, *The Churches and Rapid Social Change* (London, SCM Press, 1961) and E. de Vries, *Man in Rapid Social Change* (New York, Doubleday, 1961).

[2]   *The Kingdom Overseas* May 1954: p. 100.

because they were not in charge. Donald Childe, a missionary in south China from 1930 to 1949 and then a MMS Secretary until 1965, recalled the words of a Chinese doctor who was shown round the hospital at Kukong, Childe's first circuit:

> This is as good as it is because there are two or three foreigners in charge of it; if you were to go ... it would break up. You do not know how much this makes me hate you.[3]

It was said, wrote Childe, in friendship; the doctor recognized his own debt to the west for his education; his anger was rooted in his impatience with China's backwardness. The Chinese Communist Party shared that impatience and anger; its vision was of a new, progressive China, unhampered by foreign interference or patronage.

Most Chinese Christians and foreign missionaries had no experience of Communist rule before 1949, and did not know what to expect from the new régime, but they were inclined to fear the worst. Those who were living in areas under Communist control, however, had already discovered that the Communists were not like the inefficient and rapacious Guomindang officials; they held out real promise of restoring order to a ravaged society. At first it seemed possible that some missionaries might be permitted to continue serving in China under the new régime, and that financial support from abroad would be acceptable as long as it came with no strings attached. But the outbreak of the Korean War in June 1950 put an end to such hopes. Anyone with western friends was suspected of divided loyalties, and the missionaries realized that their continued presence was an embarrassment. With the approval of the Chinese Methodist leadership Childe, the Society's China Secretary, had the sad task of organizing the departure of the missionary personnel. Exit permits were required, and for some that entailed a long, anxious wait. Vernon Stones in Yunnan endured four-and-a-half months of solitary confinement, before deportation.[4] A yet harsher fate awaited many Chinese Christians. Elliott Kendall, Stones' colleague, told of two ministers, one who committed suicide after weeks of interrogation and another shot after a summary trial. Many more, in the years to come, would be harassed, beaten, imprisoned, or sent to manual labour in remote, impoverished rural locations. But as news of these tribulations filtered through to London, Childe recalled the minister whose last words to his departing missionary colleagues were:

> Kindly give our gratitude and affection to the Methodist Church in England; ask them to trust us; tell them that as for me personally, if in the future I have to earn my rice by selling peanuts in the streets of this city, I shall still remain the minister of this Church![5]

---

[3]   D.B. Childe, *China Now* (London, Cargate Press, 1955), p. 24.

[4]   p. 71.

[5]   Childe, p. 18.

After 1951 no money could be sent to China. It was not necessary for the government to freeze bank accounts; Christians could see how damaging to their cause continued dependence on foreign support would be, and what displeasure, both official and popular, it would incur. Indeed, any form of foreign contact was risky, and before long correspondence fizzled out, except for rare occasions when the postal service could be circumvented. A handful of visitors from Britain in 1954 and 1955 brought back news of new members and the ordination of some probationers. The ex-missionaries continued to pray fervently for their friends, but in Methodism (and not Methodism alone) Childe rued the 'negative thinking of so many people in our pews about the Church in China'.[6] The absence of missionaries, grants and news made them ask if the whole century-long enterprise been worth it. Childe himself was more hopeful. In a 1957 paper he reviewed the situation:

> The Church was suddenly thrown back on itself, and upon God. Many expected that the Church would be driven underground; that the organization of the Church would collapse, public worship cease; and perhaps only a small remnant of the faithful remain.

> But the prayers of the Universal Church were not in vain ... Today as we survey the position during a time of diminished tension, it is already apparent that the Protestant Church has emerged confident and undismayed from out of this first stage, from what has been a great trial and an experience of unprecedented difficulty.

He soon had to eat those words. The brief respite afforded by Mao Zedong's plan to 'let a hundred flowers bloom' gave way to renewed repression and economic disaster. In 1958 the Protestant Churches were 'collectivized' and all clergy were compelled to take full-time secular jobs. In 1961, Childe wrote:

> It would seem, today that the prospect for the Church is dark. Congregations in the cities are much smaller; they include very few young people. The education system is entirely in the hands of the Government. Most people must be pre-occupied with the problem of personal safety and how to subsist in the present national food crisis.[7]

The 'food crisis' was, unknown to the west, a famine in which over thirty million people died. Even before the 'Great Proletarian Cultural Revolution' was launched

---

[6] G.A. Hood, *Neither Bang nor Whimper* (Singapore, Presbyterian Church in Singapore, 1991), p. 232, quoting a letter dated 24 June 1956.

[7] MCH: Papers circulated to MMS General Committee members, dated 30 March 1957 and July 1961.

by Mao in 1966, the Chinese people experienced great suffering, the Chinese church was totally isolated and Chinese Christians endured much adversity.[8]

Donald Childe was determined that the Society's work among the Chinese should continue. Hong Kong was swollen with refugees from the mainland, living in overcrowded misery. Dispossessed magistrates, army officers, professors and others who held high positions in old China, were glad to find shelter in a shack of old kerosene tins. Childe encouraged the vestiges of the South China District – Cantonese-speaking – to consolidate its presence there, develop its social welfare ministry and collaborate with the Mandarin-speaking Episcopal Methodists. (There had been conversations in China prior to 1949 about a United Methodist Church in China. Overtaken by events on the mainland, they would eventually come to fruition in Hong Kong.) The initial joint venture was a Housing Scheme, to which American Methodism would contribute £8,000 and the MMS £2,000. In 1955 the first 'Wesley Village' was opened, on a steep hillside site provided by the government, consisting of eighty small homes for families made homeless by one of the fires that regularly destroyed the shanty towns. A church and community centre for the Village were built the next year, and other Villages followed. Both Methodist branches opened schools and evangelistic work on the flat roof-tops of government refugee settlements.

Childe also looked to the Chinese diaspora in Malaysia, Singapore and Indonesia. The American Methodist Mission Board had been working there for many years, and he negotiated an arrangement whereby some British missionaries would serve in the Chinese work in those territories. He wanted to ensure there was a new generation of missionaries who would be ready to move back into China if the door ever re-opened. The most urgent of these appointments was to the staff of Trinity College in Singapore where Anglicans, Presbyterians, Methodists and the LMS had combined to prepare ministers for work in Chinese communities throughout South-East Asia; Christopher Smith, who had cut his teeth in Yunnan, was posted there in 1955 and worked in Singapore for twenty years. Two very experienced China missionaries took up similar work: in Sarawak, on the island of Borneo, where John Foster taught at the Sibu Theological School and in Sumatra, where Cyril Baker was persuaded to come out of retirement to the Medan Bible School.

When Foster and three probationers arrived in 1957, Sarawak was still a British colony; it became independent as part of the Federation of Malaysia in 1963. Methodism had arrived in Sarawak in 1901 in the shape of a large group of migrants from China's Fuzhou province. American missionaries had brought them under their wing and also begun work among the indigenous Iban people. One of the probationers was John Hodgkinson, who later worked with Chinese congregations in Britain. Another was Geoffrey Senior, who taught both at Sibu and Medan and had a year as acting General Secretary of the Malaya and Singapore

---

[8]   For a succinct account of the 1949–1959 decade from a Protestant perspective, see D.H. Bays, *A New History of Christianity in China* (Chichester, Wiley-Blackwell, 2012), pp. 160–168.

Christian Council after Indonesia's confrontation with Malaysia compelled the evacuation of British missionaries. Later he worked for seven years in Hong Kong and was the first Methodist to return to mainland China when a chink in the bamboo curtain appeared in 1978. On that first visit he saw no signs of Christian activity, but on his fourth, in 1980, he made contact with the church in Guangzhou and just a few weeks later met two pastors who had begun their ministry in the South China District.[9]

As China's doors opened further, relations with the post-denominational Protestant Church, under the umbrella of the China Christian Council, were naturally developed on an ecumenical basis. MCOD played an active part, especially in the Teachers' Programme of the Amity Foundation. Amity, an independent Chinese voluntary organization, was created in 1985 on the initiative of Chinese Christians to promote education, social services, health and rural development. MCOD helped to select and support teachers of English on two-year contracts in Colleges in less developed areas.

Burma

Until 1942 Methodism in Upper Burma won few converts. Baptist missions in the south and east of the country were much more fruitful, especially among the Karen people. In 1919 William Goudie, on behalf of the Society's officers, removed the Chairman, complaining:

> Your returns of membership and Christian Agency give real cause for concern. Stagnation has continued for a number of years. Your full membership for 1907/8 was 449. Your returns for 1918 were 533, an increase of just 84.[10]

But annual increases continued to be counted in single or double figures, drawn not from the mainstream Burman Buddhist population, but from residents of the Mandalay Leprosy Home and others on the margins of society, and from the ethnic minority peoples. Once only, in 1926, was there a sudden and dramatic increase in membership, when 274 Lushai Christians transferred their allegiance because they drank alcohol and on that account the Baptists denied them baptism. The more relaxed view of the WMMS was summed up by Walter Noble as a 'matter of total immersion in water and partial immersion in alcohol'.

There were, at the time of Goudie's rebuke, over 2,000 pupils in thirty Methodist schools in Upper Burma. The schools were noted for their moral values

---

[9]   G.R. Senior, *Visits Through China's Opening Doors* (Hong Kong, 1981) and *For Love of the Chinese* (Hong Kong, 1989), pp. 85–9.

[10]   SOAS, WMMS/Correspondence/Burma/FBN1, Goudie to Sheldon, 11 December 1919.

and firm discipline as well as their academic standards, but they did not produce the results Thomas Thomas had hoped for when he wrote in 1892:

> The Buddhist schools … (are) the strength of Buddhism, and if we mean to overthrow it we must attack it in its strongest place … In vernacular schools we can always expect more direct fruit as we have ample time for instilling Christian Truth in to the hearts of the Young … we shall be able to counteract the work of the Buddhist Monk and reach … the 'masses'.[11]

As the nationalist movement gathered pace through the 1920s and 1930s, the schools were from time to time the scenes of protests and strikes. In 1930 a brief rebellion, largely confined to the rice-fields of Lower Burma, prompted the District Magistrate in Mandalay to ask the District Chairman, Mervyn Young, if he was prepared, in the event of major civil disorder, to be sworn in as a Special Police Officer with responsibility for the quarter where the Methodist Church was situated and where most Europeans lived. Young wrote to Noble for guidance, explaining that his responsibilities would include giving orders to fire if the situation demanded it. He concluded:

> I must emphasise that by choice I do not want anything to do with this, it holds no attraction for me. However as a minister, I cannot shirk from my duty. The duties do not and cannot involve offensive action … although I would be willing to use force to prevent a massacre.

After what was evidently a lively discussion, Noble cabled a reply saying 'Majority of WMMS officers will endorse your judgement if you feel under obligation to accept post offered'.[12] It did not come to that, but unrest continued to flare up periodically and mission schools were prey to boycotts and sometimes violence.

There were just over 1,000 members by the time the Japanese invasion compelled the hasty departure of the entire missionary body in 1942. Some were evacuated by air, others trekked across remote mountain passes; after many a hair-raising experience, all finally reached the safety of India.[13] In 1945 many of them returned to dilapidated mission houses, gutted churches and schools, a cost of living much greater than their 'Burma dearness allowance' provided for, and a nation whose travails were far from ended by Japan's surrender. The ensuing years were marked by the assassination of the Prime Minister, General Aung San, in 1947, Burma's long-awaited independence in 1948 (several months after India and Pakistan), and the revolt of the Karen people. In 1949 a battle for control of Mandalay saw the tower of Wesley Church blown up only weeks after it had been

---

[11]   Ibid., Thomas to General Secretaries, 9 February 1892.

[12]   SOAS, WMMS/Correspondence/MRP2, Young to Noble, 14 November 1930 and cabled reply 15 December 1930: see Leigh, p. 49.

[13]   Ibid., pp. 110–121.

rebuilt. At the same time there was great unease in the church. The missionaries were unhappy with the Society's officers in London, especially Donald Childe who knew much less about Burma than about China; the Society was loath to spend the Reconstruction Fund it had set aside when renovated premises were liable to fresh depredations at any time. The Burmese ministers were resentful of the missionaries, who had automatically assumed leadership from the day they returned, barely acknowledging the bravery with which the Burmese had ensured the Church's survival during the occupation; the first Burmese Chairman of the District, U Po Tun, who took office in 1950, was particularly bitter. And because many of the rebellious Karens were Baptists – and Buddhists could not be expected to make a distinction between Baptist and Methodist – they were all viewed with suspicion. In 1961 Buddhism was pronounced the state religion and missionaries began to feel that it was only a matter of time before they would be made to leave.

In 1962 democratic rule came to an end when General Ne Win, who had earlier ruled Burma under martial law, seized power again and imposed the 'Burmese Way to Socialism'. Shops and schools were nationalized, the press heavily censored, the currency was demonetarized. The Leprosy Home begun in 1891, popularly known throughout Burma as the Wesley Leprosy Hospital, was nationalized – and eventually, in 1990, the residents, comprising 300 households, were moved out of Mandalay and given plots in a village forty miles away. Ne Win foolishly declared that 'no foreigner can be a friend of Burma'. There was a large Indian population, settled in Burma on the coat-tails of the British in the nineteenth century, and some 200,000 Indians, educated people reduced to destitution by a programme of Burmanization, returned as refugees to their own country. In this atmosphere home rule was urgent for the Church. A Transfer of Authority Standing Committee had been appointed by the 1960 Synod to prepare for autonomy. Amalgamation with the Methodists of the American tradition in Lower Burma was an option, and in 1963 Donald Childe and Ruth Anstey were dispatched to Rangoon to negotiate. But the Synod would not have it; work on a constitution was rapidly completed and approved by the 1964 British Conference. The Methodist Church in Upper Burma (MCUB), with U Ba Ohn as its first President, came into being just in time, for in 1966 came the decree that all missionaries must leave by the end of May. All but three had already gone, with *L.B.* (i.e. Leaving Burma) *for good* written on the visa page of their passports. Such was the bureaucratic chaos that reigned, that while the government was bringing heavy pressure to bear on missionaries to leave from 1964, exit visas were obtained only with difficulty. And such was the fear and uncertainty in the air, departing missionaries felt obliged to burn all records that might compromise their colleagues; thus when David Turtle and his doctor wife Maureen and family left Maindaungphai, they destroyed every trace of their activities, including the medical records of the clinic, to guard against recriminations.

Notwithstanding all these traumas, membership had increased in twenty years from 1,000 to 6,000. The new converts were almost wholly Lushai people from the Chin Hills, northwest of Mandalay, and Khongsai from the Soma Tract and

Naga Hills still further north, rather than Burmans. Devout Wesleyan missionaries were uncomfortable with the Lushai Christians' charismatic style of worship, but their conversion rate was undeniable. The Conference area was divided into three Districts: Mandalay, Tahan and Homalin. Mandalay, despite its long history and far greater investment, was much the smallest, consisting largely of small scattered congregations in widespread circuits.

The departure of the missionaries did not isolate Burmese Christians as totally as in the case of China. There was no bar on overseas funding and grants continued to be sent. British representatives were usually granted visas, albeit for a week only, to attend the Upper Burma Conference. Some Burmese Methodists were from time to time allowed to travel, and a few came to study in Britain, though there were no permanent passports and permission was not granted easily. A youth exchange was arranged in 1985 when seven went to Burma and Indonesia, but the return visit eventually happened only in 1988, when just two Burmese received their travel documents at the eleventh hour. Those who represented the British and Irish Conferences at the Church's centenary celebrations in 1987 experienced a tremendous and moving welcome, but travel restrictions prevented them from visiting the tribal areas. They found simmering unrest in the country – less than a year later mass demonstrations were violently suppressed and a new military junta took power – but a lively church with a passion for evangelism. In 1987 too Dr Than Bil Luai started a Methodist Hospital in Tahan, which by 1996 had eighty-four beds and forty-six staff, all Lushais.

Thirty years after the expulsion of missionaries, the MCUB remained one of the smallest Christian Churches in Burma. Statistics were difficult to obtain and unreliable, but its numbers were at least four times the 6,000 recorded at autonomy.

Korea and Japan

A new link, with South Korea, was forged in 1973 when Choon Young Kim came to Britain and for two years ministered in Hammersmith. Soon after returning from Britain he became the Korean Methodist Church's Director of Mission and Evangelism. He held that even his fast-growing missionary-minded church could benefit from 'aliens of the same faith living and working among us as brothers and sisters'[14] and so in 1980 two British couples went to Seoul, one for three years and the other for a few months' secondment at the Theological Seminary. Priorities in both Britain and Korea changed, however, and no further appointments to Korea were made, though a youth team visited Hong Kong and Korea in 1987, while Korean congregations in Britain, staffed by Koreans and meeting in Methodist churches, multiplied. KEEP, the Korean Ecumenical Education Programme of the British Churches, was set up with MCOD backing before the 1988 Seoul

---

14   *NOW*, December 1977: p. 22.

Olympics; it sought to raise awareness of the Korean people's desire for peace and reconciliation between North and South.

The United Church of Christ in Japan, known as the Kyodan, was a union of thirty-three diverse Protestant religious bodies forcibly brought together by the Japanese wartime government. Some resumed an independent status after religious freedom was restored in 1946, but not Methodists; American Methodist missionaries returned to work with the Kyodan. In 1977 MCOD agreed in principle to send teachers to Japan but it was 1981 before David Gray, who had met his Japanese wife-to-be Keiko in London, took up a post in Okinawa. The following year the children of the Liverpool District, inspired by the story of the Japanese girl Sadako Sasaki, made 20,000 paper cranes, symbols of peace; they were hung in the Liverpool Philharmonic Hall at the District's annual Overseas Mission rally and several thousand were sent on to the Hiroshima Peace Tower where they were hung on the 37th anniversary of Hiroshima's destruction.[15] In 1986 Sheila Norris began her long service at Kwassui Women's College, originally a Methodist foundation, in Nagasaki. In 1982 a request had come for a minister, but no appointment ever materialized.

Melanesia and the Pacific

When the autonomous Australasian Conference was established in 1855, it formed its own Missionary Society, took responsibility for the Tonga and Fiji Districts, and in 1857 resumed working in Samoa where the WMMS had earlier withdrawn by agreement with the LMS. In 1874 George Brown brought Fijian and Samoan missionaries to the Duke of York Islands, and they soon spread out into New Britain and New Ireland, larger islands off the east coast of New Guinea.[16] Later, New Zealand Methodists started work in the Solomon Islands, and then on the island of Bougainville. After 1950, when the central highlands of the Papua New Guinea (PNG) mainland, inhabited by people living a stone-age existence, began to be exposed to the outside world, a new mission was begun among a handful of the country's 800 tribal groups.

The MMS was not involved in these initiatives. The main area of co-operation was in North India, where Australian missionaries served in the Lucknow and Banaras District. Invited by MMS in 1902 – the year of Methodist union in Australia – to 'come over to India and help us', the request was at first declined because of the Australian Society's Pacific commitments, but William Fitchett,[17] President of

---

[15] E. Coerr, *Sadako and the Thousand Paper Cranes* (London, Puffin Books, 1977).

[16] Pritchard, *Methodists and their Missionary Societies 1760–1900*, pp. 174–6. The islands had not yet been named 'the Bismarck archipelago'.

[17] Fitchett, for forty-five years Principal of the Methodist Ladies' College in Melbourne, was also a journalist and a naval historian held in such high regard by Winston Churchill that he ordered copies of Fitchett's books to be placed on every British warship:

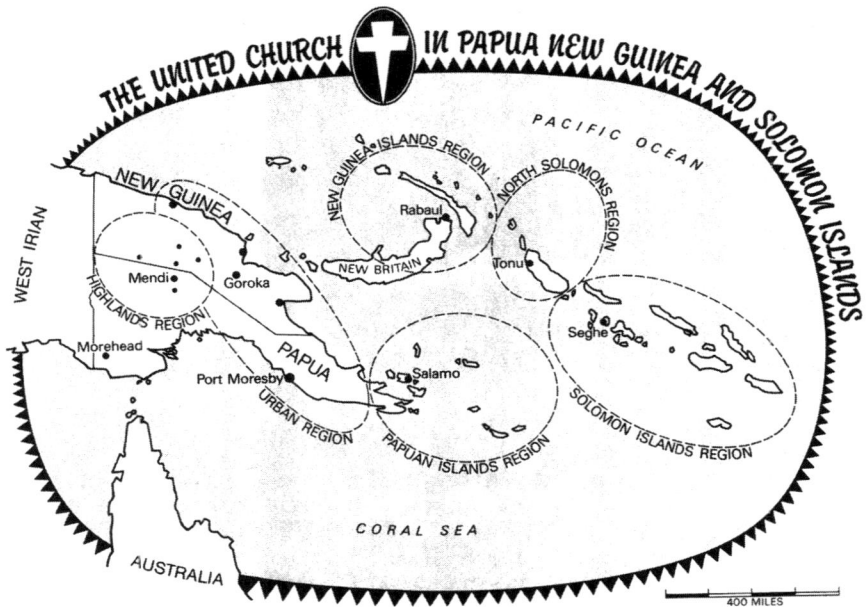

Map 15.1   Papua New Guinea

the 1904 triennial Australasian Conference, argued that 'too much money and too many workers have been given to the Pacific Islands for a population equal to two or three Sydney suburbs.'[18] There was much more to be done in India, especially in areas from which 'coolies' were migrating to Fiji. The vain hope of training catechists for the Fiji work was a factor in moving the 1907 triennial Conference to approve the enterprise and the first missionaries, John Allen and Frank Nunn, took up residence in the neighbouring towns of Mau and Azamgarh. When the CMS left Azamgarh in 1915 its High School, opened in 1837, became the Wesley High School, and in 1927 Allen founded the Azamgarh Christian Hospital for Women. British and Australian missionaries collaborated in the District up to and beyond its absorption in the Church of North India in 1970.

Meanwhile the newly autonomous Pacific Churches soon instigated new partnerships with British Methodism. One of the last acts of the Melanesian United Synod as it prepared for the merger which constituted the United Church in *Papua New Guinea and the Solomon Islands,* was to ask its Australian parent body to approach its British grandparent with a request for personnel. The MMS

A.H. Wood, *Overseas Missions of the Australian Methodist Church* (4 vols, Melbourne, Aldersgate Press, 1980), vol. 4, p. 23.

[18]   *The Missionary Review*, September 1907.

accepted the challenge and a 'missionary task force' with many different skills was assembled over the next few years. There were only ever two ministerial appointments, at separate times; the task force consisted of teachers and teacher-trainers, medical and agricultural workers, builders, administrators, even a boat-builder. They were stationed in widely dispersed places. Travel between Port Moresby and other stations was by air, village clinic patrols often by sea, and getting to a circuit meeting or regional Synod might take twenty-four hours, perhaps crammed in a canoe.

Paul Ruddick, one of the first MMS partners, described a typical few days in the Lai Valley in the southern highlands:

> First, organising the drainage system for the new hospital on our station and supervising the upkeep of the station. Second, counselling a pastor and his wife who are having marital problems. Third, walking twelve miles through the bush to question potential candidates for baptism and to supervise their continual instruction. Fourth, managing a trade store (which sells anything from tinned fish to trousers) with all the headaches of keeping accounts. Fifth, going into the school to teach Religious Knowledge. The children are taught in English, so for once I do not need an interpreter! Sixth, leading a pastors' fellowship where in prayer, Bible reading and discussion we deepen our faith and prepare for Sundays.

And when it was necessary to visit the District headquarters, 'It takes three hours by landrover to cover the twenty-six miles to Mendi!'[19]

The last MMS partners left PNG in 1992. It had been a brief period of assistance to a young Church finding its feet. A Prime Minister of PNG once referred, only slightly tongue-in-cheek, to 'a western cult known as Christianity'. It was time for a new generation of indigenous church leaders to stop looking over their shoulders and for a genuinely Melanesian Christianity to walk tall.

In both *Fiji* and *Western Samoa*, the Methodist Church became autonomous in 1964. The Free Wesleyan Church in *Tonga*, reunited in 1924 thanks to an initiative of the young Queen Salote, resumed its affiliation with the Australian Conference until the Uniting Church of Australia was inaugurated in 1977. In all three island groups the majority of the population was now Christian, and in Fiji and Tonga Methodists were the largest denomination.[20] Their ties with Australia and New Zealand remained strong, not least because of the numbers of migrants who settled in Auckland and Sydney and formed congregations there. But they also renewed their links with Britain, which led to some sharing of personnel: never more than a few, but in both directions. In 1974 Barbara Pott went to teach in Tonga and was soon appointed Principal of Queen Salote College in the capital. She served in

---

[19]   *NOW*, June 1971: p. 5.
[20]   In Tonga a significant minority refused to join the reunited Church in 1924 and formed the Free Church of Tonga, run along Methodist lines.

Tonga for thirteen years. In 1974 too Dr Philip Brakenbury went to the Methodist Hospital at Ba, on Fiji's west coast, for two years, and in 1982 Paul Greene began nine years' service with the Samoa Methodist Land Development Society on the island of Savaii. In each case they were the first missionaries from Britain to arrive in over a century. In the other direction, Akuila Yabaki moved from Fiji to London in 1979 and spent six years as a circuit minister in Hammersmith; he returned to Britain in 1990 as the Society's Secretary for Asia and the Pacific. Lalomilo Kamu from Samoa served as a tutor at Kingsmead College from 1983 to 1989. A tripartite arrangement with the German Conference brought Dr Ludwig Rott to teach at the Davuilevu Theological College in Fiji during the difficult years 1988–1994.

Fiji was a multiracial, multi-religious and multicultural society. The native Fijians of Melanesian stock were a little less than half the population; they were outnumbered by Fijians of Indian origin. The Methodist Church ministered to both groups, and to the smaller Chinese community. Two-thirds of the indigenous Fijians were Methodists, as were perhaps 10% of the Indo-Fijians, most of the rest being Hindus. These latecomers were not allowed to own land, which was under the control of traditional chiefs, but they ran prosperous businesses. A turning point in the political history of the country came in 1987 when for the first time a multi-racial coalition took office, replacing the Alliance Party which was the political vehicle of the traditional chiefs. A multi-racial government was not to the liking of indigenous Fijians. In two successive bloodless coups the army took over and Fiji left the Commonwealth. An election under a new constitution was held in 1992 and Colonel Sitiveni Rabuka, the Methodist Local Preacher who led the coups, became the civilian Prime Minister. Meanwhile there was also a church coup in 1989. The Methodist leadership was divided in its attitude to the military take-over and also on the extent to which strict Sunday observance laws should be imposed on the non-Christian population. The majority faction began to wage a Sunday observance campaign and week by week road blocks were set up, even preventing ambulances from answering calls. The General Secretary, Manasa Lasaro, was sentenced to three months' imprisonment for organizing the road blocks; but on his release he succeeded in first locking out of the office and then turning out of office the President, Josateki Koroi. Calls for tolerance from Akuila Yabaki and the former President Paula Niakula, prominent critics of the coups in both State and Church, went unheeded. Some of the better-off Indians, including several ministers of the Church's Indian Division, subsequently left Fiji. An international delegation, including the MCOD General Secretary, visited Fiji in 1993 in a vain attempt to effect reconciliation within the Church and within the World Methodist family. When Yabaki returned to Fiji in 1999 he found himself *persona non grata* in the Church; he became director of the Citizens' Constitutional Forum, working for a multi-racial democracy. Although the political scene was relatively quiet until the end of the millennium, the next decade would bring even greater turmoil. Fijian Christians were sustained by the convictions well expressed by Paula Niukula:

I often said to my small village churches as they prayed during the crisis in Fiji, 'You know that Jesus is Lord, and is in control of what is happening in Fiji. Let us not feel helpless and think that only the chiefs, or the military, or some other powers are in control. Ultimately the Christ is in control … His kingdom, and his way will win, even if right now we do not see much light in the distance.'[21]

South America

Migrant Methodists settled in the Dutch islands of Aruba and Curaçao, off the Venezuelan coast, in the 1930s and the Leeward Islands District stationed William Barrett on Aruba in 1939. The furthest south British Methodists had gone in the Americas was Guyana; there were, however, Methodist Episcopal Churches in much of the continent. The formation of CIEMAL, the Council of Evangelical Methodist Churches in Latin America, in 1969, brought the Churches and their parent bodies into a closer relationship than they had hitherto known. MMS embarked on an abortive Anglican–Methodist Project in 1971.[22] When it ended the Society's attention to the continent did not wane, especially as it became more and more newsworthy for all the wrong reasons: unrest, guerrilla activity, dictatorship, drug barons, military coups and 'disappearances'. The work of Paolo Freire, author of *Pedagogy of the Oppressed* (1970) and of the liberation theologians (including the Argentine Methodist Miguez Bonino) further stimulated interest in Latin American affairs.[23]

The appointment in 1980 of the Jamaican, Ivy McGhie, as Secretary for the Caribbean and the Americas brought a change of gear. She and her two Panamanian successors, Lesley Anderson and Luis Veagra, ensured that South America figured more regularly in MCOD plans. The chief ingredient in inter-Church relationships was no longer sending out missionaries – rather it was the Uruguayan Diego Frisch who ministered in Birmingham from 1982 to 1989 (enabling his English wife to live near her English relations for a while). Then in 1990 Margaret Valle, a British minister married to a Peruvian, was appointed to Lima: personal considerations played a significant part in both these arrangements. British mission partners subsequently worked in Bolivia and, after the dust of the Falklands/Malvinas war had settled, in Argentina. The hostilities did not undermine relations, and a letter from the Methodist Church in Argentina in 1985 said:

---

[21]   Uniting Church of Australia Mission Prayer Handbook, 1991.

[22]   pp. 171–3.

[23]   P. Freire, *Pedagogy of the Oppressed* (New York, Continuum, 1970); J.M. Bonino, *Christians and Marxists: the Mutual Challenge to Revolution* (Grand Rapids, Eerdmans, 1976) and *Doing Theology in a Revolutionary Situation* (Augsburg, Fortress, 1985).

Our two countries have recently engaged in a useless and miserable war; and the Malvinas situation is not yet resolved. It is important that as citizens of these countries, and also as Christians and Methodists, we create channels for communication and understanding.[24]

While the exchange of personnel was on a very limited scale, the Overseas Division was able to support the mission of the South American Churches with small grants. These could not, and were not intended to, compensate for the steep reduction in funding from the United States a few years earlier; the Churches were painfully working towards self-support. But they did make a difference, for example to the social work at Martinez Reina in Montevideo, inspired and led by Araceli Rochietti. In addition to serving two parishes, and chaplaincy at Uruguay's largest prison forty miles away, she was in the 1990s the Vice-Moderator of the WCC's Faith and Order Commission. But she made time for Martinez Reina, a disused knitwear factory which had been divided by flimsy internal partitions into 280 single-room dwellings, and was occupied by families made homeless when recession-hit businesses failed. The four-storey block had just three outside sinks with cold running water for laundry, and four communal bathrooms, when they were not out of order. Here Rochietti and a few of the women worked wonders to improve the quality of the children's life, issuing powdered milk to mothers too malnourished to breast-feed, and every Saturday providing a protein-rich lunch and then an afternoon of indoor and outdoor activities. She recruited two dozen high school students who faithfully came along each Saturday to run the activities and bond with the children. She got regrettably little support from local Methodists – but there were only 630 full members in the whole of Uruguay, for the political repression of the 1970s had driven some of the best trained and dynamic pastors and laypeople into exile. A small grant from MCOD – the Division's grants to South America were rarely more than a few thousand pounds – was a great encouragement. Another was made, in 1996, to help launch an ecumenical women's group in Bolivia, the Comunidad de Libertad y Esperanza de la Mujer (CLEM). In a macho society where wife-beating was common, many of these women had been victims of domestic violence. Seeking to break the cycle of deprivation, dependence and abuse, they embarked on self-help activities to raise money in order to improve the life of women in the impoverished *barrios*. (A few years later, through sheer tenacity and hard work, they opened a women's clinic in a deprived *barrio* supplying a range of basic treatments at affordable prices.)

Additionally, Second Mile Projects[25] channelled support for community development among the indigenous Mapuche in southern Chile and for text books for church-run primary schools in Bolivia, while a tripartite youth exchange took British and Portuguese youngsters to Brazil and Brazilians to Europe, formative

---

[24]   *Celebrate Partnership in Prayer: the 1985–1986 Prayer Manual* (London, MCOD, 1985), p.19.

[25]   p. 269.

experiences for visitors and hosts alike. *Encuentro* was a study pack the Division produced for the benefit of British congregations. It provided a Latin American view of the 500th anniversary of Columbus' historic 1492 voyage and the Spanish conquest to which that was the prelude. Another innovative programme took a young Brazilian theologian, Magali da Cunha, to share in grassroots community work in Britain. In the twenty-first century further initiatives would strengthen and diversify links with Latin America.

Home and Away

The expanding network of relationships and the new destinations were a practical possibility because the speed, the increasing frequency, and indeed the economy of air flights (since aviation fuel was nowhere taxed) made travel so much easier in the second half, and particularly the last third, of the twentieth century. The 'ends of the earth' were accessible. By the same token, Britain became more accessible, especially to the people of the commonwealth. The 492 Jamaican immigrants who disembarked from the *Windrush* at Tilbury in 1948 were followed by boatloads and planeloads from the Caribbean – 260,000 between 1955 and 1962 – the Indian sub-continent and Africa. The first arrivals were people with initiative, seeking new opportunities and better lives in the manner of the British who had established the colonies and dominions. Some came to study, most to find work. Later, more arrived as refugees from violent situations, as had Huguenots and Jews before them. The treatment they received in what many thought of as 'the mother country' is well documented. British congregations, Methodists not excepted, were slow (at best) to offer a welcome. But among those who had lived abroad, who knew the culture shock and homesickness of being 'strangers in a strange land' and who had received generous hospitality from some of the world's poorest people, there was real concern and a profound feeling of shame.

One of those was Hilda Porter, who had worked in China and later became a WW Secretary at Mission House. Long before the *Windrush* docked, she was befriending overseas students in London who lived in cold, damp and cramped conditions in former fire-watching stations not far from her home. She invited them to her flat on Sunday afternoons, and they began to call on her in ever greater numbers. Through her WW contacts, she succeeded in getting twenty-nine 'hospitality secretaries' appointed, who would make contact with overseas arrivals in their neighbourhood and find people to take in lodgers. She soon became the full-time co-ordinator of this work, which the MMS owned as an important element of its overseas mission.

It did not take Hilda Porter long to realise the extent of the prejudice which black people – usually called 'Coloureds' in the 1950s and 1960s – faced, and the grim reality of the unremitting, doomed search for lodgings. She determined that the church itself must open an International House, for people of any colour. After a long quest for a property, she found a hotel in Inverness Terrace, London, which the Society was able to buy with part of the proceeds from the sale of its previous Mission House.[26] It needed a lot of repairs and refurbishment. In August 1950 she moved in. Her plan was to renovate a room a day, with the help of a legion of friends she recruited to scrub, paint and fix. As each room was ready, a student moved in, and by Christmas Methodist International House (MIH) had become not just a lodging but a multi-racial home, its character expressed in its motto, 'In honour preferring one another'.[27] Students came and went; so did others, directed as often as not by taxi-drivers who knew it was one place from which they would not be turned away. They looked on Hilda Porter as a surrogate mother, and indeed she was 'mother of the bride' at several weddings; on one occasion she acted as the bride's father, when Grace Okon and Egemba Igwe (later to be Secretary of the Nigerian Conference) married and Grace insisted Hilda must do it or she wouldn't be 'given away' at all. Responsibility for MIH left little time for the Care of Overseas Students around the country, the post to which she had been appointed. The MMS was alert to the need, re-opened the office at Mission House and made a new appointment. Meanwhile, inspired by the Inverness Terrace venture, other MIHs, locally funded and managed, opened in several strategic university cities.[28]

In 1966 Eric Daniels, a Pakistani minister, was stationed in Bradford to work among immigrants, and in 1967 Byron Chambers and Alford Alphonse were seconded by the MCCA for similar work in London and Birmingham respectively, and Yuk Lun Wong from Hong Kong began a ministry to Chinese in London. These were the first appointments of black and Asian ministers to British circuits. The wheel had not yet come full circle, but it was turning.

Unreached Peoples

The greatest difference in the second half of the century was not made by the geographical enlargement of the Society's sphere of work but by a sea-change in the character of its activity. Missionaries now did what their contemporaries in Britain did, in schools, hospitals, theological colleges and circuits. There were children to teach, students to train, babies to deliver, illness and injury to treat, sermons to preach, Bible studies to lead, meetings to attend. The message 'Pastor, will you come to our village' was more likely to be delivered to an indigenous minister than to an expatriate. Grants tended to be made to consolidate and extend work initiated long before by missionaries but now under local control. The emphasis was properly on resource-sharing – human resources (people and their skills), material resources (money and its purchasing power), spiritual resources (prayer and solidarity) – and sharing meant both giving and receiving.

---

[26]   p. 41.
[27]   Romans 12:10.
[28]   Webb, *Women of our Time*, pp. 71–96.

This was in itself a full and worthwhile agenda but it left aside the call to primary evangelism. There was no doubt that the most effective evangelists were local people operating within their own culture. But there were still peoples with whom no evangelists of any culture had contact. The Church Growth movement, which took off in the 1960s, claimed that 2 billion of the global population were in that category. Its guru, the American Donald McGavran, took issue with the notion that mission is 'philanthropy, education, medicine, famine relief, evangelism, and world friendship' and held that good deeds – while necessary – 'must never replace the essential task of mission, discipling the peoples of the earth'.[29] In 1984 he called for every Christian congregation to organize

> frontier missionary societies … specifically founded to evangelize the Unreached People groups … Most mission resources – ambassadors and money – should now be spent working directly or indirectly to multiply sound churches among the two and a half billion lost men and women *who are presently locked out of and locked away from any personal witness within their group.*[30]

His arguments sparked off lively debate. Osmond Mulligan, an Irish surgeon, local preacher and former Nigeria missionary pressed the need for the Overseas Division to be more than a resource-sharing agency and take fresh initiatives in evangelism among unreached peoples. So in 1985 a letter went to the heads of partner Churches enquiring whether they had any such initiatives in mind and whether the co-operation and partnership of MCOD would be helpful. Resource-sharing and primary evangelism did not have to be in contradiction.

Almost at once a reply came from Zimbabwe. MCOD's letter had arrived just as the MCZ was being pressed by one of its ministers to develop work in the vast Nyaminyami region bordering Lake Kariba. The lake had displaced the Tonga people living on the south bank of the Zambezi and driven them to the arid, infertile escarpments that the dam waters did not reach. Given the area's practical needs as well as the almost total absence of organized Christian activity, a team ministry with evangelistic and humanitarian dimensions would be called for, said the reply. In 1986 two envoys from MCOD travelled to Nyaminyami with Zimbabwe Methodist leaders and met with local councillors, officials and people to discuss the project. They heard that two people had died at the roadside a few days earlier, trying to get to the solitary clinic many miles away. They gave a lift to some women carrying corn to the grinding mill, a twenty-two mile walk they did every three days. They saw the raised platform in every field where someone would spend the night ready to scare off invading animals for whom the boundary of the adjoining National Park meant nothing. They visited a school with a Waddilove-trained head where an English exercise on the blackboard read 'Yesterday was Sunday and we go/went/going to church' – though there was no church for many miles. They learned about

---

[29]   *International Bulletin of Missionary Research* (10.2) April 1986: p. 54.
[30]   *Journal of Frontier Missions* (1.3) 1984: pp. 252–3.

Figure 15.1   Village worship in the shade, Nyaminyami, 1988

the fear that dominated people's lives: the spirit world must be kept happy and the diviners must not be provoked. On their return it was agreed that MCZ would station a Chitonga-speaking minister in Nyaminyami and meet the basic stipend, while MCOD would fund a manse with a solar module, an initial furnishing grant, a four-wheel drive vehicle, and a grant for the minister's children's boarding school fees, such as was available for missionaries' children. MCOD would also try and recruit a nurse-midwife and provide and equip a mobile clinic as well as her house. The government would pay a driver and a nurse-aid and meet the running costs and maintenance of the mobile clinic. All this was duly realized. Within weeks Deina Smith, a nurse-midwife made an offer of overseas service and was promptly assigned to Nyaminyami; she proved an admirable person for the task. Morris Maswanise, the dynamic minister with whom the whole idea originated, agreed to take on the evangelistic work. It was a daunting prospect, but they set their hand to the plough and did not look back.

Pressed still further by some of the Committee about unevangelized people-groups, MCOD commissioned a preliminary study of the Kurds but concluded that not even an exploratory reconnaissance mission was viable. It could however point to its ongoing work with the United Mission to Nepal[31] as giving expression to God's love in Christ by practical action in a land where overt evangelism was prohibited.

Nationals in Mission Appointments

By the 1990s the shape of the MCOD budget had changed markedly from the pre-autonomy and immediate post-autonomy years. The proportion devoted to missionary costs had fallen dramatically with the reduction in the number of mission partners, both lay and ordained. In the case of lay professionals this was in part due to uncertainty about their chances in the job market after some time away, and in the case of ministers in part to the problem of interrupting a spouse's career. There was also a much-changed attitude to 'missionary work' within British Methodism, as British society became more unchurched while, overseas, people took Christ to their hearts in great numbers. In 1967 the Prayer Manual listed '300 men missionaries, 165 women missionaries and 272 missionaries' wives' – a total of 737. Thirty years later there were just 75 mission partners.[32] While terms of service and lay pension provision had improved, the overall cost of mission partners was no longer such a significant element in the budget. At the same time autonomous Churches were struggling to provide from their own resources for the indigenous personnel who had replaced them. In some cases they had imaginative plans for new initiatives and competent, committed people ready to implement them but lacked the funds to make it happen, even though the sterling amounts required were much less than the cost of an expatriate. It was in this context that a scheme to fund Nationals in Mission Appointments (NMAs) was devised. Churches that were enthusiastically self-propagating but not fully self-financing were enabled to rise to the opportunities they had identified. A novel feature of the scheme was that applications were vetted and NMAs approved each year by an international group composed of overseas representatives to the British Conference.

If it was difficult to keep up with the pace of change, the grass was not allowed to grow beneath Methodist feet.

---

[31] pp. 256–8.

[32] The *Prayer Handbook 1997–1998* listed six retired missionaries and twelve Amity Teachers from unspecified denominations in addition to the 75.

Chapter 16
Do All the Good You Can

Methodist missionaries took to heart the words attributed to John Wesley:

> Do all the good you can,
> By all the means you can,
> In all the ways you can,
> In all the places you can,
> At all the times you can,
> To all the people you can,
> As long as ever you can.

Alongside their teaching and medical ministries, they promoted agriculture and rural development, housing schemes, wealth creation projects, family planning, orphan care and skills training. Those who engaged in specialized humanitarian ministries were sometimes scornfully labelled 'do-gooders', but argued that as Christians their role was to be salt and light in society. The fierce debates about the social gospel which marked the early years of the twentieth century were not as divisive overseas as in the North Atlantic world. Hugh Price Hughes's powerful voice called his generation to recognize that the gospel was not about pie-in-the-sky:

> Let us not only save people's souls but … sanctify their circumstances … Let us, then, in the name of God and humanity, combine heartily to abolish Slavery, Drunkenness, Lust, Gambling, Ignorance, Pauperism, Mammonism and War.[1]

From the earliest days of the WMMS and its contemporary Societies, most of the activity which in the twentieth century comprised 'development' formed part and parcel of the missionary enterprise: alleviating the suffering of humanity caused by poverty, disease, ignorance, oppressive work conditions and society's injustices. Alongside the emphasis on education and health care, the promotion of efficient agriculture was a concern long before MMS decided to employ an agricultural advisor: Samuel Leigh began agricultural experiments in New Zealand in the 1820s and Thomas Birch Freeman in the 1860s introduced bullocks into West Africa to improve the local stock. The passion for social justice, which drove Hughes and became an integral part of the development agenda, motivated the campaigns to abolish slavery, cannibalism and, albeit with less energy and

---

[1] H.P. Hughes, *Social Christianity: sermons delivered in St. James's Hall, London* (London, Hodder & Stoughton, 1889), p. xiii.

less success, caste. David Hill's virtual secondment, in 1878, to the famine relief operation in Shanxi, was an early instance of emergency disaster relief. In 1920 and 1921 the Jamaica Synod twice voted £100 for famine relief in China. Mission was understood to be holistic – Douglas Thompson, in the 1930s, used the expression 'life-inclusive.'

Rural development

From their mission stations in Africa, Asia and the islands of the Caribbean, normally located in or close by market towns and other centres of population, ministers and evangelists would visit the villages round about, making regular treks, sometimes of many days' duration, through the countryside, whether open savannah or dense bush. They slept in village huts and observed village life and customs. Much of what they saw appalled them: infants playing in the dirt; older children, unschooled, herding goats or cattle; the long hours of a woman's day; the heavy loads of wood and water they carried; the injuries – a toe severed by a hoe, a wrist gashed by a machete – that, having been treated bush-fashion, left them crippled; women with fistulas from too much and too early child-bearing, and few surviving children to show for it; the indulgence in home-brewed (or imported) liquor; perhaps most of all, since it affected their personal hygiene, the absence of toilet facilities. They had limited resources but, if the quality of village life was to be improved, they had to pay attention not only to health and education: the fields and herds had to be made more productive. Education, indeed, was a two-edged sword. One deplorable but predictable result of introducing a western-style school system was that boys who completed their elementary education, let alone those who went on to secondary school, liked to think they were 'emancipated from the drudgery of tilling the soil'.[2] Somehow the rural community had to be helped to see the value of agriculture and its capacity to improve the quality of life.

A wide range of agricultural activities developed. The Society had no carefully constructed central plan, and most started as a spontaneous response to local needs, initiated and controlled by a minister with or without specialist knowledge. In time there were demonstration farms, linked with short courses for local farmers, agricultural departments in schools, agricultural colleges, seed-banks and livestock programmes. There were also commercial farms and plantations, where augmenting church funds was the aim.

In Northern *Rhodesia*, Douglas Gray could see the importance of training in agriculture. He described the way of life which had been frustrating him ever since his arrival in 1913:

> At present they have no permanent gardens. They choose a piece of bush, lop off all the branches of the trees to be found there, and piling them around the base of

---

[2]   Groves, vol. 4, p. 297.

the trees allow them to dry. Then they burn them, thus killing the trees. Then they hoe in the ash to fertilise the soil … The first year the crop may be good, so the second and third; but soon the soil is exhausted … 'The garden is finished,' they say; 'we must go and find another.' This may be miles away, and so a new village is needed near to the new gardens. Is it likely they are going to build permanent houses when those houses must be abandoned in a few years? We shall never get them to build better houses, carrying out the lessons of hygiene, ventilation and sanitation that they are taught, until they have permanent gardens. They will never have permanent gardens until we can teach them the elements of agriculture, the rotation of crops and simple manuring.[3]

The Society took note and in 1932 sent an agricultural missionary, W.H. Turnbull, to Gray's training institution at Chipembi with its motto *Atuume luteeta* – 'Let us blaze a trail'. Gray secured a government grant to fund the appointment but it was not renewed and Turnbull was transferred south to the much larger Waddilove institution. The long-awaited Chipembi Farm College eventually opened in 1964 with support from the newly independent Zambian government. Gray's son-in-law, Merfyn Temple, noted that after half-a-century the way of life of Zambian farmers had changed little: moving on when the soil was exhausted, leaving a treeless waste behind them; growing little but maize with the resulting malnutrition from the inadequate diet.

Waddilove and Tegwani, the Rhodesia District's principal training centres, both had extensive lands and from the outset courses had an agricultural component. Student evangelists and teachers were expected to spend some time each day on the farm, and grew much of their own food. By the 1930s the Waddilove tree nursery was distributing trees to the teachers who were posted to schools in the 'reserves'. In the early 1940s this work was developed more systematically, with a post-primary two-year Agricultural Training Programme and a model farm. It became a three-year course in 1953 and later a four-year course, supervised by Emery Alvord, a former Director of Native Agriculture for the colony. The syllabus included: the use of fertilisers; the care of poultry, sheep, cattle and pigs, including dosing sheep against worms, and dipping cattle against ticks; forestry; protection against soil erosion through contour ridging; the use of tools, including tractors, and simple tractor repairs; fencing. There were around thirty students in each year. Many became government demonstrators, living in the reserves and, by the way they themselves farmed, demonstrating how to improve crops and animal husbandry. At Tegwani too there was a flourishing agricultural department. The courses at both Waddilove and Tegwani continued until 1965 when the government decided that in future students would first have to pass the Junior Certificate examination. Those who had already completed up to three years, confidently expecting to become government demonstrators in their turn, were

---

[3] S.D. Gray, *Frontiers of the Kingdom* (London, Cargate Press, 1930), p. 102.

abruptly told they would not qualify. Thereafter formal agricultural training was left to government centres.

'Rural reconstruction' was a term often heard in *China* in the 1930s. Returning to Hunan from furlough in 1933, Douglas Thompson stopped off in India to learn all he could about rural development programmes. He took a particular interest in human waste. He saw how acres of desert had become fertile through 'buying the sewage of Allahabad and harnessing it through long canals on to the wilderness'. He admired a school compound at Ushagram in Bengal where they had installed septic tanks – 'the sewage was treated in them and went on to the land and solved the supply of food to the school'. During his furlough he had become an Associate Member of the Royal Sanitary Institute, and in Dichpalli he was able to design the first septic tank system for the Leprosy Hospital.[4] Once back in Hunan, he put into action a sixfold plan. Its components were adult literacy, rural credit co-operatives, local healers equipped with three months' training and a medicine chest, improved agriculture that would produce a better balanced diet, a recreational programme for young people (with drama, rather than sport, at its heart) and indigenized worship. It all depended on training local people to deliver the plan, village by village; Thompson believed that if they could be trained as Local Preachers and take the gospel message to the villages, other skills could be taught and handed on in the same way. The gospel message was 'life in all its fullness'.

The scheme was only partly successful. Agricultural development was slow; Thompson had to accept that 'farm improvement is a long and patient business'. Amid ongoing conflict between Nationalists, Communists and Japanese invaders, it took three years to get seeds from the Agricultural College in Nanjing, sow them on a mission compound, and get them out, via village chapel plots, to the farmers themselves. The farmers who were bold enough to experiment were introduced to tomatoes, broad beans, cabbage, lettuce, Irish potatoes, peanuts and two new strains of rice, all good for revitalizing the impoverished soil as well as supplying healthy meals.[5]

In *Haiti* Marco Dépestre, a trained agronomist, brought up a strict Roman Catholic, stumbled upon Methodism in his early 30s and became a minister. After studying in Jamaica he was appointed in 1948 to the Petit Goâve circuit west of Port-au-Prince, where he served for twenty-five years. For him too economic and spiritual needs went hand in hand. Evangelization entailed:

> A competent medical service available to the peasants in the rural community itself and not in town where it takes too much time to come and it cannot meet emergency cases; a scientific agricultural programme to demonstrate that

---

[4]   D.W. Thompson, *A Mountain Road* (privately published, 1983), p. 41.

[5]   Ibid., pp. 46–53; Davey, *Changing Places*, pp. 135–7.

successful farming has nothing to do with any capricious spirits man needs to propitiate; a family and social life enriched with Christian leisure.[6]

In 1959 Dépestre founded the Christian Rural Life Institute, a training centre for community leaders. Here he demonstrated the uses of compost and advocated organic farming, and experimented with household appliances such as bio-gas and solar cookers, and mobile latrines that could be moved along trenches. Retiring from circuit ministry at the age of 60 in 1973, he continued to busy himself with the affairs of the Institute.

Another Haitian minister, Alain Rocourt, concerned at the rate of land erosion in his home region of Jérémie, devised a rural rehabilitation project which obtained funding via the WCC's Inter-Church Aid network. A suite of buildings included school, dispensary, garage and home economy centre; there was a market garden, some animal husbandry and groves of rubber, cacao and sisal. Nine Swiss staff arrived in 1965; they had learned Creole even before reaching Haiti. Tragically two were killed in a plane crash in January 1966, but the team – including the director's widow – carried on developing the project.

After the Mau Mau uprising in *Kenya* was crushed in 1956, the government introduced a 'land consolidation' scheme. On the recommendation of a Royal Commission, the colonial policy of maintaining traditional systems of land tenure was reversed, and families were encouraged to exchange their scattered strips of land, often widely separated, for smallholdings of twelve to twenty acres, depending on the fertility of the area. The incentives for this peaceful agrarian revolution were the security of tenure that the new title deeds provided, the credit that African farmers were no longer denied, and the right to grow cash crops and access marketing facilities, which was previously the prerogative of the white settler minority. Merle Wilde, a deaconess from a farming family, arrived in Kenya at just the right time to give practical advice. A little later, Francis Mungania, an experienced teacher, offered himself for ministerial training and offered his land to the church. He had been one of the team translating the Bible into Kimeru and had been struck by what he read in Leviticus about proper stewardship of the land. He was concerned about school dropouts and how to present farming as a worthwhile way of life, and he wanted his smallholding to be made a rural training centre. Colleagues, concerned about the effect on his family, were reluctant to accept his land; they prevailed, for happily the District Council made over a fifty-acre plot. It was gradually cleared, by manual labour rather than machinery, and by 1962 dormitories and classrooms were ready. Soon coffee, maize and other crops were being grown and dairy farming, artificial insemination, fish farming and other skills were being taught. In the arid Tharaka region forty miles away a companion centre was begun, which was renowned especially for its honey.

---

[6] M. Dépestre, *Experimenting Rural Evangelism in Haiti* (Petit Goâve, La Presse du Sauveur, 1957), quoted in Griffiths, p. 269.

The 1920 WMMS Report from *India* described 'one feature of our work in Haidarabad' as 'absolutely unique'. A lay missionary, Ernest Bevan, had been 'appointed to take charge of and develop agricultural training', a charge he fulfilled for twenty-six years. Later Bob Livingstone, an experienced Irish minister and Principal of the Methodist Agricultural College at Gurteen, accepted a similar brief from CSI. His first assignment, in 1963, was to advise the CSI on how to turn unused church lands into productive areas, and to identify a site for an agricultural centre in each diocese. That task completed, he settled in Medak, where 100 acres lay idle on the cathedral compound, and until 1970 piloted a training centre for young farmers there. Waste land became fields of rice, millet, maize, sugar-cane and sorghum. 'Soil', he once wrote, 'is like a bank account. There are deposits and withdrawals. Every crop uses nutrients, and unless they are returned the soil is impoverished.'

A venture in which Livingstone took particular pleasure was designed to improve the quality of Indian cattle; he developed a close working relationship with Andhra Pradesh government departments and used his contacts to have several consignments of pedigree bulls and heifers sent from Ireland. With the first bulls to arrive the State Department of Animal Husbandry inseminated selected native cows. When their calves came into milk in 1969 they produced up to 250 gallons a year, compared with eighty gallons from their dams. The scheme developed with a new consignment of bulls from Lincolnshire but collapsed after the herd went down with foot-and-mouth disease.

A young Irish agriculturalist, Howard Dalziel, started the training programme in earnest. It covered crop production, animal husbandry and the use and maintenance of farm machinery. Several milk production training courses were carried out in the centre for farmers sent by the State Government and also for project managers from NGO groups from all over India. But the neediest people locally had no resources to maintain cattle. So the emphasis of the centre shifted to dry-land farming and water development, demonstrating soil and water conservation and husbandry techniques aimed at enhanced and sustainable yields of rain-fed crops. Local farmers were trained in their fields; at the centre many courses were organised, in collaboration with the All India Council for Agricultural Research, for trainers from other projects across the state of Andhra and beyond. It is testament to the suitability of the methods promoted that they were widely replicated.

Over a twenty-five year period a huge amount was achieved with and for poor people. Yet the centre was eventually closed down. Dalziel's analysis of the reasons concluded that from the outset the centre operated in a policy vacuum. The CSI had neither a clearly articulated rationale for engaging in agricultural mission nor a vision of the desired outcome. Selection of the centre's activities and priorities was left to those – in this instance, the missionaries – on the spot. They were accountable to committees who received reports and kept watch on finances but did not, in his experience, address wider issues. Furthermore – and this was not unusual, either in India or elsewhere – he was given other, unconnected, time-consuming responsibilities which impeded his primary task and he never once had a performance review.[7]

MMS had no clear policy on rural development either. Every situation was different; initiatives had to be left, at first to the missionaries *in situ* and subsequently to the inclination of the autonomous churches. By 1967, however, this *laissez-faire* attitude was felt to be inadequate. Harry Morton wrote: 'The facts of world poverty and the imminent danger of world famine are a challenge to the MMS and the churches we serve, at home and abroad.'[8] Droughts and famines were not just transient local misfortunes; the promotion of efficient agriculture was a global imperative. The UN had proclaimed the 1960s the 'Decade of Development', hoping to achieve for the poorest countries what the Marshall Plan had done for post-war Europe. The Green Revolution[9] was under way. 'Miracle rice' in India was producing ten times the usual yield. New varieties of maize and wheat, synthetic nitrogen fertilizer and chemical pesticides all contributed to a substantial rise in food production; the downside – the loss of biodiversity, the carcinogenic effects of pesticides and the long-term impact of chemical inputs and monocultures on soil fertility – was not yet apparent. But despite the many initiatives and considerable achievements, the high hopes with which the Decade had been launched were not being realized. Furthermore, Morton pointed out, the Society had seen 'many failed schemes' over the years, and it was time to add an Agricultural Advisor to the staff at Mission House.

Ralph Whitlock, who was appointed to the post in 1968, was a Wiltshire farmer, writer and broadcaster with a passionate love of the countryside. He wrote over a hundred books and for sixteen years was 'Farmer Whitlock' on BBC radio Children's Hour. He was thus well-known and could make fruitful contacts, but had little experience of the undeveloped world. However, his brief was to travel widely in the first two years and assess the needs and opportunities, then identify potential projects and seek funds from other agencies to launch them. He undertook a gruelling schedule: to East and Central Africa, to West Africa, to India, Indonesia, Haiti and Belize. He had a talent for water-divining, which was sometimes called upon, to good effect, on his travels. He wrote full reports, and did not temper his comments, some of which were unhelpful and irritated colleagues, like his hasty and ill-judged appraisal of the 'formidable difficulties' faced by a project in the Ivory Coast:

> The major handicap is that the people … are not accustomed to hard work. Subsistence farming is pretty easy in this forest zone. Villagers … would like better crops and more money, but such things are not worth much extra effort.[10]

[7]   H. Dalziel, personal communication, 27 December 2011.

[8]   MCH: paper circulated to MMS staff and committees, 30 March 1967.

[9]   The term was coined by William Gauld, addressing the Society for International Development in Washington, 8 March 1968.

[10]   MCH: Report on a visit to Lakota, 31 March 1969.

After Whitlock's five-year term the Society was no nearer to formulating policy guidelines for rural development work, and many questioned whether it was a worthwhile exercise, so the post was discontinued. His appointment had made little impact on the ground. The broad concerns he identified on his fact-finding tours were undeniably serious issues; they had also arrived on the agendas of Christian Aid and the World Development Movement (WDM) and were being pursued energetically. WDM was started in Britain in 1970 to campaign *inter alia* against the tariffs which made it uneconomical for countries producing cash crops to develop their own processing industries and obliged them to export raw produce at cheap prices fixed by western cartels. From its inception Methodists were active in WDM both nationally and in local groups.

On his tour in 1969, Whitlock noted that there were no agricultural projects in *Sierra Leone*, but he had high hopes that the recent arrival of a Yorkshire couple, the Capsticks – keen Young Farmers' Club members at home – would change that. They were stationed at Tikonko and Dwin Capstick became known as a 'reverend farmer'. He started growing rice on part of the mission land and proved to neighbouring farmers that good yields of rice could be had even from poor sandy soil, if it were properly laid out. Soon, with the collaboration of the Ministry of Agriculture, an extension programme was begun to help villagers develop their local swamps. Within a few years a small workshop was started as well, training blacksmiths to make simple tools which were not dependent on any sophisticated technology or on electricity. This Small Farm Equipment Unit moved in 1976 to premises in the nearby town of Bo which had been vacated when the country's only railway line stopped running, but it remained a unit of the Tikonko Agricutural Extension Centre (TAEC). The Centre also managed a number of micro-credit unions, aiming to widen the benefits from individual farmers to village communities.

But young farmers were in short supply. The allure of urban centres and diamond fields left the strenuous tasks of bush-clearing to an older generation, generally in poor health. For a few years TAEC flourished but by the end of the 1980s a depressed economy left a depressed population. A visitor in 1987 found 'an attitude of resignation … Shortages and failures are accepted as normal'. A rabbit hutch, doubtless in poor repair, had collapsed and the rabbits had escaped. A piggery had succumbed to disease. A crop had failed. People described these events as matters of fact without a hint of frustration.

Rural development projects in *Ghana*, too, had mixed fortunes. A number were launched in the quarter-century after autonomy: Ghanaian initiatives with Ghanaian management and staff, though helped by overseas advisers and seed-money. To translate ambitious plans into working business was a slow process, liable to encounter setbacks at any stage. One which went well was managed by Noah Kyireh, a minister who was previously a teacher of agricultural science and had studied agriculture in America. He developed a demonstration farm at Assin Nyankomasi, inland from Cape Coast, with crop production (oil palm, plantain, yam, pineapple), livestock (cattle, goats, sheep, rabbits) and pasture development

– an experimental plot growing various sturdy grasses, hoping to improve the quality of pasture. Having made good use of his two years in Georgia, he obtained funding from several sources there. He successfully resisted pressure from church headquarters to show a profit, knowing full well that training and commercial objectives were not readily compatible and that to pursue both outcomes was to court failure. Revenue from the farm simply paid the workers. He recognized that if the farmers of the region began to farm more efficiently and their income rose, they would be in a position to give more financial support to the church, and that was good enough.

In 1989 the MCCA started a training project for young farmers in *Antigua*, in co-operation with the Canadian and Antiguan governments. The Church contributed five acres for a demonstration farm, on the historic estate formerly owned by Nathaniel Gilbert, who introduced Methodism to the western hemisphere in 1759. The average age of Caribbean farmers was fifty years, and the younger generation was not interested in agriculture or its related industries. Yet the sector offered great opportunities for young people, in terms of realizing employment, raising self esteem, and providing opportunities for youths to better themselves and become productive members of society. Following the success of a two-year pilot project, the Gilbert Agricultural and Rural Development Centre was born, offering agricultural and enterprise training to young men between the ages of sixteen and thirty. In 1996 it also began targeting the training of unemployed and low-income women, with special emphasis on the use of natural resources in agriculture and other forms of rural enterprise.

Three urgent concerns came into ever more prominent focus as the century drew towards its close: well-digging, tree-planting and organic farming. Millions of women were spending several hours every day walking to a source of water and then carrying home enough for the family. The same women had to spend longer and longer hours collecting firewood as deforestation took its toll.

Wells were essential for agricultural as well as domestic purposes, and had long been an important factor in rural development. In Mysore, for example, ACRES – the Agency of the Church's Rural Extension Service – had a scheme whereby any small farmer could apply for a well. Hundreds were dug, each involving twenty or thirty jobless people for up to six months, receiving food in return. The diocese bought pumps at a discount and the bank loaned the farmer 75 per cent of the cost of the pump. Thus the church, the bank, the pump manufacturers, poor persons on relief and the government (responsible for transporting the food from the ports) all worked together on a scheme which improved the standard of agriculture as well as the quality of domestic life.

Bob Mann already had twelve years' experience as an agricultural field worker in Nyasaland and Tanzania when he was appointed to The Gambia in 1974. His brief was to establish a small demonstration plot and work alongside local farmers. After a series of meetings thirty-five decided to participate and agreed to begin with dry-season vegetable-growing. Over the next dozen years, as well as extending the farm, sharing the experience of drought, grasshopper-infestation and other setbacks, identifying preventive measures, demonstrating the importance of compost, animal vaccination, poles for climbing crops, shade for nursery beds and much else, he trained well-digging teams and by 1986 there were six teams of four working in many parts of the country.

Mann was acutely conscious of progressive desertification, caused by factors ranging from excessive logging to the appetite of goats for green shoots. Declining rainfall was directly related to the loss of tree-cover. He encouraged the establishment of orchards, or simply one or two fruit trees in the yard, to provide extra income as well as a means of carbon sequestration; he promoted alley-cropping to reduce water run-off and wind erosion and to optimize the benefit of nutrients. After handing the Gambian project on, and short assignments in Ghana and Ethiopia, he was asked by MCOD and the Methodist Relief and Development Fund (MRDF) to spearhead a West African Agroforestry Programme. He travelled through the region several times a year, motivating the Churches and their projects with the slogan 'Trees Mean Life'. A regional conference in Accra in 1990 was a spur to national seminars and initiatives such as seed banks and sustainable woodlots for firewood. He started a twice-yearly bulletin, *Africa Link*, in English and French, with news items from across the network, which MRDF continued to produce long after his retirement.

Merfyn Temple, long after *his* retirement, was an ardent advocate of organic farming. In 1965, seconded at the request of President Kaunda for government service in newly-independent Zambia, he had been dazzled by the prospects of the Green Revolution, and made small loans to some of his neighbours in Chipapa, the village where he was living, so that they could buy 'miracle seed' and fertilizers. In the first year, the results were spectacular, harvests as much as ten times the norm. But in the second year the rains failed, the crops withered, and the farmers were left deep in debt. He became a convert to the organic method:

> The organic farmer ensures that the soil's fertility is constantly renewed through the natural processes of life, death, decomposition and rebirth … The organic method of agriculture gradually improves soil fertility and is therefore indefinitely sustainable. As it requires no external inputs, it is available to anyone with access to soil, water, sunlight and a crop to grow; the incorporation of livestock into an organic farmer's system provides valuable manure for increased soil fertility.[11]

In 1989 he marked his 70th birthday with a tour of East and Central Africa, some of it by bicycle, both to look at organic farming and to encourage the friends who had taken it up. Organics were still a minority interest: he described in poetic vein the more general picture:

---

[11]   M.M. Temple, *New Hope for Africa* (Reading, Taurus, 1991), p. iv.

With their axes they have cut down the trees to plant their crops and make charcoal for their cooking fires. With plough and hoe they have scorched the earth, turning soil into dust, to be driven on the wind, or washed in muddy rivers down to the sea.[12]

In fact, he could see, the damage had two causes. There were the foreign agribusinesses, to whom he wanted to say 'Keep your dangerous herbicides to poison your own land ... and let the women and children of Zambia destroy their weeds with their own hoes',[13] and there was the pressure of runaway population growth, with so many mouths to feed making excessive demands on the soil. In this Zambia was not alone. One of the most outstanding – and provocative – missionaries in the final half-century of this history, Merfyn Temple was a passionate evangelist with a 'life-inclusive' gospel.

Urban and Industrial Ministry

Alongside all the efforts to improve the quality of village life and the productivity of the land, the rapid growth of great cities commanded attention. In 1900, only 14 per cent of the world's population lived in urban areas. By 1996, 46 per cent were urbanized.[14] Mission was concerned both with those who made good in the city and with the sixth of humanity – approaching a billion people by the century's end – who lived precariously in squalid shanty-towns. By the 1960s the concept of specialized urban-industrial ministry had taken root in places as far apart as Hong Kong, Calcutta, Madras, Nairobi, Abidjan, Kingston, the Copperbelt of Zambia and the mines of South Africa.[15] One example was described by the Ghanaian, Yedu Bannerman.[16]

Tema, fifteen miles east of Accra, was until 1954 no more than a small fishing village. Then work began to construct a major seaport, and it grew rapidly, until by 1970 there was a busy harbour, and over two hundred industrial and commercial firms operating in the zone. Shanty-towns sprang up as quickly as factories: a 1970 report spoke of an area where there were six public water-taps, not always working, for 12,000 people; where garbage heaps were taller than houses; where the local market was one of the dirtiest places in the town; where the only clinics were privately run and expensive; where there was no policing and theft was rampant; where there was no electricity, no paved road, no drainage and a paucity

---

[12]   Ibid., p. iii.

[13]   Ibid., p. 147.

[14]   By the end of 2008 less than half the global population lived in the countryside.

[15]   Davey, *Changing* Places, pp. 123–131 describes several of these ventures.

[16]   J.Y. Bannerman, *The Cry for Justice in Tema* (Accra, Ghana Publishing Corporation, 1973).

of latrines. Similar descriptions could be written of slums throughout Africa, Asia and the Caribbean.

Bannerman, a dynamic young minister stationed in Tema who later served as a mission partner in The Gambia and Ulster, became the first Urban Industrial Missioner appointed by the Tema Christian Council. The new post was funded on a shoe-string, and he gave up both the car and the telephone that the Methodist Church provided in order to take it on. He made himself everybody's friend and servant, talking with them at factory gates, in offices, shops and markets, outside the Labour Exchange and inside the Police Station, not in order to get them into church but to encourage civic consciousness, facilitate workers' education and develop cultural activities. He understood that 'it is not the laity's job to help the minister run the Church; it is the minister's job to help the laity change the world'. He was to be found acting as an 'unpaid magistrate in helping to settle disputes ranging from clash of personalities, misappropriation of funds, to indiscipline' in cultural associations and benevolent societies;[17] marching with demonstrators demanding better sewage facilities; and helping union representatives and employers' associations to organize an annual industrial exhibition. Urban mission – or urban service, the term generally preferred in India – had similar features wherever a specialized ministry was put in place.

Two projects in Kingston were renowned throughout *Jamaica*. The first started in 1940 when the church was asked to second Hugh Sherlock, a minister of eight years' standing, to work with disenchanted and unruly teenagers, many of them with criminal records, most brought up by single mothers who could not control them. Sherlock, who eventually became the first President of the MCCA and wrote the Jamaican national anthem, was not daunted by the challenge. He began with a residential centre in a borrowed Baptist church hall, which the boys trashed. To their bewilderment he did not give up on them, but in 1942 opened a bigger home which became famous as Boys' Town. They knew him as 'Father' Sherlock and for many he was the first father they had known. He ran an exacting programme of lessons, sports, camping, hiking and learning a trade in the workshop. It did not always stop boys fighting, sometimes with knives, and there were tragic incidents and disappointments, but many were influenced for good. Sherlock said that the area around Boys' Town was in his mind when he wrote

> In the streets of every city, where the bruised and lonely dwell,
> We shall show the Saviour's pity, we shall of his mercy tell.[18]

He remained in charge until 1956, when he was appointed the first Jamaican Chairman of the Jamaica District. Boys' Town was still serving young Kingstonians

---

[17] *The Kingdom Overseas*, June 1969: p. 21.

[18] H. Sherlock, *Lord, thy church on earth is seeking thy renewal*, hymn written 1959, © Trustees for Methodist Church Purposes.

forty years later, though it was twice rebuilt, after political riots in the 1970s and Hurricane Gilbert in 1988.

In another part of west Kingston, where '150,000 people lived in narrow, muddy lanes, in homes made from beaten-out kerosene tins, cardboard cartons and sacking, with one latrine for every 100 people and one water standpipe for every 2,000', a Jamaican deaconess, Julia Davis, pioneered Operation Friendship. It was a district to which people drifted from the countryside, hoping for a better life in the city, only to find little but unemployment, prostitution, drugs, crime and gang warfare. At first a play school on the church steps and a little clinic, after fourteen years Operation Friendship was running adult literacy classes, an Engineering Training School and a Health Centre with over fifty staff. Like Sherlock before her, and with his encouragement, she pestered organizations such as Rotary for financial support. She moved on to set up Operation Peace in another area of the city where unemployment, crime and gang warfare were rife. Operation Friendship continued to expand. It became a limited company with two sites: the trades school, with courses in woodwork, printing, refrigerator-refurbishing and industrial sewing on one, and on the other the health services, supported by volunteer doctors and dentists alongside the full-time nurses, together with a school for teenage mothers and day care for their children. Pregnancy testing, family planning, housecraft training were all part of a joined-up programme to transform lives.[19]

From the 1930s diamond mining in *Sierra Leone* became a big business and drew large numbers of people to the Kono area. Koidu, once a few farm huts in the bush about seven miles from the company headquarters, was transformed by the arrival of illicit diamond miners into the third largest town in the country, with a fluctuating and polyglot population. Young men by the thousand abandoned their fields – which, efficiently cultivated, could have fed the nation – in search of a quick fortune. In the classbooks of Methodist chapels the comment 'Gone to Kono' constantly recurred. The life-style they found in Koidu was that of the Wild West; their village values were dislocated culturally, morally and economically. In 1970 Methodism followed them; an agreement between the recently autonomous Methodist Church of Sierra Leone and the United Methodist Church formed the Koidu Joint Parish. A nucleus of forty-seven baptized members welcomed Ken Todd from Ireland and David Bockari, an African UMC minister; and, like Koidu itself, the little church grew apace. In five or six years over a thousand adults were baptized, twenty preaching places were opened, a radio ministry in the local language was begun and preachers in six languages had been trained. The Todds were followed by another missionary couple, Stephen and Brenda Mosedale, respectively minister and doctor, and she initiated a Community Health Programme. It began with two local women whom she trained in basic care, two mornings a week; after three months they began practical work in three locations. This work too expanded rapidly, and the Programme, managed by a committee

[19]   Davey, *Changing* Places, pp. 129–31.

of Parish members, eventually employed three State Enrolled Community Health Nurses, ten full-time nursing aides and a driver.

Tragically diamonds did not make Sierra Leone wealthy. On the contrary, from the 1980s the leone was repeatedly devalued; and by the early 1990s ministers were being paid – often not on time, and sometimes not at all – the equivalent of £4 a month, whereas a bag of rice cost £13. Koidu's population had reached half a million by the time civil war, a reaction to government corruption and the mismanagement of diamond resources, broke out in 1991. Foday Sankoh's Revolutionary United Front, with backing from Liberian rebel forces, soon controlled the eastern and southern regions. Thousands took refuge across the frontier in Guinea. The conflict lasted for eleven years, leaving the infrastructure and economy of the country in ruins, Koidu 'looted of everything useful except its mud'[20] and Tikonko desolate. Ministry to miners gave way to ministry to refugees, with regular lorry-loads of relief supplies making the hazardous journey to Guinea.

Social Welfare

The plight of orphans and street children could not fail to touch the hearts of missionaries, as it touched Riccardo Santi in Naples.[21] Papa Santi used to say, 'When a child suffers, I do not ask who the child is; I become that child'. Casa Materna survived fascist rule and two world wars. In 1938 Mussolini closed the school but the orphanage remained open. The children were evacuated in 1942 because of heavy bombardment; after the war Santi's sons oversaw rebuilding and took over the direction of the home, which remained a private institution until it was passed to the church in the 1970s.

Matthew Rusike, the first African to be made a circuit superintendent in the Rhodesia District, was, like Santi, someone who could not pass little children by on the other side. The Rusikes began caring for orphans in their manse at Kwenda in 1949, and before long they had a 'family' of sixteen. In retirement they established a Children's Home at Epworth on the outskirts of Harare, opened by the Governor-General in 1961. The National Children's Home in Britain (NCH: later renamed Action for Children) seconded a trainer to work with the staff for part of each year over a long period and provided some funds towards the extension and improvement of the Matthew Rusike Children's Home (so named after his death in 1977). As the ravages of AIDS left more and more children parentless the numbers in need of care and protection grew; the Home expanded to accommodate over 100 children under fifteen, and some older ones, in small family groups with house parents, and gradually began to develop a nationwide childcare programme.

In Ovim, Eastern Nigeria, a missionary received a letter in 1958 from a Nigerian colleague in the next circuit, saying 'A woman member of one of my churches has

---

20   Mark Doyle, BBC report 10 August 2001.

21   p. 11.

died, leaving a two week old son with no-one to care for him. Do you know of an orphanage or hospital to which the father can take him?' It transpired that

> In that area, when a woman died in childbirth, it was believed that it was caused by a Juju curse on the infant. Thus many would refuse to have the baby in their compound. This baby's father was a Christian, however, and did not fear this Juju and wanted his son to live. But without the knowledge of simple hygiene he would be unable to keep his child alive by bottle feeding. In only a matter of weeks the baby would probably die from dysentery.[22]

Alan and Doris Roberts took him home on a Thursday and by Sunday a second baby was brought. Their impromptu motherless babies' home grew rapidly; fortunately they could take over an empty mission house next door, recruit and train some local teenage girls to help with child care, and count on the support of friends at home, with contributions in some cases from the child's relatives. After the Roberts were moved to a new appointment the Home was transferred to Uzuakoli. NCH sent a Matron for two years and Bella Teite from Uzuakoli was sent to NCH in England for two years' training. The Methodist Relief Fund (MRF) made a recurrent grant to support the work. In 1966 a brand new Home was opened with Swedish funds, its capacity doubled to forty babies. But just a year later civil war broke out. The Motherless Babies' Home continued to function and took in a group of abandoned refugee children as well, but all outside aid was blocked and food became more and more scarce and costly. Then Uzuakoli was taken by Federal forces, most of the staff fled, the babies were evacuated by the Biafran Red Cross, and the new building was plundered and gutted. The ruins were rebuilt in 1973. Thereafter the Home lurched from crisis to financial crisis, but continued to care for an average of twenty-eight babies, including some left abandoned in the gutter or the bush. At eighteen months, they were either returned to their fathers or guardians, or found foster-parents; but the Home continued to monitor their progress.

In the Madurai diocese of the CSI *Arulagam*, a home for destitute women and their children, was begun in 1975. Some were unmarried mothers, some came from abusive marriages, or a life of prostitution, or prison, others fled from unhappy widowhood. At Arulagam they were given a home, counselling, education, skills training and loving care. It lived up to its name, meaning 'House of Grace'. After a few years there, most of the women were ready to leave the home and support themselves in the community, though some with learning difficulties would stay longer. In 1989 Margaret Addicott, who had earlier worked for over twenty years in the Trichinopoly diocese, was granted a visa to return to India and joined the small staff team. As the years went by, more and more women who were HIV+ arrived, often slipping in secretly, haunted by stigma and shame. In 1998 Arulagam

---

[22]   Alan and Doris Roberts, prayer letter circulated to friends, quoted in A. Cox, *Uzuakoli Miracle* (Berkhamsted, 1991), p. 11.

started a hospice for women with AIDS. Built for twenty, there were times when thirty were squeezed in and cared for.

Besides 'doing good', social welfare meant tackling what was harmful: challenging the stigmatization of leprosy and AIDS, undermining traditional beliefs about 'Juju' curses, taking issue with 'the altogether revolting and senseless mutilation of girls which takes place just before marriage'.[23] But concern with the world beyond the English Channel was not the sole prerogative of the Missionary Society. The Society was the means through which Conference administered the Overseas Districts, and the channel through which the social concerns of Methodists abroad were communicated; but those concerns were widely shared. In 1924, in the heyday of the temperance movement, an Overseas Joint Temperance Committee was established, bringing together representatives of the WMMS and of the Temperance and Social Welfare Department to combat 'the evils of alcoholism among native peoples'. Over time the scope of its interest widened, though for twenty years the agenda was dominated by alcohol issues, including rum-running in the Bahamas and the Gold Coast gin traffic. From the outset the opium trade was a concern, and in 1925 the Committee agreed to consider gambling questions, and to send a list of relevant literature to missionaries – keeping missionaries informed, at a time when communications were still quite slow, was an important element in the Committee's *raison d'être*. In 1927 there was an item about 'a book of a very undesirable character' circulating in India – whether this was pornography or some other undesirable subject the minute book did not record. (Opinion as to what constituted undesirability constantly shifted: in 1917 Edwin Smith's description of Ila life containing sexually explicit material had, for propriety's sake, been put into Latin before publication.) An issue in 1929 was 'the moral influence of cinema films in native countries': in Britain an arrangement had been reached with American film producers and distributors to cut 'bad features of American films' but no such arrangements were in place in other lands.

The agenda was by now so broad that in 1929 'Social Welfare' was belatedly added to the Committee's name. Its interests included the thorny problem of polygamy (a Conference was arranged by the Society in 1931 on Marriages in West Africa) and a memorial from the Burma Synod about the Remarriage of Divorced Persons. In 1933 the Committee decided to send to all Chairmen of the Overseas Districts the texts of previous Conference resolutions not only on alcohol and gambling but on War and Peace and on Sunday Observance. Overseas Chairmen had not hitherto automatically received Conference resolutions which were prepared in, and intended for, the British context, since it was recognised they were not automatically relevant or appropriate in very different cultures. A significant item in 1934 concerned 'Hindu and other students' in London, experiencing problems with accommodation. Discrimination was being practised. In 1936 two matters arose from Rhodesia. Legal aid for native prisoners was one

---

23   A.J. Hopkins in *Advance*, July 1931: p. 133 – but see p. 144.

of these; but it took up less of the Committee's time than a complaint from the Synod about advertisements in the Methodist press for quack remedies, which prompted the Committee into correspondence with the *Methodist Recorder*. Female circumcision in Kenya was brought up in 1937, the South African Institute of Race Relations was prophetically commended in 1938, and juvenile delinquency in Sierra Leone was a topic in 1940.

'Temperance and Social Welfare' became 'Christian Citizenship' in 1950. The formal agendas for District synods were recast accordingly, and one of the main items before the Joint Overseas Christian Citizenship Committee was consideration of the reports from overseas synods. The relevance of Standing Orders on social questions to overseas situations was kept in review, with appropriate discipline in cases of divorce still an issue. From the West Indian Districts, concerns were raised about the liquor trade in the Bahamas, about the aftercare of prisoners in Jamaica and about gambling in the shape of 'Spot the Ball' competitions in Trinidad's newspapers. The Barbados and Trinidad District ruefully reported in 1964 that 'when the results of a recent Roman Catholic raffle were announced, the winner of the first prize was a leading Methodist layman'. A substantial paper on Inter-Faith Marriages was tabled in 1965 and constantly recurred in the business over the next few years. The Committee was responsible for preparing Conference resolutions on Rhodesia after the Unilateral Declaration of Independence (UDI) in 1965 and on Nigeria at the time of the Biafran secession. But by 1970 Methodist responses to world poverty took an increasingly prominent place on the agenda.

Relief and Development

Shortly after an earthquake shook Accra in June 1939, a letter was received requesting contributions from the missionary societies to a relief Fund. MMS replied that since the Society was faced with a bill of £7,000 for repairs, it ought to be a recipient of relief rather than a contributor. The letter was an indication of the high regard in which societies like the MMS were held for their humanitarian work. Another instance was the secondment of the Irishman John Fee to Malaya in 1953, by arrangement with the Colonial Office. Fee, who had served in China and on the Mission House staff, was appointed to help re-house Chinese people fleeing Communism. Within weeks, however, he became the 'Food Control Enforcement Officer' in the State of Pahang, an immensely challenging task at a time of emergency with militant groups widely active in the region. Although he had known internment by the Japanese in China, Fee described this assignment in Malaya as the most frightening and dangerous of his ministry.

Following the devastation of the Second World War the need for relief, reconstruction and rehabilitation in Europe was pressing. British missionary agencies had only a minimal presence on the continent and were not equipped to rise to the urgent post-war demands. So the newly-formed BCC established 'Christian Reconstruction in Europe', soon to become 'Inter-Church Aid and

Refugee Service' and then Christian Aid. Around the same time the Methodist Relief Fund, with the same concerns, was set up.

It was not long before two things happened. Firstly, the new agencies swiftly recognized that prevention was better than cure. Relief in disaster situations was vital, but it was essential to set in place 'development' programmes to strengthen the poor[24] in the expectation that many disasters could thus be averted and that, when they did occur, the people on the spot would have the capacity to tackle the consequences. Secondly, the agencies determined to extend their sphere of action beyond Europe to the undeveloped, or underdeveloped, world.[25] They had proved adept at raising funds for their cause and were in a position to adopt a broader remit once the most clamant European needs had been addressed by the Marshall Plan. But the underdeveloped world was the territory where the missionary Societies were working. So when it came to social development projects or disaster relief, the overseas Methodist and united Churches, one by one becoming autonomous, had several organizations to which they could apply for funds: both MMS and one or more of the agencies.

The MRF was managed by an ad hoc committee until 1951, when it came under the aegis of the new Christian Citizenship Department (CCD). Edward Rogers (who declined to be nominated as MMS General Secretary in 1958) had joined the department in 1950 and was instrumental in bringing MRF under the Department's wing. In 1955 he wrote: 'Aid for relief is a very practicable expression of our Christian Citizenship – and is a pointer also to the co-operation which becomes essential when worthwhile Christian service is attempted. The Department finds itself working in the happiest collaboration with the Missionary Society.'[26] The distinctions between home and overseas were becoming blurred as CCD extended its sphere of action abroad while MMS developed work among overseas students in Britain. Rogers subsequently had a very wide brief as General Secretary of the CCD and then the Division of Social Responsibility (DSR), but relief and development were foremost among his personal concerns and he retained that portfolio when DSR was set up in the 1973 restructuring.

The sheer scale of human need, the ever-widening gulf between the incomes of the richest and the poorest, and a succession of disasters, 'natural' and 'man-made' – given publicity as never before by the ability of television journalists to speed images into every British household – aroused the Methodist conscience. But ordinary Methodists were becoming confused by the variety of channels through which overseas concerns could be addressed and the plethora of appeals to which they were invited to respond. The distinction between mission, aid and development was not clear. The new agencies were promoting work of the type

---

24 'To strengthen the poor' was for many years Christian Aid's strap-line.

25 There was much debate about the terminology. Many argued for 'developing' world, but the rich world's wealth was growing faster. Bosch, pp. 433–4, offers a critique of development as conceived by western governments and NGOs from the 1960s.

26 *Methodist Recorder*, 10 November 1955

that had long been a concern of missionaries. At the same time the arrival in Britain of migrants from south Asia and east Africa raised the question of how Christians should relate to people of other faiths much more acutely than the historic presence of the Jewish community had done. MMS Asia Secretary Wilfrid Pile confessed in 1969:

> We can appeal with confidence for 'aid' but find it difficult to appeal for evangelism in a way that is likely to quicken response.[27]

MRDF was formed in 1985 by the merger of MRF with a World Development Action Fund, which from 1977 had been a fund without charitable status, designed to promote global justice in ways that the Charity Commissioners deemed to be 'political' and therefore closed to charities. Both MMS (by now MCOD) and Christian Aid fell foul of the Charity Commissioners during the protracted anti-apartheid and Zimbabwean independence struggles.[28] The relationship between these later expressions of the Methodist people's global concerns and MMS/MCOD continued to evolve. MCOD put the expertise of its staff and its contacts with sister Churches at the disposal of MRDF; Area Secretaries served as advisors to the MRDF committee, and on their overseas visits often acted for MRDF in making contacts and identifying or following up projects. Because work for economic and social justice and development were widely seen as integral to God's mission, many Methodists found the structural division between 'mission' and 'development' unhelpful and confusing. There were others who found it a helpful distinction because, they argued, it should have led the MMS to concentrate on the primary evangelistic task which other bodies did not address, but it was the holistic view of mission which prevailed.

The United Mission to Nepal (UMN)

In just one instance, the Society consented to engage in 'mission without overt evangelism'. It was only in 1951, following a palace revolt and the proclamation of a constitutional monarchy, that missionaries were allowed into the Hindu kingdom. There were conditions: medical and educational work was welcomed, but they were still forbidden to propagate their faith and convert Nepalis, and their visas restricted the extent to which they could travel around the country. In view of Nepal's lack of welfare services, institutions, infrastructure and trained personnel, eight mission boards accepted these limitations and in 1954 negotiated an agreement with the government which founded the UMN as an international

---

[27]   *The Kingdom Overseas*, December 1969: p. 16.
[28]   pp. 291–2.

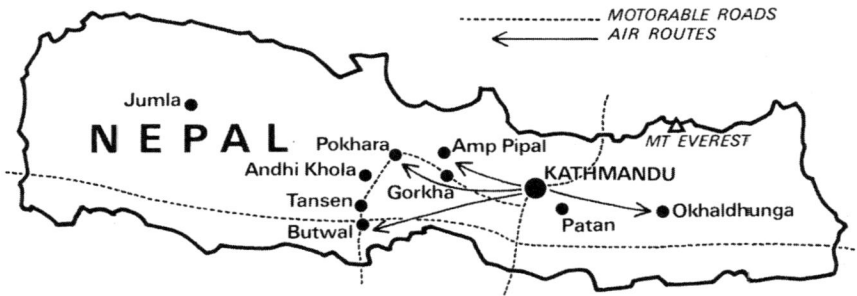

Map 16.1   Nepal

interdenominational Christian mission.[29] UMN's earliest staff worked in difficult environments, usually without the benefit of roads, electricity, and skilled workers, yet with few resources they built institutions and projects that were to have a lasting impact on the country's development. The number of participating agencies grew steadily and the first British Methodists – a nutritionist and a farmer – went to Nepal in 1978. There were questions to be faced, as every other member body had to face them, about whether it was a proper use of a missionary society's resources, when there could be no question of baptizing Nepalis or pastoring congregations. Finlay Hodge reflected, as he was about to return for a second spell in 1984:

> We went to work in Nepal because we were thankful for God's love for us. We wanted and felt able to serve the practical needs of Nepali people in the name of Christ. Our home churches, UMN, the Nepali government, the Nepali Church all have different expectations of missionaries ... God used each of us in different ways according to our gifts. As a farmer, I had to share my skills in farm management and encourage village farmers to develop appropriate farming methods. I looked to God not to help me convert numbers of people to the Christian faith but to work with sensitivity and humility.
>
> ... When we moved to the village from language school we did not think, 'Now, how can we tell people about Jesus Christ?' Lonely and lacking confidence, we depended on our neighbours to 'minister' to us while we found our feet in the community. As our friendships grew, so our understanding of each other's religion increased. This gave us spontaneous opportunities for sharing our faith and also made us look at our relationship with God in a new light.[30]

---

[29]   See J. Lindell, *Nepal and the Gospel of God* (New Delhi, United Mission to Nepal, 1979).

[30]   *NOW*, February 1984: pp. 9–10.

Figure 16.1   The Hodge family outside their home in Nepal, 1985

Alongside rural development, education (including the nation's first girls' high school), and health services (which included running four hospitals and accounted for 40 per cent of UMN's budget), almost a third of the budget and a quarter of the personnel were by the 1980s committed to engineering and industrial development. This was largely centred on the old market town of Butwal, near the Indian frontier 160 miles west of Kathmandu. In 1964 UMN set up the Butwal Technical Institute, an apprentice training school offering four-year courses in mechanics, electrical work, building, cabinet making and book-keeping. By 1978 a number of businesses had been set up providing employment in the area and on-the-job training for the boys, among them a plywood factory, a furniture making firm, a company building and maintaining biogas plants, a mechanical workshop where small suspension bridges, irrigation gates, small water turbines and sluices were built, and a company specializing in tunnelling for hydroelectric and irrigation projects. These were all joint ventures with both UMN and government representatives on the boards. As part of this work, UMN developed a full scale hydro-electric engineering sector and, through the company it had established, built and commissioned three power stations. In all these enterprises UMN tried to develop good business practice and a caring industrial environment, and demonstrate how a company can and should be run. In the mid-1980s they employed over 600 Nepali workers, and the expatriate (missionary) staff were gradually replaced by Nepali managers. By the early 1990s UMN and its associated businesses employed over 2,000 Nepalis, and the number of foreign personnel grew to over 250, a figure which did not include those described in its reports as 'unassigned spouses'. They came from over thirty member bodies and a score of different countries. Although the number of British Methodists never reached double figures, there were more mission partners in Nepal in 1996 than in any other country except Kenya.[31]

By then UMN's agreement with the government had been renewed, usually at five-year intervals, many times. The small indigenous Nepal Christian Fellowship was growing rapidly,[32] and mission partners were able to worship with Nepali believers, though in Kathmandu the weekly service in English was preferred by most. They remained untypical missionaries in that they took no leadership roles in the Nepali church, but they lent their support and encouragement and some shared in the preaching and teaching ministry. The position was well described by Tom Hale, an American surgeon who served in a rural hospital for many years and then in Kathmandu:

> There is no question that the professional services of United Mission personnel are welcomed and appreciated. Our continued presence in the country is evidence of this. But … the government cannot help but view the presence of Christian missionaries with ambivalence. Thus we have been invited to work in Nepal only under the condition that we do not 'proselytise'. This means that we agree not to persuade any Nepali to become a Christian by means of material inducement or other forms of external pressure. (This, of course, we would avoid doing in any case.) We are, however, free to practice our own religion, which includes making Christ known by word and deed.
>
> … There has never been anything secretive or deceptive about the operation of the United Mission. Consequently it has earned both the admiration and confidence of Nepali leaders.[33]

In the half-century after the country opened up in 1951, the number of Christians in Nepal grew from under a hundred in Kathmandu to some hundreds of thousands spread over most of the country. While no human would take any credit for this, mission partners who, like their Lord, 'went about doing good', were a catalyst.

---

[31]   Including spouses, nine in Nepal, ten in Kenya.

[32]   See N. Kehrberg, *The Cross in the land of the Khukri* (Kathmandu, Ekta Books, 2000).

[33]   T. Hale, *Don't Let the Goats Eat the Loquat Trees* (Grand Rapids, Zondervan, 1986), p. 11.

Chapter 17
New Name, New Mood, New Emphases

In 1973 Methodist connexional structures were rationalized by merging numerous departments into six Divisions, while the Missionary Society formed a seventh and became known as the Methodist Church Overseas Division. Many felt more comfortable with the label 'MCOD' than with 'MMS', as the new name reflected the reality that the organization was no longer primarily in the business of sending missionaries, or mission partners as they came to be called. Books with titles such as *The End of the Missionary*[1] and *The End of an Era*[2] signalled that the missionary enterprise had taken on a new shape. Overseas Mission Sundays in local churches tended to be rebranded as World Church[3] Sundays, or even completely discontinued; while the last General Secretary before further restructuring suggested that MCOD could stand for Multi-Cultural Omni-Directional, the new nature of mission.

What was happening as the century wore on was in effect what Henry Venn had once described as 'the euthanasia of mission' – not that mission itself was a thing of the past, but that in its colonial form it had been superseded by a host of missionary Churches, reaching out in the spirit of Brunner's famous dictum that 'the church exists by mission as fire exists by burning'.[4] Following the integration of the WCC and the IMC in 1961, the WCC Commission on World Mission and Evangelism held a World Mission Conference in Mexico in 1963 with the *leit-motiv* 'Mission in Six Continents'. The 'Message' of the Conference declared that:

> This missionary task in one and demands unity. It is one because the gospel is one. It is one because in all countries the Churches face the same essential task. It is one because every Christian congregation in all the world is called to show the love of God in Christ, in witness and service to the world at its doors … It must be the common witness of the whole Church, bringing the whole gospel to the whole world.[5]

---

[1]   C.M. Morris, *The End of the Missionary?* (London, Cargate Press, 1962).

[2]   R.E. Kendall, *The End of an Era: Africa and the Missionary* (London, SPCK, 1978).

[3]   The expression had a long history: the *Methodist Recorder* leading article on 16 July 1942, commenting on Walter Noble's presidential address to Conference, was headlined 'The World Church'.

[4]   E. Brunner, *The World and the Church* (London, SCM Press, 1931), p. 108.

[5]   R.K. Orchard, *Witness in Six Continents* (London, Edinburgh House Press, 1964), p. 175.

In 1964 representatives of the newly autonomous Churches in Africa and the Pacific which owed their origins to the Paris Missionary Society expressed a strong desire to change the nature of their relationship with the French churches. They wanted to be partners in mission. The first outcome was an 'Action Apostolique Commune' with an international, multi-racial team working among the Fon people of Dahomey (not yet renamed Bénin). This was not a country where the Paris Mission had worked, but French missionaries had worked in partnership with the MMS in the French West Africa District from the 1920s. Then in 1971 the PMS was dissolved and replaced by CEVAA, the Communauté Evangélique d'Action Apostolique, a federation of sister Churches in Europe, Africa and the Pacific who agreed to pool some of their human and financial resources and activities in order to respond together to jointly agreed priorities. The United Church of Zambia was a founder member and the three francophone Methodist Districts, Bénin, Ivory Coast and Togo, though not yet autonomous, became members too.

In 1977 the Churches which had grown out of the work of the LMS, the Commonwealth Missionary Society and the English Presbyterian Board of Missions took a similar course and the Council for World Mission (CWM) was created, with the aim of 'sharing money, people, skills and insights globally, to carry out God's mission locally'. In CWM and CEVAA alike each member Church had a seat in the governing body, which appointed its leadership and staff. Distinctions between 'home' and 'overseas' mission were challenged: for younger Churches Britain, Ireland, France, Switzerland are overseas. A second Action Apostolique Commune team began work in Poitou in 1970.

The MMS officers and Committee were well aware of these developments and struggled with possible ways by which they too could introduce some form of joint budget-making. Nothing similar to CWM or CEVAA seemed practicable. There were far more Churches in the Methodist orbit and the size of any resulting body would have been unwieldy. Telecommunication was unreliable and air travel expensive, so some thought it impossible to ensure the full participation of such a widespread group without incurring unacceptably heavy overheads. The united Churches in India would have had reservations about a denominational organization,[6] while the UCZ would have found itself a member of three different communities. Furthermore British Methodism was preoccupied, at first with the Church of England, and then, not for the last time, with setting its own house in order.

MMS in the Seventies

Throughout the 1960s Anglican–Methodist conversations created uncertainty about the future shape of the church. Many were confident that they would see reunion in their lifetime. The proposals which eventually went to the General

---

[6]   Both CSI and CNI met annually with agencies of several denominations in their respective Related Missions Committees.

Synod of the Church of England and the Methodist Conference were for a two-stage process of unification, so the immediate future of the MMS was not in question. There were several Anglican missionary societies, and one extra in a reunited Church would not be an unmanageable complication. But the General Synod's vote in 1972 fell short of the required majority, and Methodism had to chart its separate future.

Earlier, following a debate in the 1966 Conference, a single Methodist Department for Mission had been contemplated. This was the PM principle before 1932 and the theological rationale was plainly stated back in 1928 in the PM popular report:

> The world contains but one mission field. For the purposes of administration we may divide Home and Foreign, but we must not allow ourselves to separate them in thought. The world is one. The needs of any one people do not differ essentially from the needs of all. God's purpose concerning the whole race is the same purpose.[7]

Forty years later there was no arguing with that contention, but some feared that a single department would perpetuate an idea of mission as a separate activity and not the concern of the whole Methodist church. The massive, and well-endowed, organization which would result would set up a power structure which might distort rather than express the unity of the missionary task. So when restructuring took effect in the aftermath of the Anglican-Methodist vote, Home and Overseas were kept separate, despite the clear anomalies including MMS/MCOD's work with overseas students and ministry to immigrant communities in Britain, and the Home Mission Division (HMD)'s links with the World Methodist Council's initiatives in evangelism, including sponsorship of mission teams for short-term missions, mainly in the USA.

The Conference of Missionary Societies in Great Britain and Ireland (CBMS) was similarly exercised about its functions and relationships in this changing context. A working group reported in 1973:

> It is true that many activities belonging to the former era will continue to be necessary in fulfilment of earlier obligations, but they must not be regarded, as a result of restricted vision or nostalgia for the past, as setting patterns for the future. Only if we frankly recognize the decisive character of the change from the old to the new era [the end of the colonial period, the rise of national self-consciousness, the advent of autonomous and united Churches, the impact of religious pluralism and secularism] can we be responsive to the fresh opportunities for sharing in Christ's mission, which God is setting before Christians in Britain in this period of history.[8]

---

[7]   *The Adventure of the Road,* PM report 1928: p. 14.

[8]   CBMS, *Shaping Up to the Future* (London, CBMS, 1973): para. II.3.

There was deep-seated unease among CBMS member bodies about the reaction of their constituencies to the declining number of missionaries. 'Self-propagation' was a term that did not figure in most supporters' vocabulary. Elliott Kendall, a member of the working group, addressed the issue:

> Is it not true that the western Church will maintain its interest and support for the overseas Church so long as there are missionaries serving in it, but not if there is no missionary link? ... Most missionary societies know that their *raison d'être* and their support would disappear if they could not demonstrate that they actually supported missionaries overseas. It is not too much to say that the distortion of mission to which the West has become adjusted is that it will participate in world mission if it can send missionaries but not if it cannot.[9]

Immediately after the CBMS report was published, the Society set up its own Commission on *The MMS in the Seventies*. The timing was odd, for a new General Secretary, Colin Morris, was shortly to take the helm, but it got to work without awaiting his arrival. It was now clear that MMS would continue with a largely unchanged remit, albeit under a new name. The task, announced *NOW* magazine, was to consider

> How shall we spend our money? The question is more wide-open than that. The real questions are; 'Has the MMS any purpose today – and if so, what is it?'[10]

The Commission's report, circulated in July 1974, included a theological section on the nature of the Christian Mission, a historical review of the development of missionary societies and their relationships with the emerging Churches, a section on structures to facilitate 'two-way traffic', enabling Christians in the West to receive as well as give, and a description of the Society's responsibilities in Britain, with implications for collaboration with other new Divisions, especially the Division of Social Responsibility and its Standing Committee on World Development. Although MCOD, alone among the seven new Divisions, formally served the Irish Conference as well as the British Conference, the report made no explicit reference to Ireland.

The Commission recommended that alongside bilateral relationships with overseas Churches, relationships should be encouraged with ecumenical bodies abroad such as training institutions, national and regional Councils of Churches and organizations as diverse as the Islam in Africa Project and the Christian Institute of Southern Africa. It argued for increased funding for work in multi-racial areas of Britain. It recommended an educational programme 'designed to change attitudes (and) challenge emotional attachments to past and present relations, methods and structures in mission so far as these are tied to a situation

---

9   Kendall, *The End of An Era*, p. 112.

10   *NOW* June 1973: p. 3.

that has passed'.[11] It affirmed that 'policy decisions are to be made by the MMS and the overseas churches together' and went on:

> Little progress can come without some assault on the related citadels of decision-making and money. Until churches in other countries are involved in decisions about how to spend resources raised in Britain, all talk of the wealth of the Church being the wealth of the whole will be hollow … If power and responsibility can be shared at this point, that may also give a greater sense of confidence when difficult or controversial decisions have to be made, and remove some of the embarrassments arising from one part of the Church being so much wealthier than the other.[12]

Some of what the report advocated was already in place. The 1968 Conference had approved the use of money given to the MMS for community and race relations work. Ministers from autonomous Churches were already serving on the British stations. Other recommendations were effected within the space of a few years; on the other hand, the thorny but fundamental issue of power-sharing was not tested until 1991 when Churches were asked whether, due to difficult budget decisions, they would prefer a reduction in their un-earmarked grant, a moratorium on scholarships or the withdrawal of missionaries.

Moratorium

One of the indicators of the new mood was the proposal for a moratorium on missionaries. By 1971 the Kenyan Presbyterian, John Gatu, in Africa and the Filipino Methodist, Emerito Nacpil, in Asia, among others, were calling for the withdrawal of missionaries, and in England Merfyn Temple, who personally heeded the call and left Zambia in 1974, became its advocate. The rationale for a moratorium – indeed, for permanent withdrawal – was well expressed by Nacpil, in a presentation to a conference on 'Missionary Service in Asia Today' in 1971. He said:

> I believe that the present structure of modern missions is dead. And the first thing we ought to do is to eulogize it and then bury it, no matter how painful and expensive it is to bury the dead.

> The missionary structure had performed magnificently the role of a successful midwife in helping to bring out into the light of day a new child, which is none other than the rise of the Christian community in the hands of the Third World. But now that the child is born, there is no longer any need for the midwife! It had also performed with love and sacrifice and patience and hard work the role

---

[11]   MMS in the Seventies, para. 92.

[12]   Ibid., para. 42.

of guardian and trustee over the growing life of the child. But now the child is grown-up ... the most missionary service a missionary can do today in Asia is to go home![13]

Another strand of the argument related to the spiritual state of Britain. Christians arriving to work or study were shocked to discover how few British people were church-goers, and how unwelcoming those few were. 'Look to the heathen at home,' came the message, unconsciously echoing John Wesley two centuries before.[14] 'What will help us most is a revival of Christian discipleship and a restoration of Christian values in the economically and militarily powerful nations in the West.'

The All Africa Conference of Churches, in its 1974 Assembly in Lusaka, took up the theme:

> ... our option as a matter of policy has to be a Moratorium on external assistance in money and personnel.

> ... a halt to receiving financial and human resources from abroad will necessitate the emergence of structures that would be viably African and programs and projects of more urgent and immediate priority...

> The Call for a Moratorium may also enable the African Church to perform a service of redeeming God's people in the Northern Hemisphere whose missionary sending agencies have in many ways distorted the mission of the church in Africa.[15]

The call gave rise to much debate. The case for the wholesale and permanent departure of western missionaries was not widely supported, but a temporary withdrawal of expatriate personnel for five years would make it easier for the nascent Churches to determine their own priorities and develop their self-reliance. Missionaries were often viewed as pipelines for additional funds, particularly by those among whom they were stationed. Circuits and institutions with missionaries on the staff could benefit from direct appeals to friends at home for their projects, bypassing both Marylebone Road and national church headquarters. This easily aroused resentment in neighbouring circuits not so blessed. Inevitably, while some indigenous leaders argued that to shut down the informal pipeline would be more equitable, others were not ready to deprive themselves of valued supplementary

---

[13]   Asia Methodist Advisory Committee, *Missionary Service in Asia Today* (Hong Kong, Chinese Christian Literature Council, 1971), pp. 78–9.

[14]   Wesley to M'Allum, 14 July 1778, in J. Telford (ed.), *The Letters of John Wesley*, (8 vols, London, Epworth Press, 1931), vol. 6, p. 316; see Pritchard, *Methodists and their Missionary Societies 1760–1900*, p. 8.

[15]   *Ecumenical Press Service*, 20 June 1974, p. 11.

resources. It was too early for the staggering consequences of the enforced closure of all pipelines to China to influence the debate; the phenomenal growth of a self-propagating, self-funded church only began a decade later.

In the event there was no moratorium. Colin Morris had pointed the way forward a decade earlier:

> … there is room for European missionaries, provided that *they are responsible not to those who send them, but to those to whom they are sent.* This is one of the big problems involved in transforming the mission into the missionary Church, for more often than not, the Church cannot afford to pay the salaries of missionaries or their passages back to their home countries for furlough. But the text, 'He that pays the piper calls the tune', is not found in the New Testament. The missionary giving of the home Churches should be an exercise in stewardship for their spiritual growth, not a weapon for continued control of the work which is done overseas with the help of their money.[16]

Yet when an overseas participant in an ecumenical consultation, whose church had explicitly rejected the call, was asked 'If the missionary societies to which you are related offered to give you the money the missionaries cost instead of sending you the missionaries the money pays for, would you still want missionaries?', his unhesitating reply was 'Of course not'.[17]

Omni-directional

MCOD was from the 1970s a Resource-Sharing agency. Sharing personnel became a two-way thing when mission partners from the erstwhile mission fields were invited to serve in Britain and Ireland, not just in specialist posts but in regular circuit appointments, under the aegis of the 'World Church in Britain/Ireland Partnership'. Almost all of these were ordained, for UK visa restrictions made it virtually impossible to recruit an overseas partner for a lay post – though Ivy McGhie from Jamaica served as MCOD's Secretary for the Caribbean and the Americas while her husband exercised a circuit ministry. Ministers were chosen and seconded by their home Church and stationed by the British or Irish Conference, after extensive consultation with the receiving circuit. They had a very thorough programme of orientation, though not so extensive as the preparation most mission partners going from Britain still received in Selly Oak. It was equally vital to prepare folk in the receiving circuit to work and worship alongside a minister whose accent might be hard to tune into at first, who would not always fully understand what was expected and whose ideas and emphases might well be unusual. One or two of these appointments were such a mismatch

---

[16]   Morris, *The End of the Missionary?*, p. 56.
[17]   MCH: Graeme Jackson, paper circulated within MCOD, 28 January 1975.

that they had to be curtailed. Others led to compliments: 'We've not had such assiduous pastoral caring for a long time'; 'As an African, he talks to everyone he meets in the street. Lots more people are getting to know about our church now.'

Luis Baldeon, a Peruvian minister with a Japanese wife, Estela, and four children, had an outstanding ministry in Belfast from 1990 to 1995.

> Many have expressed concern about their personal safety, but Luis replies with examples of much greater danger at the hands of terrorists in Peru. As an 'outsider', he can go into the homes of people in Northern Ireland whom local priests and ministers dare not go near. Having been a lawyer in Peru, he is not afraid to talk with police and to enter situations where people have been victims of violence. His sensitivity makes him welcome in both Protestant and Catholic pulpits.[18]

Beside these five-year appointments, 'Mission Live' visits lasting six to twelve weeks were organized, bringing ministers or laypeople to be hosted in two or three circuits for a fortnight or more. One who made a powerful impression was Morris Maswanise from Zimbabwe, who throughout his stay steadfastly refused to drink more than six glasses or cupfuls of liquid a day, explaining that if he got used to more he would suffer when he returned to the arid Zambezi valley where that was the available limit.

There was 'South-South' personnel-sharing too. Dr Roy Goonewardene had gone from Ceylon to work at Ilesha from 1958 to 1963. The Barbadian, Eric Clarke, was appointed Chairman of The Gambia District in 1966; he was succeeded by Cyril Alleyne from Guyana and several Ghanaian Chairmen followed. The MCCA recruited ministers from Samoa, Fiji and Tonga in the 1980s; by mid-decade some twenty Fijian missionary families were scattered across the world.

A series of youth exchanges took small parties to a score of sister Churches over the years, and welcomed teams to Britain in return. The exchanges were learning experiences for the many receiving congregations and youth clubs as well as for the young people who made up the teams. The first visitors came from Kenya in 1972 – not simply to experience church life in Britain but to share their faith. Preparations for the visit prompted a provocative article by Bill Watty, then a tutor at Kingsmead and later President of the MCCA, entitled *Can a Missionary Minded Church Receive?*

> Apparently not … the whole missionary enterprise has been based up to now on a simple and neat division of the world between the 'haves' and the 'have-nots' … Missionary-minded churches cannot receive with a good grace. They can only give … I shudder that the Kenyans may just be real live specimens of missionary success. I have no doubt that they will be royally entertained. They will be given innumerable cups of tea … British Methodism will still be givers,

---

18   M. Edwards, *Bridges of the Spirit* (London, SPCK, 1994), p. 74.

and the Kenyans will return to Nairobi raving over the wonderful times they had in England. But I have little confidence that British Methodists will be listening to what God is saying to them through the visitors. I doubt whether there will be a single conversion as a result of their visit: for what can simple, rural Africans tell British Methodists which can be of real and lasting value in their modern, complex, sophisticated, technological society of the seventies?[19]

Watty's bitterness was unsurprising, given the shabby treatment West Indians were given by British churches as well as British society at large, and the chip remained on his shoulder throughout his ministry. But his forthright challenge kept the organizers of all subsequent exchanges on their toes.

Education in World Mission

The old Home Organization Department of the MMS was primarily in the business of soliciting support and encouraging supporters. MCOD's Home Education Department had a different two-fold focus. One was to enable sister Churches to share, in a spirit of interdependence, their concerns, opportunities and challenges. The other was to restore the confidence of British and Irish Methodists to engage in mission. One minister serving on the World Church in Britain Partnership spoke for all when he observed, 'Christians in Britain are very closed spiritually; they are not able to share their faith. This will hold the Church down for many years.' The challenge could not be ignored. Study, prayer, encounter and action were promoted in pursuit of the twin objectives. Information sheets and study packs, as well as magazines and prayer manuals proliferated. The periodicals had an informed, appreciative readership; other literature was harder to move off the warehouse shelves, especially as more and more publications from other Divisions competed for Methodists' attention. However, the words were made flesh as well as print.

1986 was a year of celebration. Two hundred years earlier, Thomas Coke had issued his *Address to the Pious and Benevolent* and the Conference had stationed the first missionaries in the West Indies, where they arrived on Christmas Day 1786. The highlight of the bicentenary year was a gathering on Midsummer's Day at Trentham Gardens, near Stoke-on-Trent where the Conference was meeting. One who was there recalled 'the sun beating down' and 'people, people everywhere'.

There was so much to do and see. How long could I listen to the Gospel Choir? Should I queue for the Indian Pavilion or would it be better to go straightaway to taste the spicy Caribbean food before it ran out? … Could I afford one and a half hours for a workshop when there was so much else to pack into one day?[20]

---

[19] *NOW* October 1972: pp. 19–20.

[20] Janet Patrick, in the *MLMM Newsletter*, September 1986: p. 19.

Several thousand people, mostly from Britain but seasoned by visitors from all over the world, enjoyed the day, and many more shared in other events through the year. The momentum of the bicentenary celebrations was maintained through the ensuing decade by a series of residential summer gatherings known as World Village, with an all-age programme in which mission partners on furlough, overseas students, 'Mission Live' visitors and MCOD staff mingled with campers, caravaners and others more comfortably accommodated.

It was imperative to counteract the negative picture of the global south which the public at large acquired as they read of one disaster and catastrophe after another, a picture composed of refugee camps, starving children, queues for food aid, parched earth or hurricane-hit houses. The residual impression left by constant media reports and appeals for aid was, in many minds, that the poor world was overwhelmingly a theatre of tragedy where human misery was unabated. A survey conducted in 1993 found that 81 per cent of churchgoers thought that at least half of the people in the 'third world' relied on food aid (the true figure at that time being nearer 1 per cent). The MCOD education programme sought to counter such misapprehensions. JMA posters of happy children playing in the tropical sun or families enjoying a meal outside their palm-thatched homes did not tug at the heart-strings but reflected everyday realities. Meeting visitors from abroad full of charm, humour, vigour and confidence brought home the reason why their churches no longer depended on missionary leadership. Not all visitors were of that ilk. There were some who made any visit to Europe an opportunity to solicit material help, whether a pair of shoes, presents for the family at home or funds for a church building. They played, perhaps quite unconsciously, on their hosts' uncomfortable awareness of their own affluence, and even on a vague sense of historical guilt. This undermined, if it did not defeat, the purpose, and the picture remained, in too many minds, one of need rather than self-reliance.

Some Methodists were unhappy with MCOD's financial policy, which resisted ear-marked donations. Project giving would favour 'glamorous' work rather than the continuing day-to-day activity that sustains the life of the church; and a lot of extra administrative work would be needed, at home and abroad, to see that the right gifts got to the right projects. So funds were disbursed by the officers, under the direction of the Committee, a high proportion in the form of general grants to Churches and ecumenical bodies which had full liberty to determine their use. One issue of *NOW* magazine was packed with information about the Division's many budget lines and 'the faces behind the figures'.[21] The days when the budgets of Churches overseas were decided and monitored in London were past, but it was undeniably impersonal. Some local churches had personal contacts abroad, made direct gifts to specific projects and received reports on the particular causes they supported. Others, with or without such contacts, declared a desire to be 'twinned'. MCOD produced guidelines on twinning which pointed out how easily

---

[21]   *NOW*, June 1983.

the unidirectional flow of money could reduce partners and friends to sponsors and patronized, how money generated power and dependence generated resentment.

Direct relationships between local churches were at that time few in number, but the demand to know just what £10, £100 or £1,000, made possible – a feature of many charities' propaganda – became more general and could not be gainsaid. After considerable discussion in 1984 and 1985, some of the objections were over-ruled and 'Second Mile Projects' were born. The first mile was fundamental: churches and circuits were exhorted to meet the core budget, calculated at a rate per member (steadily increasing as the budget requirement rose and the number of Methodist members declined). They were invited to go further and contribute to a project, jointly agreed by MCOD and one of its partners, with a clear purpose and a guarantee of feedback. There was a choice of project each year and a twice-yearly update. The projects varied greatly. In Nigeria the Prelate insisted that the urgent task was to build a first church in the new capital of Abuja, and the entire £150,000 target was destined for that. Ten years later, a £104,000 target was divided between seven projects in China, including library books for rural primary schools, resources for training lay leaders and an irrigation pumping station.

More Changes and Challenges

Life at the Mission House never stood still. In 1986 the only computer in the building was the Finance Department's mainframe computer occupying an entire office. Ten years later, there was a personal computer on almost every desk. Senior staff did weekend duty in rotation in case of an emergency overseas and until 1988 the duty officer, to be within reach of the telephone, was housebound. It was a liberation when MCOD acquired its first mobile phone, despite its unwieldy size. Over the years the number of staff decreased steadily, as some services were no longer needed, others were computerized and a few redundancies were enforced by financial pressures. As offices were vacated, other connexional staff moved to the building, which in 1996 – ending a protracted debate about the preferred location of Methodist headquarters – became Methodist Church House.

The multi-racial character of British society was a challenge to the church as a whole. For a decade and more the Home Mission Division argued that MCOD should be responsible for work among ethnic minorities, on the grounds that its staff and committees were well-versed in cross-cultural relationships and knew the societies from which immigrants came. MCOD replied that it was vital for HMD staff and committees to acquire the same skills and sensitivity. But it was the Overseas Division which took the initiative in setting up and resourcing the working party that produced the ground-breaking report *A Tree God Planted*[22] in 1985 and pressed for Church Councils, Synods and the Conference to have more

---

[22]   H. Walton, M. Johnson & R. Ward (eds), *A Tree God Planted: Black People in British Methodism* (London, Ethnic Minorities in Methodism Working Group, 1985).

representatives from ethnic minority groups. That report was followed in 1987 by a Conference Statement 'reaffirming that the Methodist Church is against racism in all its forms and committed to racial justice within a plural society'. It declared:

> We welcome the multi-racial nature of society in Britain and assert our unqualified commitment to it. We regard it as economically, socially, culturally and spiritually beneficial for total human development.[23]

A prominent contributor to this work was Sybil Phoenix, a trained classical singer and youth worker from British Guiana, who arrived in Britain in 1956. She had an immense influence on community relations, especially in Lewisham, south London, where she fostered innumerable children and founded a youth centre, and in Methodism where she was one of the instigators of MELRAW, the Methodist (later Methodist and Ecumenical) Leadership Racism Awareness Workshops, set up in 1981. Her companion-in-arms was Vic Watson, formerly a missionary in Panama. It became normal for MCOD officers, like other connexional staff, to attend a MELRAW course.

From 1952 the Overseas Training Fund, which began bringing potential church leaders to Britain for short periods of exposure to circuit life in 1937, became a regular feature of the Society's programme. With the creation of a course in 'church management' at Westhill College in Birmingham, many of them studied there, living at Kingsmead and sharing its community life. There was no previous educational requirement other than an adequate grasp of English, and English courses were available at Selly Oak over the summer. Since a whole batch of students now arrived together for the start of term, an event was held to welcome them; it was combined with the annual valedictory service for departing missionaries and called 'Gowelcome', later renamed 'Greeting Point'. Church management and other courses at Selly Oak lasted a full year, a long separation for married men. Family life on their return could be strained because one of the couple had a wealth of experiences of which the other had no concept. The Fund began to make it possible for wives to join their husbands for a term, usually the third when most missionaries-in-training had departed. For many of them, the English classes were a boon. The OTF was renamed the Scholarship Programme in 1988. Its beneficiaries followed a wide range of courses, some leading to degrees or doctorates, in places as far apart as Aberdeen and London as well as in Birmingham. In the 1990s it began to provide for some to study in other parts of the world, outside their own country. It was a major contribution to the life of sister Churches. Between 1977 and 1996 284 men and 67 women from forty-eight different overseas Churches were supported by the Programme. The Churches' nominations had to be vetted carefully as there were always more applications than places.

---

[23]   *Methodist Church Statements on Social Responsibility 1946–1992* (London, Division of Social Responsibility, 1992), p. 102.

Much the most important of the controversies in which MCOD was caught up surrounded the WCC's Programme to Combat Racism, which is discussed in the next chapter. Another concerned the World Methodist Council (WMC)'s proposals for world evangelism, which were on the agenda of its meeting in Honolulu in 1981. Its 'Plan for Evangelism in the Eighties' declared roundly, 'The World Evangelism Committee of the WMC has a responsibility to continue to lead World Methodism in the task of mission.' Prior to the Honolulu meeting a draft of the plan had been before the Commission on Evangelism of the British Conference, which 'wholeheartedly endorsed many of the goals' but had 'grave reservations'. The plan was imperialistic in tone and showed 'no awareness that … one of the most urgent needs at present is for the churches in wealthy Western countries to hear what the rest of the world is saying to them'. It 'assumed that renewal and growth come about through the infusion of resources from outside. There is no evidence for this.' It was a costly, centralized plan showing 'no recognition of the great variety of cultures within the human family'. It showed 'no awareness of the ecumenical movement, nor of the multitude of organizations which exist to promote justice and peace or to provide opportunities for young people to engage in voluntary service'. In sum, it was superfluous. Particular criticism was levelled at the proposal to establish a 'World Evangelism Institute': 'A centralized training resource would serve a tiny élite … The money would be better used to help people receive training in the numerous institutions which already exist throughout the world to teach the doctrines, methods and message of evangelism' – even though those institutions did not necessarily bear the label Methodist.[24]

Donald English, soon to be the General Secretary of HMD, was one of those charged with preparing the Commission on Evangelism's response; he found himself unable to subscribe to this paper. When the WMC met it approved the proposals *in toto,* with a few qualifiers reflecting the British concerns. A World Evangelism headquarters office, an Institute based in Atlanta bringing ministers and lay people 'from across the world for short and longer courses', Regional Secretaries and Committees for World Evangelism, 'New World Mission' teams crossing the globe – or at least the Atlantic – and a Director conducting 'evangelical missions around the world' were all included in the Charter. The wording was finalized by the Australian Alan Walker, the incumbent director, and Donald English. Henceforth the British Conference's links with world evangelism would be channelled through English and the HMD, while contacts with the CWME and other ecumenical bodies were maintained by MCOD: an unfortunate (if comfortable) separation of responsibilities.

Besides all this, the transfer of authority to overseas Districts continued one by one, new relationships were established and new initiatives were undertaken, Women's Work and the Women's Fellowship were merged as 'Network', several consultations between representatives of British Methodism and sister Church

---

[24]   MCH: G.C. Jackson and J.D. Bridge, for the Commission on Evangelism, restricted circulation, 1981.

leaders were held, Kingsmead College was painfully closed and the scheme for supporting Nationals in Mission Appointments was born. Meanwhile, in the late 1980s, a 'more radical enquiry' into how the connexional offices were configured, which the *MMS in the Seventies* report had advocated, was begun. Two commissions later, all seven Divisions were merged into a single connexional team, and MCOD's functions were dispersed among various offices, of which the 'World Church Office' was one.

Chapter 18
Struggles for Justice

Sharing in God's Mission was the title of an influential report published by the Home Mission Division in 1985. At the heart of the report was the affirmation that:

> Christian commitment to mission arises from God's care for his world. From the Bible in general, and from Jesus in particular, we learn about God's love for the whole creation. By mission we mean any way in which Christians are sent to share in experiencing and expressing that love. It involves *evangelism* since God has declared his desire for all mankind to know and love him. It includes *social caring* for God's mercy reaches out especially for the poor and needy. It incorporates the political *struggle for justice* in our society because God intends men and women to live at peace together. These three do not exhaust the missionary task, neither are they alternatives in our mission, for they belong inextricably together. Indeed they should be areas of passionate commitment by us, since the world is so desperately far from what God intends in all three areas. They are imperatives not options.[1]

The three areas of mission italicized echoed a statement issued by the World Evangelical Fellowship in 1983:

> The mission of the church includes both the proclamation of the Gospel and its demonstration. We must therefore evangelize, respond to immediate human needs, and press for social transformation.[2]

That declaration marked a significant reappraisal of the socio-political aspect of Christian mission on the part of latter-day evangelicals, and a degree of convergence with the ecumenical movement's commitment to confronting social evils. Like eighteenth and nineteenth century evangelicals, who were prominent in the campaigns against child labour and slavery, they had profound social concerns. For their part Methodists had neither forgotten nor forsaken Wesley's social ethic, and *Sharing in God's Mission* articulated the principles on which they operated at

---

[1]   *Sharing in God's Mission* (London, Methodist Church Home Mission Division, 1985): p. 9.

[2]   Quoted in Bosch, p. 407; cf. the four marks of mission adumbrated by the Anglican Consultative Council at Badagry, Nigeria in 1984, namely 'To proclaim the good news of the Kingdom; teach, baptize and nurture new believers; respond to human need by loving service; and seek to transform unjust structures of society'.

home and abroad. There was still disagreement about aspects of the struggle for justice; the report was published at a time when the anti-apartheid campaign was at its height, and race relations were always a particularly controversial subject. In South and Central Africa, Europeans, including missionaries, differed as fiercely as their forebears had over slavery in the early nineteenth century.

Nationalism and Independence: Raj and Swaraj

The relationship between colonialism and Christian missions is the subject of numerous studies.[3] The colonial period was a short episode in African history, and only a little longer in the Caribbean and parts of Asia. No sooner had the colonial powers consolidated their rule than independence movements emerged. The attitude of Europeans varied from outright opposition and repression – 'never in a thousand years' declaimed Ian Smith in Rhodesia – to the condescending view that the natives would not be sufficiently educated and cultured to embark on self-government for a long, albeit unspecified, period. Imperialism and racism went hand in hand. Only a few Europeans, at first, were able to read the signs of the times. Most saw God's hand in the efforts of the Christian community to bring the benefits of civilization to 'underdeveloped' lands, but failed to see God at work in the process of nation-building.

The struggle to be rid of their foreign overlords gathered pace most quickly in India. The Indian National Congress was organized in 1885 in order 'to channel popular protest into legal moderation'. But 'the Congress slowly outgrew its collaborationist boyhood and became a demanding youth.'[4]

> To most representatives of the government, Indian political agitation was a troublesome interruption, distracting attention from the more important tasks of building up a peaceful and prosperous society. Missionaries, who were well aware how precariously order was maintained, and who were convinced that if *Pax Britannica* ceased to hold India together their flocks would be among the first and worst sufferers, naturally tended to regard every Indian agitator as an enemy of the Gospel ...[5]

---

[3]   S.C. Neill, *Colonialism and Christian Missions* (London, Lutterworth Press, 1966); B. Stanley, *The Bible and the Flag* (Leicester, Apollos, 1990) and (ed.), *Missions, Nationalism and the End of Empire* (Grand Rapids, Eerdmans 2003); A. Porter, *Religion versus empire?* (Manchester, Manchester University Press, 2004); N. Etherington (ed.), *Missions and Empire* (Oxford, Oxford University Press, 2005); J. Darch, *Missionary Imperialists?* (Milton Keynes, Paternoster, 2009); J. Stuart, *British Missionaries and the End of Empire* (Grand Rapids, Eerdmans, 2011).

[4]   L. Fischer *The Life of Mahatma Gandhi* (London, Jonathan Cape, 1951), p. 168.

[5]   Neill, p. 109.

Then came the Amritsar massacre. Following the murder of three English bankers in April 1919, Brigadier-General Dyer exacted terrible vengeance when he ordered his troops to open fire on a crowd of over 10,000 people attending a meeting which he had prohibited. The crowd was given no warning to disperse. The fusillades continued for ten minutes. More than 1,000 Indians were killed and 1,200 injured. Dyer told the Commission of Enquiry that he would have used machine guns if he had been able to get armoured cars in position. He was asked to resign from the army but kept his pension. The die was cast. In 1920 Gandhi and Congress unequivocally adopted the goal of *swaraj*, self-rule.

The WMMS's work in India did not extend to the Punjab and *The Foreign Field* totally ignored the massacre. On 1 May the large advertisement which the Society placed each week on the front page of both the *Methodist Recorder* and the *Methodist Times* consisted, unusually, of comment on the news.[6] It was written in ignorance of the full story, and on the assumption that Indians were the ones behaving rashly:

> Lawlessness may be local and occasional, unrest is evidently widespread and deep – the new wine of fresh ideals in the old wineskins of outworn institutions … Were India given all she is asking she would not find in it the secret of peace but the beginning of sorrow and strife.

> For India the secret of peace and true power lies nearer home – in the emancipation of her women, the education of her children, the freeing of her serfs, the abolishing of caste, and the acceptance of the truth that makes men free, an enlightened faith and a new hope, and these can only come through the message of the Gospel and the power of God.

> India's need is England's responsibility. We are largely the authors of her trouble; we must be the makers of her peace. We have shown her wealth and power and political ambition; she needs to see Jesus. Restless she must be till she finds her rest in God…

These were commendable and timely sentiments, and the ominous phrase 'the beginning of sorrow and strife' would prove all too prescient in 1947. But there was no reference to a massacre, or to General Dyer, because the truth only came out the following December when the results of the Enquiry were published. The *Methodist Times* (though not the *Recorder*, its comment columns pre-occupied with the Treaty of Versailles and the League of Nations) then gave it full treatment. Basil Mathews' weekly column pulled no punches:

---

[6]   The front page, as with much of the press at the time, was devoted exclusively to advertisements.

We have been allowed in these last few days to have the veil drawn back so that we can see a deed perpetrated months and months ago which will go down to history as an indelible revolting stain on the record of the British Raj. I can see the articles we should have written if the Germans had done it. We should then have written: 'The Amritsar massacre is an infamy. It is a disgraceful act of gross injustice, of crass stupidity, and of bloody cruelty. It combines at their maximum the blind lunacy and the murderous ruthlessness of a maddened buffalo. It reveals a blend of the panic of the coward and the brutishness of the bully.'[7]

In contrast the WMMS remained tight-lipped. Its annual report published in 1920 had two references. From North India, no expression of horror or protest but simply:

In April 1919 riots broke out in Delhi and spread rapidly to the Punjab. This necessitated the calling out of British troops and the almost complete dislocation of our work in cantonments. As the troops were dispersed in small bodies, and located for the time in numerous and scattered places, it meant a heavy addition to the duties of the chaplains.[8]

The South India report went slightly further, quoting Duncan Leith of Madras who referred to 'the grave disorders in the Punjab and their repression' and to 'the attitude and actions of some of the representatives of Government in the Punjab' – which were a matter of concern but were not, at least in print, spelled out or labelled reprehensible.

For another thirty years missionaries, even those who were working towards united and autonomous Churches in North and South India, were divided in their attitude to the independence movement. Few took up the cause of *swaraj* as wholeheartedly as the Anglican, Charlie Andrews.[9] Many shared the indignation of the 1921 annual report, which described 'a storm of criticism, often unfair and malignant ... levelled against the Government'. But some changed their views as time went by, and new arrivals came with a different perspective.

In August 1942 Congress passed a 'Quit India' resolution which demanded the immediate cessation of British rule, undertook that a national government would align itself with the Allies, and threatened mass civil disobedience if the demand was refused. The British government preferred suppression to discussion and promptly imprisoned Gandhi, Nehru and scores of others. Violence erupted. Police stations were torched, telegraph lines severed, rail tracks sabotaged and British officials assaulted. Two minor incidents in Uttar Pradesh illustrate how Methodists were caught up in the turmoil. In Mau, a big crowd demanded to hoist the Congress flag on the new church, but were firmly told by Emmanuel Das, the

---

[7]   *Methodist Times,* 24 December 1919: p. 10.

[8]   WMMS Report 1920: p. 44.

[9]   N. Macnicol, *C.F. Andrews: Friend of India* (London, James Clarke, 1944); P.C.R. Choudhury, *C.F. Andrews: His Life and Times* (Bombay, Somaiya Publications, 1971).

young probationer-minister just out of college, that the church was neither his nor theirs but God's, and no flag would be hoisted there. The crowd moved on. In Azamgarh, a week after the arrests, the superintendent of police appeared at the mission station to say that the District Magistrate was besieged by a mob at a remote police station, and asked the missionaries to use their influence to restore order and rescue the Magistrate. David James said:

> It was a ghastly position for us all. Niblett and Wingfield were our friends, and regularly attended our English services, and here was one of them in danger and the other at his wits' end. But on the other hand we knew that if, even in this way, we were to align ourselves with government, the current feeling that missions were a branch of the Raj would be confirmed once and for all … [We told] Wingfield that while we were desperately sorry for him, we must stand aside. For a moment he seemed stunned, and then asked what our position would be if the situation became such that he had to offer us police-protection, and we said we should refuse …

> And so we had burned our boats. Immediately we got hold of some of the Indian leaders of the church, and told them what we had done. They fully agreed with our refusal to help, but were rather doubtful about our unwillingness to be protected … but we pointed out that if we weren't willing to cooperate we could hardly expect to be protected![10]

James and others did their best to identify with their Indian colleagues and made a point of frequently eating Indian food and entertaining Indian guests. It was a major breakthrough when they persuaded the senior missionaries to let the whole Synod eat together for one meal each day during its meetings, instead of being racially divided, but once a day was apparently the limit.

According to Stephen Neill, when independence came in 1947,

> no single missionary of any denomination left his post. Some in their heart of hearts felt that the granting of independence to India had been a mistake, and that the old ways were better. Others felt that the process of transfer had been unduly hasty, and that a further period of close co-operation between Britain and India would have been for the welfare of both nations. Yet others welcomed the change with enthusiasm. But all made it clear, without any exception whatsoever, that their presence in India was due to one cause only, the desire to serve Christ in His Indian Church.[11]

---

[10] D.W. James, written August 1942, in 'The Hand that Guided, the Heart that Planned', privately circulated memoir.

[11] Neill, p. 114.

African Nationalism

The Scot Alexander Mackay, a CMS pioneer in Uganda, observed in 1889: 'In former years the universal aim was to steal the African from Africa. Today the determination of Europe is to steal Africa from the African.'[12] The Congress of Berlin of 1884–1885 shared out the continent between European nations. Informed Africans did not take this quietly. The Ghanaian Methodist Casely Hayford, a son of the manse, was one of the founders of the Pan-African Association. Its goals included securing civil and political rights for African peoples, in Africa and in the diaspora, improving their conditions, encouraging them in education, industry, and business, and promoting friendly relations between races. The Association inspired the civil rights movement in the United States and the independence movements in the Caribbean as well as in Africa. A series of Pan-African Congresses in the 1920s and 1930s were largely off the radar of missionaries and mission boards, though the exceptional Arthur Cripps of the SPG, a contemporary of John White in Rhodesia, published *An Africa for Africans* in 1927.[13]

The nationalist movements, led by educated men, owed an incalculable debt to the work of the missions in the field of education. Edwin Smith suggested that Christian teaching contributed to their cause in another, even more direct and personal way: through its insistence that every person is responsible to God for his or her own actions. The missionary was concerned with individual conviction and conversion; for an African, making an individual decision apart from the clan was something never previously contemplated. This preaching of a person's right and duty to act autonomously according to Christian conscience, was one of the factors that undermined traditional chiefly authority. If such a long-standing feature of African culture could be called into question, then European authority and its moral basis were bound to be questioned and challenged.[14]

Ghana won its independence in 1957. British and French colonies in West Africa, and the larger Caribbean colonies, became independent in the course of the next decade. The struggle had been long and not entirely peaceful; demonstrators had been killed and leaders imprisoned; but it was not so bitter and violent a story as in East and Central Africa. In Kenya British rule was challenged in 1952 by a violent uprising among the Kikuyu people. Mau Mau never won mass support and as many Kikuyu fought against the rebels on the side of the colonial government as joined them in the revolt, but a state of emergency prevailed from October 1952 to April 1956. The troubles did not spread to the coast but did reach the other Methodist area of Meru. The first indication was when two young men called on Fred Valender one evening and told how they had been taken by surprise the night

---

[12]   J.W. Harrison, *A.M. Mackay* (London, Hodder and Stoughton, 1890). pp. 450–1.

[13]   A.S. Cripps, *An Africa for Africans* (London, Longmans, Green & Co., 1927).

[14]   E.W. Smith, *The Golden Stool* (London, Holborn Publishing House, 1926), pp. 255–7; see D.B. Kimble, *A Political History of Ghana: the rise of Gold Coast nationalism 1850-1928* (Oxford, Clarendon Press, 1963), p. 166.

before to a hut where they were forced to take a Mau Mau oath of loyalty and secrecy, under threat of death. They were deeply ashamed and came to confess and seek cleansing. They were the first of many; and there were some who refused the oath and were killed. Valender, a pacifist who did not believe a Christian should bear arms, was none the less required by government to take an armed escort when carrying teachers' salaries, and himself carried a shotgun which he reconciled himself to firing, if he had to, at an attacker's legs in order to stop him but not kill him. Fortunately he never had to put the theory into practice; but on one teachers' payday in 1954 a group was ambushed when returning, salaries in pocket, through the forest and four of them were hacked to death with pangas. Atrocities were not confined to the terrorists. Reprisals were equally brutal. Some 50,000 people lost their lives, all but a few score of them black Kenyans. 80,000 were incarcerated in frightful conditions in so-called 'protected villages' which were no more than concentration camps. By 1956 the uprising was crushed. Jomo Kenyatta, allegedly but improbably a Mau Mau member, was arrested on the first day of the emergency and not released until 1961. Shortly after that a brief outbreak of renewed oath-taking, led by some who called themselves 'Soldiers of Kenyatta', prompted Johanna Mbogori to write an editorial in the National Christian Council of Kenya magazine, *The Rock,* appealing for an end to it; he was summoned to see Kenyatta and warned to be careful what he wrote. After elections in 1963 Kenyatta became prime minister and Kenya became independent at the end of the year.

Kenya differed from its neighbours Uganda and Tanzania, as well as from the West African colonies, by virtue of its large settler community. In central Africa settlers were yet more numerous. In 1950 Southern Rhodesia had a population of about 3¼ million people, of whom 3 million were black Africans and 250,000 were Europeans. The Southern Rhodesia Methodist District at that time had a membership of about 21,000, of whom 1,500 were Europeans.[15] Under the Land Apportionment Act, Europeans owned 35 per cent of the land, and the land available for Africans was mostly in low rainfall areas and away from towns, roads and railways. Throughout the country there were, as in South Africa, separate facilities for Africans and Europeans, separate counters in shops and Post Offices, separate restaurants, schools, hospitals and housing areas and segregated seats in public spaces. The Education Department spent £8 per African child per year and £103 per European child per year. Europeans in Northern Rhodesia and Nyasaland enjoyed similar advantages. In 1953 these white minorities persuaded Britain to unite Northern and Southern Rhodesia and Nyasaland in a Central African Federation. The Federation was given a guarded welcome in missionary circles. A CBMS statement recognized the economic and political advantages of the arrangement, but acknowledged the objections of Africans who saw it as entrenching white power and feared the northward advance of apartheid. CBMS suggested that 'African confidence and consent should be won by patient explanation, by sympathetic understanding of their

---

[15]   Another Methodist Church, linked with American Methodism (from 1968 the UMC), was almost entirely African.

misgivings and by clear demonstrations of good faith.'[16] But none of these were much in evidence. Most Europeans, including many Methodist members, justified their prerogatives on the grounds that European initiative, knowledge and skill had created the country. The only contact most had with Africans was with domestic servants and unskilled workers. African Methodists and European Methodists worshipped in separate buildings each Sunday. This was natural, since Africans and Europeans lived in different parts of the cities and townships, and Africans were as insistent as Europeans on worshipping in their own language, but it did not foster mutual understanding. There were different conditions of membership for Africans and Europeans – for example, Africans were disciplined if they were caught drinking alcohol, but Europeans were not. The salaries of African ministers were much lower than missionary stipends. If new missionaries began to preach on racial issues, or to treat Africans in unconventional ways, they were quickly reprimanded.

But Colin Morris, posted to Chingola Free Church on the Copperbelt in 1955, was not a man to be silenced. A powerful and popular preacher, his white congregation grew rapidly at first. But his prophetic sermons on race relations[17] aroused a storm of controversy in the press and he was bitterly and even physically attacked. For a time he left the pulpit for politics. His public profile had brought him in touch with the nationalist leader Kenneth Kaunda whose declared aims were the break-up of the Federation and an independent Zambia. Morris helped to organize a Liberal Party with the objective of ensuring political justice for Africans and political security for Europeans. As its Vice-Chairman he took part in the 1961 Constitutional Conference in London which prepared the way for independence. He resigned when the Party insisted on putting up its own candidates against Kaunda's United National Independence Party (UNIP). Merfyn Temple, who had been in Northern Rhodesia since 1943, became a close friend of Kaunda. In 1957 he was seconded to the USCL in Lusaka, and in 1960 he published *Black Government?*, written by Kaunda, Morris and himself.[18] He joined UNIP and later ran the Zambia Youth Service for a spell. In Nyasaland, where there was no Methodist presence, some of the Church of Scotland missionaries, with the notable backing of George McLeod, the leader of the Iona Community to which several belonged, were equally active.[19] The Federation was dissolved at the end of 1963. The vast majority of its assets went to Southern Rhodesia. Zambia and Malawi became independent in 1964.

The Zimbabwe African People's Union (ZAPU) was founded in 1961 by Joshua Nkomo, a Methodist local preacher. The Zimbabwe African National Union (ZANU) split from ZAPU in 1963 under the leadership of Ndabaningi Sithole, a Waddilove alumnus and former local preacher. Both parties were outlawed by the

---

[16]   Stuart, p. 78.

[17]   Three were published in England: C.M. Morris, *Anything But This* (London, Lutterworth Press, 1958).

[18]   K. Kaunda and C.M. Morris, *Black Government?* (Lusaka, USCL, 1960).

[19]   Stuart, pp. 98–123.

white Rhodesian Front government, which came to power in the 1962 election. After the Federation broke up it demanded full independence from Britain and in 1965 lost patience and issued its Unilateral Declaration of Independence (UDI). Earlier that year the Rhodesia (formerly Southern Rhodesia) District's first black Chairman, Andrew Ndhlela, had taken office, appointed by the Conference on MMS's recommendation. Most Methodists first heard about his appointment through the radio and most European members and missionaries were shocked by it. But Ndhlela was a respected senior African minister, and African members welcomed the announcement. The same divisions appeared in reaction to UDI. Fred Rea, an Irish minister who worked in Rhodesia/Zimbabwe from 1937 to 1984, wrote:

> As things stand at present, if majority rule were to come to Rhodesia, the new African government would be drawn, willy nilly, into the orbit of OAU [Organization of African Unity] policy and Rhodesia would become a spring-board from which the Northern territories would seek to launch their plans for driving the Europeans out of Southern Africa.[20]

There was an understandable tendency for Irish people to read the African scene through lenses shaped by the troubles at home. However, the parallel was strongly refuted by John Truesdale, who had served in Rhodesia between 1939 and 1952. Speaking in 1969, he argued that to deny African liberation in Rhodesia was 'not only anti-social and immoral but most certainly *unchristian*'. Africans now numbered some 4,250,000 in comparison with a white population of only about 230,000, yet were denied the vote unless they owned property of considerable value and had attained a required standard of secondary education. The Land Apportionment Act ensured that the small white minority controlled 36,000,000 acres of the best land, while only 40,000,000 acres of inferior land was allocated to the huge African majority. Highly critical of police attitudes towards the African population, Truesdale quoted a case in which an African awaiting trial in a minor court had been placed in the care of a European constable known to be 'of uncertain temper'. The policeman lost his temper and 'beat the prisoner with such ferocity that he ... died.' For this he was fined £40.[21]

The MMS Secretaries in London had no sympathy with UDI and in their letter to the January 1966 Synod, dispatched quite soon after the Declaration, they wrote:

> Anyone who tries to be a world citizen knows that justice and peace can only be bought at a very high price. Today 22% of the world's peoples enjoy 73% of

---

[20]   *Irish Christian Advocate*, 30 December 1965 p. 6.

[21]   *Irish Christian Advocate*, 1 May 1969: pp. 1, 7, quoted by N.W. Taggart, *Irish Methodism and World Mission in the Twentieth Century* (unpublished monograph, 2012).

the world's wealth, and the 22% consists almost entirely of the white peoples ...
How can there be peace if black men are poor and white men are rich?[22]

There was to be no peace for another fourteen years of strife. The UN called
for economic sanctions against Rhodesia but they had little effect, since the call
was ignored by South Africa, Portugal and assorted business interests around the
world. ZANU and ZAPU had their military wings and as time went by sporadic
guerrilla activity grew into a war of liberation. The Rhodesian army forbade any
kind of gathering in rural areas and many congregations were not able to meet
for worship for several years. A number of African ministers had to leave their
stations and move into towns for safety; MCOD made grants to help with their
salaries. Some schools continued to function; one where there was also a clinic
was able to keep open because they gave the freedom fighters medical supplies. In
another place the guerrillas assembled the leaders of the community, including the
minister, and told them, 'We are not against the whites, but we want our freedom.
We are your children. People must help us. We need money, food and clothing.'
Later the minister went to the Chairman and asked to be transferred elsewhere.
Ndhlela said, 'No, you must stay where you are. We will give you extra money
to give to the guerrillas.' He took great care to keep in touch with the guerrillas,
and he tried to persuade them not to use excessive force. He also made a point of
getting alongside white people and offering them support and pastoral care.[23]

ZAPU guerrillas based in Botswana abducted a large group of students at
Tegwani Secondary School, near the Rhodesia-Botswana border. They made them
walk across into Botswana. They wanted the boys to be guerrillas and the girls
to support them. But Luke Kumalo, the headmaster, insisted on going with them
and in the end persuaded the guerrillas to let the students return.[24] Soon the whole
school was moved to a safer place in the suburbs of the city of Bulawayo. Pakame
Mission was spared – it was said that this was because it was the secondary
school where Tongogara, the head of the ZANU guerrillas, had been educated.
But, because it was spared, the Rhodesian soldiers thought the African minister in
charge was working with the guerrillas and they beat him very severely.

By 1978 the liberation movements had the upper hand. Under South African
and American pressure, the settler leader Ian Smith accepted a power-sharing
compromise with the UM Bishop Abel Muzorewa and Ndabaningi Sithole, who
had been ousted from the ZANU leadership by Robert Mugabe. It was too late.
NIBMAR – No Independence Before Majority African Rule – was the watchword
that carried the day. The 'internal settlement' was declared unlawful by the UN
Security Council and the civil war continued for a few more months. 1980 saw

---

[22]   Quoted by C. S. Banana, *A Century of Methodism in Zimbabwe* (Harare. Methodist
Church Zimbabwe, 1991), p. 134.

[23]   MCH: A.W. Mosley, report on an extended visit to Zimbabwe in January 1981.

[24]   p. 39.

Mugabe win a landslide election and Zimbabwe's independence. Like many another, Sithole paid tribute to the missionary influence:

> The Christian church has created in Africa ... a strong Christian consciousness that transcends the usual barriers of race and colour, and this Christian consciousness is based on the love of God and the love of our fellow men. It is based on a strong sense of human justice. The story of African nationalism would be incomplete if this Christian awareness was ignored ... The Christian faith may be regarded in one sense as its spiritual father and in another as its guardian angel, whether or not the Church recognizes these roles ...

> The Christian Church by sending religious, educational, and industrial missionaries to Africa broadened the outlook of many an African. It provided opportunities for many Africans to develop their latent qualities; it has discouraged tribal hatred and encouraged universal brotherhood instead ... The present enlightened political leadership would be next to impossible but for the Christian Church that spread literacy to many parts of Africa.[25]

His rosy view of tribalism was over-optimistic. Although both ZAPU and ZANU drew support at first from Shona and Ndebele alike, independent Zimbabwe was soon a theatre of inter-ethnic conflict. Thousands of Ndebele were killed in the immediate post-independence years and thousands more starved when food supplies were disrupted.

The Methodist Church in Zimbabwe became autonomous in 1977, with Andrew Ndhlela as its first President. Some of the white ministers were so uncomfortable with the new régime in church and nation that they left in the course of the next decade, well before an ageing and psychopathic Mugabe took a much more hostile stance to white citizens.

The Rise and Fall of Apartheid

Had European settlers in South Africa adopted the same policy that was applied in the Americas and Australia, history would have taken a very different course. The African peoples would have been practically exterminated, the white population with an overwhelming majority would have exercised unchallenged domination, and apartheid would not have needed inventing. But although there was plenty of fighting over land and over cattle, the settlers in South Africa did not set out to annihilate the local population. They were religious people, the Afrikaners more so than the British, and only killed in self-defence – as at the 1838 battle of Blood

---

[25] N. Sithole, *Roots of a Revolution: Scenes from Zimbabwe's Struggle* (Oxford, Oxford University Press, 1977), pp. 88–9, 94.

River, when 3,000 Zulus died. All they sought at first was space to live in and fertile land to farm. They soon realized that Africans, left alive, could be turned into a useful labour force.

By the time the British established their authority in the Cape, the Afrikaners had already been there for a century and a half. Their economy was built on slave-labour and on the subservience of the African. Within a few years slavery was abolished and in due course the franchise in the Cape was extended 'without distinction of class or colour'. The Afrikaners set out on their Great Trek, east and north, with the British following and steadily annexing the territory into which they moved, including their Orange Free State and Transvaal Republics. The Voortrekkers read their Bibles as they journeyed, and the Exodus story came alive. They were the chosen people, being tested in the wilderness, on the way to the promised land. Pagan tribes in their way must be brushed aside. Their attitude to the African hardened. The Dutch Reformed Church, which had obtained its autonomy from Holland in 1824, had in 1829 stated that the Word of God called for communion to be served to all members 'without distinction of colour or origin'. In 1857 the Synod reversed its position and segregated worship was enforced. Some Voortrekkers meanwhile formed their own, even more racist, Churches, with a platform of no equality in church or state.

Although they were defeated in the Anglo-Boer war, 1899–1902, fought to secure British mining interests in the gold and diamond fields which had been opened up in the preceding decades, the Afrikaners and their policies were soon firmly entrenched. In the new industrialized context the English-speaking settlers came to the view that allying themselves with Afrikaner interests would best serve their own. Blacks were to form a powerless labour force. They would live in separate, arid areas of the country, in townships on the edge of the cities, in spartan single-sex hostels for mineworkers, or a room at the bottom of the garden for domestic workers. The PM popular report for 1928 reported:

> ... political and economic fear operates to keep the black man under. But as the native African develops, profiting by his opportunities of education, industrial training, and so forth, his sense of justice begins to assert itself ... They consider the amount of taxes levied on them, watch the laying out of new roads for the white man's wealth-production, look at the crazy hovels provided on the locations for their own people to live on, and they say 'We want not roads but houses' ... The Revd Charles Crabtree[26] has been working heroically in the cause of the Native, notably in regard to their housing question.[27]

---

[26]   Crabtree was a PM missionary from 1922 and transferred to the South Africa Conference in 1931; he was the Secretary of the Native Welfare Society in Aliwal which brought 'Europeans and Natives together to consider matters affecting native well-being'.

[27]   *The Adventure of the Road*, PM report 1928: p. 69.

After 1932, when the Transvaal District and the PM mission were transferred to the South Africa Conference, MMS ceased sending missionaries to South Africa.[28] There were, however, ministers, ministerial students and candidates who emigrated. Some had distinguished ministries, including George Irvine from Ireland, who served as Chairman/Bishop in both Port Elizabeth and Durban, and the Lancastrian Maurice Fearns who became the Connexional Editor, while Cedric Mayson resigned when he could no longer stand being told: 'Lay off the race and politics thing: you are right but it could be dangerous: the people don't like having the Security Police in the congregation. The numbers are falling.'[29] He worked for the Christian Institute of Southern Africa until it was banned in 1977, and escaped to England in 1983 in the middle of a trial for High Treason.

Apartheid, as a comprehensive policy of separate development, was introduced by the Afrikaner-dominated National Party after its election victory in 1948. It formally classified inhabitants into four racial groups: native, white, Asian and 'coloured' – a term denoting those of mixed race, with a broad international ancestry dating back centuries. Forced removals implemented the segregation of residential areas; 'pass laws' prohibited black movement without a permit; public amenities were segregated; investment in 'Bantu education' was severely limited and would equip them for nothing but servitude. The writer Ezekiel Mphahlele put it like this:

> I've never been encouraged to think anything except that I'm black. For three hundred years this has been drummed into our heads, first by cannon fire, then by acts of parliament, proclamations and regulations. Our minds have been so conditioned that a number of our responses have become reflex: everywhere, instinctively, we look around for separate entrances, exits, reception counters, bank tellers, separate public lavatories, train coaches, platforms, hospitals. Instinctively, we make sure that wherever we are, we have permits in the form of passes ...[30]

The Methodist Church was similarly divided at local and circuit level, and although its Conference was multi-racial, leadership was firmly in white hands. It was 1963 before it elected its first black President. Seth Mokitimi had been a housemaster at the Healdtown Institution when Nelson Mandela studied there; Mandela long remembered an incident when the diminutive Mokitimi stood up to the towering Principal, and related that he 'realized then that Dr Wellington was

---

[28]   The Conference had circuits beyond South Africa's frontiers in Botswana, Lesotho, Swaziland, Mozambique and Namibia. In 1977 it was renamed the Methodist Church of Southern Africa (MCSA). In the 1980s medical missionaries served briefly at Semonkong Hospital in Lesotho.

[29]   C. Mayson, *A Certain Sound: The Struggle for Liberation in South Africa* (London, Epworth Press, 1984), p. 5.

[30]   E. Mphahlele, *The African Image* (London, Faber & Faber, 1962), p. 68.

less than a god and Rev Mokitimi more than a lackey, and that a black man did not have to defer automatically to a white, however senior he was.'[31] Mokitimi's election was well-deserved and long overdue. At the time of his presidency the MCSA had 1,364,000 members, of whom 219,000 were white, 103,000 coloured and 1,042,000 black. But the presidency was a one-year appointment and he was followed by another succession of white Presidents, while much greater power lay in the white hands of Secretaries of the Conference. In 1975, with mounting unrest throughout the country, a gathering of black ministers in Bloemfontein formed a Black Methodist Consultation (BMC), dedicated to developing black leadership and promoting black candidates for senior offices.

The Overseas Division, with its experience in Rhodesia in mind, at once saw the importance of the BMC. It made occasional grants, insignificant in amount but potent in effect, which helped them to continue meeting. In 1977 MCOD brought two emerging leaders, Stanley Mogoba and Itumeleng Mosala, to study in Bristol and Manchester respectively, and a promising young student, Mvume Dandala, to Wesley House, Cambridge. Both Mogoba and Dandala later served as MCSA's Presiding Bishop and Mosala became a leading exponent of black theology; all three were politically active in opposition parties in the post-apartheid era.[32] In 1977 too the executive staff of the Christian Institute were issued with banning orders. Two of them, Brian Brown and Theo Kotze, both Methodist ministers, sorrowfully left for Britain. Brown soon became the Africa Secretary of the BCC (and later of MCOD) and was a driving force in the Anti-Apartheid Movement and sundry associated pressure groups. Among these were Christian Concern for Southern Africa (CCSA), led by Elliott Kendall, and End Loans to South Africa (ELTSA), with David Haslam at the helm. Just as the Anti-Slavery Society and the Aborigines Protection Society in the nineteenth century had the active support of such men as Bunting and M'Arthur, Methodists were heavily engaged in the anti-apartheid and other anti-fascist, anti-racist causes of the late twentieth century. CCSA lobbied Shell and other oil companies exporting in defiance of an embargo, while ELTSA campaigned for the implementation of the UN resolution to end all new investment in and financial loans to South Africa. They pioneered the techniques of shareholder action.

The British Conference of 1980 endorsed the BCC Assembly's

> conviction that progressive disengagement from the economy of the Republic of South Africa is now the appropriate basic approach for the Churches to adopt until it is clear that all the people of South Africa are to be permanently entitled to share equally in the exercise of political power in regard to the whole of your

---

[31]   N.R. Mandela, *Long Walk to Freedom* (London, Little, Brown & Co., 1994), p. 37.

[32]   Mogoba became President of the PAC (Pan Africanist Congress), Mosala President of AZAPO (Azanian People's Organization) and Dandala was the COPE (Congress of the People) candidate in the Republic's 2009 presidential election.

country [i.e. not simply within the pseudo-independent Bantustans designated by the apartheid regime].

In its Reply to the Address of the MCSA Conference, the Conference reported this and lamely added, presumably for the benefit of white, English-speaking Methodists rather than for the million black Methodists far less likely to read it:

> We realise that it will be difficult for many of your people to understand the reasons why we have been driven to this conclusion. It is because of our deep concern for the future of your nation and our own Christian integrity.[33]

The *Kairos Document* of 1985, produced by a multiracial group of South African Christians, was a biblical and theological analysis of the crisis engulfing the country, as one black township after another revolted against the regime and the army moved in to rule by the barrel of the gun. Its call to the churches to side with the oppressed, and at times engage in civil disobedience, pointed out that 'the Church is already on the side of the oppressed because that is where the majority of its members are to be found ... By far the greater part of the Church in South Africa is poor and oppressed.'[34] The document quickly gathered the signatures of scores of church leaders; it renewed the hope and stimulated the activity of Christian people within and without the country.

The defiance of ordinary citizens, coupled with a low-key armed struggle waged by the liberation movements, the boycott of South African produce by consumers abroad, the demoralizing sports boycott and the mounting pressures on a faltering economy finally brought the end of apartheid. The MCSA made Stanley Mogoba Secretary of Conference in 1983 and his first term as President began in 1989, the year before the world's best-known Methodist, Nelson Mandela, was freed after twenty-seven years in prison.[35] Mogoba, once a companion of Mandela on Robben Island, knew more than he could say publicly about the prospect of Mandela's release. In an Easter 1989 message in a Johannesburg weekly paper, he wrote:

> Violence and war is futile ... Reconciliation remains our best hope for the future ... Now, before anyone can misunderstand me, I want to say that reconciliation is not an easy option; rather, it is a most costly one ... I have many reasons to call for war and to reject reconciliation. These include being humiliated, imprisoned,

---

[33] *Minutes of Conference* 1980: p. 43. The Address of the South African Conference and the Reply of the British Conference were published yearly from 1883 to 1987.

[34] *Challenge to the Church: The Kairos Document* (London, British Council of Churches and Catholic Institute for International Relations, 1985), p. 25.

[35] Mandela preserved the class tickets he received for the five years he was a member; he occasionally received Holy Communion while in prison; his marriage to Graça Machel was conducted by Presiding Bishop Mvume Dandala.

beaten, and losing a wife and daughter. We blacks have been trying for 77 years to bring change in our land. However, in spite of this, I still say that war does not produce the goods and I firmly believe that there can be no return to a normal way of life in South Africa without passing through the conference table.[36]

Well before his release, Mandela was already at the conference table. In 1990 the ANC was unbanned and he walked free. In 1994, with the legal props of apartheid dismantled, South Africa's first democratic elections were held and he became president.

By 1990 MCSA was greatly changed. The Conference had resolved to replace segregated with geographical circuits. Conference was no longer polarized as it had been, though white representatives still had battles to fight when they returned to their circuits. But the long years of struggle and economic hardship had left all sectors of society, including the church, weakened. Those who had overcome the handicaps of 'Bantu Education' were all too few. Infrastructure had fallen into disrepair. AIDS was taking its heavy toll. There was much to be done, both within the church and in the outreach of a church sharing in God's mission to a post-apartheid society. In the late 1980s MCSA set up three notable programmes: *Malihambe*, meaning 'let it spread', a programme of evangelism; *Ubulungisa*, meaning 'justice', a programme of Bible study, reflection, action and reconciliation; and *Zikhuliseni,* meaning 'empower yourselves', a community action programme. MCOD helped to fund these, partly through Second Mile Projects,[37] which also supported work in the Mozambique and Namibia Districts.

The Programme to Combat Racism (PCR)

The WCC Assembly in Uppsala in 1968 was deeply affected by the assassination of Martin Luther King, who was due to give a keynote speech. It urged the WCC 'to embark on a vigorous campaign against racism' and undertake 'a crash programme to guide the Council and member churches in the matter of racism'. The PCR was set up in 1969. Its mandate was to deal with racism as a world-wide problem, but much of its attention and energy was for twenty years focused on Southern Africa. It initiated research, organized consultations and published material; and it established a Special Fund from which annual grants were made to racially oppressed groups and organizations supporting the victims of racism. From 1970 to 1990 more than 9 million dollars were distributed, with the lion's share going to the liberation movements in South Africa and Zimbabwe for their humanitarian and educational work among exiles. MMS, at the urging of Pauline Webb (by then Vice-Moderator of the WCC Central Committee) sent a first grant

---

        [36]   M.S. Mogoba, *Tears of Hope* (Johannesburg, Methodist Church of Southern Africa, 1989), p. 49.
        [37]   p. 269.

of £500 in 1970. It was (with the endorsement of the Conference in 1972 and 1974) the only church body in Britain to make grants to the Special Fund – others debated whether they should, but in the end did nothing. When the first allocation was announced, with the largest grant going to the African National Congress (ANC), a storm of controversy broke out, not only in South Africa but in Britain. It was seen as funding the ANC's armed wing; 'grants to guerrillas' was the outcry. Other beneficiaries were ZANU and ZAPU in Rhodesia, SWAPO in Namibia and FRELIMO in Mozambique.

The 1970 South African Conference took exception to the WCC 'making funds available to organizations which aim to bring about political change by violent means' but resolved to continue its membership. The judgement of the 1971 British Conference, communicated in the annual exchange of open letters between the Conferences,

> differed from yours on this matter as we remembered that the organizations assisted by the grant are involved in many kinds of service and aid. We did not, by our support, commit ourselves to the principle of violence as a Christian way of solving human problems ... We offer you the support of our prayers and invite yours ...[38]

In 1972 MCSA repeated:

> The decisions of the WCC to continue and indeed to increase its support of what they term 'freedom-fighters', who are regarded as 'terrorists' in South Africa, has been the cause of much regret and concern and many voices are being raised demanding that we secede from the World Council. Some have withdrawn their membership and support from the local churches and others threaten to do so.[39]

The official position of MCSA remained uncompromising. In 1978 it recorded

> its dismay at the indications of political partisanship in the allocation of grants ... These allegedly humanitarian grants appear to go not to those who need them most but to those adhering to a particular political wing ... (and) its distress that [WCC] appears by its actions to condone the atrocities committed by guerrillas on uninvolved non-combatants and humanitarian mission workers.[40]

There was uproar in Rhodesia too. The Christian Council, chaired by Andrew Ndhlela, passed a resolution in 1970 which expressed a timid welcome to the grants

---

[38] *Minutes of Conference* 1971: p. 78.
[39] *Minutes of Conference* 1972: p. 87.
[40] *MCSA Minutes of Conference* 1978: pp. 269–70.

given to our Churches in Rhodesia by the World Council of Churches.

We acknowledge receipt in recent years of grants exceeding one million dollars for the erection of schools and colleges, for the relief of the needy, for agencies for extension of Christian work in general.

In particular we record our appreciation for the recent gesture of concern and compassion for the oppressed people of Rhodesia. We interpret the WCC action as support for the Churches' world-wide Christian Programme against Racism.[41]

The Methodist Synod of January 1971 declared:

The Synod of the Methodist Church in Rhodesia believes that Christians ought not to support violence in any form. Violence will only create further mistrust between races and amongst the people. In considering the WCC Program to Combat Racism we note that the [World] Council Executive has made it clear that it is not supporting the military purposes of the organisations to which it made grants but rather their political aims, namely justice, equality, human dignity and freedom.[42]

This appreciative assessment of PCR was not shared by some vociferous missionaries and many European members. But in a simultaneous controversy they felt it right for white Methodist ministers to become chaplains to the Rhodesian armed forces. Fred Rea expressed his

conviction that the Christian church, no less than the medical profession, has its 'hippocratic oath' of responsibility to all who are in need. If it were possible to give spiritual help to the guerrilla forces, the church would do so. Where it is possible – namely through the prison chaplaincy – the church is doing so ... That we will be accused of identifying ourselves with the establishment is a risk we must be prepared to take.[43]

The Synod debated this for several years and in the end decided that, although it would not give its backing to such appointments, it would not deny permission to any minister who in conscience felt it right to be a chaplain.

The Overseas Division steadfastly continued to make regular grants of one or two thousand pounds (no more than 0.05 per cent of its total expenditure) to

---

[41]   C.F. Hallencreutz and A. Mayo, *Church and State in Zimbabwe* (Harare, Mambo Press, 1988), p. 70.

[42]   Banana, p. 139.

[43]   MCH: Rea to MCOD, 3 August 1976.

the Special Fund throughout the 1970s, and the General Secretary's in-tray was never long without letters on the matter, most of them hostile. There were three basic arguments against the grants: MCOD was supporting the use of violence, and violence had never brought justice and peace; though the grants were to be used for humanitarian purposes, there was no check that they were in fact being so used; and in any case grants given for humanitarian purposes freed the guerrilla movements to spend more on armaments. The basic counter-argument was that although the Church believed that violence should only be used as a last resort, it had, when faced with the evil of Nazism, recognized that sometimes it was necessary to use violence. Violence was already present in Rhodesia in the racist oppression of the African people by white governments. In making the grants, the Church publicly acknowledged the liberation movements' right to share in determining their destiny and to use alternative means when constitutional reform was denied them.

Opposition grew markedly when the Special Fund made a grant in 1978 to Mugabe's Patriotic Front which was behind some murderous attacks on mission stations. Irish Methodists, in particular, were horrified. Their misgivings were inevitably magnified by the Provisional IRA's acts of terrorism in Ulster. The General Committee of the Methodist Church in Ireland called on MCOD to ensure that no money contributed by Irish Methodism to its funds should be donated to the Special Fund, and recommended the Officers of MMS (Ireland) to transfer no funds until assurances were given.[44] Complicated accounting was necessary to implement this, but the flow of funds was not held up for long. Meanwhile Ken Thompson, an Irish minister, was driven to write, in the style of C.S. Lewis's *Screwtape Letters,* a letter 'from an elderly devil to his nephew':

> I can see you have cleverly exploited fears about givings to MMS ... You are learning well, my boy, in pushing a lesser concern to the forefront in place of the Enemy's compassionate identification with the downtrodden. I was rather afraid that the Enemy might have gained ground in Ireland as a result of all the heart searching of the last few years ... It is re-assuring to find self-preservation still a dominant factor in high places. As they throw up their hands in horror at the Programme to Combat Racism, *keep them looking for perfect solutions in an imperfect world. That way nothing will get done.*[45]

In 1984 the Charity Commissioners, after receiving an anonymous complaint, prohibited further grants. The Commissioners had recently determined that

---

[44]   The Methodist Newsletter, November 1978.

[45]   *The Methodist Newsletter*, December 1978, quoted by Taggart, 'Irish Methodism and World Mission in the Twentieth Century'.

the promotion of good race relations, endeavouring to eliminate discrimination on grounds of race, and encouraging equality of opportunity between persons of different racial groups were charitable purposes in law.

But

the fact that the Commissioners have taken a decision in principle that the promotion of racial harmony is a good charitable purpose does not mean that a charity established for that purpose could then engage in the kind of activities which, from whatever motives of principle and morality, are undertaken by the PCR.[46]

Prohibition could not be the end of the matter. In due course a conduit for personal gifts to the Special Fund was established, administered through the DSR. For a few years a few individuals contributed, but the fact that contributions came from individuals rather than from central funds meant that this was no longer an act of witness on behalf of the whole Church.

It was scarcely co-incidental that WCC support for liberation movements was contemporaneous with the advent of liberation theology – the term was coined by the Peruvian Gustavo Gutierrez in 1971. In the words of José Miguez Bonino, the Argentine Methodist,

The origins of this theology in Latin America can be traced to the growing participation of Christian priests, ministers and laypeople in the life and struggles of the large poor majorities to overcome the condition of marginalization, poverty and oppression. Such participation generated a deep spiritual commitment to the poor, an awareness of the destructive nature of their conditions, an admiration for the solidarity, depth and resourcefulness which these people manifested and a need to understand better the social, economic and political structures which caused such situations.[47]

The normative biblical paradigm for liberation theologians was the Exodus story. 'Moses led his people out of the slavery, exploitation and alienation of Egypt so that they might inhabit a land where they could live with human dignity.'[48] 'Let my people go' was a battle-cry in Africa as in the Americas. But Exodus from Egypt took the escapees into the wilderness; and their Promised Land was contested by peoples unwilling to cohabit. The experience of post-colonial, post-apartheid Africa was no different. As the WCC Central Committee noted in 1995,

---

[46]   MCH: Letter from the Charity Commission to the Society's solicitor, 2 August 1984.

[47]   N. Lossky and others (eds), *Dictionary of the Ecumenical Movement* (Geneva, World Council of Churches Publications, 1991), p. 997.

[48]   G. Gutierrez, *A Theology of Liberation* (London, SCM Press, 1974), p. 294.

'Institutional racism and the ideology of racism, in their most pernicious forms, continue unabated in contemporary societies and still affect churches dramatically, while ongoing social, political and economic trends are producing new forms of racism.'

A very old form of racism victimized millions in south Asia, especially in India where Dalits and tribal peoples together constituted almost a quarter of the population. Back in 1910 Charles Monahan, Chairman of the Madras District, had written:

> I believe the chief obstacle to a true Indian nationalism with a self-governing State and an autonomous Church is caste. It must be broken before India can be free.[49]

The 1947 Indian constitution outlawed untouchability, but casteism still consigned Dalits to discrimination, exploitation, economic and psychological oppression. It was reckoned at the end of the century that *every day* two were murdered, two Dalit houses burned down, three Dalit women raped and fifty Dalits assaulted. Although the arousal of Dalit consciousness owed much to Bhimrao Ambedkar, an activist for thirty years until his death in 1956, Dalit liberation movements really began to organize only in the late 1980s. The many manifestations and offshoots of liberation theology – black, feminist, Minjung and more – were joined in the 1990s by Dalit theology.[50] The 1991 WCC Assembly in Canberra affirmed 'the growing consciousness of the indigenous peoples' struggles for freedom, including that of the Dalits of India.' The veteran Methodist anti-apartheid campaigner, David Haslam, Secretary of the British Churches' Commission for Racial Justice from 1987 to 1998, took up the cause and, after a sabbatical in India and Pakistan, was instrumental in starting the Dalit Solidarity Network in Britain.[51]

A luta continua

'The struggle continues' was the rallying cry of the liberation movement in Mozambique, and was later used across the world in connection with other socio-political struggles. In Nigeria the peoples of the Niger delta saw their environment and their health ruined by oil exploration and extraction – lands, streams and creeks polluted, toxic vapours and acid rain, frequent oil spillages and blowouts. The principal culprit was Shell; in the long campaign for compensation and restitution both the Methodist Church Nigeria and the MCOD Africa Secretary, Brian Brown, were party to negotiations with the

---

[49] *The Foreign Field* 72, August 1910: p. 351.

[50] J. Massey, *Downtrodden: The Struggle of India's Dalits for Identity, Solidarity and Liberation* (Geneva, World Council of Churches Publications, 1997).

[51] D.A. Haslam, *Caste Out.*

company. Brown's negotiating skills, well-honed in the anti-apartheid struggle, gave encouragement to the aggrieved communities, though many years were to pass before Shell accepted any liability.

In Britain Network, the successor to Women's Work which had over the years brought its efforts to bear on many aspects of women's liberation, took up such issues as domestic violence, female genital mutilation, human trafficking and child prostitution, and Nestlé's unethical methods of promoting infant formula over breast milk to poor mothers in developing countries. Groups throughout the country wrote letters and raised awareness.

A gay couple's interest in serving overseas was given careful consideration by the Candidates' Committee and MCOD adopted a controversial policy document affirming its willingness to examine such candidates on their merits, while reiterating that mission partners serve at the invitation of the receiving Church – and acknowledging that few if any sister Churches would be prepared to invite a gay couple. This affirmation of principle caused consternation in some quarters but received the backing of the Conference; in practice, no formal application was ever submitted.

The most vigorous campaign of the 1990s in which MCOD shared was for the cancellation of Third World debt. In the early 1970s oil prices rose sharply, and the oil-exporters found themselves with huge quantities of petro-dollars which they placed with western banks. The banks sent their emissaries around the world to find borrowers, in many cases without checking too carefully on the viability of the schemes they were funding. Then in the 1980s, just as repayments became due, interest rates suddenly shot up; they went up because the United States, by far the world's most heavily indebted nation, wanted to borrow yet more for a costly defence initiative (popularly derided as Star Wars), and was prepared to pay more interest to get it. At the same time world commodity prices – cocoa, coffee, copper – slumped, depleting the producers' ability to pay up. Their indebtedness spiralled out of control, and for every pound given by rich nations in overseas aid, £3 was going back in debt repayments. Fear that some big debtors would repudiate their debts and that some big banks would crash led the International Monetary Fund to intervene, giving the debtors more time to pay but imposing draconian conditions which hit the ordinary citizens of the highly-indebted nations hardest. Campaigners for the cancellation of the massive backlog of unpayable debts saw the approaching millennium as a *kairos* moment and formed the Jubilee 2000 Coalition which called upon rich world governments and financial institutions to write off the debts of the most impoverished nations.

The churches born from the pioneering missions of the MMS were now self-governing and self-propagating; but had no chance of becoming self-sufficient when the nations where they operated were in such dire financial straits. British Methodists continued to give to the World Mission Fund, and MCOD (and its post 1996 successors) continued to make grants-in-aid, but that did not address the root of the problem. Jubilee 2000 was a cause which

MCOD and MRDF invested staff time to promote, and many Methodists actively supported it. The struggle for justice was integral to God's mission, and an imperative for the whole church.

Chapter 19

Moving On

By 1996 the contours and context of Christian mission were vastly different from anything that Thomas Coke could have conceived.

The planet's population had multiplied more than seven-fold since 1800. Although people in all corners of the globe had responded to the gospel and the number of believers had multiplied too, the number of those to whom Christianity was an unknown or alien faith was greater than ever. Humans were overcrowding the earth, and inevitably its habitable areas were ever more densely populated, bringing into increasingly sharp and painful focus the scandalous contrast between the world's haves and have-nots.

The crowded planet was a shrunken planet. It was a historic occasion when a photograph of the earth from space was published: a small blue planet, seen whole for the first time, where continents and nations are bound together in geographical and economic interdependence. Wealthy people were now able to speed across oceans and continents in a matter of hours; they could communicate in a matter of seconds; an event could be viewed in real time – if the telecommunications oligarchs chose – by billions. Poorer people were on the move too: migrants and refugees, fleeing poverty or danger. Many parts of the industrialized and post-industrial world had become multi-racial and multi-faith societies.

The shrunken world was a globalized world. Even the poorest rural communities, apart from a handful of Amazonian tribes, were aware of material goods beyond their reach; the urban half of the population was prey to unbridled consumerism. Globalization was, despite the rise of China, westernization; and the English tongue, albeit with multiple local variations, had become the new Latin, the dominant vehicle of international communication.

It was still a fearful world. Old superstitious terrors of malevolent spirits were in decline, and many dreaded diseases were now preventable or curable, but terror and terrorism had not vanished (and would become yet more prevalent as the next millennium got under way). Shrinking the world had brought the possibility of enriching encounters with others, turning strangers into friends – but it had aroused, in even greater measure, suspicion, jealousy, fear and hostility. The threat of nuclear annihilation, after hanging over the planet for years, had seemingly been averted; but armaments was one of the world's biggest businesses, and there was a never-ending supply of weapons to fuel wars great and small. Competition for the resources to support so many people was becoming vicious. It was as urgent as ever to preach the gospel of peace.

All this was the product, or by-product, of a galloping technological revolution. There were other advances of equal magnitude. Darwin and Einstein, genetics and astrophysics and quantum mechanics, transformed our knowledge of the natural world. Eye-opening advances were made too in other fields of scholarship: for example in geology, anthropology and literary criticism. These in turn had a telling impact on biblical studies, producing a better understanding of the ancient texts and a wider spectrum of theologies. Science was wise to the provisional nature of its conclusions; religion is notoriously more conservative, and in every continent there were Christians who refused to abandon a literal reading of the Bible. A majority were creationists even if to most the term was unfamiliar, and they would not entertain the suggestion that Isaiah might have more than one author.

The most striking developments of the twentieth century in Protestant Christianity were ecumenism – though by 1996 it showed signs of running out of steam – and Pentecostalism. Both made their mark on Catholic Christianity too. There were Pentecostal streams in the long-established denominations and there were legions of new Pentecostal churches. In an otherwise unrecognizable world, eighteenth-century Methodists would have felt at home in the company of these enthusiastic, Spirit-filled Christians, with their ecstatic utterances, visions, prophecies and the same hysterical symptoms which frequently marked conversion experiences in Wesley's day.

World Methodism had many faces, however. Architecturally, its buildings came in all shapes and sizes. Liturgically, its worship ranged from Pentecostal freedom to very formal, and to both ends of that spectrum combined in every conceivable manner. Its theology ranged from fundamentalist to liberal. Functional episcopacy was the usual keystone of its polity; an annual presidency on the British model was as rare as Nigeria's colourful seven-fold order of ministry. Attitudes to the consumption of alcohol, and to the place of women – from where they should sit in church to what leadership roles they should be permitted to fill – were just as diverse, and, like attitudes to homosexuality, varied with local cultural norms. But while their moral teaching often reflected the prevalent culture, Methodists were not afraid to challenge it on gospel grounds.

In this end-of-millennium scene, questions inevitably arose about the place of the missionary arm of British and Irish Methodism. (The label 'Methodist Missionary Society' was scarcely used on the British side; as far back as 1955 Edgar Thompson had noted that it was not to be found in the index of the *Minutes of Conference,* its business being reported under the heading 'Overseas Missions'.) Its continuing role hinged on the Wesleyan principle of connexionalism, which itself was an expression of the unity in Christ to which the apostle Paul applied the metaphor of the human body. In the context of British or Irish circuits and in international partnerships alike, larger churches shared their resources with smaller, richer with poorer, stronger with weaker. But there are different sorts of riches and strengths, and MMS policy-makers heeded the apostle Paul's reminder that 'the members of the body that seem to be weaker are indispensable.'[1] The task

---

[1]   1 Corinthians 12.12

was to facilitate the mutual exchange of resources, all with something to offer and all with needs to be met, sharing in a common enterprise.

The resources were of many kinds. Personnel-sharing had long been two-way traffic, welcoming colleagues from abroad as well as supporting mission partners lent to sister churches. Besides secondments on a full-time basis there were short visits and exchanges, including youth teams, theological students, ministers on sabbatical, people with particular gifts for specific assignments. In many cases these were neither initiated nor funded centrally, but staff used their contacts and knowledge to provide advice and encouragement (or, if necessary, discouragement). Less of the budget went on personnel costs as the number of mission partners dwindled; more was available to support Nationals in Mission Appointments, to fund scholarships, and to make grants to sister churches, ecumenical and other bodies.

Alongside these tangible resources were others equally important to exchange. Information – publishing news about the life and concerns of overseas churches in Britain and Ireland, and passing on news to them, in print and increasingly through cyberspace. Prayer for one another, informed by the exchange of news. The theological insights that emerged from a diversity of cultural heritages, from struggling for justice and freedom, from personal and corporate experiences of joy or pain. Mutual consciousness-raising, confidence-building and questioning. It mattered little under what name this ministry of resource-sharing was exercised, since

> The MMS is none other than the Methodist Church itself organized for mission overseas; the members of the MMS shall be the members of the Methodist Church, and every member of the Methodist Church shall be ipso facto a member of the Society.[2]

Members of the Church (and therefore of the Society) were actively pursuing their calling to engage in God's mission through a wide range of commitments, often not specifically Methodist but in association with activists of all faiths and none. Such were, for example, the Jubilee 2000 campaign for the cancellation of unrepayable poor country debts, the World Development Movement, and work among refugees and asylum seekers. Two other matters were of mounting concern.

The degradation and destruction of the environment, the rapid depletion of finite resources and the effect of greenhouse gases on the global climate awoke a new regard for the planet's fragile ecosystem. Remembering the psalmist's affirmation that 'The earth is the Lord's' and that the most famous of all New Testament verses, properly translated, proclaimed that 'God so loved the *cosmos*'

---

[2]   Constitution of the MMS, Article 1, as revised by the 1942 Methodist Conference: 1942 *Minutes*, p. 6.

made care for creation a vital component of the mission agenda.[3] The hymn, 'God, in his love for us, lent us this planet,' was not confined to Harvest Festivals:

> Earth is the Lord's; it is ours to enjoy it,
> Ours, as his stewards, to farm and defend.
> From its pollution, misuse and destruction,
> Good Lord, deliver us, world without end.[4]

Then there was the puzzle over the place of other faith traditions in God's purposes. Were they deviations hateful to God, or belief-systems that, despite their shortcomings, God welcomed? It was probably the most divisive issue for world Christianity, which had shortcomings enough of its own, at the turn of the millennium. In all faiths there were those who dismissed the rest as infidels and refused to get to know them. But equally, on all sides were people who sought to understand the 'other' better and to remove others' misunderstandings of their own beliefs and practices. It could only be done by meeting respectfully.

Such respectful encounter was the usual precondition for conversion. Radio ministries played their part and some Chinese Christians, for example, owed their faith to broadcasts from Hong Kong to which they tuned in surreptitiously during the Cultural Revolution period. But conversion without conversing was rare. To meet others, to share one's faith by personal witness, was the rationale for the missionary movement from the outset. And yet, as Israel Selvanayagam[5] perceptively remarked:

> One cannot but smile sadly at the behaviour of certain churches. They support missionaries to preach and convert and feel frustrated by the absence of conversions. But they are not ready to change one iota of their institutions or patterns of worship and ministry ... Unless we are willing and able to break the stranglehold of familiarity for its own sake, do we have any right to call people of other faiths to come out of their familiar fold and join us?[6]

---

[3]   Psalm 24:1 and John 3:16.

[4]   Written (like most of his hymns) in retirement by Fred Pratt Green, and first published by the Hymn Society of America in *Sixteen Hymns on the Stewardship of the Environment*. The last verse, which disappeared from most subsequent hymnals, ran:

> 'Casual despoilers, or high priests of Mammon,
> Selling the future for present rewards,
> Careless of life and contemptuous of beauty:
> Bid them remember: the Earth is the Lord's.'

© Stainer & Bell Ltd., www.stainer.co.uk, used by permission.

[5]   p. 187.

[6]   Selvanayagam, p. 22.

The familiar structures of British Methodism were reconfigured in 1996, where this account concludes. In the new order its missionary obligations were not abandoned. The conviction that motivated the first missionaries – *for all thou hast in Christ prepared sufficient, sovereign, saving grace*[7] – was not diluted by inter-faith encounters. But the world on the threshold of the twenty-first century was an uncomfortable place. Methodists, in Britain and in sister Churches on every continent, did (and do) not lack either climate change deniers or zealots with vociferously negative and hostile attitudes to other faiths. Yet few would argue with the premise of MCOD's 1992 declaration that 'God's love is for the whole created order'[8] and the corollary that God's love affair with creation embraces all humanity. The last General Secretary of MCOD (who happens to be the author of this history) contended that those who had themselves fallen in love with God could be expected to extend their welcome, hospitality and love to others: 'We love because God first loved us.'[9]

---

[7]   C. Wesley, from the hymn 'Father, whose everlasting love' in *Hymns on God's Everlasting Love* (London, W. Strahan, 1741).

[8]   p. 50.

[9]   1 John 4:19.

Appendix 1
Principal Officers of the Missionary Societies

The WMMS, 1814–1932

1814–15	Jonathan Edmondson
1815–16	James Buckley
1816–25	Richard Watson
1818–23	Joseph Taylor
1821–23	Jabez Bunting
1824–29	George Morley
1824–26	John Mason
1826	Robert Newstead
1827–31	James Townley
1827–32	John James
1830	Thomas Edwards
1831–49	John Beecham
1832–33	Richard Watson
1833–51	Jabez Bunting}
1833–50	Robert Alder } *From 1843 the officers were styled General Secretaries*
1834–65	Elijah Hoole }
1851–67	George Osborn
1851–67	William Arthur
1859–75	William B. Boyce
1867–77	George T. Perks
1868–74	Luke H. Wiseman
1875–80	W. Morley Punshon
1876–88	John Kilner
1877–88	Ebenezer E. Jenkins
1877–90	Marmaduke C. Osborn
1881–1900	George W. Olver
1888–1919	Marshall Hartley
1888–91	John Walton
1891–1905	Frederick W. Macdonald
1896–98	B. Aquila Barber
1898–1914	William Perkins
1900–10	William H. Findlay
1905–12	John Milton Brown

1912–16	Henry Haigh
1913–29	Charles W. Andrews
1914–21	William Goudie
1919–26	Amos Burnet
1919–32	Edgar W. Thompson
1922–32	Walter J. Noble
1927–32	G.E. Hickman Johnson

From 1912, one of the Secretaries was formally designated Chairman of the Officers' Meeting, viz:

1912–14	Marshall Hartley
1915–16	Henry Haigh
1917–18	Marshall Hartley
1919	William Goudie
1920–23	Amos Burnet
1924	Charles W. Andrews
1925	Amos Burnet
1926–29	Charles W. Andrews
1930–32	Edgar W. Thompson

The Primitive Methodist Missionary Committee, 1843–1932

The first four Secretaries were at the same time the Secretaries of the PM General Committee

1843–47	John Garner (1843–5 styled 'corresponding member')
1848–53	William Garner
1854–58	John Bywater
1859–64	Moses Lumpton
1865–68	Thomas Jobling ('Missionary Secretary and General Superintendent of the Home Missions')
1869–73	Samuel Antliff
1874–77	William Rowe
1878–82	William Cutts (from 1879 'and Secretary of our African Missions'; then from 1881 'and Secretary of our Colonial and Foreign Missions and Editor of the Missionary Records and Yearly Reports')
1883–88	John Atkinson
1889–93	James Travis
1894–98	John Smith
1899–1901	Richard W. Burnett
1902	John Slater

1903–07	James Pickett
1908–12	Arthur T. Guttery
1913–17	Samuel Horton
1918–22	Joseph T. Barkby
1923–27	John H. Hirst (from 1924 'Secretary of the Foreign Missionary Committee' with no Home Mission responsibility, and Barkby as Editor)
1928–32	George Ayre

The Methodist New Connexion Missionary Committee 1842–1907

Later Minutes claim the Committee dates from 1816 but the first recorded Secretary is James Dixon, in 1838, while Jonathan Thornhill was Treasurer of the Missionary Fund, 1836–47. From 1842, a Secretary was appointed annually.

1842–49	William Cooke
1849–58	Thomas Allin
1859–62	James Stacey
1863–78	Samuel Hulme
1879–85	James Stacey
1886–90	William J. Townsend
1891	John Medicraft
1892–96	John K. Jackson
1897–1907	George Packer

The United Methodist Free Churches 1859–1907

1859–62	Robert Eckett
1862–71	Samuel Barton
1871–81	Robert Bushell
1881–89	John Adcock
1889–95	George Turner
1895–1907	Henry T. Chapman

The Bible Christian Missionary Society 1880–1907

Frederick W Bourne was the Treasurer of the Society until 1903; Foreign Secretaries were:

1880–84	William Gilbert
1885–1902	Isaac B. Vanstone
1903	James Woolcock
1904–07	Charles Stedeford

The United Methodist Church, 1907–1932

1907–32	Charles Stedeford

The Methodist Missionary Society, 1932–1972

Five Secretaries were appointed in 1932: the WM Secretaries, Edgar Thompson, Walter Noble and G.E. Hickman Johnson, the PM Secretary George Ayre and W. Alexander Grist from the UM (BC) tradition. They and their successors were all, in the Wesleyan manner, styled 'General Secretaries' until 1972. Successive Chairmen of the Officers' Meeting were:–

1932–4	Edgar Thompson
1934–42	Walter J Noble
1942–3	G.E. Hickman Johnson (Noble's year as President of Conference)
1943–7	Walter J. Noble
1947–8	G.E. Hickman Johnson
1948–9	Harold B. Rattenbury
1949–50	Frederick W. Dodds
1950–59	Basil Clutterbuck
1959–68	Douglas W. Thompson
1968–72	Geoffrey T. Eddy
1972–73	Harry O. Morton (General Secretary, with colleagues styled 'Secretaries')

The Methodist Church Overseas Division (MMS) 1973–1996

General Secretaries:

1973–78	Colin M. Morris
1978–87	Albert W. Mosley
1987–91	John E. Richardson
1991–96	John R. Pritchard

Appendix 2

Non-missionaries in Leadership roles –
The First Senior Office-holders

1872   Charles Knight, Chairman of the Sierra Leone District
1934   Shen Wen Ch'ing, Chairman of the Hupei (Hubei) District, China
        Nathaniel K. Nalliah, Chairman of the Ceylon Provincial Synod
        (1 year appointment)
1936   Paul S. Rangaramanujam, Chairman of the South India Provincial Synod
        (1 year)
        Herbert H. Cole, Acting Chairman of the Barbados, Trinidad and Guiana
        District
1937   T'ao Vuh Sa, Chairman of the Wenchow (Wenzhou) District, China
        Paul S. Rangaramanujam, Chairman of the Trichinopoly District
1943   Wong Chung Hoi, Chairman of the South China District
        Chen Sing Ming, Chairman of the Ningpo (Ningbo) District, China
        Cheng En Chih, Chairman of the North China District
        Errol S. Pilgrim, Chairman of the Barbados Trinidad and Guiana District
1944   George A.F. Semaratne, Chairman of the South Ceylon District
1946   Emanuele Sbaffi, Chairman of the Italy District
1947   Lai I-Hsiu, Chairman of the Hunan District, China
        Moses O. Dada, Chairman of the Western Nigeria District
1948   James S. Mather, Chairman of the North Ceylon District
        U Po Tun, Chairman of the Upper Burma District
1949   Gaddiel R. Acquaah, Chairman of the Gold Coast District
        Chu Shui Kwang, Chairman of the South-West China District
1950   Christa C. Pande, Chairman of the Bengal District
1955   Harold W. John, Chairman of the Lucknow and Banaras District
1956   Claude L. Cadogan, Chairman of the Honduras District
        Hugh B. Sherlock, Chairman of the Jamaica District
1958   Ephraim S. Alphonse, Chairman of the Panama sub-District
        Wong Chung Hoi, Chairman of the Hong Kong (Chinese) District
1960   Matthew S. Lucheya, Chairman of the Northern Rhodesia District
        Francis C.F. Grant, Chairman of the Ghana District
1961   Francis C.F. Grant, President of the Ghana Conference
1962   Joseph O.E. Soremekun, President of the Nigeria Conference
        Atherton Didier, Chairman of the Leeward Islands District
1964   Fred S. de Silva, President of the Ceylon Conference
        U Ba Ohn, President of the Upper Burma Conference
        Mario Sbaffi, President of the Italy Conference
        Samson Nandjui, Chairman of the Ivory Coast District

1965	Andrew M. Ndhlela, Chairman of the Rhodesia District
1966	Georges W. Gbeyongbé, Chairman of the Dahomey-Togo District
	Cyril F.H. Alleyne, first Guyanese Chairman of the British Guyana District
1967	Hugh B. Sherlock, President of the Methodist Church in the Caribbean and the Americas
	Ronald S. Mn'gong'o, President of the Kenya Conference
	W.E. Akinumi Pratt, President of the Sierra Leone Conference
1969	Jackson Mwape, Moderator of the United Church of Zambia
1977	Andrew M. Ndhlela, President of the Zimbabwe Conference
1978	Ian C. Roach, Chairman of The Gambia District
1984	Ireneu da Silva Cunha, Chairman of the Portugal District
1985	Emmanuel D. Yando, President of the Ivory Coast Conference
1992	Moïse Sagbohan, President of the Bénin Conference
1996	Ireneu da Silva Cunha, Bishop of the Portugal Conference

Bibliography

Many of the works listed, though out of print, may be consulted in the MMS Library at the School of Oriental and African Studies in London (http://lib.soas. ac.uk).

Methodist Periodicals and Reports

Wesleyan:

Missionary Notices, to 1904
Work and Workers in the Mission Field, to 1904
The Foreign Field, 1904–1932
Wesleyan Methodist Missionary Society Annual Reports, to 1932
Our Missionary Work, quarterly letter of the Women's Auxiliary, 1922–1933
What to Pray For, Prayer Manual of the Helpers' Union, 1907–1932
Minutes of the Conference, to 1932
Ministers' Missionary Union Quarterly Bulletin, 1916–1932

Primitive Methodist:

The Record of the Primitive Methodist Missionary Society, to 1904
The Herald, 1905–1922
Advance, 1922–1932
PMMS Annual Reports, to 1932

United Methodist:

Gleanings in Harvest Fields, MNC to 1907
The Missionary Echo, UMFC to 1907, UMC 1908–1932
Annual Report of the missions, UMFC to 1907, UMC 1908–1932

Post-1932:

The Kingdom Overseas, 1933–1969
Women's Work Magazine, 1933–1969
NOW, 1970–1992
MMS Annual Reports, 1933–1970

Prayer Manual of the MMS (various titles), 1932/33–1987/88; Prayer Handbook from 1988/89

Minutes of the Conference, 1933–1996

The Constitutional Practice and Discipline of the Methodist Church, revised annually from 1951

Methodist Laymen's Missionary Movement Newsletter (various titles), 1933–1986

Methodists for World Mission Magazines from 1987

Ministers' Missionary Union (Quarterly) Bulletin, 1933–1978

Other

The Missionary Review (Methodist Church of Australasia Department of Overseas Missions, Sydney), 1892–1977

Conference Reports

Asia Methodist Advisory Committee, *Missionary Service in Asia Today* (Hong Kong, Chinese Christian Literature Council, 1971)

Bate, H.N. (ed), *Faith and Order: Proceedings of the World Conference,* (London, SCM Press, 1927)

China Centenary Missionary Conference Records (New York, American Tract Society, 1907)

Conference of Bishops of the Anglican Communion: Encyclical Letter with the Resolutions and Reports (London, SPCK, 1920)

Duraisingh, C. (ed.), *Called to One Hope* (Geneva, World Council of Churches, 1998)

Engagement: the Second AACC Assembly, 1969 (Nairobi, All Africa Conference of Churches, 1970)

International Missionary Council, *Report of the Jerusalem meeting of the International Missionary Council* (3 vols, London, Oxford University Press, 1928)

Orchard, R.K., *Witness in Six Continents* (London, Edinburgh House Press, 1964)

Proceedings of the General Missionary Conference of Northern Rhodesia 1922 (Livingstonia, Mission Press, 1923)

Printed Sources

Abrecht, P., *The Churches and Rapid Social Change* (London, SCM Press, 1961)

Aitchison, R., 'The Wesley Deaconess Order in the Transvaal', in *WHS Proceedings* 58/2 (May 2011)

Allen, R., *Missionary Methods: St Paul's or Ours?* (London, World Dominion Press, 1912)

Anderson, R., *Foreign Missions* (New York, Charles Scribner, 1870)

Ariarajah, S.W., *The Bible and People of Other Faiths* (Geneva, World Council of Churches Publications, 1985)

-- *Hindus and Christians: A Century of Protestant Ecumenical Thought* (Grand Rapids, Eerdmans, 1991)

-- *Not without my Neighbour* (Geneva, World Council of Churches Publications, 1999)

Ash, G., *Ninety-Nine Not Out!* (Private publication, 2008)

Attwell, P. (ed.), *Take Our Hands: The Methodist Women's Auxiliary of Southern Africa 1916–1996* (Cape Town, Salty Print, 1997)

Balasunderam, F., *Dalits and Christian Mission in the Tamil Country* (Bangalore, Asian Trading Corporation, 1997)

Baldwin, A., *A Missionary Outpost in Central Africa* (London, Primitive Methodist Young People's Missionary Department, 1914)

Banana, C.S., 'The Politics of the Methodist Church' in C.S. Banana (ed.), *A Century of Methodism in Zimbabwe* (Harare, Methodist Church in Zimbabwe, 1991)

Bannerman, J.Y., *The Cry for Justice in Tema* (Accra, Ghana Publishing Corporation, 1973)

Bartels, F.L., *The Roots of Ghana Methodism* (Cambridge, Cambridge University Press, 1965)

Bays, D.H., *A New History of Christianity in China* (Chichester, Wiley-Blackwell, 2012)

Beaver, R.P., *Ecumenical beginnings in Protestant world mission: a history of comity* (New York, Thomas Nelson and Sons, 1962)

Bianquis, J., *Le Prophète Harris* (Paris, Société des Missions Evangéliques, 1924)

Boahen, A.A., *Mfantsipim and the making of Ghana: a centenary history, 1876–1976* (Accra, Sankofa, 1996)

Bonino, J.M., *Christians and Marxists: the Mutual Challenge to Revolution* (Grand Rapids, Eerdmans, 1976)

-- *Doing Theology in a Revolutionary Situation* (Augsburg, Fortress, 1985)

Bonk, J.J., *Missions and Money* (New York, Orbis Books, 1991)

Boocock, N., *Our Fernandian Missions* (London, W.A. Hammond, 1912)

Bosch, D.J., *Transforming Mission* (New York, Orbis Books, 1991)

Brandel-Syrier, M., *Black Woman in Search of God* (London, Lutterworth Press, 1962)

Brunner, E., *The World and the Church* (London, SCM Press, 1931)

Capon, M.G., *Towards Unity in Kenya* (Nairobi, Christian Council of Kenya, 1962)

Challenge to the Church: The Kairos Document (London, British Council of Churches and Catholic Institute for International Relations, 1985)

Chamberlayne, J.H., *China and its Religious Inheritance* (London, Janus Publishing, 1993)

Childe, D.B., *China Now* (London, Cargate Press 1955)

Ching, D.S., *Old Man Union Jack* (London, Cargate Press 1946)

-- *They Do Likewise* (London, Cargate Press, 1951)

Choudhury, P.C.R., *C.F. Andrews: His Life and Times* (Bombay, Somaiya Publications, 1971)

Church of Nigeria Inaugural Committee, Life and Mission Group, *The Way Forward: the Church of Nigeria* (Ibadan, Daystar Press, 1965)

Clayton, G.A., *Methodism in Central China* (London, Wesleyan Book Room 1906)

Coerr, E., *Sadako and the Thousand Paper Cranes* (London, Puffin Books, 1977)

Cole, E.K., *A History of Church Co-operation in Kenya* (Limuru, St. Paul's College Press, 1975)

Cox, A., *Uzuakoli Miracle* (Berkhamsted, 1991)

Cracknell, K.R., *Towards a New Relationship* (London, Epworth Press, 1986)

-- *Justice, Courtesy and Love* (London, Epworth Press, 1995)

-- *In Good and Generous Faith* (London, Epworth Press, 2005)

Cracknell, K. and Lamb, C., *Theology on Full Alert* (London, British Council of Churches, 1984)

Cripps, A.S., *An Africa for Africans* (London, Longmans, Green and Co., 1927)

Cumbers, F.H., *Richmond College 1843–1943* (London, Epworth Press, 1944)

Darch, J., *Missionary Imperialists?* (Milton Keynes, Paternoster, 2009)

Davey, C.J., *The March of Methodism* (London, Epworth Press, 1951)

-- *Rue Roquépine* (London, Methodist Church Overseas Division, 1977)

-- *Changing Places* (London, Marshall Pickering, 1988)

Davies, R.E., *Methodism* (London, Epworth Press, rev. 1976)

Davies, R.E., George, A.R. and Rupp, G. (eds), *A History of the Methodist Church in Great Britain* (4 vols, London, Epworth Press, 1965, 1978, 1983, 1988)

Debrunner, H.W., *The Story of Sampson Opong, The Prophet* (Accra, Waterville Publishing House, 1965)

Dépestre, M., *Experimenting Rural Evangelism in Haiti* (Petit Goâve, La Presse du Sauveur, 1957)

de Vries, E., *Man in Rapid Social Change* (New York, Doubleday, 1961)

Dickson, K.A., *Theology in Africa* (London, Darton Longman and Todd, 1984)

Donovan, V., *Christianity Rediscovered* (London, SCM, 1978)

Eayrs, G., Townsend, W.J., Workman, H.B. (eds), *A New History of Methodism* (2 vols, London, Hodder and Stoughton, 1909)

Edwards, M, *Bridges of the Spirit* (London, SPCK, 1994)

Essamuah, C.B., *Genuinely Ghanaian* (Trenton, New Jersey, Africa World Press 2010)

Etherington, N. (ed.), *Missions and Empire* (Oxford, Oxford University Press, 2005)

Fenton, T.F., *Black Harvest* (London, Cargate Press, 1956)

Findlay, G.G. and M.G., *Wesley's World Parish* (London, Hodder and Stoughton, 1912)

Findlay, G.G. and Holdsworth, W.W., *The History of the Wesleyan Methodist Missionary Society* (5 vols, London, Epworth Press, 1921–24)

Fischer, L., *The Life of Mahatma Gandhi* (London, Jonathan Cape, 1951)

Forward, M.H.F., *A Bag of Needments* (Bern, Peter Lang, 1998)

-- (ed.), *God of all Faith* (London, Methodist Church Home Mission Division, 1989)

Fox, A.J., *Uzuakoli, A Short History* (London, Oxford University Press, 1964)

Freire, P., *Pedagogy of the Oppressed* (New York, Continuum, 1970)

Gaitskell, D., 'Power in Prayer and Service' in R. Elphick and R. Davenport (eds), *Christianity in South Africa* (Cape Town, David Philip, 1997)

Godfrey, F.C., *Emily the Relentless Nurse* (Loughborough, Teamprint, 1999)

Graham, E.D., *Saved to Serve* (Peterborough, Methodist Publishing House, 2002)

Gray, S.D., *Frontiers of the Kingdom* (London, Cargate Press, 1930)

Green, F.P., *Methodism and the Mountain Summit* (London, Cargate Press 1932)

Griffiths, L.J., *History of Methodism in Haiti* (Port-au-Prince, Imprimerie Méthodiste, 1991)

Grist, W.A., *Samuel Pollard, Pioneer Missionary in China* (London, Cassell, 1920)

Groves, C.P., *The Planting of Christianity in Africa* (4 vols, London, Lutterworth Press, 1948–1958)

Guidelines on Dialogue with People of Living Faiths and Ideologies (Geneva, World Council of Churches Publications, 1979)

Gutierrez, G., *A Theology of Liberation* (London, SCM Press, 1974)

Hale, T., *Don't Let the Goats Eat the Loquat Trees* (Grand Rapids, Zondervan, 1986)

Haliburton, G.M., *The Prophet Harris* (London, Longman, 1971)

Hallencreutz, C.F. and Mayo, A., *Church and State in Zimbabwe* (Harare, Mambo Press, 1988)

Hares, G.B., *Journeying into Openness* (Bristol, Shoreline, 1991)

Harris, E.J, 'Wesleyan Witness in an Interreligious Context' in P. R .Meadows (ed.), *Windows on Wesley* (Oxford, Applied Theology Press, 1997)

-- *Buddhism for a Violent World: A Christian Reflection* (London, Epworth Press, 2010)

Harrison, J.W., *A.M. Mackay* (London, Hodder and Stoughton, 1890)

Haslam, D.A., *Caste Out* (London, Churches Together in Britain and Ireland, 1999)

Hastings, A., *African Christianity* (New York, Seabury Press, 1976)

Hedley, J., *Our Mission in North China* (London, George Burrows, 1907)

Hempton, D., *The Religion of the People* (London, Routledge, 1996)

Hood, G.A., *Neither Bang nor Whimper* (Singapore, Presbyterian Church in Singapore, 1991)

Hughes, H.P., *Social Christianity: sermons delivered in St. James's Hall, London* (London, Hodder and Stoughton, 1889)

Idowu, E.B., *Olodumarè: God in Yoruba Belief* (Lagos, Longman Nigeria, 1962)

-- *Towards an Indigenous Church* (London, Oxford University Press, 1965)

-- *African Traditional Religion* (London, SCM Press, 1973)

Johnson, R., 'Colonial Mission and Imperial Tropical Medicine: Livingstone College, London, 1893–1914' in *Social History of Medicine* 2010.

Kalu, O.U., *Divided people of God: Church union movement in Nigeria, 1875–1966* (New York, Nok, 1978)

Kaunda, K. and Morris, C.M., *Black Government?* (Lusaka, USCL, 1960)

Kehrberg, N., *The Cross in the land of the Khukri* (Kathmandu, Ekta Books, 2000)

Kendall, R.E., *Beyond the Clouds* (London, Cargate Press, 1948)

-- *Eyes of the Earth* (London, Cargate Press, 1954)

-- *The End of an Era: Africa and the Missionary* (London, SPCK, 1978)

Kimble, D.B, *A Political History of Ghana: the rise of Gold Coast nationalism 1850–1928* (Oxford, Clarendon Press, 1963)

Leigh, M.D., *Conflict, politics and proselytism* (Manchester, Manchester University Press, 2011)

Lewis, J., *William Goudie* (London, WMMS, 1923)

Lindell, J., *Nepal and the Gospel of God* (New Delhi, United Mission to Nepal, 1979)

Lossky, N. and others (eds), *Dictionary of the Ecumenical Movement* (Geneva, World Council of Churches Publications, 1991)

Lott, E J., 'All Loves Excelling: A Methodist Reflection on Hindu Faith' in M.H.F. Forward and others (eds), *A Great Commission: Christian Hope and Religious Diversity* (Bern, Peter Lang, 2000)

Macnicol, N., *C.F. Andrews: Friend of India* (London, James Clarke, 1944)

Mandela, N.R., *Long Walk to Freedom* (London, Little, Brown and Co., 1994)

Marioghae, M. and Ferguson, J., *Nigeria under the Cross* (London, Highway Press, 1965)

Massey, J., *Downtrodden: The Struggle of India's Dalits for Identity, Solidarity and Liberation* (Geneva, World Council of Churches Publications, 1997)

Mayson, C., *A Certain Sound: The Struggle for Liberation in South Africa* (London, Epworth Press, 1984)

Merwin, W., *Adventure in Unity, The Church of Christ in China* (Grand Rapids, Eerdmans, 1994)

Methodist Church Statements on Social Responsibility 1946–1992 (London, Division of Social Responsibility, 1992)

Mitra, N.B. (ed.), *Methodist in Bengal* (Kolkata, Shantigriha, 2007)

Mogoba, M.S., *Tears of Hope* (Johannesburg, Methodist Church of Southern Africa, 1989)

Moister, W., *Conversations on the Rise, Progress and Present State of Wesleyan Missions in Various Parts of the World* (London, Hamilton Adams and Co, 1869)

Morris, C.M., *Anything But This* (London, Lutterworth Press, 1958)

-- *The End of the Missionary?* (London, Cargate Press, 1962)

Moulton, J.H., *Religions and Religion; a Study of the Science of Religion, Pure and Applied* (London, Charles H. Kelly, 1913)

Mphahlele, E., *The African Image* (London, Faber and Faber, 1962)

M'Timkulu, D.G.S., *Beyond Independence: The Face of New Africa* (New York, Friendship Press, 1971)

Musson, M., *Prophet Harris* (London, Religious Education Press, 1950)

Neill, S.C., *Colonialism and Christian Missions* (London, Lutterworth Press, 1966)

Neill, S.C., Anderson, G., Goodwin, J. (eds), *Concise Dictionary of the Christian World Mission* (London, Lutterworth Press, 1970)

Newbigin, L., *A South India Diary* (London, SCM, 1951)

Nida, E.A., *God's Word in Man's Language* (New York, Harper, 1952)

Nightingale, E.G., *A history of Methodism in Northern Rhodesia* (privately printed and circulated, 1965)

Niles, D.T., *Upon the Earth: The Mission of God and the Missionary Enterprise of the Churches* (London, Lutterworth Press, 1962)

Noble, W.J., *Flood Tide in India* (London, Cargate Press, 1937)

Nthamburi, Z.J., *A History of the Methodist Church in Kenya* (Nairobi, Uzima Press, 1982)

O'Connor, D., *Three Centuries of Mission* (London, Continuum, 2000)

Oduyoye, M.A., 'The Value of African Religious Beliefs and Practices for Christian Theology' in K. Appiah-Kubi and S. Torres (eds), *African Theology en Route* (New York, Orbis Books, 1979)

Olusola, J.A., *Baba Mellor, Frontline Missionary in Nigeria* (Ibadan, Daystar Press, 1973)

Oosthuizen, G.C., *Theological Battleground in Asia and Africa* (London, C. Hurst, 1972)

Ormsby, F. (ed), *The Collected Poems of John Hewitt* (Belfast, Blackstaff, 1991)

Outler, A.C. (ed.), *Works of John Wesley*, Bicentennial Edition (Nashville, Abingdon Press), vol. 2 (Sermons II) (1985) and vol. 4 (Sermons IV) (1987)

Parrinder, E.G.S., *West African Religion* (London, Epworth Press, 1949)

-- *Religion in an African City* (London, Oxford University Press, 1953)

-- *African Traditional Religion* (London, Hutchinson, 1954)

-- *Avatar and Incarnation* (London, Faber and Faber, 1970)

Pearson, C.A., *Front-Line Hospital* (Cambridge, FSG Communications, 1996)

Platt, W.J., *An African Prophet* (London, Student Christian Movement Press, 1934)

Pobee, J.S., 'The Anglican Church in Ghana and the SPG' in D. O'Connor (ed.), *Three Centuries of Mission* (London, Continuum, 2000)

Pollard, E. (ed.), *The Sam Pollard Omnibus* (Pennsylvania, Woodburn Press, n.d.)

Porter, A., *Religion versus empire?* (Manchester, Manchester University Press, 2004)

Powell, A.W., *The Excelsior–EXED story* (Kingston, Methodist Church in the Caribbean and the Americas, Jamaica District, 1989)

Pritchard, J.R., 'The Untidy Beginnings of Methodist World Mission' in *Epworth Review* 26/4 (October 1999)

-- *Edward Rogers: Portrait of a Christian Citizen* (Evesham, Wesley Historical Society, 2008)

-- '1913 and All That' in P. Forsaith and M. Wellings (eds), *Methodism and History* (Oxford, Applied Theology Press, 2010)

-- *Methodists and their Missionary Societies 1760–1900* (Aldershot, Ashgate Publishing, 2013)

Race, A., *Christians and Religious Pluralism* (London, SCM Press, 1983)

Rawlinson, F.J. (ed.), *The Chinese Church as Revealed in the National Christian Conference* (Shanghai, Helen Thoburn, 1922)

Rea, K., *The Best is Yet to Be: Fifty Years in Zimbabwe with Fred and Kathleen Rea* (Harare, Munn Publishing, 1992)

Ream, W.G.B., *Too Hot for Comfort: War Years in China 1938-50* (London, Epworth Press, 1988)

Relations with People of other Faiths: Guidelines for Dialogue in Britain (London, British Council of Churches, 1981)

Rose, J.R., *A Church Born to Suffer* (London, Cargate Press, 1951)

Roux, A., *L'Evangile dans la forêt* (Paris, Les Editions du Cerf, 1971)

Sackett, F.C., *Posnett of Medak* (London, Cargate Press, 1951)

Sanneh, L., *Translating the Message* (New York, Orbis Books, 1989)

Selvanayagam, I., *Evangelism and Inter-Faith Dialogue* (Birmingham, Selly Oak Colleges, 1993)

Senior, G.R., *Visits Through China's Opening Doors* (Hong Kong, 1981)

-- *For Love of the Chinese* (Hong Kong, 1989)

-- *The China Experience* (Peterborough, Methodist Publishing House, 1994)

-- *Thomas Frank Davey* (Peterborough, Foundery Press, 1996)

Setiloane, G.M., *African Theology* (Johannesburg, Skotaville Publishers, 1986)

Sharing in God's Mission (London, Methodist Church Home Mission Division, 1985)

Sheaff, M., *From Tortoise Hill* (Leominster, Orphans Press, 2007)

Simon, M., *Souvenirs de Brousse 1905-1918* (Paris, Nouvelles Editions Latines, 1965)

Sithole, N., *African Nationalism* (London, Oxford University Press, 1968)

-- *Roots of a Revolution: Scenes from Zimbabwe's Struggle* (Oxford, Oxford University Press, 1977)

Smith, E.W., *An Ila Phrase Book for the use of Sportsmen and Settlers* (Livingstone, Administration Press, 1911)

-- *The Golden Stool* (London, Holborn Publishing House, 1926)

-- *African Beliefs and Christian Faith* (London, United Society for Christian Literature, 1936)

Southon, A.E., *Gold Coast Methodism* (London, Cargate Press, 1934)

Stanley, B., *The Bible and the Flag* (Leicester, Apollos, 1990)

-- ed., *Missions, Nationalism and the End of Empire* (Grand Rapids, Eerdmans 2003)

-- *The World Missionary Conference, Edinburgh 1910,* (Grand Rapids, Eerdmans, 2009)

Stuart, J., *British Missionaries and the End of Empire* (Grand Rapids, Eerdmans, 2011)

Sundkler, B., *Church of South India* (London, Lutterworth Press, 1954)

Telford, J. (ed.), *The Letters of John Wesley* (8 vols, London, Epworth Press, 1931)

Temple, M.M., *New Hope for Africa* (Reading, Taurus, 1991)

Theilen, U., *Gender, race, power, and religion* (Frankfurt am Main, Peter Lang, 2005)

Thompson, D.W., *Beginning at Skegness* (London, Cargate Press, 1962)

-- *A Mountain Road* (privately published, 1983)

Thompson, E.W., *The Methodist Mission House: its history and its treasures* (London, WMMS, 1933?)

Thorpe, C., *Limpopo to Zambesi* (London, Cargate Press, 1951)

Tovey, W.E., *Strangers in Chaotung* (Northampton, Little Knoll Press, 2010)

-- *Cor Blimey! Where 'ave you come from?* (Northampton, Little Knoll Press, 2011)

Trimingham, J.S., *The Christian Church and Islam in West Africa* (London, SCM Press, 1955)

Turberfield, A., *John Scott Lidgett* (London, Epworth Press, 2003)

Turner, J.M., *Conflict and Reconciliation* (London, Epworth Press, 1985)

Wakefield, E.S., *Thomas Wakefield: missionary and geographical pioneer in east equatorial Africa* (London, Religious Tract Society, 1904)

Walker, F.D., *The Day of Harvest in the White Fields of West Africa* (London, Cargate Press, 1925)

-- *The Story of the Ivory Coast* (London, Cargate Press, 1926)

-- *A Hundred Years in Nigeria* (London, Cargate Press, 1942)

Walls, A.F., *The Missionary Movement in Christian History* (New York, Orbis Books, 1996)

Walton, H., Johnson, M. and Ward, R. (eds), *A Tree God Planted: Black People in British Methodism* (London, Ethnic Minorities in Methodism Working Group, 1985)

Ward, A.M., *The Pilgrim Church* (London, Epworth Press, 1953)

Warren, M.A.C., *Social History and Christian Mission* (London, SCM Press, 1967)

Webb, P.M., *Women of our Time* (London, Cargate Press, 1963)

-- *World-Wide Webb* (Norwich, Canterbury Press, 2006)

Webster, J., *Dalit Christians: A History* (Delhi, ISPCK, 1992)

Wesley, J., *Primitive Physic* (London, J. Paramore, 1747)

Whaling, F., *An Approach to Dialogue with Hinduism* (Lucknow, Lucknow Publishing House, 1966)

Whyte, R., *Unfinished Encounter* (London, Collins Fount, 1988)

Wood, A.H., *Overseas Missions of the Australian Methodist Church* (4 vols, Melbourne, Aldersgate Press, 1975–1980)

Wright, E., *Behind the Lion Mountains* (London, Cargate Press, 1962)

Wycherley, R.N., *The Pageantry of Methodist Union* (London, Epworth Press, 1936)

Yates, T., *Christian Mission in the Twentieth Century* (Cambridge, Cambridge University Press, 1994)

Young, W.J., *The Quiet Wise Spirit* (London, Epworth Press, 2002)

Zvogbo, C.J.M., 'The Influence of the Wesleyan Methodist Missions in Southern Rhodesia 1891-1923' in J.A. Dachs (ed.), *Christianity South of the Zambezi* (Gwelo, Mambo Press, 1973)

-- 'An overview of the Methodist Church' in C.S. Banana (ed.), *A Century of Methodism in Zimbabwe* (Harare, Methodist Church in Zimbabwe, 1991)

-- *A History of Christian Missions in Zimbabwe, 1890–1939* (Gweru, Mambo Press, 1996)

Unpublished Material

Conference of British Missionary Societies, *Shaping Up to the Future* (London, CBMS, 1973)

Jackson, G.C., 'Basil', unpublished memoir of his father.

James, D.W., 'The Hand that Guided, the Heart that Planned', privately circulated memoir.

Leigh, M.D., 'Cowboys and Indians: Methodist Missionaries in the imperial high noon of Upper Burma', paper delivered at MMS History Conference 2005.

McConnell, H.O., 'Haiti', unpublished memoir, 1986.

Mole, D., 'A History of the Selly Oak Colleges', unpublished monograph.

Taggart, N.W., 'Irish Methodism and World Mission in the Twentieth Century', unpublished monograph, 2012.

Thomas, H.E., 'W.T. Balmer', unpublished monograph, 1979.

Online Resources (accessed 1 March 2013)

Biographical Dictionary of Chinese Christianity, http://www.bdcconline.net

Cawthera, A., Nijera Shikhi and Adult Literacy, 2003, http://www.eldis.org/fulltext/nijerashikhi.pdf

Dictionary of African Christian Biography, http://www.dacb.org

Dictionary of Methodism in Britain and Ireland, 'http://wesleyhistoricalsociety.org.uk/dmbi

Index

References located in the footnotes are indicated by 'n' after the page number. 'Dr' is used only of medical doctors. Places other than capitals and major cities are identified by country.